Living the Sky

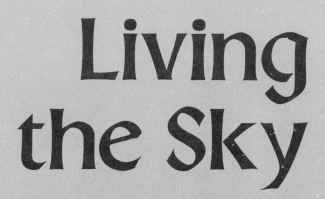

Living the Sky

THE COSMOS OF THE AMERICAN INDIAN

Ray A. Williamson

Line illustrations by Snowden Hodges

Houghton Mifflin Company   Boston   1984

Library of Congress Cataloging in Publication Data
Williamson, Ray A., date
  Living the sky.

  Bibliography: p.
  Includes index.
  1. Indians of North America—Astronomy.   2. Indians
of North America—Religion and mythology.   I. Title.
E98.A88W55 1984   970.004'97   84-4593
ISBN 0-395-35414-5

Printed in the United States of America

V 10 9 8 7 6 5 4 3 2 1

For my parents
Lois V. Williamson
Paul J. Williamson

Acknowledgments

Sometimes in the path of a human life, what seems at the time a relatively minor incident will change its entire course. Such was my first visit in 1972 to the ancient Pueblo ruins of Chaco Canyon, New Mexico. Though I reside on the East Coast, I have returned nearly every year since, and I expect to continue that practice for many years to come. My initial visit began innocently enough. Fellow St. John's College tutor Tom Simpson suggested that my family and I might want to stop off at Chaco Canyon on our way home after a summer spent teaching at the Santa Fe campus. It was a fateful visit. As we toured the ancient Pueblo buildings, hiked the sagebrush-covered mesas, and imbibed the spirit of the canyon, my family and I came to realize in our souls as well as our minds that this was an extremely special area, one in which a complex civilization had left an indelible, remarkable impression.

The remains of this civilization in Chaco Canyon and elsewhere in the Southwest pose an extraordinary, compelling puzzle for modern interpreters. What were these people doing there? What guided their lives? How did they organize their daily affairs? What was their view of the cosmos? Since that first visit, I have been privileged to play a small part in tackling some of the mystery of Chaco Canyon and other ancient Pueblo sites in the Southwest.

Comparison of my research in the Southwest with the results of similar studies in other geographical areas of North America led me to become interested in the cosmological outlook of North American native groups as a whole. As I hope this book will make clear, Native Americans throughout North America incorporated the motions of the sky into all parts of their lives. By studying the historic practices as well as the prehistoric remains, we can, I hope, begin to understand and appreciate the influence and role of celestial phenomena in the lives of Native Americans. This book draws upon, and attempts to integrate, the approaches of the disciplines of archaeology, astronomy, ethnology, folklore, and history to reach such understanding and appreciation.

Many, many people have contributed to my own intellectual odyssey concerning Native American views of the sky and their meaning for Native American culture. First and most important among these is my family, who put up with, and supported, my obsessions to wander the mesas of the Southwest and to spend many long hours, in the library and at the word-processor keyboard, studying and writing down my thoughts. Abby, my first wife, and our children Ethan and Sarah played a direct role in locating, measuring, and interpreting the buildings of the Southwest. I believe that our wanderings among the prehistoric ruins and our visits to the modern Pueblo villages have made a more vivid and lasting impression on Ethan and Sarah's lives and approach to the world than their more formal schooling has allowed.

My wife, Jean Monroe, has endured the many pressures of writing this book. Her support and thoughtful suggestions were crucial in completing the task I started several years ago. Not only did Jeanne help to type most of the manuscript, she read and commented on each iteration. She helped me organize my thoughts and saved me from sending off to Houghton Mifflin many misspellings and infelicitous phrases. I value and appreciate her continued enthusiasm, loving understanding, and patience with me.

To the numerous other people who, knowingly or unknowingly, have provided information or general support, I extend many thanks. I greatly appreciate the help of Anthony Aveni, Von Del Chamberlain, John A. Eddy, J. Heilman, Travis Hudson, and Jane Young, who all read portions of the manuscript. Their suggestions about wording and corrections of fact were extremely helpful in clarifying and improving the book's content. I remind my readers, however, that the slings and arrows for any errors or misinterpretations should be directed at me. I am grateful to Tom Simpson for suggesting that first trip to Chaco Canyon and for many later ideas about the sites therein. My good friend Clarion Cochran, who has made a lifetime of learning, provided an attitude of enthusiasm about the accomplishments of the early dwellers of Chaco Canyon, without which I might have seen and pondered too little.

I deeply appreciate the time and effort that Snowden Hodges spent in drawing the illustrations for *Living the Sky*. His ability to turn my lifeless schematic renditions into works of art that also convey the necessary information truly amazes me. For the book's title I am indebted to Claire Farrer, who graciously consented to my use of it. "Living the Sky" is the title of an article she wrote with Bernard Second for the collection of scholarly articles I edited, *Archaeoastronomy in the Americas*. Though she applied it to the Mescalero Apache, the term is in some sense true for all Native Americans who live in the traditional ways.

This book might never have been started had it not been for Joan Tapper, who suggested that I consider writing such a book and gave me early encouragement and thoughtful advice about its organization. However, she might never have known about my research had it not been for the earlier interest and support of Becky Wilson, who suggested to the Annapolis paper *The Capital* that the results of my research were worthy news to report.

I am grateful to the National Geographic Research Foundation, which provided me with research funds to pursue some of my studies in the Southwest, and to the Smithsonian Institution for a year-long fellowship to study the notes and collections of the early anthropologists connected with the Bureau of American Ethnology. I am indebted to Waldo and Mildred Wadel for their sympathetic guidance during my year at the Smithsonian. These opportunities constitute the early foundation of my learning about Native American astronomy.

I thank staff members of the Smithsonian Institution Natural History Museum for all the help they gave me in my research, especially Janette Saquet, librarian of the anthropology collection, and Elaine Mills and Paula Fleming in the National Anthropological Archives.

Many people contributed directly to my research on the prehistoric Pueblos. Howard Fisher, a colleague at St. John's College, was a thoughtful partner in much of the early work at Chaco Canyon and Hovenweep. Without the enthusiasm and energy of Craig Benson, however, we would have accomplished much less. I am especially indebted to Craig for many useful suggestions for sites to explore and for his knowledge about southwestern archaeology. Donnel O'Flynn, Jane Young, Marilyn Englander, Frances Goodwin, Cathy Leder, Bill

Haase, Doug Bacon, and Jeremiah St. Ours assisted directly in one part or another of this work.

Fred Blackburn, who has a very special and compelling vision of the Southwest as an "outdoor museum," helped me learn to experience directly the vast holdings of this area. Through him I have gained a deeper appreciation of the relationship of the land to the lives of the departed pueblo dwellers of the Southwest.

I also thank the personnel of the National Park Service at Chaco Canyon, Hovenweep, and Mesa Verde for their patience and assistance in the pursuit of knowledge. In particular, Clarion Cochran, Jim Court, Robert Hart, Walter Herriman, Debbie Krikorian, Ron Switzer, Roger Trick, Alan Wilcox, and several other park rangers gave me over the years the benefit of their wisdom, their time, and their facilities.

Florence Ellis, one of the great southwestern anthropologists, impressed upon me the importance of ethnology in attempting to interpret the ancient Pueblo world view. The shock of her sympathetic criticism of my early research encouraged me to read the available ethnologies (including most of her work), and to temper my hypotheses with actual data on the descendants of the prehistoric Pueblo people. Polly and Curt Schaafsma similarly gave me much encouragement and thoughtful advice.

I might never have pursued this subject in any depth had it not been for the work of Anthony Aveni and John C. Brandt. Tony provided all of us who work in this realm the opportunity to present papers and meet other archaeoastronomers at two early conferences (in 1973 and 1975) on Native American astronomy; Jack Brandt's interest in astronomical symbols in Native American rock art made possible some funding and a relationship that I value. Jonathan Reyman was the first person to suggest that some of the Chaco Canyon structures were astronomically aligned. Though he and I differ in many respects over methods and approach to the subject, our dialogue has been invaluable to me. His early research indirectly made it possible for Howard Fisher and me to make some of our own discoveries.

Jane Young, who started her southwestern studies as my student, is now teaching me. She provided many insights about the Zuni and other Pueblo groups and kindly shared with me her unpublished translations of Zuni poems and stories, one of which is published herein for the first time. Several other people have been generally supportive and have provided encouragement along the way. Among these are Von Del Chamberlain, John Carlson, E. C. Krupp, and Evan Hadingham.

This long list of acknowledgments would be incomplete if I failed to mention Gerald Hawkins's influence on my work. *Stonehenge Decoded*, more than any other book, sparked my interest in archaeoastronomy and in understanding the monuments of past cultures.

In preparing *Living the Sky*, I have drawn on the published results of many, many research scientists. In addition, several have shared their work with me prior to publication, especially Von Del Chamberlain, J. Heilman, Travis Hudson, and Warren Wittry. I hope I have done their work justice.

Finally, I thank literary agent Rafael Sagalyn, who encouraged my early efforts and put me together with Houghton Mifflin; editor Anita McClellan, who early on helped me organize my writing and suggested two new chapters; and editor Gerard Van der Leun, who saw the book through to publication. Their suggestions for revisions have made this a much more readable, accessible book than it might otherwise have been. I wish to thank manuscript editor Sarah Flynn for her watchful eye and thoughtful editing touch, and I am also grateful to the many other staff members at Houghton Mifflin who helped me over the hurdles of publishing.

Contents

Living the Sky

1 Myth, Buildings, and Myth Building

Archaeoastronomy in the Americas

On an isolated, windswept mountain slope high in the Wyoming Rockies, the ancient Bighorn Medicine Wheel still marks the yearly arrival of midsummer day, June 21. Apparently constructed sometime between A.D. 1200 and A.D. 1700 by Plains Indians, the 25-yard-diameter structure was built from hundreds of boulders gathered from the local area. The Indians laid the stones in a wheel-shaped pattern of straight lines that radiate from a central large cairn. A rim around the outside and several smaller cairns placed at seemingly random locations along the rim of the wheel complete the pattern. Discovered by white explorers more than a hundred years ago, this structure has long puzzled archaeologists. What sort of structure is it? What did its builders intend when they laid stone upon stone in this curious pattern? Much larger and more complex than the hundreds of tipi rings that dot the western plains, its origin and function have been unclear. The wheel is only accessible for two and a half months of the year, since it is exposed to the hazards of late spring snows in mid-June and early autumn storms in late August. It is much too large to have held down the edges of a tipi; its isolated location at the 10,000-foot level of the mountain suggests that it served a more special function.

Prior to the 1970s, the wheel led to much interesting speculation. The local Indians said it was made by "people who had no iron." Some have suggested it was somehow related to the Sun Dance ritual of the Plains Indians. Members of the Crow Nation have even called it the Sun's Tipi. These ideas are suggestive, but the usual modes of archaeological study have not explained the wheel's possible function. Archaeologists themselves ventured little beyond suggesting that the wheel probably served some sort of ritual function and that it was probably built in different stages over a period of years.

Astronomer John Eddy[1] had heard about the Bighorn Medicine Wheel, and in 1972 he investigated it to see if the structure could be explained astronomically. Thanks to his research, we now know that the Bighorn Medicine Wheel may have been a simple yet sophisticated astronomical observatory that was built to mark the summer solstice (midsummer day). Further, by indicating the direction in which to look for the first yearly appearance of the stars Aldebaran, Rigel, and Sirius, it marked not only midsummer day but also the beginning of the two lunar months immediately following.

Until a few years ago, archaeologists abruptly dismissed even the suggestion that the ancestors of present-day Native Americans were deeply interested in the intricate movements of the heavens. After all, they had not unearthed a single astronomical instrument left by the prehistoric Indians[2] of the continent. Now, however, because of recent discoveries by a new breed of interdisciplinary scholars such as Dr. Eddy, we know that the Native Americans had a keen interest in the sky. Archaeoastronomers, scientist/humanists who combine the knowledge and expertise of the disciplines of archaeology and astronomy, have recently demonstrated that these peoples, culturally a part of the Stone Age, used ritual buildings, stone and wooden circles, and large earth mounds as instruments to chart the movements of the heavens. They have shown that many different prehistoric Indian groups, from California to Florida, from Texas to Canada, made regular observations of the sun, moon, and stars with these elaborately constructed devices. Such astronomically related structures constitute part of the archaeological record throughout the Americas, from Canada to Peru.

In Mesoamerica, for example, the Caracol in the ancient Mayan city of Chichén Itzá on the Yucatán peninsula apparently served as a different sort of prehistoric observatory. A meticulously constructed building that bears a striking resemblance to the form of modern astronomical observatories, the Caracol has long been called *el observatorio* by local Mayan Indians, distant descendants of the an-

Summer solstice sunrise at Bighorn Medicine Wheel, Wyoming. This boulder structure, built by Plains Indians several hundred years ago, is aligned to the summer solstice sunrise and sunset, and to the summer predawn rise of the stars Aldebaran, Fomalhaut, Rigel, and Sirius.

cient Maya who built it a thousand years ago. Archaeologists have often speculated that it might actually function as an observatory, but until a few years ago, their speculation remained just that — speculation. Little or no measurement was attempted. In 1974, an interdisciplinary team of archaeoastronomers measured the narrow ports at the top of the Caracol and also made direct sightings through them. Anthony Aveni (astronomer), Sharon Gibbs (science historian), and Horst Hartung (architect),[3] found that the Caracol was originally built, in part, to observe the sun and the planet Venus, the latter connected by the Toltecs to their god Quetzalcoatl, and by the Maya to the god Kulkulcán. Sightings of Venus were extremely important to the Mesoamericans because they formed an important basis of their calendar, a scheme for reckoning the passage of time that far exceeded the Old World calendar in its accuracy and long-term predictive power.

Other Mesoamerican civilizations also produced numerous astronomically oriented structures. For example, the entire city of Teotihuacán in the Valley of Mexico near Mexico City was apparently originally laid out along lines perpendicular to the direction of rising of the constellation Pleiades in A.D. 150.[4] This is astronomical orientation on a grand scale. Aveni and Hartung have suggested that this was probably done because the Pleiades made its first appearance in predawn in June on the day the sun passed through the zenith at this location in A.D. 150. Zenith, or overhead, passage of the sun was of signal importance throughout Mesoamerica, for on that day at noon the sun cast no shadow and the sun god was said to descend to the earth for a time.

This same pair of archaeoastronomers has also studied the Aztec pyramid Templo Mayor, which is being uncovered in the great square of Mexico City.[5] They have concluded that it was oriented in such a way that it could be used for sighting the sun on the two days of the year when it was precisely on the equator.

In South America, the Incas, too, were astronomically adept and even planned their political and ritual centers along astronomically significant lines. With Cuzco as center, they constructed an intricate series of towers along straight lines that radiated outward to all points of their empire. Each of these lines, 328 in all, was directly related to their calendar, and some of them were oriented precisely along significant solar or lunar horizon stations. The shrines were long ago destroyed by the Incas' Spanish conquerors, but by using archaeoastronomical techniques, astronomer Aveni and anthropologist R. Tom Zuidema have pieced together evidence leading to the location of several shrines that lie along solar directions.[6]

Implicitly or explicitly, the rhythms of our lives, the movement from season to season, the patterns of the winds, and the pulse of the tides all depend on the apparent motions of the sun and moon and stars. Yet most modern urban dwellers are only dimly aware of the night sky — the stars and their myriad forms. They are only slightly more aware of the phases of the moon or the motions of the sun. Even those who take the daily horoscope seriously generally have a very poor notion of its connection with astronomical phenomena.

For Native Americans in prehistoric and early historic times, just the opposite was true. Their connections to the rhythms of the cosmos were both strong and visibly evident. It is difficult for modern urbanites to imagine that men and women less technologically advanced paid such close attention to the effects of the stars and purposely observed sunrise every day. Yet there is abundant evidence that they did and that their modern descendants still do watch the sky for such things as planting, religious ritual, and guidance in their daily affairs. Native Americans' interaction with their environment was, and still is, close and immediate. The astronomies they developed vary dramatically throughout the Americas; the systems of orientation reflect each different society and the way in which it understood its relationship to the sky and to sky beings.

In Mesoamerica and South America, people carefully tracked the positions of the celestial bodies for information on how to conduct their lives. When to plant, when to copulate, and when to sacrifice were all specified by the heavens. Further north, in what has become the United States and Canada, astronomy was less systematized, a state of affairs that probably reflected less central organization in the Native American cultures of the North American continent as a whole.

The North American astronomies and cosmological concepts were by no means primitive or undeveloped. Each Indian group on this continent developed its own characteristic response to the search for meaning in the heavens. It is to their search and their response that this book is devoted. Their use of astronomy helped them cope with an often hostile and unrelenting environment. Astronomy pervaded their lives — ritual, hunting, and farming were all affected by the heavens. Unlike their southern cousins, however, for the North American Indians the motions of the heavens were an aid to living, not a force to be feared or followed slavishly.

The Origins of Astronomy

Human beings have been observing and, in some way, charting the motions of the sky ever since they began to observe the world and reason about life. The power and beauty of the celestial panorama spoke deeply to early men and women, and they expressed their vision of the cosmos poetically in song and story. Theirs was a world peopled with fantastic, powerful sky beings who interacted directly with humans, sometimes conferring great benefits but, just as often, for no apparent reason, causing great harm.

In Homer's epic poem the *Iliad*, sky beings, personifications of the sun, moon, stars, and planets, play a direct role in the battle for Troy. Zeus, Aphrodite, and Ares, who are represented in the sky by the planets Jupiter, Venus, and Mars, play a major role in the action at Troy. They, along with other gods and goddesses, take sides in the battles and sometimes even engage one another directly on the plains before Troy. Early in the poem, at the request of the Greek warrior Achilles, Zeus sees to it that the Trojans maintain supremacy on the battlefield until Achilles receives appropriate restitution from his commander, Agamemnon. Achilles, whose honor has been slighted by Agamemnon, is only able to exact such a promise from Zeus through the direct intervention of his goddess-mother, Thetis. Appealing to the gods often has a price; in this case it is the death of Achilles' dear friend Patroklos. Here Zeus indirectly extends favor to Achilles by helping Patroklos and his fellow warriors to win entry to the gates of Troy; but he snatches total victory from Patroklos by allowing Hector, the Trojan hero, to kill Patroklos. Throughout the poem the relationships between men and women and the gods are important themes. Humans become godlike and gods act like humans. In one of the battles, the powerful Greek warrior "godlike" Diomedes stabs in the hand the goddess of love and fertility, Aphrodite, for daring to interfere in mortal combat. He also, ironically, runs a spear into the side of Ares, the god of anger and war.

In other Greek stories, the interactions between celestial gods and human beings are also strong themes. Zeus, of course, is well known for his sexual exploits among mortal women. Hera, his wife, maintains a constant vigilance to subvert his philandering proclivities. Though she is mostly unsuccessful, her wrath creates considerable problems for Zeus' hapless human consorts. In one story, Io, a beautiful earthly maiden, is taken in love by Zeus. To prevent detection, Zeus changes her into a cow while he takes the form of a bull. Hera finds out about the deception later and causes Io to be hounded by the gadfly, the ghost of ten-thousand-eyed Argos. Io's wanderings to avoid pursuit, turning in circle upon circle, mimic the celestial wandering of the planets — the images of the gods themselves.

Like the Greeks, the Pueblo Indians have characterized the celestial objects in myths. Morning Star and Evening Star are the twin war gods, helpers and protectors of the Pueblo people. With the occasional aid of other mythical creatures, or sometimes certain animals and birds, they led the Pueblo tribes to this world, conquered the dangerous monsters that threatened to harm their charges, and punished or chastised the people for untoward behavior.

We see in these myths sky gods who are directly involved with the people. Prescientific or traditional cultures depended on the position of the stars for geographic direction and on the sun, moon, and planets for organizing and defining their lives into the months of the year, the days of the month, and the hours of the day. They watched the sky for clues to tell them when to hunt, when to plant, and when to harvest. The motions of the celestial sphere also guided their ritual observances and helped them to predict future events.

The Babylonians, and later the Greeks, changed all that for Western thinkers. Their doggedly systematic charting of the motions of the sun, moon, and planets eventually led to a highly mechanized and impersonal vision of the cosmos. True, they still watched the skies for calendrically essential information, but in developing a predominantly machinelike view of the meanderings of the planets, the moon, and the sun, they began the arduous process of de-mythologizing the workings of the celestial sphere. In this system, which was highly developed by the Greek astronomer Claudius Ptolemy (circa A.D. 150), wheels turned on wheels that turned on wheels

— an intricate arrangement of cycles and epicycles. Ptolemy's conception of the sky formed a basis for our modern view of the world — organized, rationalistic, mechanized.

Of course, this view of the development of astronomy is much too simplified. The celestial objects and their motions provided ample subject matter for the poets, to be sure. However, the shift to the modern, Western, rational view of the heavens was preceded by an important development long neglected by scholars. Between the purely mythic response to the sky and the deliberate, machinelike vision of Ptolemy and his intellectual descendants, there was a middle ground of well-defined observations that had been made for centuries, perhaps millennia, in order to establish and use a calendar.

This was not true just for the early Greeks and Babylonians. It is also the case with every society for which the rhythms of the seasons must be known in order to take best advantage of the available food supplies. The cycles of the sun, the moon, the stars, and even the planets give essential clues for planting, reaping, and gathering. The regular, ordered motions of the celestial sphere provide a predictable foundation for the less certain earthly signs of seasonal change. For example, the Tapirape Indians of the Amazonian rain forests watch anxiously for the first yearly disappearance of the constellation Pleiades in the western sky as a sure sign of the end of their rainy season. Prior to that, they date the many ceremonies of the rainy season by the position of the Pleiades in the sky. Five thousand miles further north and east and some four thousand years earlier, on Salisbury Plain in England, the builders of Stonehenge apparently followed the sun and perhaps the moon in order to organize a calendar for ritual and agricultural purposes. What is true for these two disparate cultures, separated as they are by a wide gulf of space and time, is also true for traditional societies throughout the world. Even today the Hopi Indians of Arizona plant and harvest their crops by the position at which the sun rises or sets along the distant horizon.

These societies' interest in the sky is not limited to food gathering, agriculture, or other practical uses. Even social and religious ritual or acts of war have been timed by celestial movement, appearances, and disappearances. The Skidi Pawnee of the Northern Plains are reputed to have timed the sacrifice of a captured enemy maiden by the appearance of the Morning Star. According to the Greek playwright Aeschylus, the Achean warriors crouching inside the Trojan horse knew just when to burst out to conquer Troy by observing the position of the Pleiades in the night sky.

> . . . the fierce young within
> the horse, the armored people who marked out their leap
> against the setting of the Pleiades. A wild
> and bloody lion swarmed above the towers of Troy
> to glut its hunger lapping at the blood of kings.[7]

Even in this age, the Christian calendar contains the remnants of an earlier astronomical tradition. The festivals of Christmas and Easter, falling near the important solar events of the winter solstice (December 21) and the spring equinox (March 21), remind us of pagan times in which the sun was carefully watched for calendrical information. According to Biblical scholars, the dates of the pagan festivals formed the basis upon which these Christian festivals came to be observed. The Hebrew calendar, too, has a strong basis in sky watching. Determined according to the moon and the sun, Passover occurs every year on the Thursday on or after the first full moon following the spring equinox.

The Native Americans

Though the Western calendar's relation to sky watching is well known, the same cannot be said for the Native American calendar. The tradition of naked-eye astronomy has played a large role in the development of Native American thought. Still, American Indian astronomy, especially in North America, is mostly unknown, despite a strong increase in interest in recent years among laymen and professional anthropologists. This astronomical tradition is a complex but integral part of the life of Native Americans on this continent. It was well developed long before the Spanish Entrada about A.D. 1500 and the later invasion by Northern Europeans. It is still present today, though it is rapidly disappearing. We are fortunate in the Americas to be able to learn something about the very early development of the science of astronomy — to witness or reconstruct, from a rich archaeological deposit, systems of naked-eye astronomy in all their simplicity and complexity: simple, because naked-eye astronomy requires very little in the way of external aids; complex in the kinds of observations that can be made, and in the rich cultural overtones that these astronomies produced for their societies.

To the Western mind, the use of the plural in discussing native astronomies might be a little puzzling. After all, modern science is built on the understanding that there can be only one correct explanation of the universe. Anyone with the appropriate equipment can make the same observations as another and confirm or deny the conclusions the latter has drawn. Yet, there can be a multiplicity of astronomies in the sense that utilitarian observations hold the test of rightness in their usefulness and not in a theory of the phenomena. Any particular group may emphasize observing the sun primarily, or the moon and the sun as celestial counterparts. Or among some groups the stars may have predominance. The southwest Pueblo tribes strongly emphasize the sun and the moon for their calendar, while the Plains Pawnee focused on observations of the stars.

This book describes astronomical practices that were discovered only during the last decade, or recently rediscovered in the anthropological literature from the nineteenth and early twentieth centuries. Scholars are bringing new material to light every year. Today, we might even ask why so little attention was placed on the complexities of Native American astronomies prior to the 1970s and 1980s. The answer lies partly in the accident of history. It also lies in our modern blindness to the possibility that technologically undeveloped societies might have something to teach us about astronomy and its place in our lives, or that they might also be able to help us discover our own scientific origins. Yet, as will become evident later, the astronomies that were, or are, practiced by Native Americans possessed the rudimentary structures necessary for the development of a science.

We can hope to learn a great deal about the origins of the science of astronomy by studying the Native American model. Yet, we must also be especially cautious because there are very likely to be important differences — for example, between Native American astronomical practices and those of the prehistoric Greeks and Babylonians. North American astronomical observations have always, apparently, had heavy religious overtones, and this also seems to be the case in the distant Babylonian past. Just how the transition to a mechanistic theory was made is unclear. An essential missing link in this connection is, of course, the question of how Native American astronomy would have developed had Western Europeans not conquered this land and enforced their own already highly developed view of the external world on the native population.

In the eighteenth century, the Age of Enlightenment, Western thought developed fully the notion of a strong dichotomy between the world of matter, including animals and plants, and the world of spirit, which gives humans their rational powers. All outside the human spirit was part of the external world of otherness. This split aided the rise of science as a discipline and high technology as a powerful means for doing. For centuries since, Western man has sought to conquer nature, to subdue it to his ends, a view of man and the world that was expounded by the seventeenth-century philosophers René Descartes and Sir Francis Bacon, who taught that in order to make a better life for man we must learn to conquer nature. In contrast, the Indian view emphasizes participation with nature and natural effects for the mutual good of all beings. The Native American, in general, is much more closely tied spiritually and intellectually to the variety of natural effects and causes in the "external world" than the European. In fact, it is probably safe to say that the Native American does not even recognize the existence of an external world separated from the human spirit. As Frances Densmore, the noted musicologist of Indian song, explained: "The Indian waited and listened for the mysterious power pervading all nature to speak to him in song. The Indian realized that he was part of nature — not akin to it."[8]

The Rise of Archaeoastronomy

The study of archaeoastronomy, which is responsible for the present lively interest in the astronomical traditions of Native Americans of all three continents, began seriously in 1894 with the publication of Sir J. Norman Lockyer's book *Dawn of Astronomy*. To him rightfully belongs the pretentious title Father of Archaeoastronomy. However, he nearly killed the study by his inattention to numerous discrepancies in his work, and his eager embrace of specious or doubtful archaeology. *Dawn of Astronomy* was an interesting, if flawed, book. In it, Lockyer attempted to show that many of the Egyptian temples were precisely astronomically aligned to the sun and to the stars. Unfortunately for the serious study of the astronomical alignments of Egyptian temples, Lockyer's many incorrect or highly speculative remarks about Egyptian cultural history caused most scholars of Egyptian antiquity to dismiss his entire work as absurd. It wasn't until astronomer Gerald Hawkins, a recent investigator of Stonehenge, took a serious interest in Lockyer's Egyptian hypotheses that some of them were proven true. In his 1973 book, *Beyond Stonehenge*, Hawkins shows several of Lockyer's hypotheses to be false, but in the process he describes many other interesting astronomical alignments for these same Egyptian temples. Lockyer's Egyptian work, though riddled with error, paved the way for more careful research seventy years later. A similar tale can be told about his studies of Stonehenge.

Twelve years after *Dawn of Astronomy* was published, Lockyer produced a second book dealing with archaeoastronomy, *Stonehenge and Other British Stone Monuments Astronomically Considered* (1906). Earlier writers had entertained the possibility that Stonehenge was astronomically aligned, but Sir Norman was responsible for the first accurate survey of the monument and for investigating possible astronomical alignments with some attention to the requirements of the scientific approach. From his measurements, Lockyer concluded that Stonehenge was most certainly aligned to the position of the sun at summer solstice, the longest day of the year. This assertion has withstood subsequent testing by many other investigators. Unfortunately for Lockyer and for the study of archaeoastronomy, his related conclusions were quickly challenged by archaeologists; more recent studies have substantiated their criticisms. These criticisms, which centered on some claimed additional alignments, and on a specious method for dating the structure, probably stifled serious archaeoastronomical investigations for the next sixty years. For a scientist, Lockyer was remarkably resistant to criticism. Instead of considering his critics' comments seriously, he hardened his own position. This left his contemporaries and later archaeologists with a dim view of the value of archaeoastronomy for their studies, a glacial position that has only recently begun to thaw.

It is Gerald Hawkins and also Alexander Thom[9] to whom we must give credit for reviving serious interest in archaeoastronomy. Hawkins's articles in *Nature* and *Science* and finally his book *Stonehenge Decoded* (1965) drew the attention of astronomers, archaeologists, and the public to the fascinating story of Stonehenge.

Hawkins named his studies *astroarchaeology*, by which he meant the application of astronomy to the understanding of ancient structures. Hawkins found numerous alignments to the sun and moon at Stonehenge. I do not know who introduced the word *archaeoastronomy* into the literature, but ten years after Hawkins's book was published, it became the preferred term for the study of astronomical alignments of prehistoric structures.[10] Recently, the term *ethnoastronomy* was coined to refer to the study of the astronomy of living traditional groups. Often, studies in ethnoastronomy are included in archaeoastronomy.

Hawkins made a careful map of Stonehenge with a surveyor's transit and analyzed his results with a modern high-speed computer. The irony of using a state-of-the-art digital computer to analyze an ancient monument made up of crude stones cannot have escaped many readers of his book or viewers of the CBS television documentary that followed. That irony may be a strong part of the fascination the two documents still generate in the public's mind. Hawkins's work certainly drew the attention of the public, and his investigations of Stonehenge and Alexander Thom's studies of other British monuments, published in 1967 (*Megalithic Sites in Britain*) and 1971 (*Megalithic Lunar Observatories*), led to an increase in lay and scholarly interest in the astronomies of ancient and traditional cultures.

About this same time, scholars began to devote attention to the astronomical implications of the monuments of Mesoamerica. The Mesoamerican calendar developed by the Olmec, Maya, Aztec, and other groups was already known as a model of astronomical precision and was often cited as testimony to their skill and ingenuity in using pretelescopic observations for calendrical prediction. However, their intricate and precise calendar raises more questions than it answers. How did they make their observations? Did they have observatories or any sort of astronomical instruments? Were their major temples aligned to the sun or the moon, the planets or the stars? Tantalizing suggestions had been made in some of the early literature on Mesoamerica that some of the pyramids were astronomically aligned or that the Caracol had once been an astronomical observatory. Still, little in the way of sustained research had been carried out when American astronomer Anthony Aveni began his studies of the temple pyramids and buildings of Mesoamerica. His work, and that of other, widely scattered scholars, was discussed at a 1973 conference in Mexico City chaired by Aveni and architect Horst Hartung and sponsored by the American Association for the Advancement of Science and the Mexican Consejo Nacional de Ciencia y Technologia. Twenty-six scholars, who had recently begun to work on American archaeo- and ethnoastronomy, presented the results of their studies. This meeting constituted my own introduction to fellow scholars studying Native American astronomy. Though some of our work was tentative and our methodology was not yet fully developed, this small group formed the New World basis for the rapidly developing interdisciplinary study of archaeoastronomy.[11]

A second conference, held at Colgate University in 1975, was noteworthy for the increased attention to archaeo- and ethnoastronomy in North America. It presented the first detailed presentation of Incan astronomy.

The attempt to reconstruct the Inca calendar illustrates the complexities involved in the study of traditional astronomies throughout the Americas.[12] The Inca calendar system was enormously complex and is comparable to the intricate Mesoamerican calendar. It is, however, quite different. One aspect of the Inca calendar of particular interest to students of archaeoastronomy is the division the Incas made of the horizon, a complex system of lines radiating from the Temple of the Sun at Cuzco. Forty-one lines, or *ceques*, stretched out from Cuzco and intersected a total of 328 sacred shrines, or *huacas*, arranged in groups of an average of eight per *ceque*. Each *huaca* stood for a day of the year. The particular *ceque* defined by the *huaca* on that day also may have been used as a sight line for observing a particular astronomical event.

The *ceque* system clearly had ceremonial, political, and social ramifications, as well as astronomical or calendrical ones. On the summer and winter solstices (respectively the longest and shortest days of the year, which in the Southern Hemisphere occur approximately on December 21 and June 21), children were sacrificed at a great feast. Each *huaca*, or shrine, in the empire was required to send children to Cuzco to be sacrificed. Some were indeed sacrificed at Cuzco at the solstitial feasts, but others were returned home to be sacrificed near their own local *huaca*. When traveling home, these children, led by an official representative of their *huaca*, followed a straight line (*ceque*) instead of the roads, which generally took them across the local uneven terrain. Around Cuzco, this straight line of the "*ceque*" must have presented somewhat of a hardship to the messenger and the children he was leading, for not only was the terrain rough but also the children were walking to their death.

In the description of the Hopi calendar system, we will meet a system of shrines and straight lines in the southwest United States that is conceptually similar to the *ceque* system but lacks the feature of human sacrifice. For the archaeoastronomer, the study of the Incaic *ceque* system presents a problem that relates to all research in the Americas. Much of what we know of the *ceque* system and its related calendar comes from a variety of historical sources gathered in the early days of the conquest and by the Spanish chroniclers. By the time they wrote, the old system was in considerable disarray and was being replaced by a Western calendar, so much of the information the Spanish gathered was incomplete, either because those who knew about the system were dying or because the chroniclers failed to ask their informants the right questions. There is another problem in interpreting the written record of these chroniclers, one that plagues anthropologists in any research: the chroniclers' own ethnocentric bias obstructed their attempts to obtain correct and complete information.

Many early European writers simply failed to recognize that the Inca calendar was quite different from the Western one. For example, most reported that the Inca calendar was made up of twelve months and dropped the subject there, assuming that those twelve months were similar to ours. Others, better informed and probably also more intellectually tenacious, discovered that the number of days in the Inca calendar equaled the number of *huacas*. The Inca year was 328 days long, 37¼ days shorter than our Western, solar year of 365¼ days. The interesting feature about a year of 328 days with 12 months is that each month is exactly 27⅓ days long, an interval nearly precisely equal to the sidereal lunar month, or the time the moon takes to pass from a given star back to that same star. By contrast, the synodic lunar month, the time the moon takes to progress from a given phase to that same phase again, is about 29½ days long, an interval much closer to our Western month.

To observe the phases of the moon during a month and tally the number of days between identical phases is a relatively simple, straightforward observation. However, to note the precise passage of the moon among the stars is much more difficult and requires a different sort of intention on the part of the observer. He or she must watch the passage of the moon through the stars and note the particular position it takes from night to night during the month. Because there is a difference of about two days between the sidereal and synodic months, the moon will be in a different phase when it eventually returns to the same star. This must confuse the observations somewhat and make them difficult to pursue.

Because the Spanish chroniclers failed to note how the Incas determined their months, they missed an opportunity to explore the Inca more deeply. They might have been surprised that these "heathen savages" had, by European standards, an amazingly complicated and intricate yearly calendar. The chroniclers' narrow, ethnocentric bias obstructed their understanding and, incidentally, created an enormous problem for modern studies of the Incas. A similar situation occurs in most of the rest of the Americas as well. The predominant European view of the Native American as a barbaric and stupid savage obstructed the Europeans' ability to understand the intellectual accomplishments of the New World natives. As a result, much cultural knowledge is lost. Although today the anthropological enterprise has rid itself of some of the influence of cultural bias, individuals must still be wary of their own ethnocentric view when attempting to understand another culture.

Whatever the problems inherent in ethnological research, we are fortunate in the Americas to have many ethnohistorical accounts of the early astronomical practices of the Native American. These accounts, with archaeological studies and current data from members of surviving tribes, will eventually aid in reconstructing the wonderful panoply of Native American astronomies. By contrast, the task of the European archaeoastronomer is much more difficult, even impossible in some cases. The original construction of Stonehenge was begun nearly five thousand years ago, in about 2800 B.C. Any ethnographic data that could be related to the astronomical concepts incorporated into its design are long lost in the mists of preliterate Europe. Yet in investigating the *ceque* system of Incaic Peru, the archaeologists have not only the imperfect accounts of chroniclers to guide their studies but paintings and drawings of early conquest days and the archaeological remains of a few *huacas*. Thus one can hope to reconstruct the entire *ceque* system both abstractly in the calendrical and sociopolitical systems and also concretely among the numerous archaeological remains of Peru.

The Peruvian case is paradigmatic of the archaeoastronomical situation throughout the Americas — surviving records, all too few and incomplete, suggesting complex astronomical observations that resulted in a rich array of approaches to the calendar. In the highly structured and monumental societies of South America and Mesoamerica, astronomical data were sought as integral parts of the structure of their complex societies. Further north, though, where the societies appear to have been less structured and less highly organized on the whole, the native population still wove astronomy deeply into the fabric of their lives and produced noteworthy astronomies and cosmological systems. The varieties and complexities of North American astronomies were first confronted and more fully understood in the third major conference on New World archaeoastronomy, "Archaeoastronomy in the Americas," a meeting I organized at St. John's College in Santa Fe, New Mexico, in 1979. This conference demonstrated that there was lively scholarly interest in archaeoastronomy and ethnoastronomy in North American native cultures, and it also showed that different groups interpret the sky in a variety of ways and use sky phenomena for many purposes.[13] As several of the conference participants put it, "Archaeoastronomy has come of age." It has now developed a solid basis for research and for self-criticism, both of which are necessary for a mature scientific study.

This book describes the current state of our knowledge of North American astronomies and attempts to relate them to the political, religious, and social ideas of the various tribes that practiced them. By their nature, traditional astronomies cannot be separated from the cultural milieu in which they developed and flourished. In order to explain the conceptual basis of North American native astronomies, and to describe their functions, this volume also devotes considerable attention to the mythology, the religious ritual, and the geographical and social contexts of the various tribal groups.

2   The Native American

First Encounters and Reconstructions

It was July 2, 1540, by the Gregorian calendar when Francisco Vás-
quez de Coronado, governor of Nueva Galicia, and his Spanish army
who had ridden north from Mexico in quest of fortune first encountered inhabitants of the fabled Seven Cities of Cibola (the Zuni pueblos). The initial brief meeting was amicable, and the four Zuni they
met promised that the next day "the tribe would provide the whole
force with food." The Zuni quickly left. Coronado was relieved,
since his army was very short on rations, but to ensure that they were
not deceived by any treachery from the Indians, he sent a small force
ahead to reconnoiter and to hold any difficult passages for the night.
The army master in charge of these troops found a small ridge that
could have been defended by the Indians, and set up camp for the
night to prevent an attack. Though wood was scarce in the area, they
were able to gather enough twigs and small branches to build a fire.
A few hours later, the Indians crept up on this small band, attacked,
and put them to rout. Later, Pedro de Castenada, a member of the
Spanish force, wrote, "Some were so excited they put their saddles
on hind side before." The next day, despite the obvious danger,
hunger drove Coronado and his men to advance upon a village some
six miles east. Here Coronado met considerable resistance, many
bruises, and even an arrow wound from the defended pueblo before
he subdued the Zuni inhabitants and obtained the food he and his
men needed. The village he encountered was Hawikuh, one of the
six (not seven, as legend had claimed and Coronado surmised) original villages of the Zuni people. Southwest of Zuni Pueblo, Hawikuh
now lies in ruin.

Because they had no written language, we have no Zuni accounts of this first encounter. However, the Zuni have held a long-lasting antipathy toward anyone of Spanish descent; oral tradition tells that the first soldiers from Mexico burned their carved wooden war gods in a campfire. Yet, thanks to a knowledge of the calendrical customs and rituals of the Zuni and some careful historical research by an amateur historian, we can say with considerable assurance that Coronado's men had chanced upon an area sacred to the Zuni.[1] It was a place to which Zuni priests made a pilgrimage in connection with the summer solstice.

Reconstructing the probable circumstances surrounding this encounter, it appears that the Zuni first observed Coronado's men approach as they were engaged in ceremonies at their sacred lake southwest of Hawikuh. Every other calendar year,[2] the Zuni ritual calendar called for the priests to walk from the village of Zuni to the sacred lake, Kothuluwala-wa, nine days after the summer solstice to deposit prayer sticks on one day and to hunt for turtles the next. For two nights, they would camp out on the ridges near the lake. Following the turtle hunt, they would kindle a sacred fire by using a wooden fire drill and dance until midnight. Then, keeping the sacred fire going as they proceeded back to Zuni Pueblo, about a day's journey away, they would enter the village just before sunset twelve days after the solstice, and dance in the plazas.

The Zuni pilgrims apparently met the Spanish eleven days after the solstice, a day before they were due back in the village. The Zuni faced two problems. First, they had to delay the Spanish somewhat

in order to prevent their arrival at Zuni Pueblo before the ceremony was complete. Second, that night they found they had to drive the Spanish away from their sacred grounds. They accomplished both their goals. In the process they also developed a dislike of Spanish-speaking peoples that has lasted nearly four hundred fifty years. The Spanish misunderstood the Zuni's intentions and assumed that the tribe was naturally hostile to them.

After discovering that the Spanish were burning Zuni sacred war gods in their encampment on the ridge, the Zuni pilgrims must have been particularly angry, a circumstance that may account for the apparent ease with which they drove the armed Spanish from the sacred grounds. After driving them away, they quickly kindled their sacred fire with a wooden fire drill, danced, and hurried back to Hawikuh to warn its inhabitants to delay the Spaniards and allow the pilgrims to reach Zuni Pueblo in time to complete the ceremony. Apparently, the resistance Coronado and his men faced at Hawikuh was part of the Zuni pilgrims' plan. They were then able to complete their summer solstice ritual well before Coronado could reach Zuni Pueblo.

This first encounter, though hardly typical of first encounters between the Europeans and the Native Americans, nevertheless illustrates an essential difficulty in understanding precontact Native American cultures today, nearly five centuries after European explorers and settlers arrived in North America. Virtually all we have are the early European accounts, more recent observations of Native American customs, and a similar reconstruction of historic events. The vast difference between European and Native American assumptions about the nature of the world or of human nature often made understanding of each other's actions and intentions extremely difficult. The changes in both groups that have taken place in the meantime further complicate the task of fully comprehending and appreciating Native American cultures. It is a little like trying to reconstruct the original Manhattan Island.

Indeed, walking the streets of New York City today, it is impossible to strip away the forest of concrete and steel, rivers of automobiles, and streams of people, to reach back with our mind's eye to see Manhattan Island as it was four hundred years ago when the first

European settlers arrived there. The island and its surrounding rivers and shores have been so formed and re-formed that it would take a multidisciplinary research team years to reconstruct the original.

Reconstructing Native American customs and thought patterns is probably even more difficult than reconstructing Manhattan Island. In the clash of the two cultures, many Native American lifeways were lost; at the same time, the Europeans developed numerous misconceptions and prejudices about the peoples they were conquering. Such misapprehensions have stayed with us, impede our understanding, and make the task of a realistic evaluation of Native American cultural achievements arduous at best. Indeed, the very name Indian was applied to the Native Americans because of a severe misconception about the geographical placement of the New World. Our prejudices prepare us to be greatly surprised, perhaps even delighted, when we discover that the Native Americans had a well-developed astronomy, or an oral poetic lore and intricate mythology. However, though it is often necessary to interpret the early European journals, such as the description of the first Spanish encounter with the Zuni, they show that the Native Americans as first encountered by the Europeans, whether on the coasts or in the interior, possessed vital cultures of high achievement and worthy of deep respect. In studying and analyzing Native American astronomical thought, archaeoastronomers attempt to understand a significant aspect of Native American cultural achievement, one that touches most other parts of native culture.

Given the vast difference in societal organization and tribal culture among the Native Americans, it is difficult to summarize their customs and achievements. However, it is possible to illustrate the diversity of the native North American cultures and to highlight some of the most important cultural achievements as they apply to the sky, the yearly cycle of the seasons, and the task of wresting a living from an abundant but often harsh and unrelenting land.

The first European settlers saw vast wild lands that were obstructed only here and there by an occasional native village. To them it was essentially uninhabited land that was open and ripe for the taking. In general, they treated the land in that manner.

How, then, did the European newcomers view the first natives that they met? Christopher Columbus, upon landing on the island he named San Salvador on October 12, 1492, found the natives there peaceable, though "naturally timid and fearful."

> They exhibit great love towards all others in preference to themselves: they also give objects of great value for trifles, and content themselves with very little or nothing in return . . .
> I did not find, as some of us had expected, any cannibals amongst them, but on the contrary, men of great deference and kindness.[3]

In another account of the first meeting with natives of this hemisphere, Columbus's son Ferdinand noted the great expectations with which the Europeans and the natives approached each other:

> At daybreak they [the Europeans] saw an island full of green trees and abounding in springs . . . and inhabited by a multitude of people who hastened to the shore, astounded and marveling at the sight of the ships, which they took for animals. These people could hardly wait to see what sort of things the ships were. The Christians were no less eager to know what manner of people they had to do with.[4]

European accounts of many first encounters were similar. When they arrived on this continent, the tribes and the cultures that the explorers found reflected a people who used highly sophisticated stone and bone tools, a variety of well-designed and efficient hunting implements, and complicated procedures for food preparation. They also found a people with a rich oral tradition and elaborate art forms such as pottery, basketry, jewelry, and weaving. The natives possessed many of the recognized forms of civilized society, such as a complex social organization, even though they had no written language or technologies equal to the powerful European steel tools and weapons. Some tribes, such as the Iroquois, were politically well organized and united into confederacies; others, like the Apache, were more loosely organized into independent bands. All had finely developed arts of utilizing whatever abundance the land provided for them. The Spanish soldier Pedro de Castaneda, who explored the Southwest and the Great Plains with Coronado, was deeply impressed with the skill and completeness with which the Plains Indians used the bounty of the buffalo:

> With the skins they build their houses; with the skins they clothe and shoe themselves; from the skins they make rope and also obtain

wool. With the sinews they make thread, with which they sew clothes and also their tents. From the bones they shape awls. The dung they use for firewood, since there is no other fuel in that land. The bladders they use as jugs and drinking containers. They sustain themselves on their meat, eating it slightly roasted and heated over the dung. Some they eat raw.[5]

The vast majority of these characteristics and accomplishments were lost on the Europeans, whose desire for land, and for control over the environment, blinded them to the Indians' ability to live with, not in spite of, the environment. By contrast, happy to trade grain, furs, and tobacco for the horses, weapons, tools, and household implements of the palefaced settlers, the Indians initially accepted them — if not with pleasure, at least with trust that both groups might live in harmony. Yet, because the Indians were pagan and lacked European technology, they were often treated by the Europeans as subhuman, and incapable of learning European customs. Even today, nearly five hundred years later, such prejudices persist. The vestiges of conflict between the opposing notions of the Indian as noble savage and the Indian as uncivilized foe still run deep through the American culture.

During the many years that the Europeans explored and subdued this continent, they met with and conquered hundreds of different Native American groups, groups that were much more diversified in their cultural practices than the varieties of Europeans. Those who cared to observe discovered that Indian groups with as few as a thousand members had developed distinctive languages, material goods, and ways of life. Still, given the vast gulf between the Native American and the European, it is not surprising that there was very little understanding of each other's cultures. It took virtually until this century, when the Indians were thoroughly conquered and subjugated, for a few descendants of those original European settlers to turn to them and try to understand their ways. It took the development of anthropology.

It also took greed. The anthropologists often arrived after entrepreneurs and collectors had traded, bought, or stolen objects of great beauty and cultural significance from the tribes and thereby brought to the attention of academically trained men and women the wealth of material culture there was to be studied among these conquered peoples. Finely woven baskets, superb pottery, carved ritual objects, jewelry, and woven blankets form the core of the collections in this nation's major museums. The U.S. Bureau of American Ethnology in Washington, D.C. (now part of the Smithsonian Institution), the Field Museum of Natural History in Chicago, the Museum of the American Indian in New York City, and many other smaller museums hold vast collections of objects, sacred and mundane, that shed light on the life of the native peoples of this continent. These museums also contain the field notes of the early archaeologists and ethnographers, many of whom lived with the tribes for a time in an attempt to understand their ways and translate them for the newer Americans.

The study of Native Americans has proceeded along several separable but interlocking tracks — archaeology, ethnology, history. From these fields of study we derive the materials that inform us about Native American life and customs. Archaeology alone provides us with only a skeleton description of the prehistoric culture. The "likely stories" that the archaeologists construct are generally based on the material culture of the past. They therefore tend to emphasize the manner in which prehistoric groups might have made or used the implements they left behind, or the habitation patterns they developed. Archaeologists' ability to reach into the mind of the precontact Native American, to reconstruct thought patterns, or to understand spiritual activities is severely limited by what the material culture can reveal to them.

Nevertheless, during the last hundred years, American archaeologists have achieved an impressive record of scholarship. Through their work, we now know that men and women first arrived on this continent from Asia at least thirty thousand years ago, most likely across the Bering Strait, and that they dispersed throughout the Americas and developed cultures as distinctly different as the Maya and the Eskimo, the Chumash and the Pueblo.

It is impossible to say just when these first Americans developed a knowledge of astronomy that would help them survive and provide substance for their lore and ritual traditions, but we know from the archaeological remains that well before the Europeans settled here most tribes were following the regular motions of the sun, moon, and stars to regulate their own lives. Just when the peoples of this hemisphere began to incorporate astronomy into their lives is, and to a large extent will remain, a mystery. Nevertheless, thanks to the work of chroniclers and historians, occasional travelers and ethnographers, we are gaining substantial clues about the relationship of astronomy to Native American life and lore.

Living Off the Land

Although it is probably true to say that the differences among Native American groups are more evident than their similarities, it is nevertheless possible to generalize somewhat, and to summarize common traits. First and foremost, as became immediately evident to the Europeans, Native Americans lived very close to the land. Their relationship to the land and its flora and fauna enabled them to wrest an adequate, sometimes even comfortable, living from the earth. By becoming deeply sensitive to the rhythms of the earth and sky, they had adapted thoroughly to their environment. Consider the ability of the Eskimos to survive, even thrive, in the forbidding weather and landscape of the Arctic. Protected by fur-lined parkas and by dwellings of snow blocks and animal skins, they are able to survive the long arctic nights. Voyaging in the icy waters in light, skin-covered kayaks, they take sustenance from the sea.

The efficiency of Native American shelter and clothing frequently astonished the early European settlers. The fur-lined, hard-soled leather boots of the natives of eastern Canada particularly impressed the French explorers; so, too, did their canoes. Constructed from a light wooden frame and covered with layers of birch bark, the canoe was a light and efficient water craft, well designed for use in the lakes and streams of the northeastern woods.

The earth lodge of the Plains Pawnee, constructed of a wooden framework covered with a thick layer of earth and sod, was warm in winter and cool in the summer. When the Pawnee left their lodges to hunt buffalo and other animals in the summer months, they took along another highly efficient dwelling, the portable tipi. Castaneda remarked on the tipis of the Plains Indians:

> Their tents are in the shape of pavilions. They set them up by means of poles which they carry for the purpose. After driving them in the ground they tie them together at the top. When they move from place to place they carry them by means of dogs, of which they have many. They load the dogs with their tents, poles,

and other things . . . What these people worship most is the sun. The hides of their tents are dressed on both sides, free from hair.[6]

In the Southwest, the Hopi Indians of Arizona constructed thick-walled dwellings of stone. Plastered with mud made from the surrounding soil, and carefully oriented to the sun, these houses soaked up and stored the warming rays of the sun and protected their inhabitants from the cold northwest winds. The dry-farming techniques of the Hopi, which enabled this predominantly agricultural people to establish a civilization in the southwestern desert, are no less impressive than their work in stone. In his account of his explorations of the Southwest, Coronado complained about the southwest desert and the lack of abundant food for his men and his horses, yet the Pueblo people who were there well before him had managed to entice a satisfactory living from the land.

Not all Native American tribes were farmers. A higher proportion were hunters and gatherers, living directly off the bounty their gods provided. Though their overall diet would hardly satisfy Western tastes, it was generally wholesome, varied, and nutritious. The sunflower, the Jerusalem artichoke, the ground cherry, the pokeberry, and the amaranthus are just a few of the plants native to this land that were gathered and prepared by the Indian tribes. Each is edible, even delicious if gathered at the right time and prepared in the proper manner. As the writer and wild-food expert Euell Gibbons emphasized in his numerous books, many of these healthful wild foods are neglected gastronomic treasures today. Indeed, Mr. Gibbons rediscovered many of these wild delicacies by reading ethnographic accounts of Indian botanical lore and use.

In addition to gathering and consuming these wild plants, Native Americans also deliberately spread them from one habitat to another. One of the many clues used by archaeologists studying the ruins of the Colorado Plateau in the Four Corners area to locate house ruins is to search for clumps of wolfberry (*Lycium pallidum*) growing near each other. The tart, red-orange fruit of this twisted shrub was eaten by the Pueblo Indians in Arizona, Colorado, New Mexico, and Utah. Dried and eaten in winter or times of famine by the Hopi, the berries were also consumed by other Pueblo groups. The plant was considered sacred to the Bow Priesthood at Zuni Pueblo. Apparently, the prehistoric inhabitants of the region cultivated the shrub near their houses in order to have a ready supply of the fruit when it ripened in June and July.

Not all Native American foods would be considered even barely palatable today. Insects such as grasshoppers, bees, and beetles, as well as snakes and lizards, were also part of the menu in some areas. Nevertheless, even if they don't appeal to our tastes, these foods are wholesome and harmless. What they and other more commonly used foods gave Native Americans was the ability to survive and prosper in conditions that proved very difficult for the Europeans who took the land from them.

Living with Each Other

The social organization of Native American groups was as varied as their material culture. Some were highly organized into villages and towns. The prehistoric site of Cahokia, along the Mississippi east of St. Louis, represents one extreme. At one time the city on this site extended over more than thirty-seven hundred acres and housed thousands of inhabitants. By contrast, the Apache and Navajo lived in very small, highly mobile groups.

Like the Europeans, the natives they conquered generally had well-defined roles for men and women. Each sex and age group had its duties, special tasks, and rights. In contrast to European society, however, one of the striking features of Native American civilization was the frequently high status of women, particularly among the agriculturalists. Although data on the status of women are fragmentary and hard to find, it is clear that women often exercised more power in Native American communities than did their European counterparts. This was a matter often overlooked by the male travelers, missionaries, and hunters who reported their observations of the natives they encountered. It continues to be overlooked in the anthropological literature, though the women's movement in the United States and Canada has focused more attention on the role of women in Native American society. Native women in agricultural tribes often controlled the land and dwellings and passed both on through their daughters. This may have come about because the women generally tended the fields and gathered edible plants near the villages, where they could also look after the children. Women generally wove articles of clothing, blankets, and baskets and made pottery. The men did the hunting, much of the fishing, and any heavy construction, and they manufactured most of the tools needed for these pursuits.

Among the Iroquois of the Northeast, the power of women is well known. They controlled the farmland and production from it; they also had considerable say in political matters and could nominate and censure chiefs. Their husbands came to live with them, rather than the reverse.

In Pueblo and Navajo societies today, the women own the family house and its effects and, through the clans, also control the crops. If a woman is no longer treated well by her husband, she can simply set his personal belongings outside the house to divorce him.

All data on eastern tribes are much more sketchy than for those tribes that were encountered and conquered later in the history of the United States, and information on the role and status of women is very scarce. However, it is clear that in some tribes, women held public office. The Potawatomi along Lake Michigan had women chiefs, and the signatures of some of these appear on treaties with the United States. Among the Miami and the Shawnee farther south, women also had an important political role, either as chiefs or as part of other directly supportive political groups.

In hunter-gatherer societies, women generally had lower political and economic status. Among the California tribes, primarily hunters and gatherers, ownership and descent was through the male line. The exclusion of women from hunting and, often, fishing was bolstered by mythological accounts of harm that had come to women who had hunted or fished.

Although they seem to have had a small role in the political organization, Californian Indian women were highly respected and possessed a great degree of freedom and independence to tend to their own tasks. The most advanced of their handicrafts, the woven basket, was women's work. The narration of the tribal myths and singing, however, was most often left to the men.

Native American myths provide us with numerous clues to the status of women in these societies. In the Navajo creation cycle, for example, First Woman functions equally with First Man in creating elements of the physical world and instructing the Navajo people about how to live. Spider Woman has a crucial role in both Navajo and Pueblo myths in guiding wayward travelers and in helping those in need to overcome great dangers. Among some Pueblos, she is also a creator.

According to the Acoma Indians, a Pueblo group in New Mexico, the woman deity Iatiku gave them their clan names and their food, and instructed them in plying their crafts and in building methods. She thus serves the role that Prometheus has in the Greek mythology. Iatiku is even more, however; she also guides the Acoma in the proper way to worship the gods, and how to live their lives.

The Land

Ownership of the land was frequently a point of great contention between the newcomer Europeans and the natives. Indians did not own property in the same sense as Europeans understood it. For the Indians, use of the land was the important issue. Though a given portion of land was controlled by a given clan or kin group, those who controlled it were bound by custom to use it for the good of the larger entity, whether it be a village or a town. If the land was abandoned by one group, it could be used by another. The chief of a village or its elders generally had no more right to sell land or sign away the rights of access to areas traditionally used by the village than I would to sell my neighbor's property today. Further, when Europeans entered into treaties over use of the land, they most often made them with native men, little comprehending that in many cases the use of the land was controlled by the women of the tribe.

Native American societies were based on oral communications, and to a considerable extent they remain so. Although they apparently had a well-developed sign language for communicating between language groups, the Indians north of Mexico knew no writing until the Europeans arrived. This, too, created many misunderstandings between the native groups and the newcomers, for the Europeans, dependent as they were on written documents for proof of ownership, placed little faith in oral commitments. The Indians, on the other hand, derived equally little satisfaction from black scratches on paper. Time and again in the long history of the development of the United States, written agreements on land use were prepared and signed by both Indians and Europeans and then violated by the latter.

The Oral Tradition

What is especially surprising to those who are heavily dependent on the written word is the ability of those within oral cultures to remember and transmit accurately the content of a given message. Nevertheless, folklorists find a remarkable consistency between narrations recorded fifty to seventy-five years ago and their rendition today. The explanation lies in the ability of the hearer to understand the recitations in the full context of the society and all its traditions. Certain mnemonic devices help, of course, such as repeating patterns of words or using certain rhythms, but in general the transmission of an oral tradition depends on the support of the whole group. Even if the details of a given story or ritual poem are known to only a few, the society as a whole reinforces the recollection of the oral material by repeating visual symbols, dances, and songs.

Because they had no written languages, Native Americans depended on various forms of oral transmission to transfer societal norms. Ritual poems and sayings formed an important part of their oral apparatus. The winter months of storytelling also gave the elders a chance to remind themselves of their heritage and traditions, duties and taboos, and to pass these along to the younger members of the tribe. Many of our best-remembered Native American stories derive from the long nights of winter when there was little obligation to tend the fields or to hunt for animals. Mixed with the often fabulous tales were general rules for living, or moral strictures that should be observed in the tribe. Also told at these times were stories that explained the origins of the tribe and how the world came to be as it was. Creation stories and other legends are a rich source of Native American thought and philosophic expression today. They convey a tribal view of the world and describe the proper relationship of humans to the rest of nature.

One of the constant themes that appears in Native American stories illustrates another aspect in which Indians differed radically from Europeans — their intimate relationship to the animal and insect world. In their stories, not only did animals take on anthropomorphic characteristics but humans, in their turn, assumed the shapes and spirits of animals. In some stories, humans and animals mated with each other to produce offspring that could live in either world.

The Blackfoot of northern Montana tell the story of a young woman who, though she had many suitors, refused to marry any of them.[7] Her father, a widower who also had seven sons and a younger daughter, was deeply distressed at her behavior, for he thought that the older daughter should be a model for the younger. The elder daughter wanted no other lovers because she already had one, a bear, whom she met secretly every time she went out to gather wood. Each day, as soon as her father and seven brothers left to hunt, she would leave her younger sister alone in the lodge and go to meet the bear.

After some time, the younger sister grew curious, and following her sister one day to where she met her bear lover, the younger one quickly discovered the elder's secret. That night the younger sister told her father, who became enraged that his daughter would prefer a bear to one of the village suitors. He immediately gathered together his sons and others from the village to hunt and kill the bear.

Upon hearing that her lover was dead, the young woman became sad and extremely angry, but she carefully hid her anger. She became a powerful medicine woman who could work many different kinds of magic. One day, as she and her little sister were playing together as if they were bears, she turned into a real bear. Her hidden anger released, she ran into the tribal encampment and killed many people, including her father. The little sister was very frightened; taking up the smallest brother, she hurried back to the lodge. Shortly, the young woman finished her rampage in the camp and, assuming her womanly shape, returned to the lodge and threatened to kill her sister and youngest brother. The little sister took her brother and left quickly, with the excuse that they were going to fetch wood for the fire.

Several hundred yards away from the lodge the little sister met her six other brothers. They all quickly decided to run away. But since the young woman was a resourceful medicine woman, she knew exactly what her brothers and sister were doing. She took on her bear shape again in order to catch them quickly. The brothers also knew some magic, and seeing her approach, one of them poured a little water in the palm of his hand and sprinkled it before him. The water instantly became a large lake in front of the bear. While the bear ran around the lake, the brothers and sister ran on ahead. Soon, however, their sister caught up again. This time another brother threw a porcupine tail on the ground, which turned into a great thicket. On they ran, until, seeing their sister close behind them, they climbed a tall tree. Upon reaching the tree, the bear threatened to kill them all. Taking a stick, she knocked four of her brothers out of the tree. They died as they hit the ground. Though immensely frightened, one of the remaining brothers was able to shoot her in the head with an arrow and kill her.

The children who were still left then climbed down from the tree and began to mourn their siblings. But the littlest brother, who knew some magic of his own, shot an arrow into the air. When it hit the ground he found that one of his elder brothers came alive. He shot three more arrows into the air and the remaining three also revived. Rejoicing that they were all saved from the fury of their elder sister, they sat down to discuss the situation. Where should they go? What should they do? "Our people have all been killed, and we are a long way from home," said one. "We have no relatives living in the world." The youngest brother suggested that since they had no one on earth, they should live in the sky instead. After a short discussion, all agreed to this plan. Then, shutting their eyes, they ascended to the heavens, where they are now visible every clear night. The littlest brother became the North Star. Little sister and the other brothers each became one of the stars of the Big Dipper, the eldest brother and little sister being the "pointer stars." Little sister's place was closest to the North Star because she so often carried her little brother on her back.

Other stories recount humans who change into snakes, buffalo, deer, or even foxes. These stories, though understood by the tribes as mythical events that happened "long, long ago," nevertheless reflect an attitude of respect and veneration toward animals. Animals that were hunted for food were treated with particular reverence, for their souls were just like human souls, capable of deep love and self-sacrifice; when treated ill, they were likely to avenge themselves. Improperly killed and dressed, animals might inform their fellow creatures who would thereupon make themselves scarce for food. Among the Laguna Indians, a Pueblo group in New Mexico, it is proper to cover a dead deer's face before gutting it. To show love and appreciation for the deer, the hunter then sprinkles cornmeal on its nose to feed the deer's spirit. "Otherwise, the deer would be offended, and they would not come to die for them the following year."[8]

To the Oglala Sioux, in South Dakota, the buffalo was a chief source of food before they had to give up most of their lands to their conquerors. Buffalo were holy creatures, and each specific part of the buffalo symbolized a part of the universe.

Long, long ago, a beautiful woman came among the Oglala Sioux, members of the Dakota Nation. She was dressed in white buckskin and on her back she carried a bundle. This mysterious woman asked that a great lodge be built in which to meet with all the tribe. When she entered the sacred lodge, constructed from the skins and poles of several tipis, she walked in the sacred sunwise direction, around to the left.

> She took from the bundle a pipe, and also a small round stone
> which she placed upon the ground. Holding the pipe up with its
> stem to the heavens, she said: "With this sacred pipe you will walk
> upon the Earth; for the Earth is your Grandmother and Mother, and
> She is sacred. Every step that is taken upon Her should be as a
> prayer. The bowl of this pipe is of red stone; it is the Earth. Carved
> in the stone and facing the center is this buffalo calf who represents
> all the four-leggeds who live upon your Mother. The stem of the
> pipe is of wood, and this represents all that grows upon the Earth.
> And these twelve feathers which hang here where the stem fits into
> the bowl are from Wanbli Galeshka, the Spotted Eagle, and they rep-
> resent the eagle and all the wingeds of the air. All these peoples,
> and all the things of the universe, are joined to you who smoke the
> pipe — all send their voices to Wakan-Tanka, the Great Spirit.
> When you pray with this pipe, you pray for and with everything."[9]

The sacred woman, for it was now clear to the assembly that she was blessed, gave them additional instructions about living, and then, passing through the lodge in a sunwise direction, she left. However, after walking only a little way to the east, she stopped to sit down. Then a marvelous transformation took place. As the people watched, this mysterious woman turned into a buffalo calf, arose, turned to each of the four directions, and walked away.

Understanding the ability to transmit detailed information orally is of crucial importance to comprehending the ability of Native Americans to share complicated astronomical data between the generations. For example, at Zuni Pueblo, at the Shalako ceremony that is generally held in early December, the masked god Sayatasha, who has the responsibility to observe the moon in order to reconcile the lunar calendar with the solar one, recites a long ritual poem called the long talk, or Sayatasha's Night Chant.

This poem, which must be letter-perfect, is a recitation of the motions of the sun and the moon during the year, and an iteration of the rituals that Sayatasha observes throughout the year. Sayatasha (or, rather, the priest who is his impersonator) as part of his duties watches for the appearance of the first full moon after the winter solstice ceremony is over. At this time he plants prayer sticks at a sacred spring near the pueblo. Thereafter, he plants prayer sticks at a different spring every full moon until October, when he will have completed ten plantings. On the morning of the last planting, he is given a cotton string tied with forty-nine knots. Every morning thereafter, Sayatasha unties a knot until the day of Shalako arrives. On the night of the forty-eighth day, Sayatasha recites the long talk. Then he and the other masked gods (kachinas) dance until dawn. At the first sign of dawn, he climbs to the roof of the house in which he had been dancing to face the east and say a prayer to the sun while he unties the last knot.

Because the Night Chant reminds the audience of the ritual actions and the lunar and solar events that have occurred throughout the year, the poem serves to instill in Sayatasha's listeners the important observations of the ritual calendar, and to solicit their participation in them. As folklorist Jane Young discovered several years ago, his recitation also imparts significant data on the lunar and solar calendar. Formulaic repetition of certain stanzas of the poem, with slight differences to indicate the motion of the sun, sets the ritual data of each major portion of the poem and also describes the position of the setting sun along the horizon.[10] The stanzas that follow specify or describe the ritual action that took place at this time, such as the planting of prayer sticks at the sacred springs. Repeated every year at the Shalako ceremony, the words of the Night Chant thus become an integral part of each Zuni's experience.

The Sacred Clown

Native American life, in addition to being tied firmly to the land and directly incorporating the motions of the celestial sphere into religious experience, also has a playful aspect that is worth exploring. Imagine a gaily painted jester, tumbling down the aisle during an interlude in a Christian or Jewish service, singing a ribald song and making obscene gestures to the old men and women. It is likely that such a person would be quickly hustled out by the shocked and dutiful ushers and very possibly turned over to the police. Yet such is the role of the sacred clown in Native American ceremonies.[11]

The sacred clown may wear its clothes and boots backwards or ride turned around on its horse. Sacred clowns may also engage in mock intercourse or gesture obscenely at the audience. They throw objects at the onlookers or make exaggerated caricatures of the priest — anything to help the people break through to an immediate religious experience. The modes and methods differ among tribes, but the clown has a firm place in Native American religion. Clowning is a way to open the people up, to help them forget themselves and experience the mysteries of the sacred world more directly.

Iatiku, the Acoma Pueblo goddess who taught the people their roles and duties, is said to have created the sacred clown Koshari. "Koshari was kind of crazy; he was active, picking around, talking nonsense, talking backward . . . He caused Oak Man (the first priest) a lot of amusement, with his garbled speech and wisecracking and his self-confidence."[12] Acoma sacred clowns play around to a definite purpose. Often it is to aid the medicine men in their curing rituals. After Koshari had learned the rites of the medicine society, he was sent away to help the sun.

> Iatiku turned to Koshari and said, "You have done your work faithfully but you are not acting normally enough to be here with the people (all the time)." *He was different from the other people because he knew something about himself,* so Iatiku told him to go and live at ha-kuai'ch (the house of the Sun). "You are to be a help to the Sun. You will be called at times to help here. *You are not going to be afraid of anything* or to regard anything as sacred." [Emphasis mine.][13]

The comic acts of the sacred clown provide balance and relief from a sometimes overpowering sacred experience. Black Elk commented on the Sioux sacred clown Heyoka:

> I will say something about heyokas and the heyoka ceremony, which seems to be very foolish, but is not so. Only those who have had visions of the thunder beings of the west can act as heyokas.

They have sacred power and they share some of this with all the people, but they do it through funny actions. When a vision comes from the thunder beings of the west, it comes with terror like a thunder storm; but when the storm of vision has passed, the world is greener and happier; for wherever the truth of vision comes upon the world, it is like a rain. The world, you see, is happier after the terror of the storm.[14]

Thus the sacred clown reflects an essential attribute of Native American life — balance between the sacred and mundane. Its actions well up from and participate in the fundamental oneness of all nature. Folklorist Barre Toelken, who has lived among the Navajo, explains this view of oneness in describing the Navajo use of the juniper berry.

My Navajo sister says that [the] reason these beads (juniper berries strung together) will prevent nightmares and keep one from getting lost in the dark is that they represent the partnership between the tree that gives its berries, the animals which gather them, and humans who pick them up (being careful not to deprive the animals of their food). It is a three-way partnership — plant, animal, and man. Thus, if you keep these beads on you and think about them, your mind, in its balance with nature, will tend to lead a healthy existence . . . They are reminders of a frame of mind which is essentially cyclic, in the proper relationship with the rest of nature — a frame of mind necessary to the maintenance of health.[15]

Awareness of the cyclic nature of the world and of human life is evident in Native American attitudes toward stellar patterns and celestial motions. The patterns of the upper realm and the passing of the seasons are essential elements of human existence. Though the responses of different tribes or groups of Native Americans to these patterns differ in detail, they share similar attitudes — to live in balance is to observe the celestial cycles and to reflect them in ceremony, in planting and harvesting, and in daily life.

3 Celestial Motions and the Roots of the Calendar

Throughout the land, in cities, towns, and villages, well before a certain time-honored ritual began, the revelers gathered at the appointed ceremonial squares and assembly halls to assure themselves of the best location for the impending ceremony. Each wore appropriate ceremonial garb. Hours before the ritual, many people were pressed into service to prepare ritual food and drink; tables groaned under the heavy weight. As each newcomer arrived, he or she was welcomed warmly and pressed to eat and drink.

Soon the hour that they had prepared for and long awaited was upon them. In each gathering, revelers donned ceremonial hats and readied the traditional beverage. Shortly a great cry went up; the time had finally come. The ritual timekeeper announced that the sun was precisely on the opposite side of the earth. Midnight had arrived. Immediately in all the gatherings in all the towns and villages the revelers' cry rang out loud and clear. "Happy New Year!" they joyfully exclaimed. In accordance with the ancient tradition, the dutiful throngs ushered in another New Year. They celebrated, as similar crowds have in centuries past, the ending of one cycle and the beginning of another one — the yearly renewal of hopes and dreams.

Why does the Western world celebrate the New Year just as the winter season's coldest weather is about to begin? As the New Year's revelers don their party hats or take up their glasses of champagne to toast the New Year, in a distant caricature of an ancient pagan festival, few ask themselves such a question. Yet the tradition of starting the Western calendar shortly after the first day of winter has the same general roots as the new year of most Native American calendars. The Gregorian calendar that is now the world standard begins its yearly cycle just ten days after winter solstice, the shortest day of the year. Even though most of the winter lies before us, we can rejoice in the eventual prospect of longer days to come, bearing their warmth for the fields and for our winter-worn bodies.[1]

Solstice in Latin literally means "sun stand still." Winter solstice is the day when the sun halts its apparent southward journey on the celestial sphere and begins to move north again. Because of the rotation of the earth, all celestial bodies, including the sun, appear to move through the sky daily (or nightly) from east to west along well-described paths. At the same time, the earth also follows its orbit around the sun, completing a full circuit in nearly 365¼ days. This additional motion causes the sun to appear to slip eastward among the field of stars a little each day. Plato designated this apparent eastward slip "the motion of the other," and he called the east-to-west motion "the motion of the same."

The stars, by contrast, alter their position relative to the sun only very slowly. To the naked eye, this slow stellar motion, called precession, remains undetected over several centuries. Though they appear to move nightly across the sky, the stars shift very little with respect to each other. In other words, the constellations look pretty much today as they did hundreds of years ago, so much so that the Greeks called the stars the fixed stars.

The Sun's Motions

It is the small daily shift of the sun's position with respect to the stars that enabled traditional astronomers, unaided by telescopic instruments, to determine an accurate solar calendar. Not only does the sun slip backwards (eastward) against the daily (westward) movement of the stars, it does so at a 23.5° angle to the stars' "motion of the same." Therefore, as the sun shifts among the background of stars (approximately one degree per day), it also shifts its position along the horizon from day to day as it rises or sets. Thus, by standing daily in the same place and observing sunrise or sunset, an observer at, for example, 36° north latitude (about the latitude of Albuquerque, New Mexico), would see the sun execute a 60° total

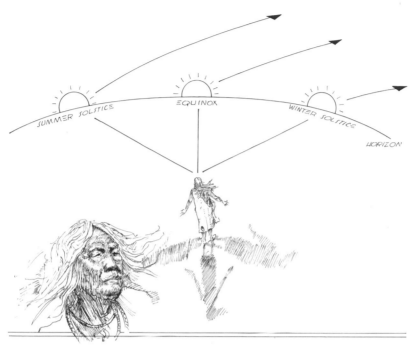

Sunrise positions along the horizon throughout the year. Because the sun's apparent yearly orbit lies at an angle of 23.5° to the celestial equator, the sun's horizon position changes from day to day. The sun appears to move slowly along the horizon from day to day near the solstices and nearly a diameter of the sun per day at the equinoxes.

angular swing between extreme positions along the horizon in the course of a year (see Table 1).

To illustrate this phenomenon: in late November, assuming a level horizon, the observer at 36° north latitude witnesses the sun rise about 25° south of east. As the days wear into December, the sun works its way further south until it appears to stop for several days on either side of the winter solstice (December 21 or 22). Its angular position would be about 30° south of east, or 120° away from geographic north. (This angle is termed the azimuth.)

Because the day-to-day motion along the horizon is so small during this period, it is not apparent to the naked eye. This was a source of grave concern to most traditional societies around the world, in-

Table 1 Rise and Set Azimuths of the Sun and Moon at 36° North Latitude
(0° Horizon Elevation)

Object	Rise	Set	Rise	Set
	A.D. 0		A.D. 1500	
Summer solstice sun	59°46'	300°14'	59°52'	300°08'
Winter solstice sun	119°21'	240°39'	119°17'	240°43'
Moon at extreme north (excursion $E+I$)	53°46'	306°14'	54°02'	305°58'
Moon at extreme north (incursion $E-I$)	67°11'	292°49'	67°26'	292°34'
Moon at extreme south (excursion $-E-I$)	127°01'	232°59'	126°45'	233°15'
Moon at extreme south (incursion $-E+I$)	113°30'	246°30'	113°15'	246°45'

E is the angular inclination of the sun's apparent celestial path (ecliptic) from the celestial equator.

I is the angular inclination of the moon's apparent celestial path from the sun's apparent celestial path.

Compared to the stars (see Table 2), the passage of years has very little effect on the rise and set azimuths of the sun and the moon.

Derived from tables computed by Anthony F. Aveni, Colgate University.

cluding many Native American groups. They feared that if the sun did not begin to move back again, the fields would remain frozen and unsuitable for planting, and all living things would die.

This cycle of the renewal of life depends intimately on the continuation of the sun's yearly cycle. Because of their concern for the sun's movements at this time of the year, many Native American groups developed elaborate ceremonies designed to entreat the sun to move northward again. The sun, as the Hopi Indians say, is inclined to wander, and must be encouraged to stay on his accustomed course.

As our hypothetical observer daily continues to watch the sun rise, he or she finally sees the sun move slowly northward until it passes the midway position on the horizon. On this day, the spring or vernal equinox, the number of hours the sun is above the horizon precisely equals the number of hours it remains below. We call this day, generally March 21 in the Gregorian calendar, the first day of spring. It is also the day when the sun moves from a position south of the celestial equator to one north of it. Thus the sun rises exactly east and sets exactly west. The careful observer would also notice an important detail of the sun's daily horizon motion. As it draws closer to its position precisely east, the sun's horizon position shift grows each day. On either side of the vernal equinox its position changes by about a solar diameter per day (about half a degree).

The sun moves quickly north, the days lengthen rapidly, and the earth begins to warm, heralding the approach of summer. In mirror image to its winter motions, the sun again begins to slow its motion, this time along the northern arc of the horizon, until it pauses and turns around to head south on the summer solstice (azimuth of about 60°). Days about the summer solstice are also the longest days of the year in the Northern Hemisphere, because the length of the sun's daily arc through the sky is greater at this time. Nights are correspondingly shorter.

After the sun has turned around at the summer solstice and headed southward again, the days begin to shorten, imperceptibly at first. Then, as the autumnal equinox approaches, the process speeds up until, at the equinox, the sun again moves very quickly along the horizon. Its southward journey continues, and by the time the sun reaches its winter solstice position on the horizon, the air and the earth have already become quite cold. Plants have died or have become dormant, and burrowing animals have retreated into hibernation. Once again, as the sun reaches its southernmost point, it slows considerably and appears to stop briefly at the winter solstice. The cycle of the sun is thus complete.

The celestial wanderings of the sun have been a fertile source of stories for centuries. They often reflect worries that because the sun god follows a wandering path, he or others who gain control of the sun disk may wander away from the proper way. Consider the ancient Greek myth of Phaëthon and the chariot of the sun. Helios, the sun god, offers Phaëthon, his son by an earthly mother, fulfillment of any wish. Phaëthon's wish is to drive the chariot of the sun in its daily journey across the sky. Helios, who normally guides the chariot himself and knows just how difficult it is to control the horses that pull the chariot, attempts to dissuade his brash offspring from making this particular request. Phaëthon insists, and Helios, bound to his own word, reluctantly turns the reins of the chariot over to him. As he drives off, the sun god warns Phaëthon to hold the reins tightly and to keep the team to the proper path. Phaëthon does well for a short time, but soon he begins to feel overconfident. Having a great desire to take a closer look at his home below, he deviates just a little from the path. Being unaccustomed to deviating at all from the usual daily path, the powerful horses charge down to earth. From then on Phaëthon loses control of the chariot and becomes an unwilling rider in a wildly gyrating vehicle. First the horses pull the sun chariot much too close to earth, causing the farmland and villages on the surface to scorch. Then they gallop too high, bringing sudden cold on other portions of the earth.

The gods high up on Mount Olympus are angered by the grief on earth caused by this boy's poor judgment. Zeus quickly hurls one of his thunderbolts at the chariot and Phaëthon falls out of the sky and tumbles to earth. Without a driver, the horses of the sun gallop home to their stables. Because of Phaëthon's ride, parts of the earth are now either covered with ice or spit forth fire and smoke. It is clear that close control and attention to duty are required to keep the sun on the proper course. As traditional societies seem to reason, any help they could give the sun god in ceremonies to remind him of his duty would ultimately help them. The Cochiti Indians along the Rio Grande in New Mexico tell a similar story, revealing their own concern with the need to keep the wandering sun under close control.

Coyote, a constant wanderer himself, arrives in the east at the house of the Sun, enters, and cheerfully greets the Sun. Sun replies pleasantly but wants to know who this stranger is. After explaining that he is Coyote-Youth, with the cheek characteristic of this mythic trickster-bungler, Coyote breezily proposes that he carry the sun disk on its westward journey.[2]

Sun is nonplused by this bold request. Taken aback and rightly doubtful, he reluctantly accedes to Coyote's desire, warning him not to deviate from the proper path and go down to the earth. Assuring Sun that all will be well, Coyote takes up the sun disk and proceeds to carry it westward. Sun directs his two sons, the Twins, to accompany him as escorts and watchguards. All is fine until Coyote arrives at the middle of his journey across the heavens. Coyote stays on the path provided by the rainbow of the sun. Then, in an action that is a caricature of the occasional actions of the real sun god who at times descends to earth to lie with women, Coyote desires to go down to the earth to see several beautiful women bathing. He pleads with the Twins to let him descend. They sternly warn him that he will make trouble.

Coyote is impervious to such warnings and plunges earthward. He is only halfway down, taking the sun and the rainbow path with him, before plants, animals, and people are severely scorched. Something must be done, and quickly. The Twins immediately turn the rainbow path back up. After they take the sun disk down in the west, pass through the underworld, and arrive finally in the east, Sun scolds the Twins for their negligence in letting Coyote carry the disk toward the earth. Coyote, for his misdemeanor, is severely punished. Sun dooms him to live the life of a scavenger. Ever after, Coyote must subsist in the desert on beetles and rotten food, on carcasses and the leavings of other animals.

The Moon

According to one version of the Navajo emergence myth, after the First People emerged from the underworld, they began to crave more light. After trying several methods of lighting up the land, First Woman and First Man finally decided to make a sun. Taking a large slab of quartz crystal, they and their helpers fashioned it into two disks. They decorated the first disk by giving it a mask of blue turquoise that would radiate light and heat; red coral they placed around the rim and tied to the ear lobes. After attaching cardinal, flicker, lark, and eagle feathers to spread light and heat in all the four directions, they attached the disk to the eastern sky with darts of lightning. After that, they decorated the second disk, the moon. The people soon began to complain that the stationary sun kept the east too hot and the west too cold. First Man and First Woman pondered how they could give it motion in the sky. How could the sun or the moon move when neither had an animating spirit? Just then, two old men appeared on the scene who were willing to give their spirits to the lifeless disks in order to allow Sun and Moon to follow their sky paths. Though the stones could now move, they faced another problem. Their bearers did not know what paths to follow. First Man came to the rescue.

> The eagle is guided by his tail feathers. We will give you each
> twelve feathers from the eagle's tail to point the correct paths you

are to follow, and the changes in the paths will mark the changes in the seasons.[3]

Enlivened by the spirit of the wise old man and with the twelve eagle feathers to guide him, Sun began his journey. Moon followed after the sun had reached the western horizon, but just as he was ready to depart, Wind Boy tried to help by pushing. The resulting wind blew the feathers in Moon's face so he could not see where he was going. As a result, the story finishes, Moon has always followed strange paths across the sky. In this Navajo account, the sun moves as it should, along twelve paths. It is the moon's motion that is somehow irregular and out of the intended order of things.

The sun's wanderings are indeed simple compared to those of the moon. In addition to continually changing shape, the moon follows three different major cycles: a monthly cycle, a yearly one, and a cycle that lasts nearly a generation. The above Navajo story explains the origins of the moon's motions, and it also provides considerable insight into the Navajos' understanding of the sun's yearly movements.

Not only does the moon change shape over a 29.5-day cycle, it also varies its relationship to the sun at the same time. When the moon is new, it stands near the sun; when full, it is opposite the sun. Furthermore, while the moon undergoes these changes of celestial place and shape, its rise and set positions along the horizon also change. Its eagle feathers are truly wind-blown!

The most obvious of the moon's cycles is the alteration of its appearance: from the invisibility of new moon through its waxing phases to full moon, it returns through its waning phases to new moon once again. This cycle, called the synodic month, lasts 29.5306 days. It is what we refer to in common speech as a lunar month. It is the basis of the month of the Western calendar. Because the phases of the moon are easy to see and to track, a monthly calendar was the easiest and simplest one to devise. It is only when one tries to fit the lunar and solar calendars together that trouble starts. Early calendar makers spent considerable effort devising ways to force the lunar calendar, with months of approximately 29.5 days, to fit a solar year of 365.25 days because the two cycles are incommensurate with each other.[4] There are 12.368 synodic months in a solar year. That and the desire to have the crucial solar events of the

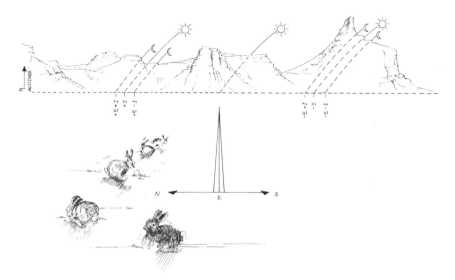

Moonrise throughout the 18.61-year lunar cycle. Because the moon's apparent monthly orbit is tilted to the sun's apparent yearly orbit, during part of its cycle ($+E+I$ and $-E-I$), the moon will rise or set outside the solstice points. Halfway through its full 18.61-year cycle ($+E-I$ and $-E+I$), the moon will always rise or set *within* the solstice points.

equinoxes and the solstices occur on the twenty-first or twenty-second of the month are the major causes of the unequal distribution of days among the months of the Western calendar.

Many Native American groups used both the lunar and the solar calendar. However, like others, they also ran into trouble when they tried to fit the two calendars together. In the best-known example, the Hopi pueblos have two sets of ceremonies, one set based on a solar calendar, and another based on the lunar calendar. In order to make the two sets of ceremonies fit each other, they add an extra month every three years. As long as one is not uncomfortable with making such ad hoc corrections when needed, the problem of rationalizing the two calendars is not severe.

The moon follows another, more subtle, cycle as well. As it slips through the heavens, it varies its position among the stars by about 13° per day. By the time it moves from a given star, around the celestial circle and back to the same star, only 27.3217 days have elapsed. Although the sidereal cycle is observable with appropriate effort, the northern Native Americans seem not to have been interested in this lunar cycle. In the Americas, only the Inca seem to have followed the sidereal lunar cycle with interest and incorporated it into their calendar.[5]

In its rambles through the heavens, the moon's complicated motions really tax the memory and ingenuity of the observer. In its monthly cycle, the moon follows nearly the same cycle of horizon positions as the sun's yearly cycle. However, the orbit of the moon around the earth is tilted by 5° with respect to the apparent orbit of the sun (the ecliptic) and this orbit as a whole completes a cycle in 18.61 years. This means that depending on which part of its 18.61-year orbital cycle it is in, during its monthly cycle when the moon reaches its own "standstill" positions, it could rise or set either inside the solstice horizon positions or outside and beyond them. The longer orbital cycle is the time the moon takes to move from a given standstill through its total cycle and back again to this same position.

To examine the moon's monthly horizon cycle, assume that it is winter and the sun is low in the daytime sky. Beginning just after new moon, we see the moon's thin sliver of light appear in the west after the sun has set. If the moon is also in the extreme part of its 18.61-year cycle, it would set to the south of the sun's winter solstice position. At a north latitude of 36°, the moon would set at an azimuth of about 306°. Then, as we follow the moon's setting positions throughout the month, it slowly moves further north, until, at full moon, the sun is just rising in the southeast quadrant. The moon is setting to the north of the summer solstice position at an azimuth of about 233°. (See Table 1.) Although the rest of the cycle of moonsets is extremely hard to follow with the naked eye because the sun is up, the moon gradually works its way south to a horizon position south of winter solstice sunset. The observer who wished to track the moon's position could, instead, observe moonrise until the moon was about to pass near the sun again at new moon. Then it disappears for a day.

Over 9.3 years, the extreme horizon positions of the moon gradually work their way inward past the solstices until they reach the maximum incursions possible — 6° north and south of the winter and summer solstices respectively.

It is highly likely that the Native American celestial observers were aware of most of these lunar intricacies. However, we do not know whether they tracked the 18.61-year cycle. This long cycle is of interest because it requires a much more sophisticated approach to observing the sky than has generally been attributed to Native American peoples.

One more lunar cycle is of great interest because of the information it conveys. Several centuries before the birth of Christ, the Chaldaeans discovered that similar solar eclipses occurred over a cycle of 223 synodic months, or 18 years 11 days. Over this interval of time, the moon and sun reach nearly the same positions with respect to one another that they had at the beginning of the cycle. Thus, if a solar or a lunar eclipse occurs, we will be treated to a repeat performance about 18 years 11 days later. Actually, the many small perturbations of the moon's motions over 18 years will generally cause the eclipse to occur at a different location on the earth's surface, so although the cycle can be used to predict the potential for experiencing an eclipse in a given local area, it is not an infallible method. Although we have several examples of Native American responses to lunar and solar eclipses, we have no evidence that they were able to, or cared to, predict their occurrence.

The Planets

The apparent movements of the planets are also quite irregular, though their cycles are entirely different from the lunar ones. The planets follow along very close to the ecliptic. Observationally, they may appear high in the night sky in winter. Conversely, in the summer months, those planets appear lower in the sky. Because they resemble stars in appearance, the planets are often confused with bright stars. Because they follow complicated paths, they were termed wanderers by the ancient Western civilizations. This distinguished them from the so-called fixed stars. The term *planet*, in fact, derives from the Greek word *planasthai*, which means "to wander."[6]

The most obvious and well known, as well as the brightest, planet is Venus, which is seen sometimes as an evening star and sometimes as a morning star. Although they did not necessarily connect the two appearances of Venus, Morning Star and Evening Star were intently observed by most Native American cultures and were sometimes used to time important ceremonies. Venus and its patterns of appearance and disappearance were of special interest to the Mayans and other Mesoamerican cultures. Venus first appears as an evening star just east of the sun a few minutes after the disk of the sun has slipped below the horizon. From then on, each night it moves farther and farther away from the sun and becomes brighter and brighter. About a month before Venus reaches its eastern extreme from the sun, it attains its maximum brightness. A full 132 days after its first appearance, Venus again begins to move toward the sun (that is, the angle between the sun and Venus begins to close). Visually, Venus is most striking as an evening star when it happens to fall close to the waxing crescent moon, a conjunction that is often celebrated in Pueblo Indian art. After approximately 263 days (the exact number depends greatly on an individual's visual acuity and the state of the atmosphere), the evening star disappears in the consuming brightness of the sun's disk. Eight days later, it reappears as a morning star, a position it maintains for approximately 263 days. Its reappearance as an evening star requires 46 to 70 days, depending again on the condition of the atmosphere and the visual acuity of the observer. The entire synodic cycle takes 584 days, or eight-fifths of a year.

At any given sun position, Venus' rise and set positions are constrained to a very narrow range of angles because Venus never moves very far away from the sun. However, because it moves with the sun, it will eventually, in its full synodic cycle of 584 days, move through the full range of azimuths available to the sun. Its orbit is inclined by a few degrees to the ecliptic, and it, like the moon, will appear inside and outside the solstice positions.

Venus is the brightest of the planets, and because of its visual association with the sun as a morning star or an evening star, it received the most attention from traditional astronomers. However, many societies also followed the movements of Mercury, a planet that also appears as a morning or evening star. Mercury is closer to the sun, and is therefore visible for only half an hour after sunset, as an evening star, or before sunrise as a morning star. Its full cycle is much shorter than Venus'. The speedy characteristics of the Roman messenger god Mercury derive from his association with the planet. Mercury completes a full cycle in 116 days.

Mars, Jupiter, and Saturn constitute a different class of planets entirely. They may be seen at any other position along the ecliptic, and as morning and evening stars. At times they appear fully opposite the sun, and take positions high in the night sky. The Greeks differentiated sharply between these planets and Mercury and Venus. The former were referred to as the outer planets; the latter they named the inner planets. Although all the planets were of great interest to the Greek and Babylonian astronomers, only Venus seems to have been of universal interest to the Native American cultures north of Mexico. To the Zuni Indians in New Mexico, for example, Venus is called Morning Star and Evening Star. Though they are considered separate celestial beings, they are twins, suggesting that the Zuni realized their essential unity. Sometimes, however, the demands of certain ceremonies related to Morning Star require the appearance of a morning star when Venus is an evening star or not visible. The Zuni then substitute any other convenient planet or bright star.

The "Fixed" Stars

Because the patterns of the stars seemed unchanging, and because each individual star seems to the unaided eye to rise and set at precisely the same location, year after year, the positions of the stars were originally thought to be fixed. Indeed, over many years they are. Yet the astronomer of fifth-century B.C. Athens would be quite surprised to find Polaris being used today as the north star. Two and a half centuries ago, Polaris was fourteen degrees from the earth's geographic pole. Today, it is slightly less than one degree away. Twenty-six thousand years from now it will again serve as pole star. This long-term shift of the pole star is called precession and is the result of the wobbling of the orbital axis of the earth. The change of position from year to year is not very great, but when added up over the centuries, these minute amounts of stellar wanderings grow large enough that it is impossible to observe a structure against today's sky and determine directly whether it might be aligned to the stars or not. For the sun, moon, and planets, the case is rather different. The relative shifts of orbits between members of the solar system is very small from century to century. It is therefore possible to observe their phenomena directly today, if the time between construction and the date of observation is less than a thousand or fifteen hundred years. Because most of the North American sites are less than fifteen hundred years old, direct observation of the sun, moon, and planets at a site is certainly possible — and desirable. Archaeoastronomers have

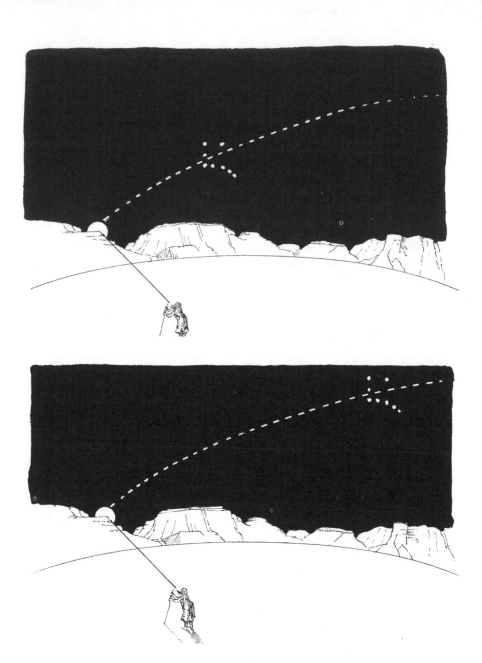

Upper drawing: heliacal rise of a constellation. Lower drawing: several weeks later. The first time in the year a star or star group is seen in the eastern predawn sky is termed heliacal rise. Several weeks later, it will have moved farther west and be seen for a longer period before dawn. The last time it is seen, just after sunset in the west, is termed heliacal set. Heliacal rise or set can be used to calibrate a yearly calendar.

found the effects of light and shadow from the sun or the moon can be quite complicated. Where possible, direct observation of celestial phenomena is an extremely important factor in interpreting a suspected archaeoastronomical site.

The annual apparent journey of the sun through the stellar background makes it possible to use the stars for calendrical purposes. As the cycle of the seasons progresses, and stars in the western part of the sky fade because the sun has entered their realm, new eastern stars become visible in the early dawn. At their first appearance, stars rise above the eastern horizon and can be viewed briefly before the rising sun snuffs out their light. As the sun slowly works its way further eastward day by day, the stars appear to move higher in the sky each morning before light from the rising sun overwhelms them. It is this first appearance, or heliacal rise (from the Greek *helios*, or sun), that was a useful calendar determinant.

In the Western world, heliacal risings of certain bright stars were used by the Greeks, Egyptians, and others to set calendars. In his classic study of the Peloponnesian wars, for example, the fifth-century B.C. Greek historian Thucydides dates the building of a certain wall this way. He tells us that when the Thebans were battling the small city of Plataea, north of Athens, the wall of circumvallation they constructed around Plataea was "completed by the rising of Arcturus." Thucydides here refers not to a certain time of night, but to a specific date in the year when Arcturus rose heliacally. Unfortunately, because of precession, such a calendar is only generally accurate over a century or so. In time, some stars move enough to rise several days earlier than they had previously, and parts of the calendar are then out of phase with other parts.

Thirty-five hundred years earlier than Thucydides, the Egyptians used the heliacal rise of the bright star Sirius to signal the arrival of summer solstice and, coincidentally, the season that marked the yearly rise of the Nile. Some Navajo medicine men also watch for heliacal rises of certain constellations in order to set their solar calendar. The Navajo constellation Old Man with Legs Spread (the Western constellation Corvus) serves as the "feather," or indicator, of November. When Old Man with Legs Spread is first seen in the east, the Navajo know it is time for hunting and for preparing for winter. When the Navajo constellation First Big One (part of Scorpio) is first visible, December has arrived. The feather for January is the Milky Way, and is called Which-Awaits-the-Dawn. Other months are similarly indicated for the Navajo by the feathers that appropriately announce them.[7]

Archaeoastronomical Measurements

Determining a building's alignments is essentially a problem in surveying. The basic methods are those known and used daily by surveyors; the tools are surveyors' tools — a transit or theodolite, a chronometer, measuring tape, and an accurate topographic map. One problem faced in studying a building for possible astronomical alignments is establishing the direction of each building feature, as accurately as possible, relative to geographic north. Geographic north, rather than magnetic north, must be used as the reference because of the large deviations in the earth's magnetic field across the surface of the earth. In the area around Dayton, Ohio, for example, the correction that must be added to a compass reading is generally less than a degree. In the Southwest, however, such deviations typically range from 12° to 14°, twenty-four to twenty-eight times the diameter of the sun and the moon. Near Washington, D.C., it is necessary to subtract about 7° to correct the compass.

In the city, the survey crew that measures out a land plot uses standard features, or benchmarks, for which true astronomical north has been determined many years ago. In most parts of the world where archaeoastronomers are likely to operate, however, such survey benchmarks are rare. So in setting up the transit, they must first determine true north by sighting the sun or some other celestial object. Though the stars, the planets, or even the moon can be used for the purpose, most researchers use the sun because, obviously, working in daylight is more convenient.

The procedure of using the sun to find true north is a little like finding positions at sea. First, the archaeoastronomer sets up a transit beside the wall or other feature to be measured and levels it, a procedure that ensures that the base of the transit lies in the local horizontal plane (that is, it is perpendicular to the force of gravity). This means that with the transit telescope set precisely horizontal, the telescope will sweep a circle that, if the horizon were level all the way around, would meet the intersection of the sky and the earth. Because of the bending effect of the earth's atmosphere, and the fact that the earth is spherical, not flat, a few extra complications creep in that make this account too simple in actual practice. Those effects are generally small, however, and corrections for them can easily be applied in the calculations.

After leveling the transit, it is most often convenient for the surveyor or observer to align the transit compass to magnetic north. Then the observer swings the telescope around and centers it on the sun, taking care to use a solar filter to protect the eyes. By timing the exact moment when the sun passes the center of the cross hairs in the transit telescope, recording the angular bearing of the telescope from magnetic north, and finding its altitude above the horizon, the observer is prepared to calculate the direction of geographic north. The National Bureau of Standards broadcasts the time every second, 24 hours a day, 365 days of the year, over station WWV (2.5, 5, 10, 15 MHz), so most archaeoastronomers carry a short-wave radio receiver tuned to this broadcast frequency or a highly accurate quartz clock that has been calibrated to WWV. Once the time of the observation is known, a detailed calculation based on published tables of the sun reveals the true geographical bearing (azimuth) of the sun for that particular time of day. The difference between the *observed* magnetic bearing of the sun and the *calculated* bearing of the sun yields a precise measure of the magnetic deviation of the earth's magnetic field at that particular time and place. "All is in flux," said the Greek philosopher Heraclitus, and that is certainly true for the magnetic field of the earth. It varies from time to time as well as from place to place; next year the magnetic correction is likely to be slightly different than it is today.

It is advisable to take a sun reading each time the transit is moved to a different location, even if the magnetic correction from a previous measurement is known. The complete calculation to find geographic north is complicated, but well within the capabilities of most portable programmable calculators. Before these electronic marvels were available, it was necessary to carry the field data back to a computer — a procedure that often resulted in considerable confusion if even small mistakes were made in recording them.

Knowing the exact correction to apply to measurements of the structure in question, the archaeoastronomer can now determine the average magnetic bearing of the wall. Walls, even modern ones, can be rather crooked, so any determination of the wall's direction will be a mean of several values. Generally, the perpendicular distance from the wall to the transit is noted, and markers are placed at the same distance from the wall at intervals along it. The angular bearing of each marker is then recorded. The average of these bearings, corrected for the calculated magnetic deviation, results in an average value of the azimuth of the wall, the true bearing from astronomical or geographical north.

Now the archaeoastronomer has nearly all the necessary data for one wall. Assuming the horizon is visible from the transit, the observer should also measure the altitude of the local horizon, both along the "forward" direction and 180° from it. These measurements are vitally important, for generally the purpose in making them is to discover whether a given celestial object rises or sets along the wall extended to the horizon. Any change in horizon altitude will alter the angle at which a given celestial object is seen to rise. For example, at a latitude of 36°N, a 3° horizon results in a southward shift of slightly less than 3°, which is very nearly six diameters of the sun. A 3° horizon is not uncommon and would correspond to a hill nearly 100 yards high, one mile distant.[8]

Once all the walls and all other significant features are measured in this manner, the last step in the process is to discover, by using the appropriate celestial tables, whether any bright stars or planets, the moon, or the sun rise or set along the horizon at those azimuths and altitudes. It is often said in criticism of the methods of archaeoastronomy that if you choose stars that are faint enough, some star will rise along any given line. However, since only the brightest stars can be seen *at or near the horizon* without a telescope, even on a very clear night, we are limited to a practical list of about twenty-five that ancient observers might have used for their naked-eye astronomical alignments.

For the sake of convenience, astronomers have established a set of imaginary coordinates in the sky to which to refer the positions of celestial objects, coordinates that are analogous to latitude and longitude on the earth's surface. *Declination* is measured in degrees along the hour circles; these lines are perpendicular to the celestial equator and pass through the pole. *Right ascension* is measured in hours of time (one hour equals 15°) eastward along the equator from the intersection of the celestial equator and the ecliptic. This point, called the First Point of Aries, is the place at which the sun crosses

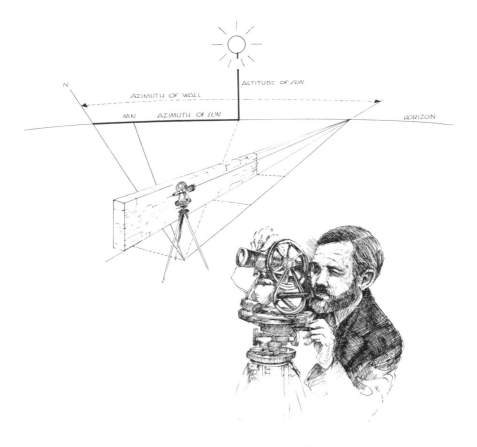

Determining the angular bearing (azimuth) of a wall from true north, using the sun as standard. Angular measurements of the sun and a record of the exact time of measurement can be used to calculate true north at a given place, a crucial measurement for archaeoastronomical studies.

the equator in its northward journey. By convention, it is also at the edge of the constellation Aries when the zero point of the zodiac was set several thousand years ago. The angles of declination and right ascension correspond respectively to earthbound latitude and longitude.

Celestial tables for archaeoastronomical use soon become extremely complicated because not only do we need to account for the motions of the wandering bodies and their major "stand stills" but, because of precession, we also have to work backward in time.

A typical table of celestial positions for archaeoastronomy illustrates the case. Unless we happen to be interested in the time that particular objects rise or set, we need only list their declinations, since any two objects at the same declination will rise or set at identical azimuths, no matter what their right ascension. For example, in A.D. 1250, the star Arcturus had nearly the same declination as the summer solstice sun; it therefore rose at nearly the same azimuth. But Arcturus was and still is a summer star, the brightest one in the Western constellation Boötes. Thus, it lies far away from the summer solstice sun, on the opposite side of the celestial sphere. Today, because of precession, Arcturus is positioned at a declination of +19°, about 4.5° north of the summer solstice sun (+23.5°).

In computing potential astronomical alignments to the stars it is useful to know the right ascension for one specialized use: computing the potential heliacal rises of certain bright stars. Knowing the

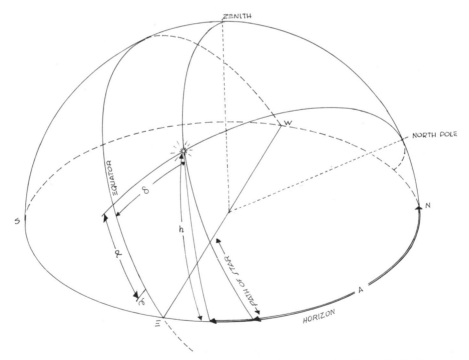

Celestial coordinates of a star: α, right ascension; δ, declination; ♈, First Point of Aries; h, altitude; A, azimuth.

Table 2 Declinations and Rise Azimuths for Selected Bright Stars (at 36°
North Latitude, 0° Horizon Elevation)

Object	A.D. 0		A.D. 1500	
	Declination	Azimuth	Declination	Azimuth
Aldebaran	10°15'	76°54'	15°23'	70°28'
Altair	5°44'	82°32'	7°39'	80°09'
Antares	−19°41'	114°11'	−25°11'	121°18'
Arcturus	30°31'	50°38'	21°50'	62°12'
Betelgeuse	4°24'	83°56'	7°11'	80°44'
Deneb	39°24'	37°42'	43°34'	30°52'
Fomalhaut	−39°05'	140°56'	−32°14'	130°44'
Pleiades	15°58'	69°44'	22°26'	61°25'
Polaris	78°14'	circumpolar	86°35'	circumpolar
Regulus	20°16'	64°14'	14°21'	71°46'
Sirius	−15°58'	109°29'	−16°08'	109°41'
Spica	0°10'	89°50'	8°31'	100°09'
Vega	38°29'	39°07'	38°24'	39°15'

Derived from tables computed by Anthony F. Aveni, Colgate University.

right ascension of a star allows one to compute the time it will rise. Comparing that time with the time of sunrise allows one to compute the date it will rise heliacally.

The relevance of heliacal risings or settings for the archaeoastronomer is important but subtle. Without Thucydides' written account, it would be impossible for the modern researcher to know that the Plataeans dated the beginning of their demise as a city from the heliacal rising of Arcturus. However, if that date had happened to coincide with an important ceremony, the Plataeans might have built a temple to celebrate the ceremony in line with the rising of Arcturus. A possibility that has not been explored adequately by modern archaeoastronomers is Lockyer's suggestion that variations among orientations of certain Egyptian temples could be explained by their alignment to stars that rose heliacally. As a given star was no longer usable to time a ceremony, another star would have to be chosen, necessitating a different temple orientation. Lockyer's hypothesis, enmeshed as it is in his idiosyncratic and often mistaken notions of Egyptian prehistory, has never been fully tested, partly because of the prejudices his theories engendered.

In the Americas, although the possibilities of alignments to stars or constellations that might rise heliacally are generally explored, very few examples are known. One of the most striking is the alignments of the Bighorn Medicine Wheel in Wyoming. There, astronomer John Eddy has postulated that the alignments indicated by three pairs of rock cairns in the wheel mark the heliacal rise of Aldebaran, Rigel, and Sirius. Astronomer Jack Robinson has suggested that yet another pair of cairns at the Bighorn Medicine Wheel align to the heliacal rise of the star Fomalhaut.

4 Southwestern Children of the Sun

This day,
> My sun father,
>> You have come out standing
>>> To your sacred dwelling place,
>>>> Where we find our sacred spring.

I give you
> prayer meal here.

>> A finished road,
>> old age,
>> sacred water,
>> ancient corn seeds,
>> good fortune,
>> spiritual power,
>> strong thoughts,

>>> Grant these to me.[1]

The Zuni, the Pueblo tribe from whom this prayer was learned, like all the Pueblo people, have a special relationship to the sun. He is the most powerful deity in their large pantheon of gods. When Sun comes up each morning, each Zuni who keeps the old ways faces him and offers a pinch of cornmeal while reciting this or a similar prayer.

The sun and its power dominates the Southwest. In recent decades this has made the region a leader in developing solar-heated buildings. For much of the year, the Southwest experiences cloudless or only scattered cloudy skies, allowing the sun to shine with relentless intensity most of the daylight hours. Because of this, it is not surprising that a sun deity dominates the religious experience of Pueblo life or that their calendar is largely sun-based. We see numerous representations of the sun in traditional native art, and a recognition of the sun's heating powers in the orientation and placement of their buildings. The Pueblo people were apparently the first Americans to practice the techniques of passive solar heating in a systematic way. This solar influence has even been extended to Anglo-American symbolic systems in the Southwest in the form of the New Mexico state flag, the emblem of which derives from the Zia Pueblo sun symbol.

Sun also dominates the lives of the native peoples of the Southwest. Sun Father the germinator, Sun the provider, Sun the lifegiver, is a major force in the lives of the Pueblo and Navajo, the Apache and Ute, the Pima and Papago. His yearly journey causes the seasons, bringing summer warmth and winter cold, the promise of spring, and the fulfillment of autumn. His warming power causes plants to germinate and grow to fullness. And when he withdraws his warmth, the earth grows cold and barren.

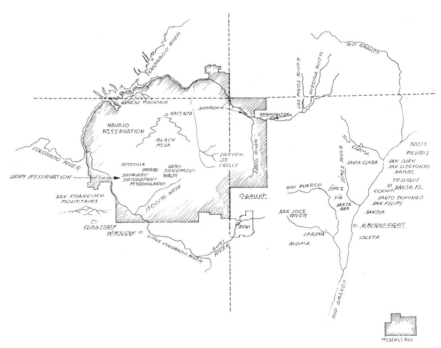

The region of the Navajo, Pueblo, and Mescalero Apache.

This is a land of desert flora and fauna. As the unwary traveler whose radiator runs dry or who fails to take sufficient water on a canyon hike will soon discover, there is very little extra water anywhere. High mesas, deep canyons, sagebrush, piñon pine, and juniper form the characteristic features of Pueblo and Navajo country. The greater Four Corners area where these Indian peoples now live is well known in financial and energy circles for the enormous wealth of coal, oil, gas, and uranium that lies beneath the ground. Although the land where Arizona, Colorado, New Mexico, and Utah meet is now coveted by corporate energy conglomerates, it is also the home of an estimated 46,300 Pueblo and 146,000 Navajo Indians. The Pueblo people, who have lived in the region since before the time of Christ, number many fewer today than at the height of their ancient civilization some eight hundred years ago. The Navajo are latecomers to the area, having probably pushed down from the north sometime during the fifteenth or sixteenth century, and their numbers are still on the increase.

The Pueblo Villages

In contrast to the Navajo, whose archaeological remains have been studied less, a great deal is known about the early history of the Pueblo Indians from the material culture their ancestors left behind. Though the different tribes and language groups are widely scattered geographically from the Rio Grande to the Colorado River, their legends show a remarkable similarity. According to these stories, the Puebloans emerged from the underground, well below this present world.

Throughout, their stories often refer to the sun and other astronomical objects. Sometimes those astronomical references are explicit; sometimes they are submerged in the poetic metaphor of the action in such a way that the uninitiated would miss the point. For example, the continual Pueblo emphasis on the number *four* suggests the four cardinal directions, which are astronomical in origin.

For the Puebloans, their emergence is more important to their concept of self than is their creation. The various Pueblos do have stories about the creation of the world, but these are considerably fewer and less elaborate than their accounts of the emergence and subsequent search for their place in this world. Clearly, what is

Pueblo petroglyph of Kokopeli, the humpbacked flute player.

central to their own understanding of themselves is their process of becoming. Until they finally emerge in this present world and settle down, they are continually becoming; before that time they are partially, but not quite, human. The metaphors that the storytellers use to describe the states of humankind before and after emergence, interestingly, are related to plant growth. In the underworld, men and women are soft and pliable, and unripe or unfinished. After emergence, the human state is variously described as ripe, cooked, or finished. The several worlds through which humans pass are also sometimes described as being spongy, flooded, burning, or soft, an indication that those worlds are not fit dwelling places. It is part of the Pueblo concept of becoming complete human beings that they establish biological and social order in the journey through the layered underworlds. The stories vary from pueblo to pueblo, but in their original state, human bodies were either soft, as in an Acoma legend, or unfinished, as at Zuni (they had tails and webbed feet), or they lacked social order, as at Hopi (men and women cavorted indecently in the sacred rooms, and copulated indiscriminately, or gambled with abandon).

Some of the original people perceived the need to leave the unfinished or disordered state, and they began to search for a way out. As one Hopi version of the story goes:

> In the Underworld all the people were fools. Youths copulated with the wives of the elder men, and the elder men deflowered virgins. All was confusion, and the chief was unhappy. He thought, and at sunset proclaimed that on the morrow all the people should assem-

ble around him. On the following morning all came into the court. They said, "We heard you announce, you have sent for us. What is it you wish, perhaps you wish to tell us something." "Yes," said the chief, "I want to tell you that I have been thinking much and I am saddened by your evil actions. Now, I announce that tomorrow morning early, all the women, maids and female children and infants, all females, shall remain here in the village and all the men, youths and male infants, all males, shall cross the river and remain there on the other side."[2]

The men and women separated, and the men swam to the other side of the river. In time, both the men and the women began to be very unhappy about this arrangement and they agreed to move in together again. The women swam across the river and the men received them with happy hearts. During their separation, the men had prospered. They had built fine dwellings in which they now housed the women, and there was an abundance of corn and animals. But in other respects the land was a frightening place in which to live.

At that time, at sunrise the sky was wide, the horizon was far around, but at noon the sky vibrated, it alternately compressed and distended. The horizon was not so far around as it is in this world. In the daytime, in the Underworld, it was beautiful, there was bubbling water in commotion, all around the landscape; but at night the sky contracted and it was disagreeable. There were both sun and moon at that time. Then the bubbling waters increased and encroached upon the dry land and pressed close up toward the people. They became sad. The chief thought and said, "Perhaps there is a doorway in this sky."[3]

The people sought help from Spider Woman and from Pöqang-whoya and Palöngawhoya, the twin war gods, sons of the sun and closely connected with solar ritual. In some of the stories, Spider Woman causes considerable grief for the Hopi by her occasionally playful ways. In most others, she functions to help or protect humans when they find themselves in insuperable difficulty. She offers advice, occasional magical potions, and, in other ways, generally serves as the keeper of ancestral wisdom.

There were four mountains, at the cardinal points, and at the mountain at the Northeast lived Spider woman and Pöqangwhoya and Palöngawhoya. The Hopi War chief made a war prayer-stick for Spider woman and a nodule club for the Twins, and prayer-feathers, and sent a youth with these to the mountain. Spider woman thanked the youth for the prayer-stick and prayer-feathers and asked what he wanted. The Twins danced with glee on receiving their presents. "What do you wish for these things?" asked Spider woman. The youth said, "We are surrounded with bubbling water and it is covering all our land. Where is the good place to go to, the good houses, perhaps you know." "Yes," she said, "I know. In the above is a good place, tell all your people to hasten and come here." The youth returned and after the elders assembled and smoked, he told all that had occurred. Women prepared food for the journey, and then all the people started, carrying the altar slabs on their backs, and went to the mountain, the house of Pöqangwhoya. They all went up the mountain to its summit, and the water followed close behind covering everything, but the mountain grew a little faster than the rise of the water and after a time the mountain summit was almost touching the sky. Spider woman planted a spruce plant and it grew up against the sky, but the sky was hard and the spruce could not penetrate. Again Spider woman thought, — perhaps reed will pierce through. So she planted a reed, and it grew four days and reached the sky and found a small crevice which it penetrated. Badger climbed the stalk and reached its tip, but he could not get through to see anything, so he returned saying, "I am very tired, I could see nothing but earth." The elders thought. "What man knows? Perhaps Locust? So they asked him and he said yes he knew. Locust is very brave, he never winks his eyes. (They are like the eye glasses of the American.) So he climbed the stalk and went through and reached the tasselled tip of the reed, and looked around, and there was water everywhere. Locust carried a flute, flung on his back; he drew it out and began to play upon it, and at the Northwest the Yellow Cloud chief appeared. He was very wroth and darted yellow lightning at Locust which went close past the eyes of Locust, but he never winked, and went on with his flute playing. Yellow Cloud said, "What kind of man have we here? For sure he is brave, for sure he is a man!" Next to the Southwest, Blue Cloud appeared and he too was wroth and flung his blue lightning at Locust and it passed through him from side to side, and he only continued to play as before, and Blue Cloud said the same as had Yellow Cloud. Then at the Southeast, Red Cloud came up very wroth and darted the red lightning which passed through Locust from belly to back, and he continued playing as if nothing had occurred. Red Cloud expresses his wonder and admiration as the preceding Clouds had done. At the Northeast, White Cloud arises and casts white lightning which passes through Locust from head to tail, and he continued playing as if nothing had happened to him. The four Cloud chiefs drew together and came close to Locust and talked with him, demanding to know from whence he came. They said, "This is Cloud land; what do you here? You are a good man and brave, perhaps you are an orphan?" "No," said Locust, "I have many people behind me in the Below." "It is well," said the Cloud chief, "you are brave and deathless; your heart and those of your people must be good; go tell them to come and all this land shall be theirs." "Thanks," said Locust, who then returned and told his people. Then Badger went up and widened the crevice so that people could pass through, and while he was doing this, Locust told his adventures to the people, and said the place above was just like the place they were then at, all water. The people were saddened at this, but the chiefs thought, and said, "Well, it is no worse than here, and may be better, let us go up and see." The people climbed up the reed for eight days, stopping each night at a joint from which a great leaf grew out and the people slept on it. That is why these leaves are called sleeps.

When all had emerged, the Twins who each had the resilient lightning, shot it in every direction and made canyons and through these the water flowed away. The Twins then made all the rocks of mud, and made all the mountains, made everything that is of stone. Finished.[4]

The Center and the Four Directions

In this particular version of the Hopi emergence from the underworld, the traditional four underground worlds are compressed into two. But in most pueblos, as at Hopi, there is a strong tradition that the number of levels is five — four underground and one, the fifth world, the world of the present. Their understanding of the fifth world refers not only to the present time but also to the particular places in which they live. For not only do the Pueblo people pass through the four worlds before emerging to a fifth, they also wander to the four points of the compass before finding the Middle Place, the Center. Much more than merely a geographical notion, the Center is the proper place for them to be, the place in which they will prosper and thrive as a people — the place where their heart resides.

To the Zuni, the Center is expressed metaphorically as a place where, unlike the rest of their new world, there will be stability and peace. In their creation story, after a long and tiring search for the Center, they met to deliberate.

Nay, they called a great council of men and the beings, beasts, birds and insects of all kinds; these were gathered in the council.

After long deliberation it was said:

"Where is K'yan asdebi, the Water-skate? Lo! legs has he of great extension, six in number. Mayhap he can feel forth with them to the uttermost of all the six regions, thereby pointing out the very Middle." And K'yan asdebi, being summoned, appeared in semblance, growing greater; for lo! it was the Sun-father himself. And he answered their questions ere he was bespoken, saying, "Yea, that can I do." And he lifted himself to the zenith, and extended his finger-feet six to all of the six regions, so that they touched the north, the great waters; and to the west, and the south, and the east, the great waters; and to the northeast the waters above; and to the southwest, the waters below.

But to the north, his finger-foot grew cold, so he drew it in; and to the west, the waters being nearer, touched his finger-foot thither extended, so he drew that in also. But to the south and east far reached his other finger-feet. Then gradually he settled downward and called out, "Where my heart and navel rest, beneath them mark ye the spot and there build ye a town of the midmost, for there shall be the midmost place of the earth-mother, even the navel; albeit not the center, because of the nearness of cold in the north and the

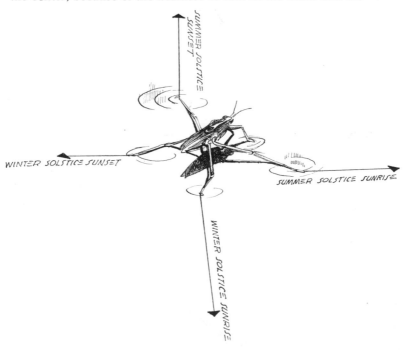

Water-Skate finding the Center. According to the Zuni creation myth, Water-Skate was asked by the wandering Zuni to find the Center, where they could settle down. Water-Skate stretched his legs to the four solstice directions; where his heart lay was the Center.

nearness of waters in the west." And when he descended (squatting), his belly rested over the middle of the plain and valley of Zuni; and when he drew in his finger-legs, lo! there were the trail-roads leading out and in like stays of a spider's net, into and forth from the place he had covered.[5]

Again and again, in their stories and in all phases of Pueblo ritual and secular life, the importance of the number *four* is evident. There are four underworlds, they travel in four directions, and in the Hopi story, there are four mountains. Contained within the number is another important aspect of the Pueblo world concept. There are four directions on the earth — front, back, and either side (at times, particularly among the Zuni, the above and below are also included to make six directions, but the use of four predominates). The Pueblo people illustrate their ties to the earth by using the number in many phases of their lives. At Zuni, even the language reflects this understanding, for the Zuni word for earth ("the ground on which we stand and in which we plant") contains as a root the word for four.[6]

There are four primary astronomical directions as well, and when we speak of the cardinal directions we refer to directions determined directly from observations of the sun or stars. Without either form of celestial aid, we would be truly directionless on the earth. Without them, direction from any particular place would be totally arbitrary, as any mariner who has experienced solid cloud cover for days at a time will attest. At such times, even the relative comfort of a magnetic compass is lost, for without the familiar celestial globe to act as a known reference, even the compass becomes suspect.

Because they have an earthly as well as a heavenly referent, Puebloans have no such problem as mariners. The boundaries of the Pueblo world are circumscribed literally by the surrounding mesas and mountains that can be seen from the Center. They also serve as figurative or psychological boundaries of Pueblo life. Everything and everyone outside those boundaries is other. Inside the boundaries, ties of blood, clan, and fraternity link them to their world.

Having thus located the Pueblo people in space, the stories of the Pueblo origin and development go on to locate their place in time. Their legends then take on the character of histories, and tell of individual clan migrations and their arrival at the Center — stories that are soon followed sequentially by the arrival of the Spanish conquerors and conflict with the Western European world.

Pueblo Prehistory

As is often true of myth, the Pueblo story of emergence and subsequent trials on this earth is a rich metaphorical reflection of their history and their coalescence and emergence as a people. The ancient Pueblo people, or Anasazi ("ancient ones"), as the Navajo have named them, developed common traits nearly two thousand years ago. They lived in an area that is drained by the upper Rio Grande, the San Juan River, and the Colorado River.

Their predecessors had moved into the area much earlier than the first century A.D., where they lived as hunters and gatherers, depending mostly on the grace of nature to provide their daily needs from wild grains, leafy plants, and animals. We would not recognize these people as Puebloan at all today, for they built no permanent houses and the remains of their early settlements exist mainly in the form of stone and bone tools and manufacturing chips, which are found in considerable profusion throughout much of the area. This early form of Pueblo life has been designated the Basket Maker phase by archaeologists — a name given these people by the famed rancher, explorer, and entrepreneur Richard Wetherill, who, in 1893, discovered a group of ninety preserved bodies in Grand Gulch, Utah, accompanied by a profusion of finely woven baskets. Wetherill coined the term to distinguish these people from the much later Cliff Dwellers of the Mesa Verde to the east.

Eventually moving from caves and temporary shelters, the Basket Makers began to build pit houses, structures measuring some three to eight yards on a side, and to group them together in family units and small villages. The pit-house walls were made of sticks tied together with yucca twine and plastered over with adobe. The inside of the pit was often lined with sandstone slabs also covered with adobe. Roofs supported by log posts were made of twigs and mats, and these, too, were plastered with adobe. It certainly made a tight, weather-resistant structure, though the lack of windows must have made it rather dark and uninviting as well. One village of such pit houses was built high on the mesa above Chaco Canyon in north-central New Mexico. At its height, the village, known as Shabik'eshchee by the Navajo who now live in the area, may have sheltered a hundred or more inhabitants.[7] This village was built late in the pit-house stage, the Anasazi having by about A.D. 700 also acquired beans to augment the protein in their meager diet. Though not a luxurious diet by any measure, the protein-rich trio of corn, beans, and squash, supplemented by grains and greens gathered in the area and by occasional small animals, was sufficient to enable these early Anasazi to prosper and expand. By this time they had added pottery making and weaving to their skills. They also began to use more stone in constructing their houses. As with the introduction of corn and beans, the advent of skilled pottery making was likely the result of influences from the south, ultimately from Mexico. Some anthropologists have speculated that this was also true for building techniques, which underwent a radical change during the next century or two.

Between A.D. 800 and 1000, the Anasazi began to design and construct the buildings we now recognize as characteristically Pueblo. Building techniques varied with time and place, but certain features were basic to Pueblo construction from this time into the historic period. Where masonry was used extensively, as in the western Pueblos, slabs or blocks of quarried sandstone were dressed and laid up with a bit of mortar and then plastered over with adobe to make them airtight and watertight. These masonry walls, pierced by ports

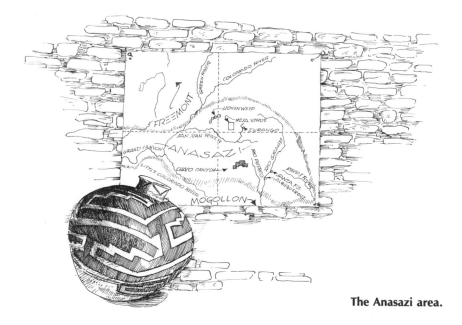

The Anasazi area.

or by larger openings probably functioning as windows, were capped with roofs constructed of wooden beams overlaid with twigs, split beams, or mats. The builders then covered these basic ceiling supports with stone slabs and adobe to form the floor of the room above, or simply a flat roof for sleeping and working. In other areas, generally along the Rio Grande, adobe was the predominant wall material, but the ceilings were constructed nearly the same as in the western Pueblos.

It is the large roof beams that usually provide an archaeologist with the best and most reliable dates for prehistoric structures. In the late 1920s, a very precise sequence of tree-ring dates was worked out by the astronomer A. E. Douglass and his students, and the sequence now extends more than a thousand years into the past.[8] If the exterior bark of the log is still intact, its cutting date can be determined with an accuracy of one or two years. In many cases, this is also the construction date of the particular room, though one must be cautious in applying such a direct correspondence since, in the arid climate of the Southwest, logs may have been used more than once. One of the logs used by Douglass to extend his tree-ring sequence to prehistoric times was originally cut in A.D. 1260, though it was found in a historic house.

Though by A.D. 1000 the Pueblo houses were built above ground, one form of room characteristically remained below the surface, most probably for religious reasons. However, its structural origins may have played a part in the reasons for its special status in the pueblo. The kiva, a Hopi name for the ceremonial room characteristic of the Pueblo, attained its special form as the pueblo structural form itself was being developed. Often round, though in some areas it was square or rectangular, the kiva was placed below or partially below ground level. From a developmental standpoint this was probably because the original kivas were constructed and used during the pit-house phase. Several kivas are known at Shabik'eshchee, the Basket Maker pit-house village in Chaco Canyon, including a very large one, a so-called great kiva.

From a religious standpoint, too, the underground nature of the kiva is entirely appropriate, since it reminds the Puebloans of their original emergence into this world. The Acoma, whose traditional village is high atop a mesa west of Albuquerque, New Mexico, explain that the kiva came about because after they emerged from their underworld, they needed a sacred place to house their gods when the gods came to visit. The mythical leader of the early Acoma, Iatiku the mother, said:

> "So far all is well but there are some things needed yet. We have no sacred place, we have no kiva." Iatiku said, "This is the way I emerged, so I guess we will make a house in the ground, which we will call kiva. This will be the sacred place for the katsina when they come." (The kivas were round at first, now they are square. At the foot of the mesa where the old town was all washed away the kiva was round.)
>
> When they began to build the first kiva, Iatiku told Oak Man that it must be done in a certain way. Then she told him just how it was to be done. The whole kiva was to represent Shipapu, the place of emergence.[9]

As they exist today prior to excavation, Anasazi kivas are often recognized by a circular depression in the earth a few yards in diameter in a ruins area. Excavated, they show that they were generally made of masonry-lined pits and four to six wooden or stone pilasters to support a roof. Wooden beams, which were then covered with twigs, mud, and stone, were laid across the pilasters. A hatchway through the roof, a fireplace on the floor below, a ventilator shaft to feed oxygen to the fire, and a raised bench around the wall between the pilasters completed the basic structural elements of the kiva. Some kivas also contained wall niches for the deposit or storage of offerings or ceremonial objects. In addition, kivas generally included a small hole in the floor near the fire pit. Often found with bits of turquoise that had been placed there as offerings, such a hole, called a Sipapu after the Hopi name for the Place of Emergence, was an additional symbolic reminder of the journey from the underworld. Imagine what it must have meant to the Anasazi to climb the ladder through clouds of purifying smoke from the fire. Each time, they were emerging once again from the underworld, a ritual which was repeated over and over in the course of a day whenever anyone left the kiva.

The Pueblos and the Sun

Ritual observances of all kinds are now and undoubtedly were in Anasazi days an essential part of life. Sun Father and the rituals attending his worship are an especially strong part of Pueblo life, a fact deriving from their belief that in some way or other the sun is directly responsible for all life.

This is expressed metaphorically in a number of stories in which the sun descends at noon and impregnates a maiden. Some Puebloans still say today that sexual union between a man and a woman during the daylight hours will result in twins — one child conceived by natural means, one the result of union with the sun.

Among the Zuni, Sun is said to have existed always. For the Hopi, in some myths Sun is already present in the underworld, suggesting that he is eternal; but in other stories, he is created. In one of these myths, when the Hopi reached the fourth world, there was no sun. They consulted with the god Maasaw to see whether they could not just go ahead and make one similar to the sun that they had in the underworld. The Hopi made their sun from a piece of buffalo hide stretched over a wooden ring, but only after trying an earlier model that turned out to be the moon. The moon, they discovered, did not supply enough light or heat.

At Zia Pueblo, two sisters, the first humans created, who then go on to lead the people up from the first world, are also responsible for creating the sun (note the use of the number *four here*).

> "Now all is covered with darkness, but after a while we will have light." These two women . . . created the sun from white shell, turquoise, red stone, and abalone shell. After making the sun they carried him to the east and there made a camp, as there were no houses. The next morning they ascended a high mountain and dropped the sun down behind it, and after a time he began to ascend, and when the people saw the light their hearts rejoiced. When far off his face was blue; as he came nearer the face grew brighter. They, however, did not see the sun himself, but a mask so large that it covered his entire body. The people saw that the world was large and the country beautiful, and when the women returned to the village they said to the people: "We are the mothers of all."[10]

Whether he was created or has existed eternally, worship of the sun is a major element in Pueblo ceremonialism and, in turn, in Pueblo life. The sun is also carefully observed in order to set the dates of the major ceremonies.

It is these ceremonies, accompanied by elaborate dances, that most clearly signify Pueblo culture to the tourist in the Southwest. In them, masked figures called kachinas dance ritual patterns that are centuries old. Though the forms of the kachinas and their dances vary throughout the year, they are all in one way or another directed toward imploring the gods to send the warmth of the sun or the moisture of the rain in order that the crops may thrive and the pueblo prosper.

The kachina cult is strongest in the western pueblos of the Hopi and Zuni, but it is considerably attenuated in the Rio Grande pueblos, perhaps because of the markedly stronger Christian influence there, following the Spanish Entrada into the Southwest. Only men participate in the kachina cult. From December until July, at times prescribed by the sun priest, men in the several religious societies don elaborate and beautifully painted kachina masks and dance in the village plazas. It is these gods that are probably the best-known part of the Pueblo pantheon of gods by outsiders, for the Hopi make representations of these kachinas in the form of dolls in order to instruct their young. They also sell them to tourists.

The dances are an important affair in the life of each village, and whether participant or merely onlooker, each villager takes the dances seriously. I was particularly fortunate to be present at a Niman kachina ceremony at Hotevilla, a Hopi village of Third Mesa, Arizona.[11] Non-Hopis are generally welcome at the public part of the ceremonies as long as they respect the kachinas and keep to the rooftops or the edges of the plaza, for these are religious rites, not tourist displays.

Hotevilla is typical of the historic pueblos — stone houses with ground-level doorways and dirt paths and walkways. Modern four-by-four framed windows are common these days, though numerous ladders to the flat rooftops announce that it is indeed a Pueblo town. At Zuni, by contrast, more and more of the houses in the old town sport sloped or peaked roofs, a development many traditionalists in the village look upon with disfavor. At Hotevilla, the occasional TV antenna seems remarkably out of place, especially when it is explained that there is no electricity available in the old part of the village — by deliberate choice of the town elders. The TVs are battery powered.

At dawn, taking our place on the rooftops along with the Hopis and a few other pahaana (white) observers, we await the arrival of the kachinas. At the rising of the sun, a muted rattle is heard and soon a bareheaded, barechested, barefoot priest appears, followed by a second priest and a score or so of Hemis, or Niman, kachinas, each wearing a brightly painted mask topped by a wooden "tabletta."

Six additional kachinas dressed in traditional cotton capes, white leggings, and moccasins follow, each carrying a notched stick and the scapula of a deer. They are called Hemis kachinmana, or kachina maidens. Save for the muffled click-rattle of tortoise shells that are tied to the calf of each leg, the kachinas enter the plaza soundlessly. Arranging themselves in a semicircle on the north side of the plaza, they begin to dance a complicated shuffle-step sharply punctuated by the intermittent staccato calls of the two priests who continually circle the dancers to sprinkle sacred cornmeal on them and bless them. In their circuit, they each make a brief detour to cast a pinch of cornmeal on a small spruce tree that has been set up in the plaza. Families and visitors crowd the plaza to watch the dancing and listen to the singing. Actually it is more like chanting, for to untrained ears, any tuneful qualities it might have are submerged in the rhythmic necessities of the dance.

The semicircle of dancers is open to the south, with the "female" kachinas dancing on the inside near the center of the curved line. After ten minutes or so of dancing, their rhythmic motions ease and the Hemis kachinmana kneel in front of the other dancers to rub their notched sticks and scapulas together, producing an unearthly scraping rhythm to which the kachinas now dance.

This sequence of dancing continues for another five minutes; then suddenly it stops and the dancers reposition themselves on the west side of the plaza with the semicircle opening east. There they repeat the rhythmic dancing.

Though this is a religious ceremony, an air of festival pervades the plaza. Hopi adults chat with one another, commenting on the skill of the dancers and on the care with which they have painted their masks. Small Hopi children, unable to contain their energetic bodies, play on the edges of the plaza, seemingly oblivious to the presence of the dancers. Yet, for each dancer, wearing the kachina mask is a sacred trust as well as a sacred duty. Each man, as he dons his mask, assumes the spirit of the mask and "becomes" the kachina he impersonates. Kachinas are gods from the west who, in the Hopi pueblos, come to dance from November through July (that is, from a month before winter solstice to a month after summer solstice). With

today's set of dances the kachinas complete their yearly cycle and
return home to dwell in the San Francisco Mountains. The kachinas,
who dance in a yearly cycle of ceremonies determined by observations of the sun and the moon, are also the ancestral spirits, or
"breath-bodies," of Hopi long dead.

After completing the third dance sequence, the dancers position
themselves on the plaza's east side with the semicircle opening west.
After the last dance of this set is over, the two priests lead the
dancers from the plaza to breakfast together outside the village. During the short breaks between each set, the kachinas give gifts of
brightly colored bows and arrows or kachina dolls to the Hopi boys
and girls standing and playing on the edges of the plaza. After the
kachinas leave, it is open warfare between the boys. As for the tourists, it is pahaana beware, as the children's toys become instruments
of playful annoyance to hapless passers-by. The kachinas continue
to dance in much the same manner for the rest of the day, entering
the plaza a total of eight times before the sun sets behind the distant
western ridges.

The final dance and departure of the kachinas brings an enormous
crowd. Hopis from neighboring villages, Navajos, and tourists inter-
mingle and strain to see over their neighbors for a glimpse of the final
ceremony. This time, after completing their dance cycle, instead of
leaving by the eastern entrance, the kachinas file off the central plaza
in a southerly direction to dance on a narrow plaza just south of the
main one. Here they stretch out in a long line, and men and women
carrying flat baskets of cornmeal file out of a nearby kiva to dance
with them and bless them with cornmeal. This year the kachinas
quickly return the blessings. A cloudy western sky of deep pink and
pearl gray brings the promise of rain, which shortly turns to reality,
lightly pelting kachina, priest, Hopi, and visitor alike. No one seems
to mind, though the wind-whipped drops are cold on bare arms and
through thin summer garments, for the kachinas have fulfilled their
promise. The rain they have brought is much needed for the crops in
the fields below the village. The Hopi men and women, for their part,
acknowledge the gift by blessing and thanking the kachinas with a
sprinkling of sacred cornmeal.

Shortly before sunset the dancers stop, and while they stand in
single file facing him, the priest addresses them in Hopi. He urges
them to return in a few months, but while they are away in their

western home, they should ever think of the Hopi who are needful of their bounty of rain and blessings for a full harvest. After hearing the priest, the kachinas take their leave, walking southward with slow deliberate step. All watch, respectful and thoughtful, though now the rain has increased, until the last kachina has disappeared. Then, as if a silent signal has been received by everyone, at once the spell is broken. All begin to stir together. The lusty crank of a pickup starter motor breaks the mood and everyone seeks shelter from the rain and chilly wind. The kachinas have left the village for the season, to return again a month before the winter solstice.

5 Pueblo Sun Watching

Each morning, too, just at dawn, the Sun Priest, followed by the Master Priest of the Bow, went along the eastern trail to the ruined city of Matsaki, by the riverside, where, awaited at a distance by his companion, he slowly approached a square open tower and seated himself just inside upon a rude, ancient stone chair, and before a pillar sculptured with the face of the sun, the sacred hand, the morning star, and the new moon. There he awaited with prayer and sacred song the rising of the sun. Not many such pilgrimages are made ere the "Suns look at each other"; and the shadows of the solar monolith, the monument of Thunder (Corn) Mountain, and the pillar of the gardens of Zuni, "lie along the same trail." Then the priest blesses, thanks, and exhorts his father, while the warrior guardian responds as he cuts the last notch in his pine-wood calendar, and both hasten back to call from the house-tops the glad tidings of the return of spring.[1]

The author of this passage, Frank Cushing, a flamboyant ethnologist with the Smithsonian Institution Bureau of American Ethnology, lived in Zuni Pueblo for five years in the 1890s. During his long stay, he had ample opportunity to observe and report on daily affairs. While a resident of the pueblo, Cushing was honored by being made a member of the tribe and was even inducted into the order of the Priesthood of the Bow. This position within a religious society allowed him to observe and to participate in Zuni ceremonies and to record numerous myths and legends.

As is clear from Cushing's description, the sun priest made direct observations of the position of the sun each day as it rose along the horizon. On one level, at least, such observations were made in order to keep a calendar. The sun priest was watching for a particular day in mid-February when the shadows of a natural feature on Corn Mountain (the Zuni sacred mountain) and a manmade pillar line up at sunrise. He knew from his own long experience and that of previous sun priests that when the sun reached this position along the horizon it was time to begin preparing the fields for planting. We know from several anthropologists that such observations were a daily occurrence and that, traditionally, the sun priest kept careful track of the position of the sun each sunrise and sunset.

Following the observation described by Cushing, the sun would have slipped slowly northward day by day until it passed the midway position on the horizon. Because the sun moves quickly at this time, the sun priest must watch carefully each day to find the proper time to announce when planting is to begin. Sun watching of this sort requires a constant and well-defined place to stand; and, because of the sacred nature of the relationship between the sun and the sun priest, this was generally a sacred place or shrine. At Zuni near the turn of the century, the sun priest observed the sunrise from the sacred shrine at Matsaki. That shrine was dismantled years ago by the Zuni, who no longer employ a sun priest, but anthropologist Matilda Coxe Stevenson of the Bureau of American Ethnology obtained a photograph of it in the 1890s in which can be seen an image of the sun pecked on the surface of a sandstone slab — a circular face from which extend short rays reminiscent of the Zia Pueblo sun symbol.

As the sun priest continued to watch the sun, he saw that its northward journey along the horizon slowed and eventually came to a halt. At this time, the summer solstice, the sun appears to rise and set in the same place for several days in succession. According to Pueblo tradition, it is stationary for four days. Though this period might be expected from Pueblo ritual interest in and use of the number *four*, it is also a fair estimate of the observable period during which the sun changes neither its rise nor its set position.

The summer solstice is a time of ritual dances for the Pueblo, part of the object being to celebrate the turning of the sun and to encourage him to remain northward and high in the sky for a long period in order to provide warmth and light for the crops. Still, the primary purpose is to encourage the kachina spirits to bring the rain. It is also a time to manufacture and deposit prayer sticks in the sun shrines. At Hopi, these shrines are often many miles away from the pueblo to which they belong. As viewed from the pueblos, they lie along the line at which the sun appears to rise or set. There are Hopi shrines at other important calendrical horizon positions as well, especially at winter solstice.[2] Like most traditional societies, the Hopi, the Zuni, and the other Pueblo groups have developed elaborate ceremonies to entreat the sun to move northward once again.

Turning Back the Sun

Winter solstice ceremonies at all the pueblos, though they differ in detail, are uniformly designed for the purpose of turning the sun around and setting him on his true northward course. They involve planting of prayer sticks, which are feathered messengers to the sun, and elaborate private and public ceremonies. The knowledge of sacred matters about the eastern pueblos along the Rio Grande is thin, probably because after their early unfortunate experiences with the Spanish, the Pueblo people are less open to persistent questions of anthropologists. But in the western pueblos of Hopi and Zuni, anthropologists observed the winter solstice ceremonies and described them in detail. The most elaborate descriptions were made near the turn of the century when non-Indian access to the ceremonies was easier. The accounts, therefore, may not be representative of current practices. However, they do vividly illustrate the Native American concern with ritual related to the calendar and metaphorical enactment of the forces of nature.

Alexander Stephen, a young man who, like Cushing, also worked for the Bureau of American Ethnology, was present for the Hopi winter solstice ceremony and the related preceding ritual, which took place in the village of Walpi in 1891. The sun priest had been watching the sunset daily, and when the sun finally set at the appropriate notch at Eldon Mesa southwest of Walpi, he instructed the town crier to announce that the sun had reached his house in the west. A few days later, after they had planted prayer sticks, refurbished the ritual paraphernalia, and conducted other preparations, the solstice arrived. Part of the solstice ceremony, which took place in one of the several village kivas, involved a dramatic enactment of the sun's indecision about assuming his proper yearly path. In this and other similar ceremonies, the chief of one of the societies carries a shield, on the front of which is a painting of the sun. On his head,

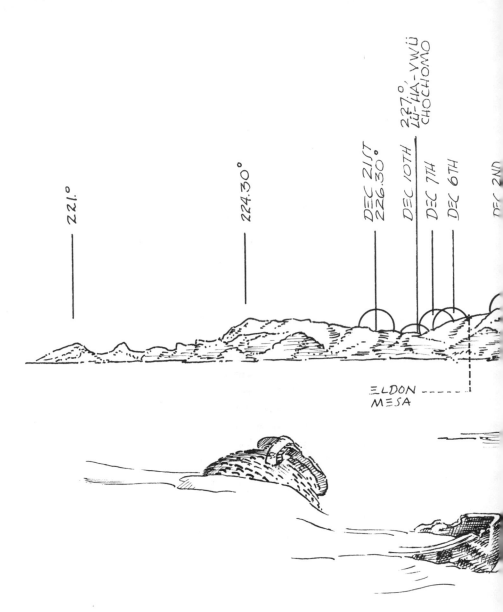

221.°

224.30°

DEC 21ST
226.30°

DEC 10TH

227.°
LÜ-HA-YWÜ
CHOCHOMO

DEC 7TH

DEC 6TH

DEC 2ND

ELDON
MESA

he wears a tablet decorated with the rain cloud symbol. Novices who are being initiated into the society stand at the four cardinal points, and each in turn chants invocations to the gods for rain and good crops.

The concerted song and invocations occupy five minutes. At 1 o'clock the shield bearer stamps upon the sipapu where he has been standing and posturing beautifully, throughout, and at this signal nearly all of the Singers (whose place of cult is this kiva) arrange

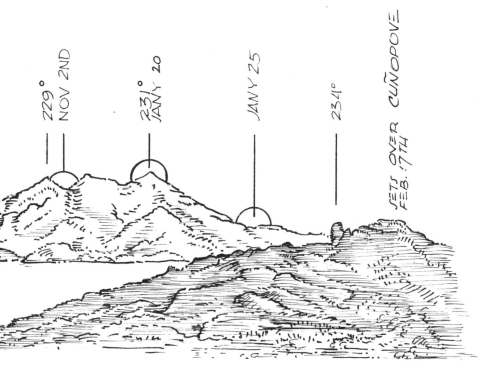

Hopi solar calendar. Horizon calendars such as this one at the Hopi town of Walpi allow the Pueblo Indians to determine the appropriate times for ceremony and for planting and harvesting. For example, when the sun sets in the place known as Lu-há-vwü Chochomo, the Hopi know that winter solstice will occur about eleven days later. (After Alexander Stephen, *Hopi Journal of Alexander M. Stephen.* Edited by E. C. Parsons. *Columbia University Contributions to Anthropology* vol. 23 [2 vols.]. New York: 1936. Map 5.)

themselves in two irregular groups on the north and south side of the main floor, facing each other, and all burst forth into song, shouting vehemently, the shield bearer making eccentric dashes among them, first to one side, then to the other. While this ecstatic song lasts he continues these short swift rushes, and the groups, although in constant vigorous motion of low, rebounding springs, restrain themselves in crouching postures, as if in expectancy, and meet his onrushes by springing erect and repelling him to the sipapu. Thus from right to left, i.e., to north and south, he continues his mad oscillations, but throughout he swings his shield in rhythmic motion, and the dancers beat their feet in astonishing unison to the impetuous movement of their frantic strains.

They will not permit me to light candles which we brought, and an old man maintains a light by steadily feeding the fire with dry twigs of greasewood, but this small fire with the crowded numbers present brings the kiva to a glowing furnace heat. Hence this violent drama is of short duration. In less than three minutes the shield bearer staggers with exhaustion and the supe runs forward and receives his shield and he disappears up the upraise, where some of the men of this kiva are in readiness to receive him. He faints and they carry him up the ladder.[3]

Stephen, who described this particular dramatic performance, later commented:

All of the posturing has been superb, and as a mimic assault the dramatic action intensely exciting, but there is no real conflict. The light feather-rayed shield is dashed from face to face, and the groups make as if they would seize it, but they no more than touch it with their outspread hands. But although to the observer this so vividly suggests an assault, yet the motive of this primitive drama is quite the opposite; it represents the Sun deity beginning his yearly shield-bearing journey, but hesitating whether or not to travel over the Hopi region, and this religious society of Singers thus display or typify their efforts to constrain him to his accustomed path.[4]

At other Hopi villages, the details of the dramatic presentation were different, but they were still related to the sun's journey. At Oraibi, a village on Second Mesa, the star priest appeared at the appropriate point in the kiva ceremony. On his head he wore a four-pointed star representing the morning star, and he carried in his hand a disk on which the sun was painted. A prayer stick was tied to the back of the sun shield. Shortly, the priest twirled the sun disk and pointed it toward each of the four cardinal directions to dramatize Sun Father's yearly path. To complete his journey, Sun Father must stop at all of the solstitial points to which the star priest pointed the sun disk. But here, as in most Hopi and Zuni ritual, the cardinal points are not the familiar north, south, east, and west we recognize, directions that are tied to the apparent rotation of the celestial sphere. In their ritual observance, the Pueblo tend to refer to the northwest, southwest, southeast, and northeast, the points of solstice standstill as Sun Father proceeds on his yearly journey.

The ceremonies I have referred to took place in the kiva at night and were attended by only one or two women who had a part in the ceremony, a few male society members, and several young initiates. The dawn brought a public ceremony in which the sun's arrival was dramatically represented for all the pueblo. At sunrise, a masked god carrying symbols of the sun entered the pueblo. Two men dressed as women walked along with him, carrying basket trays. In each tray were ears of corn set on end and arranged in a circle enclosing representations of sprouting vegetation. Fertility elements were a strong part of the ritual. By including repeated symbolic references to plant growth and to a plentiful harvest here and in other ceremonies, the Hopi emphasize the intimate connection between the sun's timely return to northern skies and abundance of food.

At Zuni, fertility rituals involve planting prayer sticks in the fields on the winter solstice. We can witness an instance of the winter solstice plume-planting ritual through the eyes of Matilda Coxe Stevenson, who was there in 1891 to see priests plant prayer sticks in sacred shrines and the rest of the people deposit prayer sticks in their own fields.

> The sun rose in splendor on the morning of the fifth day, making brilliant the mantle of snow that covered the earth. The valley was sparkling white, and the mesa walls were white, with here and there a patch of dark blue, the pines veiled by the atmosphere. The snowy plain was a vast kaleidoscope from morning until evening, the devotees in their bright clothing going to and returning from their sacred mission.

Families, including infants, deposit their prayer plumes in shallow excavations in their own fields.

> The tiny babies have their hands dipped into the meal and held over the plumes. These plumes remain uncovered until sunset the following day, that the Sun Father, in passing over the road of day, may receive the prayers breathed upon the meal and into the plumes, the spiritual essence of the plumes conveying the breath prayers to him. The excavations are afterward so covered that no one could discover that the earth had been disturbed.[5]

At Zuni, as at Hopi, the sun priest had been watching the horizon intently each morning and at the right time he announced that in ten days Sun Father would reach the Middle Place, the winter solstice house of the sun. They then started serious preparations for the winter solstice ceremonies.

In contrast to Hopi, at Zuni there is a strong emphasis on lighting the New Fire, a symbolic gesture to ensure that the new year, which for the Zuni begins on the winter solstice, gets off to a good start. On the day before the solstice, the new year fire maker (a boy) tours the village to collect a cedar fagot from every house. Each person who gives him wood offers a prayer that the crops will thrive in the coming year. The fire maker visits each house systematically and carries to the kiva the fagots he has gathered in bundles. After depositing the last load of wood, he collects coals from the nearest house to the east of the kiva and at sunset lights the sacred fire, a fire that is kept going all during the remainder of the winter solstice ceremonies. Ten days after the winter solstice, a New Fire celebration is held.

> Large fires burn in every house and bonfires light up the village everywhere. This is a real gala time for the youngsters, who are permitted to keep the fires blazing. All hands pelt the Lhe'lele (men covered with buffalo skins) with coals of fire as they pass through the streets, calling for fire: "More fire. Give us more beautiful flowers," referring to the coals of fire. The dancing continues in all the kivas until long after midnight, when the gods depart over the western road.[6]

While the people engage in this fun, kachinas visit each kiva and present seeds to everyone there. These are later planted, for they "are sure to yield bountifully if those to whom they are given have good hearts." Kindling the New Fire at the winter solstice is another way of suggesting to Sun Father that it is time to move northward once again to rekindle the warmth of the earth.

Ancient Practices

Whether at Hopi, Zuni, or the eastern pueblos, the winter solstice and the turning of the sun is still an important event among the Pueblos, and we may safely assume that it was also vitally important to their predecessors, the Anasazi. If they watched for the arrival of the winter solstice, the Anasazi most certainly also developed ceremonies to encourage the sun's northward return. We can only speculate about the form of their ritual practice, for what ceremonies they may have had died with the Anasazi.[7] But we might ask if they left other evidence of their sun watching activities. Cushing's account of sun watching at Zuni takes us back nearly a hundred years. How much further into the past are Pueblo sun watching traditions likely to extend? In spite of drought, migrations, and disruptions by Western culture, some aspects of the ancient culture persisted into the historic period, and still exist today. Ancient and historic kivas may contain nearly the same structural features, and ritual objects such as prayer sticks are found in great quantities in excavations of Anasazi ruins. Until very recently, even the form of the pueblos themselves conformed to the pattern of the ancient structures.

Given these facts, it seems likely that at least a few ancient sun watching places might be marked with sun and other celestial symbols such as Cushing observed at Zuni. There is no better place to begin to look than Chaco Canyon, New Mexico, the site of a major Anasazi civilization. Now a National Historical Park protected by the National Park Service, Chaco Canyon boasts eleven major Anasazi ruins and hundreds of minor ones.

The archaeological treasures of the canyon lay unknown to archaeologists until the 1870s when W. H. Jackson camped for several days in Chaco Canyon and made simple ground plans of eleven ruins in the area. Soon after, archaeologists turned their attention to the larger pueblo buildings, the impressive products of the eleventh century A.D., the "golden age" of Chaco Canyon Anasazi civilization. Structures such as Pueblo Bonito, the largest single building in the canyon, and its sisters Chetro Ketl and Pueblo del Arroyo, were excavated, sifted, sorted, and then reconstructed for modern tourists to marvel at and examine. But it was not until the early 1970s that anyone made a comprehensive and detailed survey of the entire canyon, searching for all signs of human habitation, ancient and modern.

The survey and the work that followed it turned up evidence that by A.D. 1100 Chaco Canyon had apparently served as a focal point for a broad Anasazi trading network. Chaco-style towns are known as far as 150 miles north in southwestern Colorado and 100 miles southwest near Zuni. There is also strong evidence for an intricate and elaborate network of ancient roads that once connected the nearby towns and villages, presumably for trade and ritual commerce. Mysteriously abandoned by the Anasazi about A.D. 1300, this canyon was dwelt in by the Navajo in the 1800s and later. Today, Navajo graze and farm the surrounding area and eke out a precarious living in the high desert environment. Sagebrush, cactus, piñon, and juniper form the major floral components of the mesas, though willow and cottonwood are often found in profusion in the wetter areas along the Chaco Wash, which flows down the center of the canyon in the rainy season. The canyon walls themselves are buff or reddish sandstone, both of which were used extensively as construction material in the pueblos.

One day in 1972, the National Park Service archaeological survey crew came across an interesting and unusual pictograph in an isolated spot in the northwest part of the canyon. Carefully executed in red paint on the narrow ceiling of a shallow sandstone overhang, the crew found a star, a crescent, and a handprint. Just below these on the vertical wall was a traditional Pueblo sun symbol — three concentric circles with a dot in the center. According to the interpretation by modern Pueblo informants, the three circles represent the rays of the Sun Father and the central dot his umbilicus, from which his power emanates.[8]

It is intriguing that the Chaco symbols are virtually identical to those described by Cushing at Zuni. (The sun symbol is stylistically different, but the two representations carry identical meanings to the historic Pueblo people.) Chaco Canyon is ninety miles northeast of Zuni Pueblo; this is a good distance even by today's standards. However, the Village of the Great Kivas at Zuni was built in the eleventh century in a style that is unmistakably Chacoan. Whether colonists from Chaco or a local group simply emulated the Chaco example, the pottery and other material items found there show that they traded with Chaco Canyon. Thus, an ideological connection between ancient Chaco Canyon and historic Zuni also seems plausible.

Whether the identity of the symbol complexes in the two places is merely coincidental or indicative of a real cultural connection across space and time, on the basis of the symbols alone, the Chaco Canyon site seems a likely possibility for an ancient sun watching station.

That the Chaco paintings are special is clear from a cursory survey of the rock art of the canyon, the walls of which are liberally decorated with thousands of petroglyphs (rock peckings or carvings) and a few pictographs (rock paintings). Some are clearly Navajo and date from the historic period, because they include horses, cows, or other animals introduced by the Spanish. Most were painted, pecked, or incised by the Anasazi sometime between A.D. 700 and 1300. These particular paintings are unique among Chaco Canyon rock art. Though there are other pictographs, nowhere else in the canyon is there this particular collection of symbols that is so reminiscent of the Zuni group of symbols. Also, they are located in what seems to be a special place, a well-sheltered area near one of the ancient roads that crisscross the canyon. This particular road segment leads east from Penasco Blanco, an eleventh-century ruin, over the mesa, then down and across the canyon bottom to emerge in a series of stairs leading up the other side, opposite the pictographs.

At first I was puzzled about how the Anasazi might have used the location for sun watching. An observer standing below the sun symbol and looking east across the canyon sees only a relatively flat, featureless horizon. There is little there to mark either the solstices or the equinoxes. But as Donnel O'Flynn, a St. John's College graduate who had won a Thomas J. Watson Foundation fellowship to travel and study archaeoastronomical sites, first pointed out to me, the situation changes twenty yards above the site, on the mesa top. From there the horizon has considerably more structure and there are peaks and notches that can be used to mark sunrise on both solstices and the equinoxes, though the most uneven terrain is in the direction of the winter solstice. One bitter winter morning near the solstice, while taking a position above the site I believe to be a shrine, O'Flynn was able to witness the sun emerge from behind a sharp edge of the distant mesa. As he discovered, even the local terrain from that position makes it an excellent place in which to sit or crouch to wait for sunrise, especially during the bitter cold around the winter solstice. There is plenty of low-level shelter to shield the sun watcher from the prevalent northwest winds.

If the mesa above is such a good place from which to observe the sun, why not put the paintings there instead of below, a twenty-yard steep drop into the canyon? In other words, why not put them where they would mark the exact place to stand? The answer, at least in part, must be that in the area below the rim of the canyon they are well sheltered from the elements. It is also the best stone surface for painting. The surface of most of the rimrock along the ancient road above is just too rough for painting or even for pecking petroglyphs.

We can imagine how the observations were made. The sun priest might awaken before sunrise and, making his way quietly out of Penasco Blanco, walk the two hundred yards to the edge of the mesa east of the pueblo. Crouching in the shelter of the rimrock ledges above the shrine, he awaits the rising of the sun. Then, after carefully noting just where the sun rises and saying his prayers to Sun Father, he makes his way back to the village to announce the new day. If Sun Father has reached the appropriate point on the horizon, his priest would also tell the village that it was time to prepare for a festival or to plant certain crops.

How can we be sure that the paintings are connected to Penasco Blanco? The best way to test the hypothesis would be to date the paintings and compare that date with the known date of Penasco Blanco (circa 1100). But rock art is notoriously hard to date. In the case of the Penasco Blanco pictographs, any attempt to date them by chemical means would probably destroy them. Other Anasazi glyphs nearby are lightly pecked designs typical of the oldest Anasazi style in the region. There are also a few Navajo glyphs as well, but we can say with considerable assurance that the paintings are not Navajo. The form of the sun is typically Puebloan, and painting or carving a hand at sacred locations is also a Pueblo trait. From the archaeological evidence we can be reasonably sure that there has been no sustained Pueblo occupation in the canyon since about A.D. 1300, so it seems probable that the symbols belong to the early Anasazi occupation of the canyon.[9]

Eastern Chaco Canyon

At the other end of the canyon, a few hundred yards east of Wijiji Pueblo, the archaeological survey turned up another sun symbol. Painted in white, and in a form more reminiscent of the Zuni portrayal of the sun because of what appear to be four feathers protruding from its disk, this sun symbol is also adjacent to an ancient roadway.

While searching the records in Chaco Canyon for other possible Anasazi sun watching sites, O'Flynn discovered this pictograph noted on the Park Service maps and hiked out to find it. He quickly realized that it is ideally suited to aiding sun watching, especially near the winter solstice, for the southeast horizon carries a particular bonus for the experienced watcher. At eye level, about five hundred yards away across a shallow rincon, are a sharp break in the mesa profile and, to its right, a nubbin of rock that projects above the line

Sunrise behind sandstone pillar, as seen from a painted sun symbol east of Wijiji Pueblo, Chaco Canyon, New Mexico. By watching the progression of the sun along the horizon prior to the winter solstice it is possible for someone with the proper training to anticipate the day of arrival of winter solstice. This site may have been used by the Anasazi a thousand years ago and in more recent times by the Navajo.

of the horizon. This sandstone projection is the very top section of a high natural stone pillar.

O'Flynn was there on the winter solstice. By standing several yards north of the sun symbol itself, he was able to witness the winter solstice sun just barely peeking out on either side of the tiny nubbin as it rose, making this feature an excellent sighting device from which to determine the winter solstice precisely. However, I suspect that it was not used that way at all, for, by crouching directly in front of the sun symbol and watching the sun rise on successive days near the winter solstice, the Anasazi sun priest could have seen the sun frame the stone pillar sixteen days *prior to* the winter solstice. This would have been a much more accurate solstice device because the sun priest could have anticipated winter solstice by watching ahead of time and then confirmed it by watching the sun rise behind the pillar on the day itself.

The useful horizon features that make winter solstice so easy to anticipate are virtually absent for the summer solstice and equinox sunrises. And in fact, at the summer solstice, the sun is well above the distant horizon before its rays can even reach the painted sun symbol.

Of course, it is not necessary that the site work well for the full scope of the year. It is entirely possible that this site, if used as I suggest, was employed solely for winter solstice determinations and for no other solar anniversaries. The problem with these hypotheses, however, is that the painted sun symbol, in spite of its similarity to other Pueblo renditions of the sun, appears to be a Navajo painting. This identification is rendered particularly plausible by the presence of a small painted glyph next to it that is clearly Navajo, a fact that a sharp-eyed amateur discovered while investigating the site during a research tour that I conducted. However, there are also many indications of Anasazi use of the area. Pottery, tool flakes, and petroglyphs typical of the Chaco Anasazi abound. When I made this discovery known, the question of whether it was an Anasazi or a Navajo sun watching site, or both, became the subject of a lively scientific interchange.[10]

Convinced by my studies of the site that the sun pictograph was a Navajo painting, I mentioned this finding to astronomer Michael Zeilik. On a subsequent visit to Chaco Canyon at winter solstice, Zeilik found additional evidence that the site as a whole might have served the Anasazi nearly as I have described. In addition, he and a colleague noted an additional possible orientation to the winter solstice sunset, an occurrence that we had missed in our earlier investigations of the site. Zeilik suggests that the proper area to stand is along the ledge to the north of the petroglyph, where Anasazi petroglyphs mark places to witness sunrise on or just prior to winter solstice, depending on the needs of the observer.[11] It now appears that the dual hypothesis — that the Anasazi used the site for sun watching sometime during their occupation of the canyon, and that the Navajo used it much later in a similar way — provides the best fit to the available data.

Near the winter solstice the site provides an extremely precise mechanism for calculating the exact day of the solstice. The problem at the solstice is that the sun's daily motion along the horizon is very slow, and as we've seen before, for two or three days on either side of the solstice, it actually seems to stand still. That fact makes it virtually impossible to pick out the true solstice by watching where the sun stops and turns around. However, if the sun is observed carefully on one year several days before and after the winter solstice, and a record kept of the number of days it takes to reach a given place on the horizon once again after it has passed that point on the way south, then the observer would be able to pick out the solstice by taking half the number of days between the two events. For example, at the Wijiji site, for an observer crouching in front of the sun painting in 1979, the sun would have risen directly behind the stone pillar on December 6 and again on January 7. There are thirty-two days between these two dates. Thus the sun watcher would know that winter solstice occurred on December 22 that year.

Some training in timing the solstice and other important dates may be necessary to keep an accurate calendar. This constituted an important part of the training of a sun priest. The Zuni tell a story regarding the first sun priest (Pekwin).

> The man who went to the Sun was made Pekwin. The Sun told him, "When you get home you will be Pekwin and I will be your father. Make meal offerings to me. Come to the edge of the town every morning and pray to me. Every evening go to the shrine at Matsaki and pray. At the end of the year when I come to the south, watch me closely; and in the middle of the year in the same month, when I reach the farthest point on the right hand, watch me closely." "All right." He came home and learned for three years, and he was made Pekwin. The first year at the last month of the year he watched the Sun closely, but his calculations were early by thirteen days. Next year he was early by twenty days. He studied again. The next year his calculations were two days late. In eight years he was able to time the turning of the sun exactly. The people made prayer sticks and held ceremonies in the winter and in the summer, at just the time of the turning of the sun.[12]

The Anasazi sun priest of Wijiji Pueblo probably underwent just such training in order to find the winter solstice with accuracy. At Hopi today, we see a similar situation. There, the announcements for summer solstice and winter solstice alike occur several days prior to the actual event, a circumstance that is only possible when the sun priest knows in advance how many days there are between sunrise at a given point on the horizon and the solstice.

In telling of horizon calendars, I have concentrated largely on the three major solar events — summer and winter solstice, and the equinoxes. But societies that used or still use the horizon directly for calendrical information seek far more detailed information than those four essential dates in observing sunrise or sunset so intently. As we saw at the beginning of this chapter, the Zuni observed the sun in order to know when to begin preparing their fields for planting. All the pueblos, historic and prehistoric, seem to do the same. In a remote corner of southeastern Utah, we discovered remarkable evidence of an intricate Anasazi calendar for planting and sowing, one in which lighting effects assume an important role.

Sunlight and Sandstone

The play of sunlight and shadow along a wall in a room or across a landscape may deeply interest or even visually thrill us, but for a people who live by the sun and depend heavily on it for knowing the seasons, the day, or the time, the interaction of light and shadow takes on a much deeper meaning. For them, the displays of light and shadow may extend into the realm of the sacred; they constitute a sacred appearance, or hierophany (from the Greek words *hieros*, "sacred," and *phaino*, "to reveal or make appear").

Around A.D. 1000 the Mayan builders of Chichén Itzá in the northern Yucatán of Mexico may well have had such a hierophany in mind when they constructed the imposing pyramid called the Castillo. There, at sunset only on the equinoxes, the northwest corner of the pyramid casts an undulating shadow against the western side of the north stairway. The curvy shadow terminates at a carved stone serpent head on the lower end of the stairway's balustrade, creating the striking illusion that a serpent is lying head down along the stairs.[13]

No one is sure just what caused the Mayans to build the temple this way. One thing is certainly clear. This serpent shadow could hardly have gone unnoticed by the thousands of Mayans who inhabited Chichén Itzá. A great undulating serpent appearing along the temple steps only two days out of the year must have had deep religious connotations for the people, whether or not they understood the appearance's connection with the calendar dates. One can imagine, however, that for the Mayan priests, who were precise astronomers, the shadow had a different sort of meaning — sacred, to be sure, but also practical. With its appearance they would have found confirmation or correction of intricate calendrical calculations. By the shadow they were able to determine the exact day of the equinox.

The serpent's appearance on the side of the Mayan pyramid is an event that is both remarkable and beautiful as well as practical. Yet one need not construct an imposing edifice in order to experience the power and beauty of the sun's yearly journey. Seven centuries ago, on the side of a small canyon in what has become Hovenweep National Monument in Utah and Colorado, Anasazi dwellers marked the passing of the year in a different way. Here, two enormous boulders about one hundred yards south of Holly House stand in mute testimony to the Anasazis' powers of observation and to their ingenuity. The two form a natural narrow corridor some eighteen feet long that opens to the eastern horizon. The western horizon is almost fully blocked by another large boulder. On the southern side of this natural corridor, below a rooflike overhang, the Anasazi pecked several shallow petroglyphs. Above and to the east are two spirals, about one foot in diameter, one now half-eroded by time and seeping water. Three feet to the right of this is a typical Pueblo sun symbol — three concentric circles with a dot in the center. Its appearance in this place clearly demonstrates that the connection of this symbol with sun watching was widespread; the celestial sun interacts with this earthly one in a manner that leaves little doubt about the site's use for sun watching.

Doug Bacon, a seasonal park ranger at Hovenweep, pointed out this panel to me several years ago, but it wasn't until later that I was able to witness the thrilling and compelling sequence of events that constitutes the summer solstice sunrise there. After the conference "Archaeoastronomy in the Americas," which I organized in Santa Fe, New Mexico, I led a tour of fellow archaeoastronomers and friends to Chaco Canyon and Hovenweep. Knowing from previous work my colleagues Jane Young and Craig Benson had done there with me that the summer solstice sunrise might prove to be a significant event, I took the archaeoastronomers to see the sunrise at the Holly House site.

We observed a striking and moving interplay of light and shadow. About forty-five minutes after the sun had risen above the local landscape, a narrow sliver of sunlight begins to enter the long, narrow corridor from a natural slit in the northeast and cuts across the left-hand spiral. As it elongates and reaches across the second spiral, a second knifelike light beam begins as a tiny point of light far to the right of the sun symbol. It, too, extends but moves to the left toward the sun symbol and the first sword of light. In a minute or so, the second narrow streak of light cuts the sun symbol just below its center. Shortly afterward, the two extended streaks of light join in the space between the sun symbol and the spirals, broaden, and move downward across the rest of the petroglyph panel. It takes only seven minutes for this compelling drama of light and shadow to play out, but in that time even the modern secular observer is drawn into it, feeling a sense of wonder and an unusual oneness with the cosmos.

All the intricate and fascinating display of light is caused by the interaction of a moving sun and the complicated three-dimensional geometry of the boulders — boulders placed there by nature, and used by human beings. The streaks of light were entirely natural phenomena — until noticed by the Anasazi who pecked the glyphs strategically on the face of the southern boulder.

After the glyphs were in place, the sun priest, by very carefully observing the interaction of light and shadow over a few years, would have easily been able to determine the date of the solstice within three or four days. For, although a series of investigatory observations revealed that a similar phenomenon of light and shadow occurs at sunrise for perhaps twenty days on either side of the solstice, each day's appearance is slightly different, and the practiced eye should be able to distinguish the day of the solstice from the others with high enough precision to set a calendar. Here, the sun priest would likely have been able to forecast the arrival of the summer solstice days ahead of time and check this prediction by watching for the characteristic pattern of light on the actual solstice.

In addition to the sun symbol, there are also other petroglyphs on the panel. To the right of the sun symbol a pecked wavy line extends vertically from below the sun and terminates in what appears to be a head. Although the upper end of the line is heavily eroded and difficult to see, the "head" has a projection attached to it that seems

Petroglyphs near Holly House, Hovenweep National Monument. The narrow corridor formed by these two large boulders lies along the direction of equinox. When the sunlight first falls along the corridor at sunrise, it is time to begin to prepare the fields for planting (about February 20). Shortly after the vernal equinox, the sun has moved too far north to light up the entire corridor. Around the summer solstice, in a dramatic display of light and shadow, sunlight forms two serpents of light, which fall across the two spirals and the three concentric circles (a common Pueblo sun symbol) and meet between them.

to be a horn similar to the plumed or horned serpent that, in Mexico, was associated with the cult of Quetzalcoatl. The plumed or horned serpent is a common artistic motif throughout the Southwest. Along the Rio Grande, the serpent is called Awanyu and appears on pottery, among the numerous petroglyph panels, and also on war shields. There, and in the western pueblos of Hopi and Zuni, the plumed serpent is a major mythological character.

Snakes or serpents in the pueblo bring to mind the snake dances at Hopi in which the priests handle dozens of live, fully venomed rattlesnakes in an elaborate and bizarre ceremony. The Hopis' trust in their serpents may appear foolhardy to some, since Christians and Jews are taught by both Biblical tradition and recent folklore to fear and even hate snakes. Although the Hopi as well as all the other Pueblo tribes recognize the potential danger of rattlesnakes, they also respect their role in the balance of nature and venerate them as symbols of fertility and war. This symbol must certainly go back to A.D. 900 or 1000 in Pueblo culture. Images of snakes are a common occurrence in the rock art near Hovenweep. They are also found in Chaco Canyon. A snake effigy found in Pueblo Bonito in Chaco Canyon suggests that the Bonitians venerated snakes and may have used them in ceremonies. The effigy, which was carved from a cottonwood root, is carefully smoothed and painted with black and white pigment.[14]

The cult of the plumed serpent must also be very old in the Anasazi area. In the abandoned pueblos along the Rio Grande near Albuquerque and Santa Fe, New Mexico, images of a horned or feathered serpent begin appearing in the rock art by A.D. 1400. Plumed serpent iconography was clearly an import from the south, and its northward progression from Mexico can be readily traced through time along the Rio Grande. There may have been another route north for the feathered serpent cult, as well. Less than twelve miles from the Holly House petroglyphs at Hovenweep, in a remote canyon, is a remarkable wall mural. Painted on the second-story wall of a cliff dwelling that was probably built prior to 1300, the mural includes an excellent example of a plumed serpent, reminiscent of similar early images near El Paso, Texas.[15] From this, and other evidence in the Four Corners area, it appears that the plumed serpent cult may have moved northward from Mexico along a more westerly route somewhat earlier than along the Rio Grande. It was probably well established by the mid thirteenth century, a time by which most of the Hovenweep towers were built.

In the historic pueblos, the plumed serpent is deeply respected as having an essential part in the balance of the world. Known as Kolowisi at Zuni, Palulukong at Hopi, and Aywanu in the Rio Grande pueblos, the plumed serpent is the beneficent guardian of pools, waterfalls, and springs. He is also potentially destructive —

just as violent storm water is sometimes destructive. During the vernal equinox ceremony called Palulukonti, as it was celebrated at the turn of the century at the Hopi village of Walpi, an effigy of Palulukong overthrows young corn plants set out before him. Only after being offered prayer meal does Palulukong withdraw to interfere no longer with the growth of the young corn.

The anthropologist Jesse Fewkes offered a compelling description of the ceremony:

> The act opens with a song by the chorus, and as it progresses the six disks bearing the sun emblems, which are seen to be hung by a hinge on one side, swing open from below. As they do this there protrude through the openings the blackened heads of six effigies of the great serpent, one of which, larger than the others, has udders and is called the "mother serpent." As the songs begin, these effigies move their heads back and forth, darting at each other as if attempting to bite their neighbors, while from the rear of the screen issue sounds made by concealed actors imitating the fancied roar of the horned serpent. As this continues, the song rises higher and higher, and the attacks of the serpent effigies on their fellows become more and more vicious. Suddenly the head of the mother serpent sweeps down to the floor of the room over the imitation field of corn, overthrowing the hills and scattering them right and left. These realistic movements of the snake effigies are caused by men concealed behind the screen, who handle their charges by means of a stick called the "backbone." After the field of corn has been overturned and the serpent effigies raise their heads, there passes before them the man dressed as the Earth woman, who offers prayer meal as food to the enraged serpent, after which the effigies are withdrawn, the disks fall back in place, and the chief gathers up the scattered clay cones with the sprouting corn plants and distributes them among the audience.[16]

After a long wait, a group of actors from another kiva appears to perform a second act, this time dramatizing directly the opposition between the sun and water. In this drama, the Hopi Sky God stands near the center of the kiva and struggles with an effigy of Palulukong. The serpent realistically twists around the masked god, and fights with him. Then suddenly, without warning, it sweeps down upon a group of young corn plants and knocks them over amid loud cries of protest from the audience. Palulukong wins a momentary victory before he is subdued by the Sky God.

The potentially destructive quality of Palulukong has a counterpart in nature, for the same spring rains that are needed to ensure the growth of crops can also be enormously destructive if they fall too fast or hard. The Hopi feel a balance must be struck, and by repeating this ceremony, they seem to be instructing the sun to stay on his proper path throughout the year.

The plumed serpent has also had a prominent place in the winter solstice ceremony at Hopi. At this time, an effigy of the serpent appears in a central location on the winter solstice altar as the most conspicuous feature of that altar. Here, too, the opposition between the water serpent and the sun is dramatically represented, each personifying essential elements in the fructification and growth of life. In this ceremony, a figure carrying a painted sun shield beats back a menacing plumed serpent and subdues him in mock combat. The success of the sun in this enterprise represents an assurance that the sun will again triumph in his yearly journey and turn northward to illuminate and warm the earth.

The presence of a plumed serpent next to a sun symbol on the Holly House panel implies that not only was the plumed serpent present in the Four Corners area by the thirteenth century but it was already associated with the sun and sun ceremonies. The glyph panel itself is impossible to date directly, but it exists in the midst of a grain storage area that was likely in use during the occupation of the nearby towers and boulder houses at the head of the canyon. These towers apparently date from the thirteenth century.

Below the sun on the petroglyph panel at Holly House are a pair of connected circles that may also have astronomical significance.

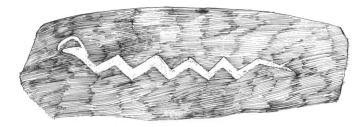

Plumed serpent (Hopi petroglyph). Believed to be related to the plumed serpent of Mexico called Quetzalcoatl, the Pueblo plumed serpent is the guardian of sacred springs and waterfalls. Rock paintings or carvings of this sacred being are found throughout the Southwest.

When you look closely at the pair, they give the distinct impression that they possess heads and legs; they may therefore represent anthropomorphic beings of some sort. Their bodies are made up of circles with a central dot, which seems to relate them to the sun pictured above them. They thus can be readily interpreted as twin beings associated with the sun.

In Pueblo mythology, the Twins, helpers and protectors of the Pueblo people, figure prominently. The Twins are represented in the sky by the morning and evening star. A charming and explicit Hopi myth that was collected by Alexander Stephen at the turn of the century describes the conception and birth of the Twins, sons of the sun:

> A Hopi maid longed for copulation, because she had heard it was sweet, but she knew nothing of it, for sure she was a virgin. She was constantly longing, and one day while she was seated in her house she spread wide her legs, and drew up her dress, uncovering her person. She cried, "Sun! my father! for sure you do not (love) care for me." There was a crevice in the house roof, and through it the sun rays penetrated and fell upon her exposed vulva, and the sensation was pleasant and she moved with delight. This was in the early summer when the corn was knee high. Clouds came up and the rain fell and the maid went under a projecting cliff for shelter, and again she longed, and she drew back her dress, exposing her person, and spread her legs apart. The falling rain collected in a pool on the edge of the cliff and flowed over in drops, and there fell upon her vulva, and again the sensation was pleasant and she moved with delight. Like the antelope, she gave birth to two upon the same day; the first born was the child of the Sun, Pöqangwhoya, the other twin was also the child of the Sun, but is also called the child of the Water, Palöngawhoya, Echo.[17]

Interestingly, the myth indirectly connects the Twins with the plumed serpent. Thus, the sun—plumed serpent duality that is present in the various solar ceremonies appears in the very genesis of the mythical beings who did so much to aid the Pueblo people.

Two faintly visible lazy S's and a geometric figure complete the Holly House panel. Thus, except for these latter symbols for which we have no astronomical explanation, all the elements work together to constitute a conceptual whole related to sun watching. This and the fact that the corridor itself opens only to a narrow band along the eastern horizon that frames the position of sunrise for only two

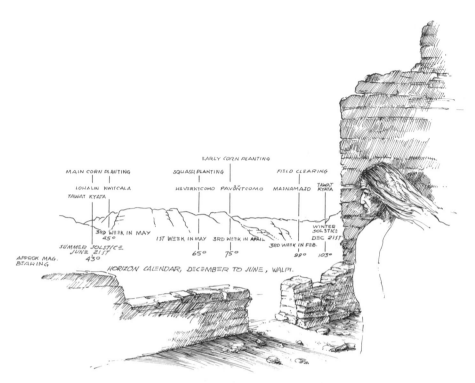

Sunrise horizon planting calendar from the Hopi pueblo of Walpi. When the sun reaches the appropriate place along the horizon, the Hopi know it is safe to plant certain crops. (After C. Daryll Forde, "Hopi Agriculture and Land Ownership." *Journal of the Royal Anthropological Institute of Great Britain and Ireland* 61 [1931]: 357–405.)

months of the year were the first clues that the site might have functioned as a solar observation station for setting the agricultural and ritual calendar. As the sun appears on the horizon from February 20 to March 21, and from September 22 to October 20, its light streams into the corridor and lights up portions of the panel. Between February 20 and March 20, the sun's light illuminates the lower part of the petroglyph panel, but it cannot reach the sun symbol because it is blocked by the rock overhang, or "roof," above the petroglyphs. Finally, just around the vernal equinox, the sun reaches far enough north for the suns to "look at each other" briefly at sunrise. It does this for a day or two until at sunrise the sun is once again blocked by obstructions along the horizon, this time by a large boulder to the northeast. After about March 23, this boulder effectively blocks the sun from reaching the sun symbol until around April 10, when the suns look at each other again for several days.[18]

The dates that are defined by the combination of boulders and the sun along the horizon at this place are extremely significant in the Hopi agricultural calendar. The Hopi, who live a hundred miles southwest of Hovenweep, still employ many of the same agricultural techniques used by the Anasazi who inhabited Hovenweep in the twelfth and thirteenth centuries. Archaeologists working in the Hovenweep area have discovered systems of check dams, small field terraces, and field outlines remarkably similar to those on the Hopi mesas.[19]

The Hovenweep Anasazi also grew many of the same crops as the Hopi; corn, beans, and squash are still staple foods of the modern Pueblo, as are piñon nuts gathered in the fall. Like the modern Hopi, they also seem to have been masters of the techniques of dry farming, making use of every available drop of water in their desert environment. The Hovenweep region, then as now, probably received less than twelve inches of precipitation a year. Although these similarities do not constitute proof that the Anasazi of Hovenweep and the Hopi are related, such a conjecture is supported by Hopi tradition, which says that some of their people came from the Hovenweep–Mesa Verde area.

We may follow another line of evidence in the Hopi agricultural calendar. By February 20, the date on which the sun first enters the narrow corridor, it would be time to begin preparing the fields for planting. A month later, on March 21, when the sun first illuminates the sun symbol, the Anasazi sun priest would know that the sun had arrived midway on its northward journey and that it was time for the vernal equinox ceremony. He would also know that in about twenty days, the first corn planting could be made. On that date, around April 10, as we have seen, the sun symbol is again lit by the rising sun. It remains lit for a brief time each morning until about May 20, when, for a period, sunlight is again blocked from reaching the carving of the sun by the northeast boulder. For the Hopi, the main corn planting should be completed by this date. Likewise, if my hypothesis about the meaning of this panel is correct, the Anasazi sun priest, who no doubt had been keeping careful track of the count of days since the first planting of corn was begun in April, would know by the absence of sunlight on the sun symbol that it was time to complete the spring planting.

Is there clear evidence that this area was ever used this way by the Anasazi? Unfortunately, here, as in so much of archaeological research, most of our conjecture must remain only that. The best we can do in this inquiry, and indeed anywhere in science, is to highlight the results of converging lines of evidence and let that evidence speak for itself.

First, the dates defined by the sun's interaction with the complex geometry of the site and the glyphs on the panel relate rather well to the historic Hopi agricultural calendar. Second, most of the elements of the glyph panel are related to one another in historic Pueblo ritual and mythology, so their nearness to each other seems appropriate to the sun watching aspects of the site.

In addition, the canyon in which the panel is located would be an excellent location for growing the traditional corn, beans, and squash of the Anasazi. Narrow but shallow, the canyon is oriented nearly north-south and therefore both slopes receive sun for most of the day. Ancient terraces on the canyon slopes and several check dams across the drainages about the canyon attest to its intensive use for agriculture. And where there is agriculture, there is special need for a precise and accurate calendar.

In emphasizing the need for a precise celestial calendar for agriculture we must not lose sight of the possible sacred nature of this and similar sun watching sites. No calendar stations are purely secular to the Pueblo. Among the historic Pueblo Indians, the symbols of this petroglyph panel are also sacred symbols having great power. It would be astonishing if they were not so for their prehistoric brethren as well. Imagine, then, the sacral power of Sun Father, first appearing along the corridor in mid-February to announce the approaching spring, then later by his explicit presence across the sun petroglyph guiding the planting and harvest of the fruits of his light and warmth. In this context, the connections, so obvious to the Pueblo people, between the sun, corn, and the self, take on a fundamental meaning that can only be glimpsed by our modern society.

The Pueblo signify the explicit connection between them through color symbolism. To each direction they assign a color. And for each directional color they associate a variety of corn. For the Zuni these colors are: north, yellow and yellow corn; west, blue and blue corn;

south, red and red corn; east, white and white corn; zenith, black and black corn; nadir, all colors and speckled corn. Corn quite literally brings life; corn becomes flesh, an understanding reflected in the Pueblo saying "We are corn." But of course it is only through the power of the sun that corn will grow to feed the people. Sun — corn — people — Sun. They of the corn return their thanks for life in the form of prayers and supplications to the sun — and the cycle is then complete.

A Noontime Marker

In their pursuit of a calendar, the Anasazi were wonderfully inventive. High atop a lonely butte in Chaco Canyon stands a different, apparently Anasazi, calendar device.[20] Unlike most of the other suspected ancient sun shrines we know of in the Southwest, Fajada Butte functions when the sun is near the meridian, rather than on the horizon. The butte has long been of archaeoastronomical interest, because its height raises it well above the local mesas and makes it an excellent platform from which to watch the sun rise or set along the horizon. The butte holds ample signs of prehistoric use; its various sandstone outcroppings are the backdrop for ancient petroglyphs, and just below the summit on the south side, the remains of several rooms attest to its use as a place of habitation. The lack of water on the butte and the difficult climb from the canyon floor 450 feet below make it unlikely that it supported many people. It appears a spot more likely for ascetics, hardened to a frugal, lonely life.

Finding the calendar device was a mixture of good luck and insight. As part of a team making a major rock art survey of the canyon, artist Anna Sofaer was recording the rock art at the top of the butte. While investigating a large pecked spiral hidden behind three large stone slabs on the southeast side of the butte, she was astonished to see a narrow dagger of light appear on the spiral and begin to move downward across it just to the right of center. In about twenty minutes the spectacular daggerlike appearance was over and the lighting around the spiral had returned to its normal dimness. The fact that she had been there to witness this remarkable event an hour before noon a few days after the summer solstice was a stroke of good luck. Her previous acquaintance with archaeoastronomy made her wonder if it was a marker similar to other shadow-play markers in the canyon, deliberately designed to act as a summer solstice device.

Encouraged by several of us who had seen her photographs of the event, she joined forces with two others and returned the following spring to document the appearances before, during, and after the summer solstice. There were several questions to investigate in detail. First, though there was already ample evidence of the Anasazis' interest in horizon observations for the calendar, no one had found a noontime device — nor had anyone looked for one. It took Sofaer's accidental discovery and her pursuit of its possibilities to suggest that the Anasazi might also have made meridian observations of the sun in addition to the more common dawn or dusk observations.[21]

Previous archaeoastronomical investigations in the Southwest have concentrated on horizon observations because there are so very many data on historic horizon observations in the pueblos. Most writers on southwestern astronomy had overlooked the fact that noon has also been of interest in Pueblo calendar keeping and in their mythology as well. In fact, it can be said that the sun's entire journey, day and night, is of interest to the Pueblo, for when Sun Father retires to his western house, he has not completed his entire twenty-four-hour cycle. Just as he shines down upon us during the day, so does he shine up from below to illuminate and warm the underworld while the stars shine above. At Hopi, this conception is even extended to the cycles of the months; when February is above, November is below; when winter is here, summer with its mature vegetation is below.

At Isleta Pueblo south of Albuquerque, the return of both summer and winter solstice involves midday ceremonies. During each ceremony, after the chief (sun priest) receives a basket of cornmeal from one of the "corn mothers," who represent the six colors of corn, he breathes upon it and then waves it in the anti-sunwise direction, that is, northwest, southwest, southeast, northeast. After laying prayer feathers on the basket and sprinkling them with meal, he begins the rite of drawing down the sun:

> In the roof of the ceremonial room there is a hole through which at noon the sun shines onto a spot on the floor near where the chief now stands. In front of the chief stand his assistants, then the row of the other men present, and then the row of women present. All turn to face the east, singing to call the sun. This is repeated in the

anti-sunwise circuit, before each song each sprinkling meal from the meal basket or pollen received from the chief assistant. All return to their places, except the chief, who makes drawing-in motions from all the directions from the corn mothers, throws pollen up toward the roof hole, and points upward with his stone knife. All sing the song of "pulling down the sun," while the chief makes the motions of drawing something toward himself. Now the sun drops down on the spot of sunlight on the floor. It is a round object, white as cotton, which opens and closes. To this the chief ties the prayer feathers, as all sing. All stand and throw pollen toward the sun object. The chief waves the sun object which shines so brightly you can hardly look at it. (The room has been darkened by closing windows.) All breathe on their clasped hands. As the chief waves the sun around his head the sun goes back through the roof hole. This is noontime when for a little while the sun stands still.[22]

The same sort of recognition of the sun's noon passage through the meridian occurs in Isleta mythology. Their version of the conception of the Twins by the sun's agency make the visitation occur explicitly at noon. As in most of the Rio Grande versions, a maiden who has refused the advances of many suitors is confined by her father to a dark room.

> The old man got mad at her. He scolded her; tried to whip her; and the old woman was protecting her. The old man got so mad he locked her into a cellar. He kept her there all the time. Her mother took the food in to her. It was dark in there, but somewhere there was a little hole (as big as this match). At noon the sun shone into this crack. On the floor when the sun shone, she used to come and lie, looking at the sun outside. She stayed there a long time. Once when her mother took in her food, her father came in to see her. He saw she was big with child . . .[23]

In other stories, the sun's noontime appearance is made explicit. To an observer, for about an hour on either side of noon, the sun seems to cease its vertical motion and therefore, in a sense, to stand still. In another Isleta story, one son of the sun helped his father move the sun disk across the sky.

Nashon'uchu helped Sun with his kick stick. Each morning before dawn, Nashon'uchu would emerge from his cave in the west before sunrise and cast pollen to the rising sun, his father. Then, placing his kick stick between his toes, he would kick the stick toward the east. As the bright, multicolored kick stick, painted with zigzag patterns, hit the ground, lightning flashed to let Sun know his son was working for him. By the time he reached the east to recover his kick stick, Sun had reached the middle. It was noon. Again, Nashon'uchu kicked his stick and again he caused lightning. Then Sun stopped in his travels and descended to thank his son.

> That's why people say the sun always stops a while at noontime and comes down and meets all his sons. Nashon'uchu had some prayer feathers for the sun. (They are what we clothe the sun with.) Nashon'uchu sprinkled some pollen and got his kick stick, while the sun started to the west. Nashon'uchu threw his kick stick to the west, and the kick stick and the sun met again, at sunset.[24]

These and many other stories describing the sun at noon, and the Isleta noontime solstice ceremonies, may be a remnant of an earlier Anasazi tradition.

The Fajada Butte site, discovered in 1977, probably some eight to ten centuries after it was used, suggests that certain Anasazi also had some interest in noontime observations. It presents a challenge to archaeoastronomers. Where else in the prehistoric record was the solstice sun observed at noon? Are there other, similar sites elsewhere in the Southwest? How does it relate to the other solar sites in Chaco Canyon? For several years after it was found, it remained a singular find. Now, however, several other rock art images, apparently also designed for sun watching, are known and are being investigated in detail.

At Fajada Butte, the streak of light is caused by sunlight passing between two of the three upright sandstone slabs that lean back against the ledge upon which the spiral is carved. The sequence of events near noon is dramatic. On the summer solstice, at 11:05 local solar time (the time that would be determined by a sundial placed on the butte), a small spot of light forms above the center of the spiral. It soon lengthens into a dagger shape and begins to move slowly downward through the center of the spiral. Eighteen minutes later, the streak has moved completely through the spiral and faded away.

A few days before and after the solstice, the sun dagger falls to the east of the spiral, a progression in space that allows one to determine the solstice within several days. Sofaer, Rolf Sinclair, and Volker Zinser have suggested that the individual or group that made the glyph and used it was able to determine the solstice within a day. In rebuttal, astronomer Michael Zeilik has pointed out that the dagger's horizontal motion across the spiral over the period near the solstice is so minute as to make it extremely difficult to determine the day of solstice that accurately.[25] He argues that it is more likely that the site was used, if at all, to celebrate the arrival of the sun. In that, it probably functioned much as the Holly House site at Hovenweep. Because the sun enters the Fajada Butte site near noon every day of the year, it can be used to follow the full scope of the year, whereas the Holly House site only functions from February through October.

The single dagger of light is itself quite enough to allow an observer to find the summer solstice within a few days, but a second one may have allowed the date to be determined even more precisely. At noon on days to either side of the summer solstice, this second streak of light, which appears to the left of the large spiral, cuts across a second smaller spiral. But on the day of the solstice and for a few days on either side of it, the second one is almost completely extinguished. This second dagger is formed by the narrow slot between the second and third sandstone slabs. Anna Sofaer and her colleagues have postulated that the declination of the sun was such at about A.D. 1000 that the spot totally disappeared on the solstice. If so, it would have served as a precise and sensitive indicator of the day of summer solstice.

The site also works to define the equinoxes and the winter solstice. By the autumnal equinox, the second dagger of light has worked its way across the small spiral to bisect it, while the first dagger has moved right to cut across the outer rings of the large spiral. By the winter solstice, the two patterns of light frame the side of the large spiral.

The evidence that Sofaer and her colleagues have gathered supports the hypothesis that these appearances were not accidental occurrences; the spiral was deliberately placed where it could be used to record the solstice for the Anasazi sun priests. Sofaer and her colleagues raise several interesting questions about the site. Were the slabs smoothed and abraded to make the daggers move in the precise way they do? Or were the slabs themselves moved to construct the entire solstice marker on the mesa? Sofaer has insisted from the beginning of her studies that the stone surfaces were worked — smoothed and abraded — and that the stones were put there by human beings. Others of us are not so sure.

The archaeologists and geologists who have inspected the site have agreed that the surfaces that delineate the slots responsible for the daggers of sunlight could have been shaped by man, but since the natural effects of erosion often mimic manmade abrasion it is difficult, if not impossible, to prove it. Nor can it be proved that the slabs had or had not been placed there by human agents. Their position, lying vertically against the mesa face, suggests to the eye unfamiliar with the spectacular rocky formations of the southwest mesas that they were deliberately dragged there and propped up to create the solstice marker. However, such vertical slabs are seen elsewhere in the canyon and through similar terrain in the Southwest, though their context is generally such that there is little question that they are the products of nature rather than of humans.[26] Most archaeologists and geologists familiar with the region whom I have queried deem it highly unlikely that the stones were placed there deliberately. They point out that formations quite like it without a spiral or other designs connected with them also exist in the canyon. Certainly, considerably more evidence would be needed to support any claim that these slabs had been placed there by humans.

Whichever opinions are supported by future work at the site, it is clear that Sofaer and her colleagues have raised interesting questions about Anasazi astronomy. The minimum hypothesis for the site is that the construct marks the sun near noon on the critical days of the year, and that the turns of the spiral could be used to calibrate the year with a minimum accuracy of several days. For that alone their work is significant.

A Sun Watching Experience

Sun watching, though an intensely practical pursuit, is also deeply religious. As with much of Pueblo life, past religious practices have either died out as the old priests have died or been radically altered by the pressures of modern living. Thus, in order to construct Pueblo astronomy we depend heavily on reports from the early observers of the Pueblo. The notebooks and articles of anthropologist Jesse Fewkes, whose observations and descriptions of Hopi and Zuni life were made in the 1890s before the heavy influx of tourists and anthropologists to the pueblos, are an invaluable resource today. During one summer solstice period, he watched priests make feathered prayer sticks, or ba-hos, to present to the sun in thanks and supplication.

Then, shortly after daybreak on the summer solstice, Fewkes climbed with one of the priests to the Hano sun shrine ba-ho-kia near Wal-la, a gap in the nearby mesa. The shrine, a simple affair a few feet in width and depth, was open to the east and had no roof. It was framed on the west by a large boulder set against the mesa itself, and on the north and south by two smaller stones. The da-wa-ba-hos (sun prayer sticks), which he planted in the sandy floor of the small shrine, were made of sticks of cottonwood a few inches long and somewhat greater in diameter than a pencil. One was male, one female. In other ceremonies of other pueblos the prayer sticks are slightly different, but they all have in common that they sport eagle or turkey feathers so the prayers they represent may reach their destination — the sun.

Following the wagon road for a short distance, he suddenly stopped, and without a word mounted a trail formed by steps cut in the rock. For a few feet it was like climbing the vertical wall of a precipice. After some trouble I succeeded in following him, and we made our way to a small, simple shrine or enclosure facing the east, backed by a huge boulder. The sun had just begun to redden the east, and the morning star was very bright. Without a word he planted the line of da-wa-ba-hos in the back of the shrine, so that

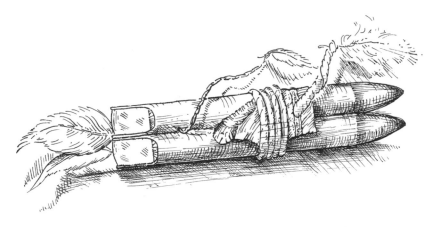

Hopi prayer sticks to the sun. The Pueblo groups present prayer sticks to the sun as offerings. These prayer sticks were offered at a sun shrine on the summer solstice. (After J. Walter Fewkes, "A Few Summer Ceremonials at the Tusayan Pueblos." *Journal of American Ethnology and Archaeology* 2 [1892]: 27.)

they faced the point where the sun was to appear. He then sprinkled them with sacred meal, and the string with the attached breathfeather was extended at right angles to the line of ba-hos, in the direction of the point of sunrise. The tur-nop-na (an offering of food) was placed in front of the da-wa-ba-hos, at the entrance of the ba-ho-kia, and a line of sacred meal was then drawn along the string, and a pinch thrown to the point from which the sun was to rise. We then awaited the appearance of the "orb of day"; Ka-la-cai sitting in front of the shrine, facing the south. Before the sun had appeared, Ka-la-cai offered a short prayer, and then chanted, or half intonated, in a low, melodious voice.

Just as the sun appeared, and while it was rising from behind the distant hills, before its lower limb had left the horizon, Ka-la-cai addressed a few words to it, casting meal on the feathers and towards the east. He then immediately left the place.[27]

Sun watching is a ceremony itself, but it is often done for the sake of ceremony. At Hopi, the major ceremonies Wuwuchim (the beginning of the ceremonial year when the kachinas return), Soyal (the winter solstice ceremony), and Niman (the date when the kachinas return home) are all set by noting the arrival of the sun at certain horizon features, just as the planting and harvest dates are set. Each of these ceremonies celebrates the Pueblo connection with the natural world of sunlight, rain, and the cycle of the crops.

At Hopi, in addition to the sun shrines that exist near the pueblos, it is customary to erect shrines at the spot on the horizon at which the sun seems to rise or set at specific times. Though these are sometimes five to fifteen miles away, the shrines are tended by runners from the pueblos and prayer sticks are "planted" in each on the day at which the sun rises or sets over the shrine. In conjunction with the sighting place, the shrines constitute a group of sacred places and a long set of straight lines that are highly reminiscent of Incan *huacas* and *ceques*, though I do not suggest that one set of ideas derives from the other. They are, however, conceptually related and demonstrate how similar ideas may spring up in widely separated locations. The young Hopi initiates run in as straight a line as possible to the shrines and back in order to plant their prayer sticks. They follow, as it were, literally, the straight road of a beam of sunlight.

Hopi sun watching is highly accurate. Historian Stephen McCluskey has shown that the date the sun priest determines for a given ceremony each year normally differs by only a day or two from the average over many years.[28] Of course, the sun watcher may occasionally be wrong. When that occurs, the people are highly critical. The Hopi Indian Crow Wing wrote in his journal for April 18, 1921: "We think the Sun-Watcher is not a very good man. He missed some places, he was wrong last year. All the people think that is why we had so much cold this winter and no snow."[29]

6 Ancient Pueblo Sun Buildings

Preceded by graduate student Craig Benson, I reached along the narrow ledge on the south side of Hovenweep Castle and pulled myself through a narrow cliffside doorway.[1] We had journeyed some two thousand miles from our East Coast homes to be at this remarkable Anasazi site during the period of the summer solstice. Our first day of transit measurements was complete, and now the sun was just a few minutes away from setting on the western horizon.

I had begun our season's work at this building in Hovenweep National Monument because it was, quite frankly, the easiest to reach. I could hardly believe our good luck. Though they were the only two ports in the first room we investigated, both seemed to be sun ports; the northwestern one appeared to point roughly to the summer solstice sunset and the southwestern one to the winter solstice sunset.

Although we were confident of our equipment and the calculations we had made earlier in the day, we did not know exactly how the sun would interact with the building, nor exactly where on the opposite wall the sunlight would fall. Nor could we tell from our measurements just how precise this alignment would be. It is hard to convey the excitement we felt as we watched the sun and the building perform their roles.

By the time we climbed into the room, sunlight was already streaming through the port and falling on its interior northern wall just to the east of the doorway to the D-shaped tower. The sun was still several solar diameters above the horizon. Then, as we watched in awe and great satisfaction, the spot of light slowly worked its way

Hovenweep Castle, Hovenweep National Monument. The canyons in and around Hovenweep National Monument contain numerous towers such as this, which were built by Anasazi groups related to the people living at Mesa Verde. Precariously perched on large boulders or on the edge of the canyons, these towers and their companion boulder houses are distinctive Anasazi architecture.

eastward in a shallow arc and eventually came to rest on the lintel of the doorway to the next room to the east. Just before the sun reached the horizon, a portion of the beam reached into the next room and fell on a spot on the floor in the northeast corner. Then, as the sun set, its image fell upon the doorway lintel once again. As we looked from the doorway toward the port, the apparent width of the port was just a trifle greater than the angular width of the sun. We were able to confirm observationally what our measurements told us — the proper way to look for the sun through these ports is diagonally. The opposite corners of the ports define the directions. We felt that we had just been made privy to a secret locked in these walls for seven hundred years. The room functioned then as a calendar device and so it acts still.

I was reminded of another portion of *My Life at Zuni,* written by Frank Cushing when he lived at Zuni Pueblo:

Nor may the Sun Priest err in his watch of Time's flight; for many are the houses in Zuni with scores on their walls or ancient plates imbedded therein, while opposite, a convenient window or small port-hole lets in the light of the rising sun, which shines but two mornings in the three hundred and sixty-five on the same place. Wonderfully reliable and ingenious are these rude systems of orientation, by which the religion, the labors, and even the pastimes of the Zunis are regulated.[2]

Wonderful and ingenious indeed! This observation of Cushing's provided an essential clue in the investigations of the mysterious towers and boulder houses at Hovenweep National Monument.

In the dusty interior of an Anasazi dwelling or ceremonial room a narrow beam of sunlight would be exceptionally bright and highly visible. The story of the sun impregnating a young maiden is known throughout the pueblos in several different versions and shows the power such sunbeams were believed to have. One Zuni account begins, "They were living at Matsaki," the same ancient Zuni pueblo at which the sun priest had his shrine.

> The daughter of the village priest never went out. She lived in the fourth inner room and went outside only after dark. She made baskets all the time. Everybody in the village wanted to see her but they never did. One day just at noon, while she was making baskets, the sun shone into the inner room through the hatchway and fell upon her lap. She became pregnant and in ten months it was time for her baby to be born. One night she took the sweepings from her room and bundled them in a blanket and took them out to the river. She felt her pains coming and she found shelter by the edge of the river and put down a big piece of bark. Her baby was born. Pretty soon she had another baby. There were both boys.[3]

A metaphor of the fruitful powers of the sun, this story is played out in real life in the growth of the crops after the return of the sun. To ensure the best use of the sun, it is essential to derive and keep an accurate calendar. The towers and boulder houses at Hovenweep National Monument demonstrate Anasazi ingenuity and inventiveness in using their buildings to accomplish this task.

At Hovenweep, the main sources of ventilation and light in the Anasazi buildings are small ports or loopholes similar to the ones also used at Zuni a hundred years ago. During the day, as the sunlight falls through various of the ports, bright spots of light move along the opposite wall. The particular port through which the light passes and the precise place the spots of light fall depend directly on the time of year and the time of day, just as we had observed, so a calendar exact to a day or two could be devised along the lines that Cushing tells us the Zuni used.

Oddly enough, what had originally drawn me to study the Hovenweep ruins for evidence of Anasazi astronomy were not the ports at all, but the suggestion that the towers there, tall buildings that had puzzled archaeologists for nearly a century, might be astronomical observatories. Apparently, the sole reason for that suggestion was their shape. According to this thinking, unusual, tall buildings must be astronomical observatories. Interestingly, some of them probably did function as observatories, but not because they are towers. As will soon become clear, the ingenious Anasazi used a variety of ways to pursue their astronomical observations, none of them related to or dependent on the tower shape.

Precariously perched on the rims of narrow box canyons in southeastern Utah and southwestern Colorado, the towers, boulder houses, and small pueblos of Hovenweep National Monument have been an enigma for archaeologists since they were first photographed and documented in the late 1800s by William H. Jackson.[4] This famous photographer, as part of a U.S. Geological Survey team exploring the entire West, carried his huge box camera and heavy glass plates through the mountains, along the mesas, and down into the canyons of much of the Southwest as well. His photographs were an extremely useful instrument in alerting the federal government to the wealth of ancient Native American remains in the area and also in helping to establish our present system of national parks and national monuments.

After the Hovenweep towers became known from Jackson's photographs and drawings, several early archaeologists[5] attempted to explain their function, but since they did scant excavation and collecting in the area, they really had little data on which to build viable, consistent hypotheses. The towers occur most often in small groups or clusters at the heads of the canyons where there is, or was in Anasazi times, a steady supply of water. These interesting buildings are typical of construction called Mesa Verde style — large, loaf-shaped blocks, dressed and laid up with a bit of mud for mortar, and plastered over with the same adobe mud. Most of the plaster has long since washed away, but here and there in protected spots, bits of it still adhere, providing important clues to how the Anasazi finished their walls. Because of the construction techniques they used and the pottery they made, the Hovenweep group of Anasazi appear to be closely related to the same Indians who inhabited Mesa Verde and built the impressive cliff dwellings there. Although there is a wealth of small buildings, storage units, and other signs of Anasazi activity in the region, most of the archaeologists' attention has focused on the towers, a form of Anasazi architecture that occurs from west-central New Mexico into eastern Arizona and north into southern Colorado and Utah. The Hovenweep towers have been variously described as storage granaries, defensive fortresses, signal towers, and, lastly, astronomical observatories. The latter suggestion, to be sure, is what interested our archaeoastronomical team, and enticed us to examine the towers — measuring, hypothesizing, and testing.

Hovenweep Castle

Hovenweep Castle is the first building one passes in the self-guided trail from the visitor's center at the monument. It is also one of the largest surviving towers at Hovenweep, and the one with the most ports to measure. But by the end of our first day of working in the monument, our team had already established that one of the rooms in Hovenweep Castle had probably functioned as an observatory of the sun and contained the essential elements of a complete yearly calendar device.

The "sun room" of Hovenweep Castle, for so we soon called it, is one of about ten rooms that were added on to the original D-shaped tower. The D tower itself was at one time two and a half or three stories high, as were the connected rooms. But many years ago all of the second-story floors and ceiling collapsed and fell in upon the lower floors; now, the remaining unexcavated rubble lies a foot or two deep on the ground story of the building. It is on this ground level that the sun room lies, adjacent to the south, linear side, of the D tower.

Determining the azimuths of all the ports at Hovenweep Castle and other Hovenweep buildings was not an easy matter. First of all, the ports are at many different heights and the confined quarters of the small rooms generally prevent placing the transit in such a way as to sight through the port. Also, the height of the existing walls serves to block the sun from the transit so it cannot be used to determine north. Using the transit for direct measurements of the ports was impossible. By employing a bit of Yankee ingenuity, however, we derived a workable indirect method. We obtained a general correction for magnetic deviation by observing the sun on the mesa away from the building. (In order to stabilize the towers from further deterioration, archaeologists often use steel rods, which may alter the local magnetic field near the building.) Then, while one person inside looks out through the port, a companion outside looks back through a sighting compass. The first observer guides the second to a place on the mesa in a direct line with the orientation of the port. The compass measurement derived from this procedure (a so-called reverse bearing) is 180° out of phase, so to speak. The observer inside the tower then measures the altitude of the horizon from the port along the same line with a portable sighting level.

The results of this procedure, though not as accurate as those derived using a transit, are entirely adequate for survey. Any alignments that look particularly promising can be remeasured with a transit, or, as in the case of the solar calendar room at Hovenweep Castle, the phenomena suggested by the measurements can be observed directly.

Using these methods, later checked by direct observations where possible, we discovered that all four major solar events are commemorated in the room — summer and winter solstice and spring and fall equinox. The equinox alignment falls between the inner and outer doorway uprights and the eastern inner doorway. On a winter observing trip to Hovenweep, Benson and I clinched our suspicion that on and near the winter solstice, the winter solstice port worked exactly like the summer solstice one. As the sun set, a beam of light entered the port and fell on the east corner of the doorway leading into the D tower. While observing this, we also noticed another curious fact that we might not have discovered by measurements alone: the west edge of the exterior doorway casts a shadow to the east upright of the door to the D tower. To the right of the shadow, sunlight streaming through the exterior door illuminates a wide portion of the north wall. That event would not be particularly remarkable in itself, but when it is combined with the equinox alignment that also exists in the room, a rather interesting fact emerges. As the sun works its way back north, the beam of light passing through the port falls progressively further east on the wall and finally disappears. But the shadow cast by doorway A also works its way east. As

The solar observing room, or sun room, in Hovenweep Castle. Two ports and a doorway define a complete solar calendar.

it does, the beam of light that passes through the doorway narrows until, near the equinox, it becomes a very thin sliver. After the vernal equinox, the sun is too far north to shine through the doorway.

Because all three major solar directions are integrated into the structure, it appears that the Anasazi were observing the four solar events associated with those directions. But what are the chances that they are accidental alignments? If there were just one solar port in the room, or one doorway aligned to the sun, then assuming we allow a 1° mean error* in the placement of the port, the chances of finding an accidental solar alignment are 1 in 60. In another way of looking at it, if we measured sixty structures each with a single randomly oriented port, by the laws of chance alone, we would expect to find one aligned to either the summer solstice, the equinox, or the winter solstice. This is because there are 180 possible 1°-wide positions on the western horizon and there are three possible major solar alignments to act as benchmarks for the solar calendar. However, in this room of Hovenweep Castle, there are only two ports, each of which has a solar orientation. The probability of finding only those two port alignments and no other is 1/60 × 1/60 or 1 in 3600. If we add the equinox alignment in the total, that probability jumps to $(1/60)^3$ or 1 in 216,000. So we can assume with considerable assurance that the alignments we have found are intentional.

The Anasazi seemed to have placed the external door in such a position that they could take advantage of it to keep a daily calendar along the northern interior wall. Unfortunately, the plaster and any marks painted or engraved on it have long ago washed off the wall, so we will never know whether they actually used this feature, but it seems possible that they did.

One of the most interesting features of the room's alignments is that the doorway alignment is not quite equinoctial. This may prove to be of major importance in understanding the Anasazi calendar, for it seems entirely plausible that in order to find the equinox, they may have counted days.

Geometrically, the equinox is the halfway point between the solstices if the horizon is level. But the western horizon from Hovenweep Castle is not at all level, nor is it from most locations in the

---

* A mean of 1° is chosen because the placement of the existing solstice ports without additional plaster ranges between 0.5° and 2°.

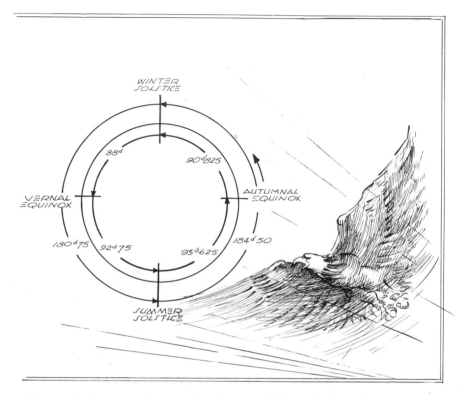

The yearly day count. Because the distance of the earth from the sun varies throughout the year, the day count between winter solstice and summer solstice differs from the count between summer solstice and winter solstice.

Southwest. By counting days between the solstices and taking the halfway point in time, it is possible to come close to the equinox. However, this determination will be several days off because the sun's apparent motion along the ecliptic varies slightly throughout the year. The sun's trip from winter solstice to summer solstice takes only 180.75 days, while the balance of its journey occupies 184.5 days. What is of interest at Hovenweep Castle is the duration of the sun's trip from solstice to equinox and then from equinox to solstice. There are 88 days between winter solstice and vernal equinox but almost 5 more between vernal equinox and summer solstice, for a total of 93 days. Now, if instead we assumed that the vernal equinox was precisely halfway between winter and summer solstice, we would reckon it to be 90 days after the vernal equinox, or on March 24 instead of March 21. If we were designing a building feature to commemorate the date, we would orient it so that the sun's light would fall along that path 3 or 4 days after the vernal equinox. That is nearly what happens at Hovenweep Castle. The "equinox" alignment at Hovenweep Castle occurs 4 days *after* the vernal equinox. This indicates that the Anasazi may have kept records of the count of days throughout the year.

To carry this argument further, we must also examine what happens at the fall equinox, since the same alignment that works for the vernal equinox must also work in the fall as well. Based on taking one-half of the count of days from summer solstice to winter solstice, the autumnal equinox would appear to occur nearly 2 days prior to the actual day when the sun is on the equator. However, the Hovenweep Castle alignment happens 4 days ahead, not quite as good a case as we could make for the vernal equinox. As a result, our conjecture that the Anasazi were counting days between solstices must remain a suggestion until we have more evidence. The interesting thing about this site is that if the Anasazi tried to find the appropriate equinoctial horizon point by locating the apparent halfway point between solstices geometrically, at this location they could have found the equinox exactly. This is because, by chance, though the western terrain is uneven, it so happens that the winter solstice, equinox, and summer solstice horizon altitudes are at nearly the same height — quite a unique occurrence.

Archaeologically, the striking thing about this room and the room above it is that they were later additions to the original D-shaped tower. The solstice room is of generally poorer construction, and the western wall that joins the D tower is not interlocked with the D tower walls. This lack of interlocking construction is fairly common among Anasazi buildings. When adding a room to an existing structure, they often simply laid the blocks of the new wall against the old without attempting to anchor the new wall to it. Unlike most of the other buildings at Hovenweep, not only do we know that the solar observing room was built after the tower, we also know when both were likely built. Tree-ring dating of a timber from the D tower indicates that it was built around A.D. 1166. Timbers used in the construction of the addition (which includes several other rooms) yield a date of A.D. 1277 or an interval of 111 years. From other evidence, archaeologists can supply the clues to understanding why this room might have been added at this time.

Apparently the community in Square Tower Canyon was well established by A.D. 1200. Sometime earlier, probably in the mid 1100s, the widely scattered family groups had begun to consolidate at the heads of narrow box canyons such as Square Tower Canyon. Prior to that, they tended to live on the mesa tops in small, so-called unit-type houses — small buildings that must have housed one, two, or even several families. The area's population density was certainly high at the time, for in walking across the region today one finds the remains of these houses on nearly every hillock or local rise. There the Anasazi did their farming, depending on their skill at dry-land farming to provide their entire crop. Whether because of increasing drought or for social reasons, they began to move toward the canyon heads and settle there in small communities, building the towers and boulder houses we see today. They chose their dwelling locations well — where there were (and generally still are) springs or seeps to provide water for consumption and for irrigation.

Apparently by A.D. 1200 or so, they were comfortably settled in and along the canyons. One hundred years later, they had abandoned the area. Answering why this happened has troubled archaeologists for years. There is little evidence that they were pushed out. No burnt towers or hasty burials are found, and though several investigators have suggested that the purpose of the towers and boulder houses was for defense, there is little auxiliary evidence to support that hypothesis. It is true that the towers, built where they are grouped together on the edge of the cliffs and perched on boulders, would provide better defense against invaders than the isolated mesa-top structures. However, no one has been able to demonstrate persuasively why they might have needed defensive structures in the 1200s when they lacked them in the 1100s.

The discovery of the solar observing room and other calendar-related structures at Hovenweep may provide one clue as to why the Anasazi moved into the canyons in the first place and also why they eventually left for good. The area around Hovenweep, and indeed the whole Southwest, suffered from periods of prolonged drought between 1200 and 1400. Because of the drought, mesa-top farming would soon have become untenable, but the heads of canyons, with their adequate supply of water, would have remained viable places for some time. As a result, some Anasazi may have moved away from the area soon after the cycle of droughts began; but many others surely migrated to the canyon heads and set up a new way of life in larger community groups. There they not only learned to live in close proximity to other families, they also developed new farming techniques — using terraces, check dams, and whatever else they could to conserve the little rainwater they did get. They also then began to pay much closer attention to the calendar for predicting when to plant and when to harvest. In a land where there is plenty of rainfall, planting a few rows or even a field of corn before a killing frost will not be disastrous because the later plantings will make up for the loss. In a period of drought, however, the available tillable land shrinks; more time must be taken tending less acreage, because the wide-open expanses are impossible to irrigate adequately from a spring. Although, as we have seen, horizon calendars can be quite accurate for much of the Hovenweep area, in or near the canyons, the horizon from Hovenweep Castle is relatively featureless.

A building especially designed for solar observation would be a considerable asset in setting up and following a calendar, and the calendar room of Hovenweep Castle would certainly play that role extremely well. Convenient marks on the plaster of the north wall would have served to calibrate the movement of the band of light as it progressed from the doorway leading to the tower and narrowed day by day after the winter solstice. When the band of light had moved within twenty inches from the east doorway it would be time to begin preparing the fields. By the time the band had reduced to a sliver and disappeared, the vernal equinox would have just passed. A count of days from there on would suffice to time the various plantings.

Our survey of the rest of the ports and the walls at Hovenweep Castle turned up no other significant alignments save for a row of three ports on the east side of the original building. Because some of the intervening walls are currently in a shambles, the eastern tower now appears to be a separate building. Originally, it was part of a single structure that included the D tower and the solar observing room. It has three ports that open to the winter solstice sunrise. Other ports on the now-ruined eastern walls could certainly have been used to time a planting sequence. In examining the three ports still remaining, it is now impossible to determine their original function.

Though the three "winter solstice" ports certainly open to the winter solstice at sunrise, there is no indication that they might have been used for calendrical purposes. The back, or west, wall of the room has fallen, so no architectural features are left to indicate an alignment. If the ports' orientations are intentional, they may have served to celebrate, rather than determine, the winter solstice. This distinction is an important one to make, for there are probably many buildings that were deliberately aligned to the sun but were not used to set a calendar. Such alignments would have functioned in a ritual way, the sun's entrance being a palpable sign of its presence in the ritual. In such cases, of course, there may be very little need for precision, since the precise date could have been determined at a different site.

Cajon

Hovenweep National Monument is a collection of small holdings spread out over a vast area. One interesting group of houses and towers is located about half an hour's drive southwest of Hovenweep Castle, at the head of a small canyon on Cajon mesa. They are arranged around a spring that today serves the local Navajo sheep and horses.

These ruins demonstrate a highly unusual means of keeping a calendar, reminiscent of the effects of the Castillo at Chichén Itzá. It took some time for us to realize how these calendar alignments work because they depend on the interaction between two buildings. First, a port survey revealed that two ports in the ground-level room of one of the two towers at Cajon are oriented to the summer and winter solstice sunsets respectively. These alignments, while probably intentional, are not very convincing to skeptical eyes. The sun enters at the solar extremes right along the axis of each port, but the beam of sunlight falls on the opposite wall in no particular place. As the original plaster that might have served as the base for calendar markers has washed away, we cannot make as tight an argument for sun watching with these ports as we can for Hovenweep Castle. However, two other associated facts make this room similar to the sun room at Hovenweep Castle. It was added after the original higher tower was built, though because there were no wood fragments to analyze for tree-ring dates we are uncertain about when it was added. The south wall of the tower is oriented almost precisely east-west, so the sun would rise and set nearly along the wall at the equinoxes. From looking at the total assemblage of aligned features, together with the fact that the room was a late addition, we suspect that it indicates the same sort of attention to sun observing as at Hovenweep Castle.

The fascinating fact about the Cajon ruins is that their builders were not content to stop with a single observing room. They apparently used two entire buildings to keep their calendar. We began to get an inkling of this when we used the transit to take the bearing of the south wall of the tower. A line extended beyond the south wall nearly intersects with a corner of the building west of it. Only later, when we made direct observations at the winter solstice as well as at the summer solstice, did we understand the whole picture. Looking out the tower's winter solstice port toward winter solstice sunset, it is clear that a corner of the western building would have blocked the vision of the setting sun when the latter's wall was at its original height. The winter solstice port could not have operated when the southeastern corner of the western building was intact. At sunset on the winter solstice, that corner casts a vertical shadow right along the southwest corner of the tower. This fact means that if the winter solstice port in the tower was ever operative, it was built prior to the corner of the western building. Unfortunately, no dating is available for either room, so there is no way to check the possibility at this time.

There is much more to the shadow casting than our first analysis revealed. A closer look showed that the two buildings operate with respect to each other as a giant yearly sundial, marking the seasons for all to see. Beginning at the autumnal equinox, as the setting sun passes the equator moving south, it also passes south of the line defined by the south wall of the tower and the northeast corner of the western building. Thus, on the evenings after the equinox, this building casts a shadow on the tower. Each successive day from the autumnal equinox, beginning at the south end of the tower, the shadow moves slowly northward until it completely shadows the tower. This shadowing continues through the fall until, at the winter solstice, the shadow falls only on the west wall of the tower; the

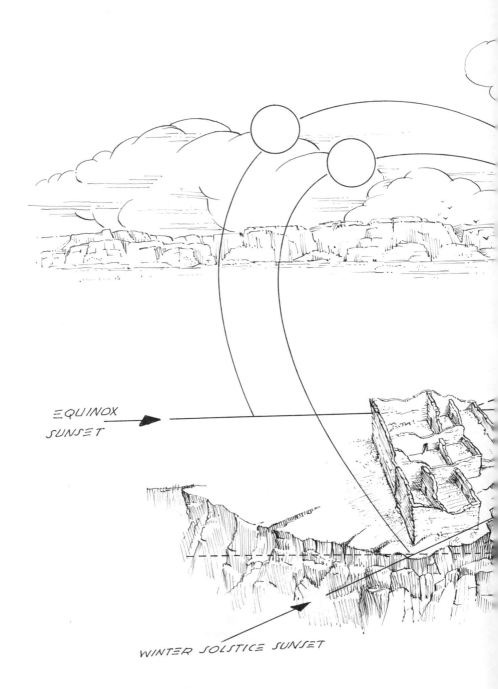

EQUINOX
SUNSET

WINTER SOLSTICE SUNSET

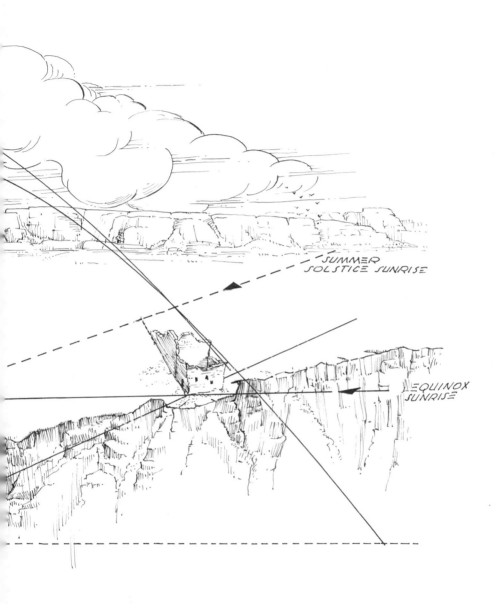

Within the illustration:

SUMMER
SOLSTICE SUNRISE

EQUINOX
SUNRISE

Solar alignments, Cajon Ruins, Hovenweep National Monument. Shadows cast between these two buildings at sunrise and sunset throughout the year define a solar calendar that would be obvious to all the dwellers of this isolated set of buildings overlooking the Aneth oil fields to the south.

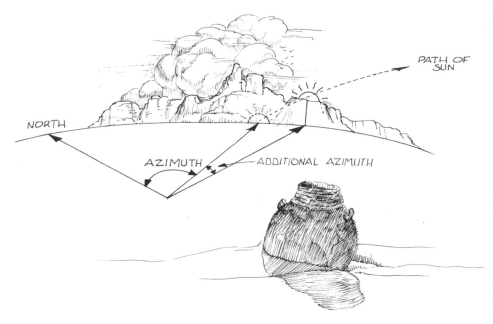

The effect of a high horizon on azimuth measurements. The greater the altitude of the horizon, the further south is the sun's rise position. This effect requires measurement of the horizon altitude as well as the azimuth along a given structural feature.

south wall receives sunlight because the southern edge of the shadow falls vertically along the southwestern corner of the tower. Then, as the new year proceeds from the winter solstice, the process is reversed until the vernal equinox, when the tower receives no shadow from the other building at all.

Now an interesting thing happens. After the vernal equinox, the role of the buildings is reversed and the tower casts a shadow across the western building at *sunrise* from the vernal equinox until sometime near or on the summer solstice.[6] Unfortunately, short of excavating the structure, it is impossible to pinpoint precisely the northern end of the sequence of events because the north end of the tower is in ruins. This much, however, is clear: throughout much of the spring and summer, the tower casts a shadow on the western building at and just after sunrise each day. The equinoxes themselves are marked by the observational fact that only then, neither building casts its shadow on the other.

Though not charged with the heavy overlay of symbolism that the serpent's appearance at the Castillo in Chichén Itzá gives the equinox shadow, the Cajon shadow effects are quite striking. The interaction of these buildings represents a public display of calendrical information we have not seen elsewhere in the Southwest.

Looking at the Cajon data a bit more closely, we again see evidence there that the Anasazi may have been counting days in order to find the equinox. The last time the western building shadows the tower occurs at sunset three days after the vernal equinox. If, in constructing the shadow relationship between the two buildings, the Anasazi had simply bisected the angle between the sun at summer and winter solstice, they would have placed the northeastern corner of the western building exactly along the equinox line. This is because the horizon along the summer solstice line is 2° higher than it is along the winter solstice line. Because the effect of raising the horizon is to push the apparent sunset southward, the angle between summer and winter solstice is now smaller than it would be for a strictly level horizon. This has the effect of making the point at which you expect the sun to set at the equinox too far south, in this case, by about two days. However, because the horizon along the equinox line is about 1° higher than along the winter solstice line, the two effects cancel each other out and the line in question would very nearly coincide with the equinox. Here again, though, the alignment is too late by three days, indicating that they may have taken the halfway point in the count of days. The data here and at Hovenweep Castle, though tenuous, seem worth exploring in more detail in future attempts to understand the exactitude of Anasazi astronomy.

Unit-Type House

The variety of ways the Hovenweep Anasazi found to keep a calendar are truly astounding. They used ports, doorways, walls, and even the relative orientation of two buildings. We began our study at Hovenweep by looking at towers exclusively, but the possibility that other buildings with ports might also have been used for sun watching soon occurred. This indeed proved to be the case for a boulder house not far from Hovenweep Castle. Dubbed unromantically but unambiguously Unit-Type House, this group of rooms probably housed one or two families. It is similar to many of the unit-type houses that occur throughout the Hovenweep region.[7] Most others, though, are situated along the mesa tops, well away from the canyons; therefore, they tend to be older buildings.

A few hundred yards east of Hovenweep Castle, Unit-Type House is built from the same sort of loaf-sized blocks so typical of construction in the area. It is remarkable for its placement and for the strict symmetry the Anasazi observed in its design. Six rooms and a kiva perch on a single boulder. One room lies east of the kiva, a nearly identical one to the west; the remaining four rooms are arranged along the north side of the building. The outer walls of the eastern room are still intact, as are four ports and a single exterior doorway. The four ports are what drew our attention to this building, for they all open eastward. Three of the four ports are solar ports, opening respectively to the summer solstice, equinox, and winter solstice. The fourth could be a lunar port; if so, it would be the first such find in the Anasazi area.

Discovering the astronomical alignment of Unit-Type House was largely an accident, one of those happy circumstances in the pursuit of science when serendipity combines with the proper awareness and openness to new possibilities. We had not planned to study all the Hovenweep buildings. While surveying the canyon east of Hovenweep Castle one December morning near the solstice,[8] in an attempt to assess just how many towers there had been in Square Tower Canyon, we noticed that of the four ports in the east room of Unit-Type House, all of them pointed east. The low morning sun shown brightly on the eastern wall and highlighted those ports. Without hesitating, Craig Benson and I climbed up toward the building and did a quick but thorough compass survey. It was immediately clear that one port faced the winter solstice sunrise and another the equinox sunrise. But a large boulder a few yards northeast seemed to block any possible view of the summer solstice sunrise. As at Hovenweep Castle, our measurements of the structure, though severely limited in accuracy because of the physical difficulty of making transit measurements, indicated that the remaining port was oriented to the summer solstice sunrise. Because of the boulder, sunlight could only enter well after sunrise. Confirmation of the summer solstice orientation had to wait until six months later, but we were there at sunrise the following morning to observe the winter solstice sun appear above Sleeping Ute Mountain

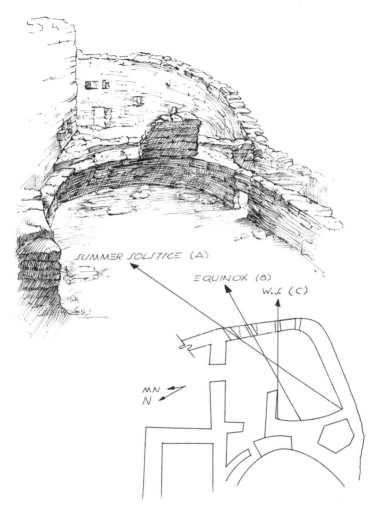

Labels within figure:
SUMMER SOLSTICE (A)
EQUINOX (B)
W.S. (C)
MN
N

Solar alignments at Unit-Type House, Hovenweep National Monument. Sunlight entering through three of the four ports found in the eastern room of this small building can be used to define a solar calendar.

to the southeast. We watched with great satisfaction as sunlight pierced the "winter solstice" port and fell against the opposite corner.

Observations over the following six months demonstrated that here also was a calendar room, similar to that of Hovenweep Castle, yet accomplished by using only three ports. At summer solstice, about an hour after sunrise elsewhere in the canyon, the sun finally rises above the massive boulder to the east and streams through the northernmost port to fall on the southwestern corner of the room. On the winter solstice, the sunbeam falls in the north corner of the interior western wall of the room, next to a small, low wall jutting out from it. The equinox beam lights up a spot midway between this small wall and the southwestern corner. According to the archaeologists who have examined this room in detail, there seems no functional reason for the small protruding wall, save to define the winter solstice direction. Here again is a potentially accurate calendar device using ports and architectural features to define the passing of the year. By narrowing the size of the ports sufficiently with plaster, accuracies of a day or two in determining the solstices would be possible.

In my view, the placement of the kiva immediately adjacent to this solar room is far from accidental. Calendar watching in the historic pueblos is inseparable from ritual practice; and, because of this, it is not surprising that there is a kiva nearby. Elsewhere in the Southwest we find the connection between ritual practice and the calendar even stronger than at Hovenweep.

Casa Rinconada

We have now seen in some detail how the Anasazi near Hovenweep responded to the demands of developing a calendar for agricultural and probably ceremonial use. Two centuries earlier, a quite different group of Anasazi had established a major civilization in Chaco Canyon, nearly 125 miles south of Hovenweep. Although the Chacoans probably made excellent use of horizon calendars, they also incorporated solar and other astronomical alignments in some of their buildings. Perhaps the most striking of these buildings, as well for its sheer beauty as for its astronomical associations, is Casa Rinconada — a great kiva situated near the center of Chaco Canyon National Historical Park. Casa Rinconada is a massive circular wall pierced north and south by two T-shaped doorways. Everything about it is impressive.

First and foremost, Casa Rinconada is a religious structure; it is called a great kiva because of its size — some 60 feet across and 12 to 16 feet deep. It literally and figuratively stands apart from the other kivas in Chaco Canyon and even from the other great kivas by its striking location; though stylistically a part of the same "classic" age of construction as the large villages of Pueblo Bonito, Chetro Ketl, and Pueblo Del Arroyo, it is set well apart from them on the south side of the canyon. All other buildings contemporary to Casa Rinconada and constructed in the same classic Chaco style are either on the north side of the canyon or on top of the mesa. Because of its setting atop a low knoll on a spur of the nearby mesa it can be seen readily from most of these large pueblos. Except for a few attached rooms, which could have served as dwelling places for a few persons, there are no related buildings nearby. Within a few hundred yards' radius from the kiva are several small groups of rooms scattered about with no obvious pattern. Though these "room blocks" were apparently occupied in the same era as Casa Rinconada, their radically different architecture suggests that their inhabitants were not directly related to the builders of Casa Rinconada. In contrast to Pueblo Bonito and other "classic phase" buildings, these rather small units were poorly constructed of random-sized stones and relatively thin walls. Casa Rinconada, then, seems a structure deliberately isolated from the other great buildings of the canyon.

How can we understand Casa Rinconada? Why did the Anasazi build it and place it where it stands? Until recently, archaeologists have lacked the means to answer these questions with any strength of conviction. As a great kiva, Casa Rinconada is a member of an elite group of buildings, all related to one another by size and structural components, but all of which differ radically in detail. It is clear that they are all religious structures, and anthropologists believe that because of their size they served several religious fraternities. Ordinary kivas, at least in historic times, are built and used by only a single religious group within a pueblo.

Yet, in Chaco Canyon, within a radius of several hundred yards, there are five great kivas — three in Pueblo Bonito, one in Chetro Ketl, and, standing alone, Casa Rinconada.[9] The great kivas of Pueblo Bonito and Chetro Ketl, as village great kivas, can be understood as centralized religious buildings, ones that served to unite the pueblo ceremonially and perhaps politically as well. Casa Rinconada and the two other known isolated great kivas in the Chaco area probably served several villages, and indicate an intervillage level of sociopolitical organization. There, until recently, must the explana-

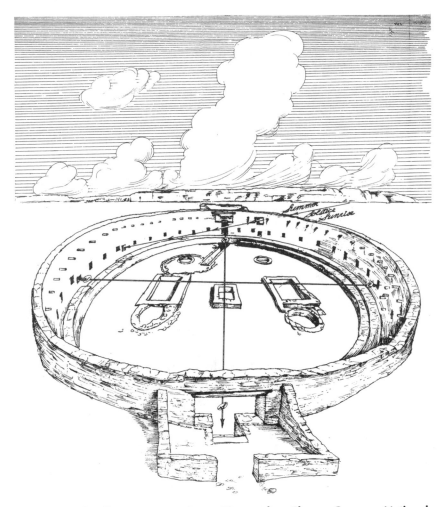

Astronomical alignments at Casa Rinconada, Chaco Canyon National Historical Park. The entire great kiva is astronomically aligned to the cardinal directions. Built in the late eleventh century, this building was probably the site of major Chaco Canyon ceremonies.

tion of Casa Rinconada be left — a ritually related building that served several canyon villages. Recently, however, by applying the methods of archaeoastronomy to the structure, we can now dramatically extend this suggestion to include a hypothesis regarding the cosmological outlook of the Anasazi priesthood.

Lacking written documents of some sort, it is normally impossible to reach inside the minds of a prehistoric people to derive some of their thought patterns. However, the artifacts they left behind can be "read" to some extent, and certain extraordinary buildings or other objects will often give us special clues to their thought patterns. Casa Rinconada appears to be such a building. Set apart from the other canyon buildings in an imposing setting, it commands attention and invites close scrutiny. Upon seeing it, one is immediately struck by the awesome grace and beauty of its features.

In addition to two T-shaped doors, the circular wall also contains twenty-eight small niches set at regular intervals around the kiva and six larger but lower niches, four symmetrically placed on the west side of the kiva and two on the east side. Originally, the twenty-eight small upper niches were probably twenty-nine, one having been lost in the process of reconstruction. The kiva has an opening that could be a window or small doorway in the northeast quadrant, and a large high shallow wall-niche directly opposite it across the kiva. There is an ambiguity about the function of the opening into the kiva — sometime in its use, the kiva had an exterior room just outside that opening. In addition to the large fireplace south of the kiva center, the floor vaults, and the low bench along the kiva wall, one important kiva feature needs to be mentioned. Below the staircase that leads into the kiva by the north entrance is a second narrow staircase that terminates in a long narrow trough. Archaeologists surmise that the function of this rather special entrance was to allow ceremonialists — masked dancers, perhaps — to enter or leave the kiva entirely unseen by its other occupants. Whatever its function, it is a feature not found in any other excavated kiva, great or small — a fact that lends weight to the apparent special quality of this particular kiva.

In investigating Casa Rinconada for astronomical alignments, we quickly came to the realization that its structure was remarkably symmetric. Even unaided, the eye can easily pick out one major axis of symmetry — the line between the north and south doors. Most of the features on either side of this line would fit counterpart features on the opposite side of the kiva. But what is certainly more remarkable is that the line of symmetry is also a true north-south line! My colleague Howard Fisher and I discovered this on our first trip to Chaco Canyon. Since we had only hand-held compasses with which to measure orientations, we could hardly believe what they were telling us. That evening, with permission from the National Park Service, we returned with camera in hand, and setting up the camera's tripod along the line of symmetry, we took a time exposure of the kiva against the stellar background. With this simple technique, we were able to determine the axis of the line of symmetry with greater accuracy than the magnetic compass would allow.

Later, after making a detailed transit map of the kiva's interior, we concluded that the designers and builders of Casa Rinconada had taken unusual pains to construct a geometrically precise building unlike any other building in the Southwest. Consider these attributes determined by transit and steel tape:[10]

1. *The kiva itself is a carefully made circle.* In order find the center, we merely had to stretch a tape measure between each matched pair of small niches across the kiva and drop a plumb bob from the half-diameter point.

The center so defined falls within a circle 4 inches in diameter. The sole exception to this experience was the pair of niches numbered 14 and 28, counting clockwise around the kiva. A line between these two niches extends much too far east of the average center, a situation that puzzled us until I later located some original excavation data in a forgotten file in the Museum of New Mexico. Those field notes indicate that there was a niche between the present niches 27 and 28, which would have been the appropriate one to pair with niche 14. Unfortunately, its precise location was unknown at the time of excavation, although the excavators noted there had been a niche there originally.

2. *The angular distance between each small niche and its nearest neighbor varies little around the kiva.* The center-to-center average angular distance from one niche to the next is 11°07′ ± 19′.[11] Notice that 22°16′, the angular distance between niches 27 and 28, is almost exactly twice the average distance between niches, further confirming the existence of a niche between these two in the original building.

3. *The four holes that served as sockets for the four large beams supporting the massive original roof of the structure nearly form a square, the center of which falls within the 4-inch circle defining the center of the kiva.*

4. *The sides of the square defined by the post holes A, B, C, and D are close to cardinal lines,* extending east-west and north-south, thus joining the astronomical orientations with the geometrical design.

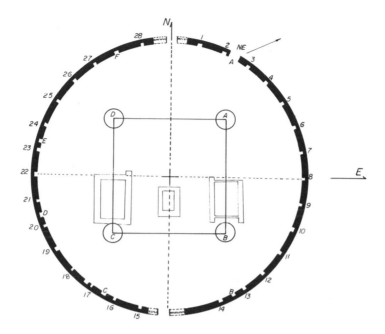

Ground plan of Casa Rinconada showing cardinal alignments. The major and minor axes of symmetry fall along cardinal lines, as do the four post holes that once held beams to support the massive roof.

5. *The line between niches 8 and 22 is also an east-west line, in addition to passing through the center of the kiva.*

6. *The major axis of symmetry, which, as we have seen, is also a cardinal north-south line, intersects the east-west line at the center of the kiva.*

One last but important astronomical alignment must be mentioned, because although it does not relate directly to the set of geometrical / astronomical patterns, it is the only alignment that could have been directly observed inside the kiva after the builders added the roof. On and near the summer solstice, the light of the rising sun enters the northeast opening and falls against the opposite wall. Shortly after sunrise, it lights up the wall above small niche 24, then moves slowly down the wall across that niche to settle for a short while in niche E, one of the large, special niches lower down on the wall.[12]

This is a remarkable set of geometrical / astronomical data about a single prehistoric ritual building. The most important questions to answer are whether they add up to a consistent whole and are consistent with other known facts about Anasazi culture.

I suggest that Casa Rinconada, taken as a whole, is a metaphor of the cosmos in stone, adobe, and wood — an image of time and space as seen by the Anasazi. To understand this fully, we need to make ample use of the clues provided by the ethnographic record. An account from the people of Acoma Pueblo, some sixty miles southeast of Chaco Canyon, suggests a way to understand Casa Rinconada. The Acoma emergence myths describe the "first kiva" in some detail:

> When they built the kiva, they first put up beams of four different trees. These were the trees that were planted in the underworld for the people to climb up on. In the north, under the foundation they placed yellow turquoise; in the west, blue turquoise; in the south, red, and in the east, white turquoise. Prayer sticks are placed at each place so the foundation will be strong and will never give way. The walls represent the sky, the beams of the roof (made of wood of the first four trees) represent the Milky Way. The sky looks like a circle, hence the round shape of the kiva.[13]

This description sounds remarkably like Casa Rinconada. The Acoma do not build kivas like this today. Their kivas are rectangular and lack roof posts. It is possible that the myth contains a view of kivas that prevailed in Anasazi days. The plausibility of this suggestion is reinforced by other historical data. When the Hopi sun priest begins a prayer he casts sacred cornmeal to the four cardinal directions, northwest, southwest, southeast, northeast, in turn. Although his gesture is outward, it is in supplication to the Sun Father, whose power emanates from the edge of the rim of the world inward toward the center.

The spatial image these gestures convey is that of a square whose diagonals intersect at the center, where the priest stands. In Casa Rinconada, the four posts supporting its massive roof were located precisely at the corners of a square whose center coincides with the geometrical center of the circular outer wall. However, in the kiva the center is undefined by any structural feature. This is consistent with historic Pueblo conceptions. The center is simply "where the heart is." Expressed in other terms, the center is the intersection of the four directions.

In Casa Rinconada, interestingly, both the four cardinal points and the intercardinals are represented. The cardinal points are, of course, represented by the major and minor axes of symmetry; the intercardinals find representation in the roof posts, which stand halfway between the cardinal points.

The skeptic may doubt any intentionality behind the astronomical directions contained in Casa Rinconada because, except for the summer solstice sun alignment, none is connected to visual phenomena within the buildings. Why build an observatory in which none of the alignments, or only a very few, can be observed directly? The answer to this very appropriate question, I strongly suspect, is that Casa Rinconada was never meant to be an observatory. Even the solar "events" that can be observed in or with the building principally served ritual rather than calendrical needs. The calendar was undoubtedly kept by making horizon observations in another part of the canyon where the entire yearly horizon journey could be easily observed by the sun priest. In this view, once the Chaco Anasazi knew of the arrival of the summer solstice, for example, they celebrated it in Casa Rinconada with ceremonies designed around the beam of summer sunlight streaming through the northeast doorway.

Though they were not used for sun worship and therefore lack the deliberate orientation to solar events, some European cathedrals were oriented for similar reasons — to be in tune with the cosmos. The cathedrals are astronomically aligned because it was appropriate that they be so oriented. These orientations symbolized the connection to the cosmic order. The city of Washington, D.C., is another prime example of this sort of alignment. It was laid out along carefully surveyed cardinal lines, since it was important for the capital city of a new nation to be appropriately planned — that is, in harmony with the cosmos. Hence the grid pattern of streets running east-west / north-south. Even the Capitol Building is carefully oriented along the cardinal lines. And the Washington Monument is situated directly west of the Capitol Building; in astronomical terms, on the equinox, the sun sets precisely behind the Washington Monument.

In Casa Rinconada, the equinox, nearly midpoint in time, has a spatial image as well, which is conceived on a grand scale in the very placement of the entire kiva. The kiva is situated due west of a mesa-top shrine area at the head of one of the staircases that are an integral part of an ancient roadway system running through the canyon. At dawn near the equinoxes the mesa edge east of Casa Rinconada casts a shadow across half the kiva, the shadow line falling roughly along the line between niches 8 and 22. Thus, halfway between the solstices the sun shines along a line marking the middle way in space and nearly the middle way in time. In this, and several other ways, the kiva unites space and time through visual phenomena. From this point of view, the summer solstice orientation takes on new meaning. The light of the summer solstice sun, streaming through the northeast portal, delimits the northern spatial boundary of the sun's motion, just as it also represents the halfway point in the course of the year.

One of the major concerns in investigating Casa Rinconada is the fact that it has been reconstructed since it was excavated in 1931, and no matter how accurately the work was done, some error must unavoidably creep in. Inevitably, reconstruction requires judgments about the extent and shape of missing pieces, and even the best of judgments may be guesses. For example, in Casa Rinconada, over each low large niche, there was a major wall break; and there is some slight evidence that there may have been openings above those niches similar to the northeast openings above niche A. But when it was reconstructed, the walls were filled in. That may indeed have been the right choice, but no one can now be sure. Fortunately, with Casa Rinconada enough of the features were still intact when it was excavated to assure that our measurements of the reconstructed kiva reflect the state of the original structure. Furthermore, by some persistent searching, I was able to turn up original field notes containing original measurements of the excavated building *before* reconstruction. These measurements confirm our own more recent ones and underscore the care the archaeologists took in reconstructing the kiva.

When confronted with such a remarkable structure as Casa Rinconada, one is drawn to ask whether there were any abstract conceptual bases for their building techniques. In other words, were they guided by a set of the notions of geometry — the right angle, parallel lines, regular right triangles? We remember that long before Euclid codified and arranged the axioms and propositions of plane geometry, the Egyptians, by trial and error, had developed a useful geometry in which 3-4-5 triangles were used to construct right angles for surveying purposes. The Egyptians were masters of applied geometry, a skill that served them well in constructing the great pyramids along the Nile. The Pueblo buildings, though not of the monumental cast of the Egyptian buildings, are nonetheless the products of an inventive and ingenious people, men and women who had a strong aesthetic and practical sense. Pueblo Bonito, Chetro Ketl, and any of the classic Chaco buildings, as well as the extraordinary cliff dwellings in the Mesa Verde, amply exhibit both traits. In designing their buildings, did they begin with a concept of mensuration? Did they have a standard measure? Casa Rinconada alone shows that they knew full well how to *construct* a right angle, but did they have a generalized *concept* of the right angle, or any other angle as well?

These questions, though they may seem peripheral to archaeoastronomy, are actually of central concern and are at the foundation of such issues as how they planned for the alignment of their buildings. We don't know how they aligned Casa Rinconada. The alignments may have been carried to the structure from some more appropriate observing station, or perhaps they were generated at the site before construction. As with most puzzles of this sort, the early answers are no more than informed conjecture; but we may hope that by continually asking them, the questions will generate new approaches and new research that will, in turn, ultimately generate better answers than we have today.

When faced with attempting to reconstruct the way in which the Anasazi might have oriented their buildings, we immediately realize that the answer to this question also contains within it the seeds of answers to other questions about their cosmological view and about the sophistication of their astronomical knowledge as a whole. In constructing likely scenarios about their building practices, we begin to separate the merely possible alternatives from the likely ones. To do this we must necessarily rely somewhat on the experience of the modern, historic Pueblo. We must also ask how, bereft of all our modern instruments but possessed of the knowledge of astronomy that an observant, intelligent Anasazi may have had, we might proceed to lay out the astronomical directions we needed. In asking such a question we need to consider two classes of astronomical directions: first, those direct observational orientations such as the winter and summer solstices; and second, directions that must be derived from measurement as well as observation, the most obvious examples being the perpendicular cardinal directions. In building a structure, both classes of alignment are likely to involve some complex observations, but the secondary orientations may also involve some rudimentary geometrical construction — and it is this possibility that makes Casa Rinconada such an interesting structure. The care with which it was built suggests a high level of intentionality on the part of its builders. Before tackling the more difficult questions this building implies, we should look at a simpler structure.

In building the sun room at Hovenweep Castle, discovering where to put the solstice ports would have been a fairly straightforward procedure. Given the D tower, which was built much earlier than the sun room, it would have been relatively easy to establish the port position by direct observation of the solstice sunsets. The same is true of the equinox doorway orientation. Once the day of equinox was known from observations elsewhere, or from counting days, the equinox sight line could have been easily set up at sunset on the day of equinox. This seems terribly inefficient, involving as it does observations at the site over a six-month period. It seems much more likely that they used other astronomical observations to find the sight lines. The experienced observers at Hopi know precisely which horizon features correspond to the equinoxes and to the winter and summer solstice as seen from their usual watching place. Though we have no evidence that the Hopi or any other historic Pueblo group ever connected the positions of the stars to solar positions, by watching at night and seeing which bright stars rise or set at those same spots, they could have carried the information about solstices and equinoxes to any other geographical location. In A.D. 1250, near the time when the sun room was constructed, this would have been particularly easy, for Antares, the brightest star in the Western constellation Scorpio, had a declination of $-24°27'$, only 55' arc south of the sun's winter solstice declination on the same date. Similarly, in A.D. 1250 the zero-magnitude star Arcturus possessed a declination of $23°14'$, only 18' arc south of the sun's summer solstice declination. Even the equinox direction could have been so determined. The "belt" of the Western constellation Orion was only about a degree from the equator in A.D. 1250. A very important winter constellation for the historic Pueblo, Orion was very likely important for the Anasazi as well. Because it is an easily recognizable winter constellation, it today serves as a timing device for winter kiva ceremonies. When it appears above the eastern horizon, when it is over-head, and when it sets are all important milestones in the course of Hopi kiva celebrations. In constructing the solar room at Hoven-weep, it would have been particularly easy to use Antares and Arc-turus, and the constellation Orion, for in the late summer all are visible in the course of a single night.

Returning to Casa Rinconada, we are faced with a different problem. Only the summer solstice alignment could have been built directly from observations. The cardinal directions require a greater degree of abstraction. It seems unlikely that the Anasazi used Polaris, for in A.D. 1100 the present north star was nearly 6° from the pole, or about twelve moon diameters distant, hardly near enough to the geographi-cal pole to serve as an accurate determinant of north.

There is a simple method for finding north that uses the sun and that the builders of Casa Rinconada might well have used. The method, which requires only a stick, a string, and a level piece of ground in which to place the stick, is an integral part of modern Boy Scout lore.

Just after sunrise, the stick will cast a long shadow westward. As the sun climbs upward and moves south, the shadow shortens as the sun moves ever closer to the local meridian line. The shortest shadow will, of course, lie precisely along a north-south line. How-ever, it is very difficult to pick out the shortest line, because when the sun is near the meridian, it moves very little in altitude and therefore all the shadows appear to be nearly the same length. By the same token, it is very difficult to determine noon precisely by ob-serving the sun directly and attempting to pick out when it reaches its greatest altitude above the horizon. But suppose one chooses equal shadow lengths on either side of noon. Then the center of a line stretched between the end of each equal shadow will be pre-cisely on the meridian. A line connecting the midpoint of the stretched line and the base of the stick will be the required north-south orientation for the kiva.[14] It will, of course, also lie along the shortest shadow. We can now easily find our east-west line, for it is coincident with the segment connecting the two shadow endpoints. As a by-product, this method also allows for directly constructing a right angle; it might even be considered a natural right angle, reflec-tive of the original construction of the cosmos.

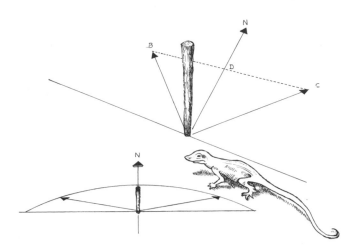

Finding north by the sun. It is possible to determine geographic north with an accuracy of a degree or less by setting up a stick perpendicular to the ground and marking shadow lengths on either side of noon. North can be found by bisecting the line between the endpoints of shadows of equal length (B and C) and connecting this point with the base of the stick.

We cannot be sure whether the Anasazi ever actually used such a technique; their descendants are much more haphazard in the construction of kivas and dwellings than were the Anasazi. Still, it at least seems plausible that they used a method like this, for without it they could not have laid out the kiva so precisely along cardinal lines.

Pueblo Bonito

In the course of our early studies of the Chaco buildings, we discovered that, like Casa Rinconada, one of the two great kivas in the village Pueblo Bonito[15] was aligned north-south along its axis of symmetry. But there the similarity ends. The Bonito great kiva has thirty-four small wall niches arranged nearly symmetrically around the kiva, but not in patterns that are astronomical. The four sockets for the roof beams are arranged at the corners of a quasi parallelogram, the long sides of which are parallel to the major axis of symmetry. The shorter sides are not quite parallel to each other and are several degrees away from being east-west lines. It appears to be a caricature of Casa Rinconada, with features that superficially match

Painted sun symbol in Chaco Canyon, New Mexico. Probably Navajo in origin, this sun symbol (far left) marks an excellent place from which to witness sunrise near the winter solstice. By watching the sun rise along the opposite horizon, an experienced observer can anticipate the arrival of winter solstice to within a day. On the right of the sun symbol is a faded painting of Born-for-Water, the younger of the Navajo Twins.

Below: Rock painting (pigment probably hematite) in Chaco Canyon, New Mexico, thought to be of Anasazi origin. The star and crescent may represent the appearance of the Crab Nebula supernova next to the waning crescent moon on July 4, 1054. According to Pueblo tradition, the concentric circles may represent the sun, and the hand marks the site as sacred. This site may mark the presence of a sun watching station on the mesa above.

Native watercolor of the Hopi kachina A'Hote, which appears in the Mixed Kachina Dances. The star represents Morning Star. Stars and moon are common symbols on Hopi kachinas. (Courtesy National Anthropological Archives, Smithsonian Institution.) See J. Walter Fewkes, "Hopi Kachinas," *Smithsonian Institution Bureau of American Ethnology Annual Report* 21 (1903).

Navajo rattle with constellation patterns. Pattern to lower left represents Dilyehe, the Navajo name for Pleiades. The six stars left of center may represent the Navajo constellation First Big One (upper part of the constellation Scorpio). (Photograph by Clarion Cochran.)

Seven-inch model of Kiowa war shield commissioned by James Mooney, Smithsonian Institution. The red center represents the sun, and the red and brown stripes represent the rays of the sun. The blue stripes and circles represent the night sky and stars respectively. The group of dots above the crescent represents the Pleiades. (Courtesy Smithsonian Institution.)

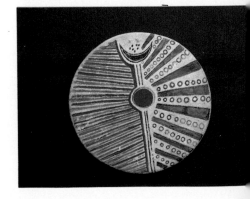

Unit-Type House, Hovenweep National Monument. Three of the four ports visible in the wall of this building face respectively the summer solstice, equinox, and winter solstice sunrise.

Hovenweep Castle, Hovenweep National Monument. The corner room facing the viewer contains two ports that align to the summer and winter solstice sunset directions.

Fajada Butte, Chaco Canyon, New Mexico. Near the top of this butte, which commands a panoramic view of Chaco Canyon, is the site of a large spiral petroglyph that may have functioned as an Anasazi device to mark or celebrate the arrival of the solstices and the equinoxes.

Below: Casa Rinconada, Chaco Canyon, New Mexico, looking from south to north along the axis of symmetry. Built by the Anasazi about A.D. 1100, Casa Rinconada is a great kiva aligned along the cardinal directions. The four circular holes to the right and left of the fire pit (center) once held large posts to support the massive kiva roof. These holes form a square that is nearly aligned along the cardinal directions.

Casa Rinconada. The summer solstice sun appears in the northeast passageway as seen from the low wall niche across the kiva.

A late-thirteenth-century cliff dwelling in a remote canyon of southeastern Utah. Note the large petroglyph above the cliff dwelling. This wall contains three ports aligned respectively to the summer solstice, winter solstice, and equinox sunsets.

Large petroglyph (2½ feet in diameter) above cliff dwelling in southeastern Utah. The circle may represent the sun and the crescent shape may represent the moon.

Anasazi petroglyph, south of Albuquerque, of Morning Star and a coiled snake. The claws on the star symbolize Morning Star's warlike nature. He is thought of as the war captain by some Pueblo groups.

Sunlight at summer solstice sunset streaming through port in cliff dwelling in southeastern Utah. This illustrates how plaster on the wall can be used to narrow the port and make the alignment more precise.

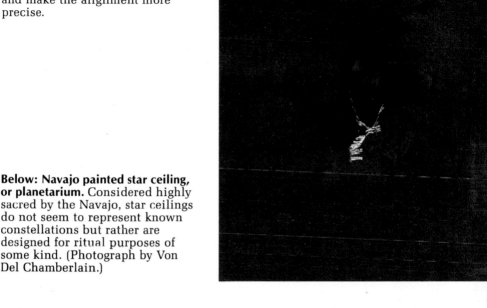

Below: Navajo painted star ceiling, or planetarium. Considered highly sacred by the Navajo, star ceilings do not seem to represent known constellations but rather are designed for ritual purposes of some kind. (Photograph by Von Del Chamberlain.)

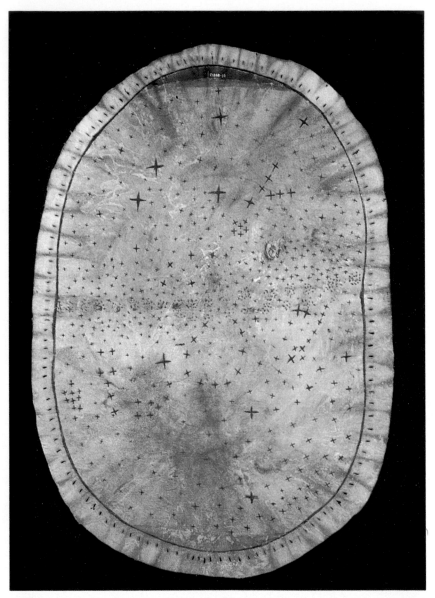

Skidi Pawnee star chart. On display at the Field Museum in Chicago, this leather star chart was apparently once part of a Skidi sacred bundle. On it are represented many of the known constellations of the Skidi Pawnee. The group of small dots across the center of the chart probably represents the Milky Way, which is called the Pathway of the Departed Spirits by the Pawnee. At death, the spirit walks this path on its way to the Southern Star. (Photograph by Von Del Chamberlain.)

those of its sister across the valley floor but lack Casa Rinconada's precision of astronomical and geometrical detail.

Looking at Pueblo Bonito as a whole, however, we see that the entire village is astronomically aligned. For example, as Howard Fisher and I found, the wall that divides the pueblo into western and eastern halves was constructed very nearly along the meridian. We also determined that the western half of the south wall is nearly a precise east-west line.[16] However, the eastern section of this wall is set at an angle 3° north of the latitude line, a deviation for which there does not seem to be any astronomical explanation. As with Casa Rinconada, Pueblo Bonito's careful orientations may be of deep ritual significance, but they are coincidentally of enormous practical value. Pueblo Bonito seems to have been deliberately designed and built to capture as much of the sun's vast radiative energy as possible for the direct benefit of its dwellers.

The amount of solar energy the Southwest receives daily makes solar-heated buildings an attractive possibility for architects working in the Southwest. Over the last decade they have been particularly interested in passive heating concepts, which require no moving parts or fluids to distribute the collected heat. Thus, it is ironic and rather surprising to some to discover that the Anasazi also employed passive heating concepts in their buildings.

I became suddenly aware of this possibility some years ago while taking nighttime photographs at Pueblo Bonito. Though the dry desert air had begun to cool quite rapidly as soon as the sun disappeared behind the distant western mesa, the sandstone walls radiated considerable heat onto the plaza where I was standing. This phenomenon continued for several hours and made my evening task much more pleasant than it might otherwise have been.

A complete village in one building, Pueblo Bonito once contained eight hundred rooms and housed a thousand or more people. Its unity of form and graceful design caused the Navajo guide who named it in the last century to give it a graceful Spanish name — "beautiful town." Not only was it an attractive place to live, but it also must have been rather comfortable, for its form and construction made it energy efficient as well.

The present form of Pueblo Bonito is shaped like the letter D. Its success as a solar collector is based on four factors. First, the pueblo is oriented in such a way that its curved wall opens south. Second, the rooms were stepped so that the northernmost part of the curved wall was four stories high, while much of the southern part was only one story. This "stair-step" design allowed the sun's energy to be reflected onto the central plaza, making it pleasantly warm even long after sunset. Third, it was located against the high north wall of the

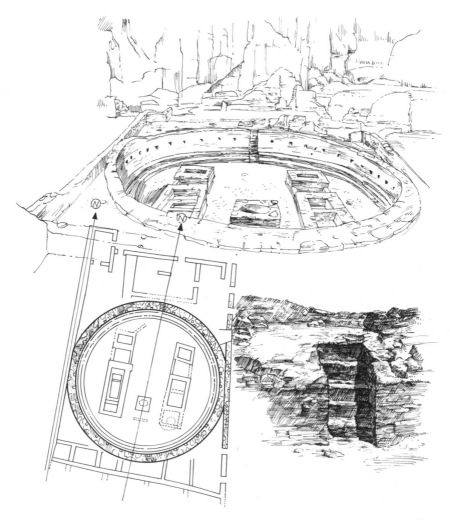

A great kiva in Pueblo Bonito, Chaco Canyon National Historical Park. Like the great kiva Casa Rinconada, situated across the canyon, this kiva is aligned along the meridian. However, there is no apparent east-west alignment between wall niches such as is found in Casa Rinconada.

canyon, which provided the shadowed exterior of the north wall of the village with reflected heat. Fourth, it is an extremely massive structure and therefore changes internal temperature only slowly even as the external temperature gyrates wildly.

From fall to late spring, the pueblo enjoys the heating effects of the sun all day long. As sunlight streams down, part of it is soaked up or absorbed by the sandstone walls of the structure and converted to heat. The remaining light is reflected. Throughout the day, the sun's warmth works its way through the massive walls and warms the cooler interior. Even very early in the morning on winter days, the air on the plaza would have warmed quickly because of the sunlight reflected from the walls of the northern rooms. Since much of the cooking and other activities were probably done outdoors, this would have been a most welcome feature of the structure. By the time the interior of the building was required for sleeping in the evening, it would have heated to a tolerable level and remained warm a substantial portion of the night.

Several years ago, in an attempt to discover just how comfortable the Bonitians might have been, I made quantitative temperature measurements of two rooms in the north side of the building.[17] One room, an interior one, received sunlight from the top. The other room, on the outside edge of the building, received no direct sunlight, but only reflected light and reradiated heat from the mesa wall north of it. In the summer, both rooms were predictably cool during the day and comfortably warm at night when the desert almost always becomes cool. Interestingly enough, the total temperature range in both rooms was quite small. For the inside room, the temperature throughout the twenty-four-hour period varied by only 4°F while the exterior air cycled through 38°F. In the winter, the equivalent temperature range was a mere 2°F for a 33°F exterior swing. The exterior room suffered a much greater temperature range because the door leading outside was left uncovered. My research at this stage has been exploratory only. Nonetheless, these data are indicative of what more extensive investigations would undoubtedly substantiate — that Pueblo Bonito was a surprisingly comfortable place to live year-round.

The small internal temperature swings are primarily caused by the building's great mass. As the seasons progress, it only slowly heats up and slowly cools down. The earth beneath also serves as an enormous heat reservoir, which also tends to moderate any internal variations. Because of the shape of Bonito and its geographical placement near the north wall, it was vastly more comfortable to live in than a building of comparable mass elsewhere in the canyon oriented at random.

Was this orientation and placement intentional? Once again, we do not know for certain, but the available facts certainly point in that direction. For one thing, the building has a long history of construction and reconstruction, each phase of which supported or improved upon its solar design. Unlike the historic pueblos in which rooms are added to the existing structures pretty much as they are needed, the large pueblos of Chaco Canyon were constructed in well-defined massive building phases. Nowhere is this more evident than in the construction of Pueblo Bonito. Today, even the inexperienced visitor can easily pick out four different masonry styles. Each different style represents a distinct building phase.

Pueblo Bonito began around A.D. 820 as a small crescent-shaped building. Its builders situated it near the high north wall of the canyon and oriented it so the concave side of the crescent opened to the southeast. Their plaza lay within the curving arms of the crescent. Although there is some doubt about the actual extent of the crescent because later construction phases obliterated parts of that first building, it is clear that even in the crescent stage, the building was well designed to capture and hold the sun's heat. Because the crescent was open to the southeast, the plaza received sunlight immediately after sunrise from late summer through late spring. The plaza continued to be illuminated for the rest of the day. During the summer, when shielding from the intense heat of the sun would be most appreciated, the high canyon cliff on the northeast prevented sunlight from reaching the plaza for about an hour after the sun's rays had crept above the canyon rim and struck the center of the canyon. Although the plaza was necessarily in full sun for most of the day, it was again protected from the sun for the last few hours of daylight by the height of the building itself in the northwest. But as the sun worked its way south, the plaza once again remained in sunlight from dawn to dusk.

For nearly two hundred years, the pueblo seems to have changed little and its people seem to have lived pretty much as they had when they first began to live there. But early in the eleventh century,

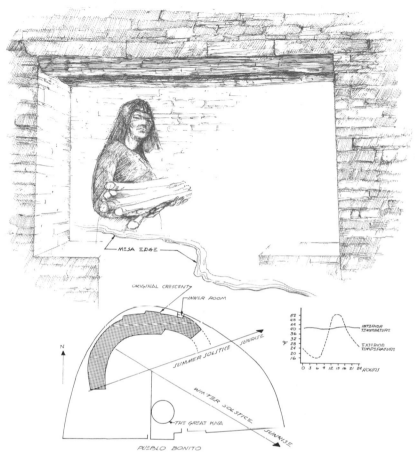

Pueblo Bonito as solar collector. The design and placement of Pueblo Bonito make it an excellent solar collector and passive storage structure. During one winter day, as the exterior temperature changed by over 35°F, the temperature swing of one of the interior rooms was only about 2°F. The average internal temperature was about 10°F higher than the average external temperature.

a period of vigorous growth began. Perhaps a new group entered and took control of the village. Or perhaps the old group simply underwent a rapid cultural advancement influenced by visitors who built elsewhere in the canyon. Whatever happened, it is clear that a major alteration of the pueblo took place, exemplified by a change in masonry and in construction techniques as well as in pottery styles and other aspects of the village's material culture.

In this second phase of construction, the old walls were covered up, the crescent was extended around to the southeast, and the plaza was enclosed with straight walls connecting the ends of the crescent. This brought the axis of symmetry of the pueblo around to a more southerly orientation, which considerably improved the solar heating effect on the plaza, since the afternoon sun was reflected back onto the plaza by the new walls in the east.[18]

Further massive construction on the pueblo was begun again in comparatively few years. Starting about 1040, the crescent shape was expanded many yards further south in both the east and west sections of the building. The great kiva, the north-south dividing wall, and the western section of the southern enclosing walls were all added at this time. It is this third-phase masonry that most intrigues the visitor to Pueblo Bonito. The Anasazi builders used narrow bands of large, reddish sandstone blocks interspersed with wider sandstone bands made up of smaller buff-colored chips and pieces. The overall effect is quite pleasing, although when the pueblo was inhabited it was most surely plastered over, causing the pattern to be lost. This third building phase gave the pueblo its present form. The last major addition or alteration to the pueblo merely extended it slightly to the east and added height to the rooms. The masonry characteristic of this last phase is composed of small slabs of the dark reddish sandstone laid up with very little interspersed mortar. Interestingly enough, the architects of the third phase had extended the foundations of the pueblo far to the east, but neither they nor the later builders carried through with this plan. Instead, they curved the building around and enclosed it. Was this because they realized that the addition would prevent them from constructing an energy-efficient building? Here again, we may never resolve this question, but this notion seems at least plausible in the context of their other construction efforts.

Such considerations are just part of the total puzzle surrounding the construction, use, and eventual abandonment of Pueblo Bonito. In the thirteenth century, the pueblo was apparently abandoned peacefully and by small groups, each leaving for their own reasons, but probably related to the increasingly hard life the canyon dwellers faced when the effects of the great southwestern drought began to be felt strongly in the area. In the meantime, successive generations of Bonitians had lived a seemingly comfortable life in a well-designed and beautiful Pueblo town.

7 The Navajo:
In Beauty May They Live

When the Dineh, or Navajo people, first emerged from the four underworlds through which they had passed, they found a barren world: neither plants nor mountains, nor even sun, moon, and stars. From the underworld they had brought nothing — no food, clothing, or shelter. Before they could sustain themselves they first needed to learn how to start plants growing. They also needed to form the earth and make it livable. First Man and First Woman thought. Before they could plan anything, they needed a dwelling place in which to meet and to establish the order of the world. So, right where they emerged, before making any more plans, they built a hogan.

First Man dug a shallow pit and placed poles in each of the four directions — east, south, west, north. Then he began to sing about building the hogan. For the two main poles First Man used Black Bow, which symbolized the overthrow of evil. He then cut two other poles, one from the male reed and one from the female reed, symbols of the male and female principles. Everyone who came up from the underworld helped to build the hogan. From the eagle they learned to build it round like the horizon and the face of the sun. From the beaver they got smaller logs for the walls. The swallows contributed adobe and straw for the walls and floors.

First Man blessed the hogan with cornmeal ground by First Woman, saying, "May my home be sacred and beautiful, and may the days be beautiful and plenty."[1] In some versions of the story, instead of using earthly materials, they covered the hogan with sunbeams and with rainbows, which in those days were pliable films that could be used like blankets. First Man covered it over by first laying two sheets of rainbows from north to south. He then laid the two sheets of sunbeams from east to west. Then, after bringing all their belongings into the first hogan, the Holy People sang the songs that accompany the building of hogans.

Next, they built a second hogan, or "planner's hogan," in the form of Fir Mountain (Gobernado Knob), one of the so-called inner mountains of the Navajo landscape. Fir Mountain was the home of Changing Woman, the creator of human beings. She directed the building of this hogan. Then Changing Woman directed that "when you build homes in which you are going to live, you must mark them in the four directions, just as was done for my home on Fir Mountain."[2] Today the newly built hogan — whether built in the shape of Gobernado Knob, which has a peaked shape, or more gently rounded, like Mountain Around Which Traveling Was Done (Huerfano Mountain, northwest of Chaco Canyon) — is also marked or blessed with white cornmeal, starting from the east and moving sunwise around to the south, west, and finally north. As the builders construct a traditional hogan they sing the Hogan Songs, which originated with the first hogan, as they raise the poles.[3]

Five-log Navajo hogan.

Along below the east, Earth's pole I first lean into position.
As I plan for it it drops, as I speak to it it drops, now it listens to
  me as it drops, it yields to my wish as it drops.
Long life drops, happiness drops into position, *ni yo o*.

Along below the south, Mountain Woman's pole I next lean in
  position.
As I plan for it it drops, as I speak to it it drops, now it listens to
  me as it drops, it yields to my wish as it drops.
Long life drops, happiness drops into position, *ni yo o*.

Along below the west, Water Woman's pole I lean between in
  position.
As I plan for it it drops, as I speak to it it drops, now it listens to
  me as it drops, it yields to my wish as it drops.
Long life drops, happiness drops into position, *ni yo o*.

Along below the north, Corn Woman's pole I lean my last in
  position.
As I plan for it it drops, as I speak to it it drops, now it listens to
  me as it drops, it yields to my wish as it drops.
Long life drops, happiness drops into position, *ni yo o*.[4]

After the hogan is completed, other songs are sung:

May it be beautiful, my house;
From my head may it be beautiful;
To my feet, may it be beautiful;
All above me, may it be beautiful;
All around me, may it be beautiful.[5]

This prayer, one of many that may be sung, captures in a few lines
the traditional Navajo's attitude toward life. For him or her, living in
beauty means to live harmoniously with nature, participating in the
cosmic plan laid down by the gods in the beginning of time. Living in beauty is also to live in accordance with the rhythms of the
heavens.

The Navajo and two other linguistically related Athabascan tribes,
the Apache and the Utes, entered the Southwest five hundred to six
hundred years ago. Related by culture as well as language to each
other and to Athabascan groups further north, these groups migrated
south from what is now Canada. The century of their arrival is in
considerable doubt. Navajo tradition indicates that they might have
arrived when the Anasazi still inhabited the great pueblos. Modern
archaeology does not support that suggestion; nevertheless, the ar-

chaeological record makes it clear that they were certainly well settled in the Rio Grande area sometime around the Spanish Entrada.

Navajo is the name given to this native group by the Spaniards. They call themselves Dineh, which, loosely translated, means "the People." The early history of the People is uncertain because until they entered the Southwest they were probably constantly moving, settling only long enough to plant a few seasons' crops before picking up again. Their dwellings were very simple summer brush shelters and skin or log-and-earth winter huts. Therefore, few early archaeological remains are available for study. What evidence we do have suggests that the People slowly migrated south, traveling in small, materially poor bands, and lived mainly by hunting and gathering and by planting only a few crops. This view is also supported by their own legends in which their ancestors journeyed from world to world and eventually reached their present home from lands in the North. When the Navajo arrived in the Southwest, they found a well-developed Pueblo culture — men and women who lived in villages and who had developed great material and cultural wealth; they found corn, architecture, pottery, weaving, and a host of rituals, myths, and legends. They must have been impressed, for their own tales of the early days in the Southwest refer to the Pueblo people as wealthy and sophisticated. Navajo legends credit the Pueblo with introducing them to corn and to the secrets of its cultivation. A remarkably adaptable people, the Dineh settled near the Pueblo and began to incorporate Pueblo ways, ritual, and mythology into their own cultural framework, changing and adapting it to their own requirements as it suited them.[6]

Though they borrowed heavily from the Pueblo, their culture remains distinctly Navajo. It is characteristic of the Navajo to borrow some customs and change them to their own usage but sternly and stubbornly reject cultural components that cannot be adapted to the Navajo way.[7]

Although the Navajo as a tribe are well known for their sheepherding and cattle raising, they only developed these skills after the advent of white settlers who brought sheep, cattle, and horses to the New World. By that time, the Navajo had developed their own agricultural techniques and elaborated on methods borrowed from the Pueblo groups that preceded them into the Southwest. The introduction of horses to their lives gave the Navajo great mobility. Yet they were not nomadic. Even the Navajo of early historic times maintained fixed winter abodes, although they used their horses to range far and wide to collect, hunt, trade, and raid other tribes and white settlers.

Much of the Navajo's mobility and associated raiding activity was sharply curtailed by the systematic, savage war led against them by Kit Carson and others of the U.S. Army. After being conquered, moved, and imprisoned in 1864 under harsh and cruel conditions, the Navajo were finally allowed to return to their lands in 1868, much depleted in numbers. Today most Navajo live on reservation land in Arizona and New Mexico. Though forced to cede much of their best agricultural and grazing land to white settlers, they now, ironically, own some of the richest mineral deposits in the nation. Oil, coal, gas, and uranium are among the most important of their resources. Thus, as a tribe they are potentially very rich materially. However, it could be said that their greatest riches are cultural — their close connection with the land, their distinctive art and oral literature, and their religious practices.

As we might expect, because the traditional Navajo live in scattered family groupings, rather than in villages or towns as do the Pueblo, and because they derive their livelihood primarily from ranching rather than from raising crops, their relationship to the sky and their use of celestial motions for regulating a calendar are somewhat different from their Pueblo neighbors. They depend upon the stars more heavily, and de-emphasize the use of the sun and the moon. The Navajo observe the sun throughout the year; but, because they live in isolated dwellings rather than in towns, their uses of the sun for calendrical purposes tend to be highly localized and depend on the varying shapes of light and shadow in their dwellings, or on a nearby canyon wall throughout the year.

Because the sky and sky phenomena are an essential part of the Navajo universe, references to sky phenomena are common in their art, stories, and ritual. Just as with the Pueblo and other Native American groups, the Navajo distinguish but little between the sacred and the secular. Life itself is sacred, and to live it right is a sacred act. Their use of celestial motions to set the times for ritual acts is simply a recognition of the sacred order of things. Human and animal life, plants, the rocks and streams as well as the sky, are all part of a grand scheme ruled by numerous gods or natural forces whose requirements must be divined and propitiated by the correct ritual practices. Those who discover the means of establishing and maintaining order hold the key to life's problems. As the myths tell so eloquently, the Navajo's ritual surroundings are part of this ordering. Ritually important mountains lie in each of the four directions and bound the Navajo universe. Cited in these myths of creation and ordering of the world, each mountain also has its earthly counterpart.

The Hogan

The hogan, the traditional Navajo dwelling, is also highly ordered. Built of logs and chinked with mud to form a watertight, windproof structure, the hogan (it literally means "place home") is, in its own way, a model of the cosmos. The gods themselves decreed the methods of building a hogan and specified that the Navajo follow the plan of the "first hogan," which had upright logs at the four cardinal points and a doorway facing east.

Proper hogan construction varies somewhat according to the particular locale within Navajo country and to the era during which it is built. The traditional five-log hogan results in the type resembling the conical shape of Fir Mountain. Other hogans are made somewhat differently, and may resemble the rounded shape of Mountain Around Which Traveling Was Done instead, but the basic adherence to a cosmic plan is retained.

Building a Hogan

Traditionally, the hogan is built in a single day, though circumstances often force a longer construction time.[8] When building a five-log hogan, after selecting an appropriate site and gathering together a party of helpers, the builder searches for trees appropriate for the five principal beams of the hogan frame. Any logs large enough to support the weight of wood and earth can be used, save only those trees struck by lightning or from hogans within which a death has occurred. In most areas, piñon trees would be selected, although in higher, wetter elevations, ponderosa pine might be used instead. Three of the five principal logs must terminate in a fork to allow them to lean against one another when the hogan is constructed.

After the three forked logs are dressed and hauled to the building site, they are laid on the cleared site with the forks together and their butt ends toward the south, west, and north. The builders lay two additional straight logs from the forks toward the east and as far apart as the intended width of the entry. At this stage, the direction

Floor plan, five-log hogan. One of the principal traditional hogan designs, the design of the five-log hogan is specified by the origin myths of the Navajo. The five-log hogan has a major supporting beam in the south, west, and north. The door — which, according to the origin myths, should face east — is framed by two smaller logs.

of the doorway is carefully checked, for it must be laid out to face east.[9]

After the logs are laid out in their proper orientations and placements, their positions are marked and the logs removed. Forthwith, the builders strike a circle well within the circle delimited by the butt ends of the timbers and then excavate the earth within this circle to a depth of a foot or so to create a level floor. The result of this stage of the building process is a narrow (18- to 24-inch) bench around the interior of the hogan upon which the family will later be able to store various domestic items. In the next stage, the butt ends of the forked timbers are placed carefully in their appropriate positions, starting with the north and south ones and then adding the west timber. It is important that the butt end be placed on the earth, for this part of the timber, when growing, came up from the earth. To turn the log around would be to upset the balance and proper order of things. The forks of the three timbers interlock to make a rigid tripod. Next, taking great care to place them on either side of the proper sunrise position, the builders add the doorway timbers. These rest at a slight angle to each other in such a way that their larger butt ends rest about 3½ feet apart and their smaller ends rest on the trio of forked timbers about 2 feet apart.

When the family and their helpers have completed their five-timber frame, they fill the sides between the timbers with smaller upright limbs of piñon and cedar. In most hogans of this type, the family would also include a slight extension on the western side of the hogan about 1 foot deep and 3 to 4 feet wide. They would extend the poles along this side outward appropriately. On the inside of the hogan, this extension provides a recessed compartment for storage. During ceremonies, this recess is kept covered with a cloth and used by the Singer to deposit masks and other paraphernalia.

To make the entryway, the builders select two slender, straight posts about 4½ feet long with forked tops and place them upright between the doorway timbers. These are connected to the doorway timbers and a lintel placed horizontally between the forks. A flat roof formed of split poles or small limbs completes the entranceway, which juts out from the round hogan much like a dormer on the roof of a conventional Anglo house. In this form of hogan, the builders include a hole above the lintel to allow smoke to escape from the central fire. Where necessary for strength, or to hold them in place, the workers bind the logs or sticks together. At this point in the process, the structure looks rather like a large, crude basket turned upside-down. Traditionally, the only openings in the structure are the doorway and the smoke hole. More recently, some hogans also include windows and stovepipe holes.

Two final building stages remain. In the first, the builders cover the entire structure with strands of cedar bark, filling every possible hole. Next, they cover the whole with earth, enough to make it sturdy and wind- and waterproof. Though rain seldom falls for very long in this dry country, it can fall fast and hard. This rounded structure, however, sheds water easily.

After the addition of the family's belongings, the completed hogan is ready to use, but only after it receives the proper blessing. This structure, considered quite beautiful if it is roomy, sturdy, and warm, is never decorated either inside or out. It is beautiful because it adheres to the cosmic plan; decorating it would imply that the cosmic plan is insufficient in some way.

When the new hogan is structurally complete, its owners bless the main beams by anointing each with white cornmeal in a clockwise ceremonial circuit, starting with the eastern doorway beams. From the east, through the south to the west and north, each receives cornmeal in turn as prayers are said to invoke the gods' blessings on the new home.

> Far in the east, far below, there a house was made;
> Beautiful house.
> God of Dawn, there his house was made;
> Beautiful house.
> The Dawn there, his house was made;
> Beautiful house.
> Soft possessions, for them a house was made;
> Beautiful house.
> Water in plenty surrounding, for it a house was made;
> Beautiful house.
> Corn pollen, for it a house was made;
> Beautiful house.
> The ancients make their presence beautiful;
> Beautiful house.[10]

In addition to the conical-roof hogan, the Navajo build and occupy many other types of hogans.[11] Some are variations on the style just described; others are radically different. All, however, are thought of as embodying cosmological principles in their construction, since by definition a hogan is built on a cosmic plan. Not all Navajo still dwell in hogans, since Anglo-American-style homes have gained considerable favor in recent years. When a family keeps the traditional ways, even though it may actually live in a contemporary home, it also maintains a hogan for ritual purposes. Only there may the ceremonies be performed. Even when a family chooses an Anglo-style home, the house generally faces sunrise and is likely to exhibit Navajo, as well as Pueblo or Spanish, characteristics.

Another form of vertical-post hogan, one that is built to resemble a palisade, also demonstrates the cosmic plan inherent in constructing a hogan. Instead of employing leaning timbers as with the conical-roof hogan, the builders place logs upright in a circular or polygonal trench, much as a wooden palisade is built. The posts may be of uniform size, each of which contributes to supporting the roof; alternatively, the builders sink large posts (four, six, or eight) into the earth in order to support the roof and place much smaller posts between. The decision about which building method to use depends as much on the availability of materials as on preferences of the future owner. If large posts are used, they are placed into the earth beginning with the southeast and proceeding sunwise around to the southwest, northwest, and northeast. The builders may also place precious offerings corresponding to the directional colors in the bottom of the holes. In a four-post hogan, they would deposit white shell in the southeast, turquoise in the southwest, and abalone and jet in the remaining two post holes. After the uprights are placed, the roof is added, and the holes are chinked, the walls will normally be covered with mud. The roof of a palisaded hogan will be either flat or corbeled. If corbeled, the logs are laid around the hogan in such a way that each successive ring of logs leaves a smaller area to cover. The resulting roof attains a rounded shape that resembles the silhouette of Mountain Around Which Traveling Was Done.

The other major variation on traditional hogan building methods is the stacked-log hogan. It may be constructed using corbeled, cribbed, or abutting-log techniques. Generally, this style of hogan is polygonal, most commonly hexagonal or octagonal, and the larger the hogan, the more sides it tends to have. One advantage of the stacked-log hogan is that it can be built quite large; diameters upwards of 25 feet are not uncommon in contemporary examples.

Stacked-pole hogan with corbeled roof. This is also a common Navajo design for a hogan. Its advantage is that it allows much more floor space than the five-log hogan.

Built and blessed in a ritual way to cosmological specifications and displaying a cosmological orientation, the hogan is truly a grand astronomical symbol. Most of all, a Navajo hogan is a place of life, of birth, meals, sleep, and family plans and tribal ritual. It is not, however, a place of death. According to the Navajo view, the only proper place for the deceased is in the earth as soon as possible after death. If a family has had the misfortune of having one of its members die within a hogan, the remaining family members abandon the hogan and burn it. Thereafter, the remains of the "chindi" hogan and its surroundings are scrupulously avoided by them and other members of the tribe, now the place of the chindi, or spirit, of the departed.

The Navajo and the Stars

The hogan appears in the creation myths as the home of many different creatures, but it is significant that in some stories it is also a place of creation. The stars, for example, are created there. The story of the creation of the stars is central to the Navajo conception of the universe, a universe that is essentially ordered just as the hogan is ordered but which also contains mischievous forces of disorder. In this story, Coyote, the trickster, introduces disorder into the heavens by upsetting the intended orderly arrangement of the stars.

In the hogan of creation before the stars are made, "the sky and earth lay on the floor of the hogan with heads pointing eastward, the sky on the south and the earth on the north. Both had received the 'breath of life' with various winds, though they were not 'dressed' as yet."[12] In one version of the story, it is the Navajo god Black God (or Fire God, for he also brought fire to the world) who orders the heavens by placing the stars.

In the days of creation, when Black God entered the hogan of creation, the small group of stars known to the Navajo as Dilyehe was attached to his ankle. Several of the other creators present remarked on the fact, whereupon Black God stamped his foot vigorously and Dilyehe jumped to his knee. Another stamp brought the stars to his hip. The assembled gods nodded approvingly. He stamped once more and brought Dilyehe to his shoulder. A fourth and final stamp of his foot caused them to lodge along his left temple where, he said, "it shall stay!" There it remains today. The constellation Dilyehe, which we know as Pleiades, is displayed on the left temple of the mask of Black God.

By his feat of placing Dilyehe where he wanted it, Black God demonstrated to the other gods assembled in the hogan of creation that he had the power to beautify the sky (the "dark upper") by placing stars in ordered patterns. Impressed, they encouraged him to continue. Black God owned a fawnskin pouch that contained crystals for making the stars. Standing under the dark upper, he reached into his pouch, drew out the crystals one by one, and carefully and deliberately placed them in the sky. Moving in a clockwise direction from the east, through the south to west and north, he first placed the constellation Man with Feet Ajar (a large irregular square in Corvus). Then slowly in succession, up went the constellations Horned Rattler, Bear, Thunder, and, in the south, First Big One (Scorpio). In the north, he stationed Revolving Male (Ursa Major plus the pole star), Revolving Female (part of Cassiopeia or of Ursa Minor); Slender First One (part of Orion); Pinching or Doubtful stars (Aldebaran, lower branch of Hyades); Rabbit Tracks (near Canis Major); and, finally, Dilyehe. None of these constellations, however, could shine without an igniter star to furnish their light. This, too, he added once the pattern was right. After he had established the star groups and their igniters in ordered patterns, he sprinkled the heavens with a band of fine crystal chips that became the faint track of the Milky Way.

Having completed this part of his task, Black God was about to rest for a bit when Coyote, the mischievous troublemaker, approached him. Coyote complained that he had not been consulted about placing the stars. The creator of the star patterns knew that Coyote meant mischief, but before he could prevent him, Coyote grabbed the pouch of crystals, emptied it, and blew the contents across the sky. As the Navajo who told this version exclaimed, "That explains why

Black God and his Pleiades. According to some versions of the Navajo origin myths, Black God, or Fire God, created the stars. When he entered the hogan of creation, Black God carried the constellation Dilyehe (Pleiades) on his ankle. He demonstrated his mastery of the stars by stamping his foot four times and causing the constellation to settle on his forehead. (Reprinted with permission from Fr. Berard Haile. *Starlore Among the Navaho*. Santa Fe: Museum of Navajo Ceremonial Art, 1947: 3.)

only the stars put there by Fire God [Black God] have a name and those scattered at random by Coyote are nameless."[13]

Then, in a sudden reversal of his careless behavior, Coyote took out the one crystal remaining in the pouch, and located it very carefully in the south. This star he called the Monthless Star (perhaps Antares). Today the Navajo refer to this star as Coyote Star.[14]

This intriguing story illustrates the considerable attention the Navajo pay to the stars and to naming many of the patterns. In addition, the patterns of the stars contain their rules for living.[15] As the myths expound, each constellation forms a celestial pattern for life on earth, and every earthly creature has his celestial counterpart. The Navajo think of the stars as friendly beings. They are considered to be "good medicine," especially when fighting a battle at night. They are also thought of as friendly because of their potential for calendrical use. Although the forms of many Navajo constellations are familiar to Western eyes, some are not. In general, the Navajo organize the stellar patterns differently than did the early Greeks and Babylonians who gave us most of the European constellations.

The order that Black God created in making the stars extends to their apparent motions as well. Not only do they stay in ordered groups, their motion is regular and can therefore be used to define a calendar. The appearances and disappearances of certain stars serve to mark the seasons and to announce the times for planting or for ritual celebration.

The Navajo have developed their star watching skills to the point that they know when to prepare their fields, plant their corn, and start their harvest by the appearance of the heavens. It may seem surprising to think of the Navajo as agriculturalists, since they are known especially as sheepherders and cattlemen; however, the Navajo have tilled the earth since they first settled in the Southwest, using many of the same dry-farming techniques that their Pueblo counterparts employ. For the same reasons that the Pueblo developed their lunar-solar calendar, the Navajo also investigated ways to use the stars.

The Stellar Calendar

The motions of the stars are simpler than those of the sun and the moon and they must be treated differently. Thus the Navajo know it is time to plant when their constellation Revolving Male lies parallel to the horizon in early evening (late May or early June).[16] In the spring, he is overhead; when he "slants down to the east, it is winter." The position of Revolving Male also indicates to those Navajo who are familiar with his motions when different animals are likely to mate, and when they will bear offspring.[17]

The appearance of the constellation Dilyehe (Pleiades) illustrates the use of stars that rise and set as a calendar marker. When Dilyehe first reappears in the early morning sky to the northeast, after an absence of several months from the night sky, the Navajo know that it is now too late to plant any longer and still be able to harvest before the first frost. This reappearance of Dilyehe occurs near the summer solstice and near the horizon position of the summer solstice sun, a fact that has made this stellar group highly useful as a calendar device all over the world. For the Navajo, the constellation not only announces when to cease planting but, when they see Dilyehe in the northeast in the early evening, it tells them that the first autumn frost is not far off. This occurs in late September, near the autumnal equinox, when, at about ten o'clock at night, the constellation can be seen just rising in the northeast.

Dilyehe is very well known by all the Navajo, if only for the relatively mundane reason that it also provides a nightly "clock" in the fall and winter. For some, its position above the horizon indicates the proper time to start the Nightway and the Mountainway ceremonial seasons.

In addition to the creation story, Dilyehe also figures in other Navajo stories. The stars that make up this constellation are the black dancers in the Enemyway Chant, or the seven Hard Flint Boys, warriors in several stories. Though to the naked eye the stars of this constellation appear as a sort of tiny dipper, the Navajo depict them as three pairs of stars with a seventh star that "always follows the six important stars of this constellation."[18] These seven stars are shown in this way as running and dodging just as the Navajo used to do when fighting with bows and arrows, before they had rifles as weapons. Warriors would run in a zigzag or dodging motion while shooting their arrows at the same time. The Hard Flint Boys, in drawings of the constellation Dilyehe, are practicing their running, dodging, and shooting. These same Hard Flint Boys are also known by the name of the Milky Way Boys and Rainbow Boys because in the Navajo myths they often travel on either of these sky phenomena.

The constellation First Slender One follows Dilyehe in its journey across the sky. When First Slender One is setting just at twilight (late April or early May), the Navajo begin to plant. A curved line of stars to the right of the figure is a digging stick; above the digging stick is a circle of stars that represents a basket full of corn seeds.

According to Navajo legend, the stars are made of crystal; and, just as crystal gleams and shines only by means of another light source, each of the constellations has its own igniter star to cause its stars to shine. The connection between the stars and earthbound crystal is most evident in the name the Navajo give to glass — "rock star."

They make a more explicit connection between stars and earthly rock crystals, translucent rocks, or even glass prisms, in a practice known as stargazing. Certain diviners gaze through any glasslike material at the brightest stars in order to determine the right ceremony to choose to solve a given problem. Though this practice may date from historic times, it apparently also reflects ancient beliefs that earthbound crystals are directly related to the stars. The colors seen refracted through the crystal are used to guide the diviner, or star reader, to choose the proper ceremony with which to cure ills, locate witches, or find stolen goods.

The precise reason the Navajo emphasized the use of stars in developing their calendar is probably hidden deep in their past. However, there may well be functional reasons related to their lifestyle that make the stars a more reliable standard for constructing a calendar than the sun. The fixed and regular nature of the stars' apparent positions make them much more appropriate for a people who shift their abodes from winter to summer, or who may pick up and move at any time. Determining ceremonially or agriculturally important days by following the movements of the sun or moon requires a fixed horizon and therefore a fixed place from which to view them. Alternatively, it requires a structure that is lived in during summer and winter and over a span of several years. By learning the positions of the stars throughout the seasons and the times of reappearance or disappearance of certain stars, the Navajo calendar maker could carry his calendar with him, whereas the Pueblo sun chief relied on a horizon calendar related to the geographical position of his pueblo. In order, then, to use the sun as a calendar, the Navajo need only relate the stellar indicators to the daily change in the patterns of sunlight in order to generate a place-specific solar calendar.

Other Calendrical Methods

Navajo calendrical methods are not solely confined to using the stars. The Navajo are also familiar with using the motions of the sun and the play of light and shadow across stationary objects to determine the date. The methods they use vary considerably, and depend highly on local topography or special conditions. For example, one family in northwest New Mexico was able to determine the time for planting by the changing path of sunlight that entered the smoke hole of their hogan. Several weeks after the sun passed north of the celestial equator (that is, after the vernal equinox), sunlight entering the smoke hole (in the ceiling) would begin to fall only on the east side of the central fire and not cross it. When this happened, the family knew that it was time to begin planting. Alternatively, families could and did watch the progress of the sun along the horizon from day to day. Just as their Pueblo counterparts have done, they determined when to plant or harvest by the sun's angular position along the horizon at sunrise or sunset.[19]

Where the canyons are deep and narrow, another method becomes possible. For example, in Canyon de Chelly and the nearby Canyon del Muerto, in Arizona, the proper times for planting are indicated by the downward progress of the shadow cast by the south wall of the canyon against the north wall. When the sunlight first reaches a certain position on the north wall, those who dwell there know that the day it will reach into the bottom of the canyon to warm the newly planted crops will not be far behind.

One major difference between Navajo and Pueblo methods of keeping the calendar is that the former have given us little evidence that they might have purposely constructed a means to do so, such as placing a porthole at a specific angle or carving a petroglyph for sunlight to illuminate. The sole interest the Navajo seem to have in aligning their structures is in constructing the hogan or summer shelters (the latter are also aligned very roughly to open to the east). Though highly important ritually, and as evidence that the Navajo have a deep interest in harmonizing their lives with the cosmos, the hogan is apparently used only incidentally for calendrical purposes, and in ways that are not amenable to archaeological investigation. They are much more temporary than the stone buildings of the Pueblos.

Astronomical Symbols

Astronomical symbolism, so evident in the very houses that traditional Navajo erect, is even more apparent in many of the elaborate dry paintings that the Singer constructs for curing or blessing ceremonies. In these paintings — most properly labeled dry paintings rather than sand paintings, since the pigments may derive from many other substances in addition to sand — representations of stars, star constellations, and the sun and moon are frequently present. They are used not for decoration, but because these celestial objects have a direct connection to the substance of the celebration or curing ritual.

> [T]he main purpose of the Navaho sand paintings is . . . to identify him [the patient] with the images of power that are represented in the paintings . . . Every sand painting is a pattern of psychic energy. The painting focuses the power, and the medicine man transfers it to the patient through the physical medium of sand. The patient not only makes use of the power of the figures in the painting, he becomes that power.[20]

For example, in Big Starway, the big star is one of the holy beings also found in other Navajo curing rituals. By tradition, the songs of this ceremony were given by the star people who, after making a journey to the earth, return to the sky. To the stars are attributed directional colors, in Big Starway as well as in other ceremonials such as the Navajo Shootingway, Nightway, or Windway. In some dry paintings, big (bright) stars are represented by a single diamond shape, and small (faint) ones by an equi-armed cross. In Shootingway, even big stars are represented by a cross. Other stellar representations are possible; for example, in one of the Downway dry paintings, stars are represented in different colors by four-pointed stars that have circular centers. Many variations are possible, and their precise shape and associated attributes depend on the meaning that is intended and the style of the particular artist. Star images that figure as a major part of a given painting may be depicted without a black background and in association with stellar assistants or particular symbolic attributes.

Comets or shooting stars sometimes occur in dry paintings but seldom in paintings used in ceremonies of healing, because they are understood to be abnormal and acting contrary to the ordered laws of nature.

The stars have the ability to assist in healing. For example, in the Great Star Chant, the stars of the dry painting receive their healing power from a bright star that shines through the smoke hole in the roof of the hogan.[21] As this star helps the patient directly, it is important to complete the healing ceremony before the star passes out of sight. Constellation groupings appear in dry paintings done for some of the chants, such as Shooting Chant, or the Hail Chant, but seldom in the Star Ceremony. What star patterns there are in this healing ceremony are chosen by the Singer for their particular healing power or influence over the patient's disorder.

Mother Earth and Father Sky are two of the best-known paintings because one or both are often reproduced in copies of sand paintings for sale to tourists. Together, they represent the entire physical universe. The black body of Father Sky is decorated with numerous stars in the shape of the major constellations; the sun, the moon, and the Milky Way are also generally included, the latter as a band of crosses on the chest or along the arms. The sun and moon are nearly always drawn with horns, a mark that they possess extraordinary powers.

Astronomical symbolism in art is not confined to dry paintings. Ceremonial rattles, frequently used in curing ceremonies, may also carry constellation patterns. At a Night Chant Ceremony held near the turn of the century, anthropologist Alfred Tozzer witnessed the Singer of the chant make a ceremonial gourd rattle.[22] After fitting a wooden handle to a hollow gourd, the Singer deftly drilled several small holes in the gourd's surface, seemingly at random. However, when he examined the completed rattle later, Tozzer was astonished to find that the holes were placed in the pattern of important Navajo constellations. Tozzer never, however, obtained the Navajo names of the constellations. Later work by others identify these patterns as Revolving Male, Slender First One, Dilyehe, and the Doubtful Stars.

In my own researches, I have examined several rattles that also contain similar patterns. One such rattle is particularly interesting; on the gourd it is possible to make out five distinct groupings: First Slender One, Dilyehe, Pinching or Doubtful Stars, Revolving Female, and Revolving Male. In addition, there is one isolated hole that might represent the Coyote Star.[23] These patterns are clearly similar to those Tozzer described some eighty years ago. The small differences between them are unlikely to be of consequence for several reasons. First, we can attribute some differences to the difficulty of transferring patterns from a sphere to a plane surface, or to small errors in Tozzer's notes. Since the rattle from which he copied the patterns is not available for comparison, it is impossible to reconstruct exactly what Tozzer was looking at. Second, it is not possible to compare the rattle patterns with the stellar patterns themselves because many of the constellations are rendered in a subjective, stylized form that has more to do with the stories about them than with an objective view of the sky. Differences between Navajo and Western renditions of constellations become particularly evident when comparing the stellar patterns of a dry painting with the sky. This has made identifying some stellar groupings especially difficult in the absence of direct information from the artist about which ones he was trying to portray.

However they are identified, the experience in examining these rattles has helped me to understand some puzzling petroglyphs in Chaco Canyon, New Mexico, that came to my attention some years ago. While we were investigating pictographs and petroglyphs in the area near Wijiji Pueblo in the eastern part of the canyon, a colleague drew my attention to several groups of holes in the horizontal sandstone surfaces of two large fallen boulders.[24] The holes, which range from ¼ inch to ½ inch in diameter, appear to have been drilled into the sandstone, perhaps with a steel implement. They form patterns resembling several Western constellations, but we knew from the nearby petroglyphs that they are likely to be Navajo. At the time, I thought that they were singular examples of constellation patterns in Navajo rock art. Because I had little supportive evidence that these patterns might represent constellations, I filed the information away for possible future use. However, in the intervening years, I learned two important related facts: these glyphs are very similar to the constellations depicted on Navajo ceremonial rattles; and other Navajo petroglyphs similar to these have been recorded in Blanco Canyon, northeast of Chaco Canyon.[25]

The drill holes in Chaco Canyon are found on the top surfaces of two boulders that rest directly beneath several crude Navajo glyphs of a horse and a Yei (a Navajo god). Some of the holes forming the

Navajo petroglyph of the sun, Chaco Canyon. This rock carving is found on a boulder east of Wijiji Pueblo. The three concentric circles with a central dot form a typical Pueblo symbol of the sun. However, the horns and the style of the petroglyph are typical of a Navajo rendition of the sun. (Drawing by Jean G. Monroe.)

patterns fall across shallow abraded depressions that appear to be axe-grinding grooves. The grooves were probably made by the earlier Anasazi, though they could also have been made by the Navajo.

These patterns seem to represent Revolving Male, Revolving Female, the Rabbit Tracks, and First Slender One. They are particularly interesting not only because they reproduce patterns found on ceremonial rattles but also because they confirm that this area is highly sacred. Other Navajo glyphs, found a few yards from the site, also suggest the area was sacred to the Navajo. A large boulder southeast of the constellation patterns serves as the medium for several striking glyphs. On it is a Pueblo-style sun symbol having three concentric circles and a central dot, but with horns more typical of Navajo art. To the right of the sun symbol is a rendition of one of the Navajo twins, Born-for-Water. Born-for-Water, and his elder brother, Monster Slayer, are the result of the union of the Navajo deity Changing Woman with the sun and a waterfall. As in the Pueblo myth from which the Navajo borrowed, the Twins clear the newly formed land of the terrible monsters that prey on the Navajo people. Monster Slayer confronts and kills the enemy. His brother scalps them.

This glyph is recognizable as Born-for-Water by the hourglass figures that ring its face. According to Navajo tradition, the hourglass

Navajo petroglyph of Born-for-Water, the younger of the Navajo Twins. This is found next to the sun rock carving. The hourglass shapes that ring the face identify this incised figure as Born-for-Water. It symbolizes the scalp knot that he tied after his brother Monster Slayer killed the monsters that plagued the Navajo after their emergence from the underworld. (Drawing by Jean G. Monroe.)

represents the scalp knot that Born-for-Water ties after scalping his brother's victims. He is presumably represented here beside the sun because he is related to the sun through his elder brother. Why is Monster Slayer not also represented? One likely possibility is that Monster Slayer is there in the guise of the sun. In a sort of economy of symbols, the sun and his son are merged together. Both represent different forms of power: Sun, the power to cause growth on the earth; Monster Slayer, the power to make the earth safe for humans.

Typically, Born-for-Water is painted in red. In 1981, while investigating the Wijiji site, I had a surprise that altered markedly an earlier theory I had developed about a nearby sun glyph. Painted in white and very similar in form to the Zuni sun from Matsaki near Zuni Pueblo, this second glyph is what drew me to the site originally. Seen from a spot near the sun symbol, on the winter solstice the sun rises directly behind a rock pillar that extends above the horizon to the southeast. Because the painted sun is so similar to Pueblo renditions of the sun, I made the assumption, corroborated by several anthropologists, that it was likely to be an Anasazi glyph. The possible meaning of a small red patch next to it had escaped me. However, the red painting and the Navajo symbols nearby made me later wonder whether the sun might be a Navajo representation of the sun.[26]

During the course of an educational tour of the Four Corners area, I wanted to re-explore the Wijiji site to investigate the constellation patterns. After photographing the petroglyphs of the sun and Born-for-Water, our group moved on to look at the white sun symbol and the faint red glyph next to it. One of our group, who had taken particular interest in the rock art, carefully examined the faint red patch next to the sun and noticed that it had several hourglass shapes scratched into it. It was Born-for-Water again — here in the form of a painting rather than a petroglyph.

The hourglass figure also appears several times among the constellation patterns, and in another example of the economy of symbolism often practiced for ritual purposes, these, too, represent Born-for-Water. The presence of Born-for-Water and the sun twice in the same location, along with his appearance among the constellation patterns, confirms that this site must have been highly sacred to the Navajo. The area is particularly interesting to ethnoastronomers because it is a possible example of a site devoted to Navajo sun watching. By watching the sun in its course along the horizon from this site, the Navajo would have been able to mark the winter solstice precisely.

The Blanco Canyon constellation glyphs are also of interest because that site, too, has connections to sacred ritual, indicated by a nearby sun petroglyph and the hourglass of Born-for-Water. Essentially ignored by rock art enthusiasts because of the more spectacular

Navajo petroglyph of a Yei, or Navajo god. This is found on the same panel in Chaco Canyon as the sun and Born-for-Water. (Drawing by Jean G. Monroe.)

Navajo pictograph and petroglyph of Born-for-Water. The shaded part is painted deep red-brown; the feather is scratched; the hourglasses are scratched and incised. This faint pictograph is found in Chaco Canyon a few yards from the petroglyph panel depicting the sun, Born-for-Water, and the Navajo Yei. It is next to a painted sun symbol that marks an excellent spot to watch for winter solstice sunrise across the canyon. (Drawing by Jean G. Monroe.)

glyphs nearby, these glyphs are formed of shallow pecked dots on sandstone. In addition to Dilyehe, First Slender One, and the Doubtful Stars, there is also a pattern I have never seen on a Navajo rattle or sand painting. A simple circle of dots, to the left of the pattern believed to be Dilyehe, appears to represent the Western constellation Northern Crown, or Corona Borealis. I am not aware that this constellation is of interest to the Navajo, but it could also represent the basket of seeds that is associated with First Slender One and a constellation that represents the digging stick.[27]

Astronomical symbols are found on other Navajo items as well. For example, a Navajo war shield on display at Canyon de Chelly depicts the moon, Dilyehe, First Slender One, and the Doubtful Stars, in addition to many other random stars. Also, a ketahan, a small hollow reed used for ritual purposes, is sometimes decorated with stars. Finally, some Navajo rugs have woven into their patterns crosses that may represent stars.

Star Ceilings

One last major source of star symbolism remains to be mentioned. Throughout the area drained by the rivers feeding into the San Juan in northwest New Mexico, and also in Canyon de Chelly further west in Arizona, the Navajo have left numerous pictograph star panels.[28] Containing from a few tens to nearly a hundred stars, these panels are located on roofs of shallow caves in the canyons — hence their name, star ceilings. Between fifty and one hundred such panels are known to exist. Some are as high as 50 or 75 feet above the surface and make one wonder how the painter or painters could possibly have reached the roof to do the painting.

Star ceilings are sacred to the Navajo even now, though apparently the tradition of painting them has disappeared. In Canyon de Chelly, for example, Navajo medicine men are known to visit the sites of some star ceilings as part of their religious observances. Precisely what significance they have, however, is not understood by anthropologists. Since the medicine men are very secretive about the nature of the observances they make at the sites of the star ceilings, the ordinary Navajo know few details about these sacred sites.

One informant, for example, declined to say anything about the significance of the star ceilings on the grounds that the information was highly secret and closely kept; great harm might come to anyone who disclosed their secrets. Medicine men who know about star ceilings are as reluctant to speak about them as they are about details of certain ceremonies, and probably for the same understandable reason. To learn the proper way to conduct a particularly detailed healing ceremony may take years of apprenticeship and practice. Widespread knowledge of the details of these ceremonies might cause the medicine men who have worked so hard to learn them to be less in demand. The payment for a given ceremony can range up to a thousand dollars, depending on how complicated and uncommon it is. Thus, knowledge of the ceremonies' details could create significant loss of income for the Singer. Of more importance, though, widespread knowledge could also take power from the ceremonies by making them common rather than unusual rituals. Because of the Navajos' belief that the laws by which they should live are written in the patterns of the stars, it is not hard to see how a star ceiling would also have deep significance for the Navajo. Properly trained medicine men would be able to use the star ceiling as an earthly reminder of the laws carried by the stars.

Star ceilings are often called planetaria in the literature, apparently based on the notion that the stellar patterns represent certain constellations. However, although it may be possible to recognize constellation patterns in some star ceilings, other ones contain no such obvious patterns. This may be partly because, as in dry paintings, the pattern used is conventional and not necessarily representative of the actual visual pattern (the representation of Dilyehe is just such a case). The symbolic elements used in the star ceilings to represent stars vary considerably and range from simple crosses to much more elaborate shapes. In Canyon de Chelly, they are most often executed in black pigment. Elsewhere, red, orange, and gray pigments are common.

However they are understood, star ceilings, as well as other rock art, both petroglyph and pictograph, contain many of the symbolic elements that are evident in later dry paintings. Just as each symbol of the dry painting has a common meaning to the maker, so the stars of these star ceilings also must have had a meaning to the painters.

Left: **Jackson Staircase, Chaco Canyon, New Mexico.** The Anasazi carved stairs and handholds out of the living rock in order to make their access to various parts of Chaco Canyon easier.

Below: **Overview of Pueblo Bonito, Chaco Canyon, New Mexico, seen from the mesa north of the pueblo.** The circular rooms are kivas; the rectangular ones, living quarters and storage rooms. This building was once four stories high in the north. Constructed in stages between about A.D. 850 and 1050, it contained some eight hundred rooms and housed perhaps a thousand people in the eleventh century, when it reached its present form. The straight wall that divides the plaza in half is oriented nearly north-south. The great kiva to the east (left) of the dividing wall is also aligned north-south.

Above left: **A corner passageway in the southeast part of Pueblo Bonito.** One of six known corner passageways in the Pueblo, this one opens to the winter solstice sunrise. Although it appears to be in an inner room, light from the winter solstice sun may once have entered the passageway by means of a port in the outer wall.

Above right: **The corner passageway in Pueblo Bonito as seen from inside.** Note that the southeast horizon is readily visible. At winter solstice, the sun rises just to the right of the small break on the horizon.

Left: **The great kiva in Pueblo Bonito as seen along the axis of symmetry, which is also a north-south line.** Kiva features visible in this photograph include the north staircase, wall niches, and floor vaults. Visible in this photograph are two of the four (square) sockets that once held the massive posts that must have been used to support the kiva's heavy roof.

Left: **Drilled depressions in a sandstone boulder near Wijiji Pueblo, Chaco Canyon, New Mexico.** These are apparently of Navajo origin and may represent the Navajo constellation Revolving Male (Ursa Major). Patterns in the shape of the Navajo constellations Dilyehe (Pleiades) and the Doubtful Stars are also evident on the boulder. Similar constellation patterns are found on sacred rattles and in dry paintings. The sacred nature of this site is proclaimed by an hourglass shape representing the Navajo twin god Born-for-Water carved in the same boulder.

Below: **Boulder house or tower near Holly House in Hovenweep National Monument.** Note how the masonry conforms to the contours of the boulder upon which the building rests. Most of these towers and boulder houses were apparently built between A.D. 1170 and 1290 by Anasazi groups related to the builders of the cliff dwellings at Mesa Verde.

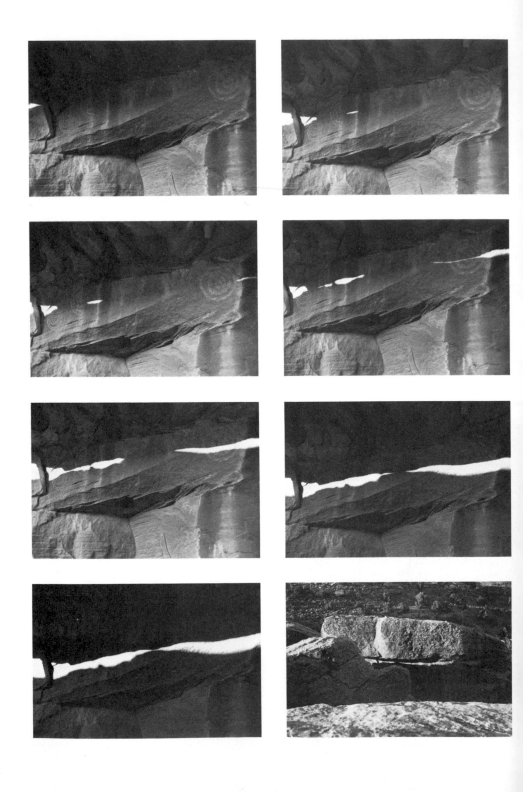

Opposite: **Petroglyph panel near Holly House, Hovenweep National Monument.** About an hour after sunrise on and around the summer solstice, a long serpent of light falls across a sun symbol (three concentric circles and a central dot) on the right of the petroglyph panel as another serpent of light falls across the two spirals on the left. The entire light display, from the time light first penetrates the narrow corridor containing the petroglyphs until the serpents of light touch each other, takes about seven minutes. Also on the panel is a twinlike petroglyph, below and to the left of the sun symbol, that may represent the twins of Pueblo lore, and a plumed serpent to the right of the sun symbol.

Opposite, bottom right: **The serpents of light as seen from a boulder above and to the north of the petroglyph panel near Holly House, Hovenweep National Monument.**

Below: **A partially reconstructed and preserved kiva in Lowry Ruin, a Chaco-style pueblo near Hovenweep National Monument.** Remnants of the plastered and painted interior are still visible along the kiva bench. Logs between stone pilasters may have been used to store ritual paraphernalia. Some archaeologists believe that Lowry Ruin may be an outlier of a vast trading network centered in Chaco Canyon, some 200 miles south.

Petroglyph (on basalt) south of Santa Fe, New Mexico. The quartered circle to the right of the flute player may represent the sun. The quartered circle is a common rock art motif in the Southwest.

Anasazi petroglyph (on basalt) south of Santa Fe, New Mexico. Shield may represent the rays of the sun. Inscribed in the center is Morning Star, the war captain of some pueblos. The figure bearing the shield apparently carries an arrow in one hand and a quiver of arrows on his back.

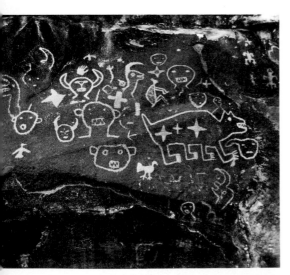

Anasazi petroglyph panel (on basalt) south of Santa Fe, New Mexico. In addition to several stars, the panel contains renditions of the plumed, or horned, serpent, and several kachina masks.

Anasazi petroglyph of shield and warrior (on basalt) south of Santa Fe, New Mexico. The outside of the shield may represent the rays of the sun. The center of the shield carries Morning Star and Evening Star, two other bright stars, and two circles that may represent the moon. The rim of the shield carries faint evidence of what may be feathers.

Left: **Paintings (white pigment) on vertical sandstone wall near small ruin (foreground) in southeastern Utah may represent the phases of the moon.** The diameter of the paintings is about 18 inches.

Below: **The log remains of a palisade-style Navajo hogan near Nageezi, New Mexico.** Originally, the hogan was plastered over. Note the corbeled roof.

Wall painting of Kolowisi, the Zuni plumed serpent. Kolowisi is the guardian of sacred springs, and a sacred being to be respected. He is also a powerful symbol of fertility, both at Zuni Pueblo and at the Hopi pueblos, where he is named Palulukong. The figure standing on the extended tongues of the Kolowisi is probably a horned toad. (Courtesy Smithsonian Institution National Anthropological Archives.)

Zuni Pueblo as it appeared in 1879. Today, most houses have peaked roofs. Note the pottery chimneys on the roofs, and the *ristras* of dried chiles hanging on the exterior walls. The dome-shaped object in the lower left is a Zuni oven. (Photograph by John K. Hillers. Courtesy of the Smithsonian Institution National Anthropological Archives.)

Frank Hamilton Cushing, anthropologist with the Smithsonian Institution Bureau of American Ethnology, posing at Zuni Pueblo. Cushing arrived at Zuni Pueblo in 1879 and stayed four and a half years. He learned the language and became a member of the tribal council and a Priest of the Bow. He gathered tales, learned Zuni ritual, and collected numerous objects of material culture in his stay at Zuni. His published writings and unpublished notes constitute some of the primary source material about life at Zuni Pueblo. (Courtesy of the Smithsonian Institution National Anthropological Archives.)

Painted wall decorations in the "animal room" at Zuni, a ceremonial chamber. Among other animals depicted are deer, a rabbit, and an eagle. Numerous painted pots are on the floor. (Photograph by Adam Clark Vroman, 1899. Courtesy Smithsonian Institution National Anthropological Archives.)

Hopi mudhead kachinas struggling with Palulukong, the plumed water serpent, at the Hopi pueblo of Walpi. This struggle dramatizes the opposition between the dual forces of fertility provided by the sun and by water. Too much of either and the crops will fail. They must struggle with each other to strike a balance that will promote growth. In this portion of the Palulukonti ritual held near the vernal equinox in the 1890s, the serpent protrudes through the painted symbol of the sun, pushing the sun's face upward. (Drawing by M. Wright Gill. Courtesy Smithsonian Institution National Anthropological Archives.)

Painted wall decorations in a kiva at Walpi Pueblo. Shown are clouds, lightning, an eagle, and a Hopi clown. (Courtesy Smithsonian Institution National Anthropological Archives.)

Niman kachina dance at Shungopavi, a Hopi pueblo, in 1901. After the Niman dances in July, the kachinas return to their home in the San Francisco Mountains until they reappear at the Soyal celebration at the winter solstice. (Photo by Adam Clark Vroman. Courtesy Smithsonian Institution National Anthropological Archives.)

Soyoko, or ogre, kachinas seen during the Hopi Powamu ceremony in February. Powamu is a ceremony of renewal and preparation for the coming spring planting. The purpose of the Soyoko kachinas is to encourage correct behavior in children. They appear in the village and demand food and small tasks of the children In preparation for adulthood. If the children fail, the Soyoko threaten to kidnap the children. (Photograph by James Mooney at the Hopi pueblo of Walpi, February 1893. Courtesy Smithsonian Institution National Anthropological Archives.)

Acoma Pueblo woman in costume for the Fiesta de San Estevan, held on September 2 each year. Note the four painted lines across her hands, and the tabletta with a star, cloud symbol at the top, and a rainbow or crescent. (Photo taken prior to December 28, 1938. Courtesy Smithsonian Institution National Anthropological Archives.)

Below: **Navajo woman weaving a rug in the traditional manner outside a five-pole hogan in late 1800s.** Three large poles stand in the south, west, and north, respectively. Two smaller poles frame the doorway, which traditionally faces east. (Courtesy Smithsonian Institution National Anthropological Archives.)

Manuelito Segundo, son of Chief Manuelito, a well-known Navajo warrior of the late 1800s who long opposed peace with the Americans on the grounds that they could not be trusted to keep their word. Note the star design on Manuelito Segundo's arrow case. (Courtesy Smithsonian Institution National Anthropological Archives.)

Below: **Mescalero Apache Spirit Dancers.** Note repeated use of motifs grouped in fours, symbolizing the four directions. These are benevolent spirits that dance for the good of the tribe. (Photograph by General Timothy E. Wilcox, circa 1887. Courtesy Smithsonian Institution National Anthropological Archives.)

Navajo dry painting for Male Shooting Way. Mother Earth is blue, and Father Sky is black. The crossed zigzag lines across Father Sky's chest represent the Milky Way. Stellar patterns on the body may represent known Navajo constellations. The lowest two groups appear to represent Rabbit Tracks (lower part of Scorpio) and Dilyehe (Pleiades). (Courtesy Smithsonian Institution National Anthropological Archives.)

Timucua Indians in Florida celebrating the end of the winter season. According to the French artist Jacques Le Moyne, who accompanied French explorers in 1564, every year in late February the Timucua would stuff the skin of a stag with the best of edible roots and other food, and hang wreaths of fruit around its neck. Then, placing it atop a tree with the head and breast facing the sunrise, they would offer prayers to the sun for fertility and increase in the coming growing season. (Courtesy Smithsonian Institution National Anthropological Archives.)

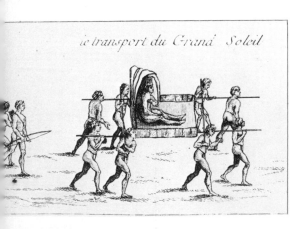

le transport du Grand Soleil

Conveyance of the Great Sun of the Natchez Indians (after Du Pratz, who was in Louisiana from 1718 to 1734). This drawing depicts the manner in which Great Sun, the chief of the Natchez, was conveyed to the harvest festival. The chiefs of the Natchez were thought to have descended from the sun. Their dwellings were built on top of artificially constructed earthen mounds. Each morning, Great Sun would come to his doorway as soon as the sun appeared and, turning himself to the east, howl three times. Then he would smoke tobacco and blow it first to the sun and then to the other three directions. (Courtesy Smithsonian Institution National Anthropological Archives.)

Exterior of Pawnee earth lodge in which Buffalo and Lance dances were held. According to the Pawnee Owen Echo Hawk, this was one of the last earth lodges to be built. The Pawnee thought of their earth lodges as models of the cosmos. Traditionally, the roof of the Pawnee earth lodge was supported by four large posts representing the stars of the four directions. The circular roof represented the sky, and the doorway opened to the east and Morning Star, the most important and powerful Pawnee star god. (Courtesy Smithsonian Institution National Anthropological Archives.)

Serpent Mound in south-central Ohio. Built by the so-called Adena culture, which flourished in the first millennium B.C., this is perhaps the most unusual and beautiful of the earthworks found throughout the central and southeastern states. Although this effigy mound has no obvious celestial connection, it was built by a culture whose burial practices suggest a marked concentration on ritual. The Adena built hundreds of conical burial mounds and circular earthen embankments. None of these have been adequately studied for their possible astronomical connections. (Aerial photo by Dache M. Reeves, January 20, 1934. Courtesy Smithsonian Institution National Anthropological Archives.)

A reconstructed house (House I/71) at the Incinerator Site in Dayton, Ohio. This thatched-roof dwelling represents archaeologists' interpretation of the original house form at the site. This house contains a hole for a small post that, on April 24 and August 20, lines up with the hole for a much larger post in the village plaza. These dates signal, respectively, the appropriate times in this region to start planting corn and to harvest the green corn used in a green corn ceremony. (Courtesy Dayton Museum of Natural History.)

Newark Earth Works, Newark, Ohio. Built by the Hopewell people, a culture of mound builders that came after the Adena, this site and a related one nearby may be astronomically aligned. This one has been used for a golf course since the 1930s. These and similar earthworks often enclose areas of up to 50 acres. The circular earthwork encloses about 20 acres and the octagon about 50 acres. Although several investigators have suggested that these and other earthen mounds might be deliberately astronomically aligned, relatively little systematic research has been done on these unusual structures. (Aerial photo by Dache M. Reeves, January 31, 1934. Courtesy Smithsonian Institution National Anthropological Archives.)

8 Omens of the Sky: Bright Star and Crescent

A Remarkable Celestial Appearance

Reckoning by the Julian calendar, it would have been the morning of July 4, 1054; the place, a fertile canyon in western New Mexico. Well before dawn, the sun priest arose quietly from his thin sleeping mat, and wrapping himself in a turkey feather blanket to ward off the early morning chill, he passed through the doorway and out onto the plaza. The stars shone with their customary radiance. There was not a cloud in the sky. He could easily make out the constellation Seeds in the brightening eastern horizon.[1] As the priest strode through the plaza, taking by long habit the swiftest route to the eastern side of the Pueblo village, he witnessed the waning crescent moon just peeking above the horizon. In two more days, he figured, the moon's cycle would again be completed. As he walked quietly along the path leading to the sun shrine that had been visited each morning by his father and his father's father, and countless generations before that, he thought about the summer solstice festival that had ended eight days earlier. The gods had entered the spirits of the dancers who impersonated them especially strongly this year. Already the effects of the rain they had brought with them had produced striking results on the corn. The lamb's-quarters and the rice grass that they normally gathered were more abundant than usual this year. The harvest would be especially good. Usually, at this time of year, the priest's thoughts would be centered on the ripening crops. By now his eyes would be intent on picking out the best patches of squawberry along the trail for his mate to gather for their family. But today was different. Today was special.

Thoughts of the harvest had taken second place to his fascination with the strange phenomenon he had been watching in the sky for the past few mornings. A thrill of excitement gripped him and he increased his pace. For several days now, he had been watching an unusual new star, one that grew brighter each day. What would he see this morning? As he mused, he nearly passed beyond the sacred spring to the right of the path. Stopping short, he drew cornmeal from the pouch at his waist and, following his usual ritual, cast a pinch to each of the six directions in turn — northwest, southwest, southeast, northeast, up, and down. Schooled by long habit, the priest's motions were smooth and swift. Automatically and almost absent-mindedly, he said the usual prayer and walked on. As he left the spring, he noted that the crescent moon was fully above the horizon and its light now nearly obscured the star group Seeds. His excitement grew rapidly. Just peeking over the horizon less than a thumb's breadth to the south of the moon, the brilliant star rose once again. He stopped momentarily to watch, transfixed and fascinated by the colorful spectacle. As the star moved upward through the thin haze along the horizon, it took on the most dazzlingly radiant colors. First red, then green, then blue, just as Morning Star often did as it rose preceding Sun Father. He nearly ran along the last few yards to his usual sun watching place.

As the puzzling star continued to rise above the horizon, moving slowly up and to the right, the rapid color changes ceased and it now shown with an unexcelled luster. Startling were the conjunction of the crescent moon and this unusually brilliant star. A feeling of awe and wonder awoke within him. Then his analytical bent, which made him such an accurate forecaster of the winds and rain, the canniness that made him the most respected member of the village, took over. What could this mean, this strange appearance? This was surely a sign! But whether it was for good or ill he could not yet decide. It was not Morning Star, of this he was sure. Nor was it any of the other bright wandering stars that he had observed. None of these stars was ever *this* bright.

The moon, changeable creature that she is, moved slowly away from the new star until she, at sunup, was nearly a hand's breadth away. Sunrise was almost a disappointment after the thrill of watching this remarkable conjunction of the crescent moon and the bright interloper appearing along the horizon. As he prayed to Sun Father, he watched him dutifully, first a bright speckling gleam above the distant hills, then blinding, furious incandescence. Carefully noting the place of Sun Father's first gleam, he cut another notch in the pinewood calendar he kept at the shrine and, more thoughtfully than usual, returned to the village.

With the new star still shining brightly in the morning sky, the sun priest hurried into the pueblo to announce the new day and to call the village elders into consultation. The arrival of the star was surely a significant omen, but what it meant was still not clear to him. In all of his years as sun priest (he had now seen thirty-two winter turnings of Sun Father), nothing quite like this had ever appeared in the sky. Whatever he and his fellow priests decided about the significance of the star, he had already determined to paint a record of it on the canyon wall at the sun shrine.

That same morning, far, far to the west, Chinese astronomers to the Emperor Chih-ho prepared to retire, their nightly watch nearly complete.[2] The eastern sky was already brightening and the crescent moon was high in the sky. Pen and ink in hand, the scribe was completing the night's report when the eastern observer noticed an odd brightening on the horizon. His attention drawn by the unusual light, he watched in fascination as the same bright star that the Anasazi priest much further east had witnessed near the crescent moon rose above the horizon. Knowing by experience that it was no planet, he watched the bright object closely. Because the eastern sky had been rather cloudy for the past several mornings, he could not say whether or for how long it had been there before this first appearance.

A great excitement took hold of him. This interloper, or guest star, was brighter than Venus. It was near T'ien-kuan (the Western star Zeta Tauri in the constellation Taurus). Carefully noting its position in his observing book, he turned his attention to its color. Yes, he could detect an unmistakable yellow tint. This was indeed a good omen.

In their excitement, the Chinese observers did not connect its appearance to the crescent moon, which had risen much earlier than the star. Their interest, unlike the North American sun priest, was in finding its place among the stars for future reference. The moon moves around too much to serve as a steady reference for other celestial appearances.

As the sun rose and caused all other stars to disappear, they were surprised to see the new star still shining brightly against the blue sky. Truly this was a remarkable object, one that was later much discussed throughout the empire, for its appearance was also noticed by the common man as well. It stayed visible even in day-time for another twenty-two days. The guest star continued to be the source of considerable interest and curiosity for the Chinese as-tronomers even longer, for it did not disappear from the night sky for almost two years. Never in any of their lifetimes had they witnessed such a bright star. As they all knew from the histories, some forty-eight years earlier a very bright "auspicious star" had appeared that had portended good tidings for the emperor and the state. As profes-sional astronomers, appointed directly by the emperor, these men were charged with the duty of observing the heavens, especially in order to watch for portents or signs from which to predict the future. They had recorded comets, meteors, and new stars of all descrip-tions; their political import had been read and evaluated by the emperor's special advisers. This guest star was certainly no excep-tion. They read its appearance as an omen that "there was a person of great worth" in the empire (the emperor). They were especially excited because the yellow color of the guest star was also the impe-rial color for the Sung dynasty.

The Supernova:
From Ancient Observations to Modern Astrophysics

The preceding hypothetical accounts are based largely on a histor-ical Chinese sighting of a "guest star" that was originally recorded by Chinese astronomers on July 4, 1054. Astronomers still find the de-tails of their sightings fascinating. Western astronomers first became interested in the Chinese account when they discovered that it was probably the precursor to the Crab Nebula, a bright, rapidly expand-ing gas cloud in the constellation Taurus.

Originally discovered by the telescopic observations of amateur British astronomer John Bevis in 1731, two centuries later the gas-eous object was shown by American astronomer John Duncan to be expanding outward. Shortly afterward another American as-tronomer, Edwin Hubble, suggested that the expanding Crab Nebula and the Chinese guest star that had been seen in the same part of the sky were different stages of a vast stellar explosion called a supernova.

From the available evidence of recent stars that have suddenly brightened and then faded slowly from sight, astronomers postulate that a supernova occurs when a massive star has used up most of its energy-producing capacities and collapses upon itself. The resulting implosion produces an enormous density in the star's core that results in an extremely high temperature near the center. Such a sudden increase in temperature causes the star to explode and throw off much of its outer envelope. The result of such an energetic explosion is an expanding gas cloud such as the Crab Nebula, and a central star that is then reduced in mass. The extreme loss of energy and mass causes the star to collapse a second time, this time to form a pulsar, or possibly even a black hole.

The Crab Nebula today is an unusual celestial object and is the target of a great deal of astrophysical research. It is composed of an outer shell of bright red filaments expanding rapidly at about 1300 miles per second, and an inner core that is also expanding but has an amorphous blue-white structure. At the speed at which the Crab expands it would take an object leaving the earth somewhat over two hours to reach the sun 94 million miles away.

For our purposes, it is the early stages of the supernova explosion that are of most interest because only then was it visible to the naked eye. Who was looking at and recording celestial phenomena in A.D. 1054?

Nearly the only written accounts of its sighting are found in the Oriental records. This may be because Western Europe was in the throes of the Dark Ages, and scientific observation and discovery were at a low ebb. By contrast, for unscientific reasons, observational astronomy flourished in the Orient. In addition to keeping the calendar, teams of astronomers were charged with recording every single changing or unusual sky event for divinatory purposes. As with European astrology, the Chinese and Japanese believed that the workings of the celestial sphere could be read for clues about the future. They methodically recorded and transcribed the occurrences of such diverse and physically quite different phenomena as eclipses of the sun, aurorae, unusual noises, extraordinary clouds, comets, novae, and supernovae. The latter were characterized in their records as "auspicious stars," "ominous stars," or simply "guest stars," depending on their physical appearance, duration, and the prevailing political situation.[3]

Everything we now know about the early stages of the Crab Nebula and many other supernovae derives from chronicles compiled by Oriental astronomers. There is an unexpected amount of scientific data in those records. Not only did the Oriental astronomers map positions of sky objects with great care, they were skilled at estimating stellar magnitudes as well. Both the Chinese and the Japanese observed the guest star in Taurus at different times; when a few apparent transcribing errors are taken into account, their stories are consistent with each other and with the identification of the guest star as the supernova beginning of the Crab Nebula.[4]

The Japanese made the first recorded sighting of the supernova about a week before it reached maximum intensity. They compared the light of the new star to Jupiter's magnitude ($m = -2.6$), which is never as bright as Venus can be. Surviving Japanese records fail to mention the star again; the Chinese annals not only record its brightest appearance on July 4 but also note its eventual disappearance from the night sky 653 days later. As the *Sung-Hui-Yao Annal* declares:

> During the 3rd month of the 1st year of the Chia-yu reign period the Director of the Astronomical Bureau said, "The guest star has vanished which is an omen of the departure of the guest." Earlier, during the 5th month in the 1st year of the Chih-ho reign period [the guest star] appeared in the morning in the east guarding T'ien-kuan. It was visible in the daytime, like Venus. It had pointed rays on all sides [literally, "in the four directions"] and its colour was reddish-white. Altogether it was visible for 23 days.[5]

Taken together, these Japanese and Chinese written records tell us that a few days prior to July 4, 1054, a star as bright as Jupiter appeared in the constellation Taurus. Around July 4, it reached its maximum brightness (probably somewhat brighter than Venus) and remained visible in the daytime sky for twenty-three days. The guest star slowly faded in brightness until April 17, 1056, when it finally disappeared from the night sky.

There is a remarkable bit of astrophysical data here, all gathered without benefit of a telescope. Because of these observations, we are able to date the birth of the Crab Nebula quite precisely. In addition, we can also match its observed brightness at different times with "light curves" of recently studied supernovae in order to determine its type and, from that, to guess at its early physical characteristics.

A Near Eastern Record of the Supernova

The brightness of the supernova and its long stay in the sky make it especially puzzling that so few records of its occurrence exist in the world. Indeed, until a few years ago, it was thought that the only historical records of its existence were from the Orient. It now seems as though we have looked only at one mode of chronicling. To argue that in 1054 Europe was in the middle of the Dark Ages hardly seems persuasive. After all, the comet of 1066 was clearly recorded on the Bayeaux tapestry, an impressive artistic rendering of the events surrounding the Norman invasion of England. Only twelve years separates these two events. It is conceivable that parts of Europe were

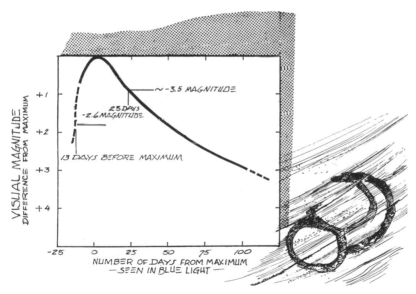

Light curve of Crab Nebula supernova inferred from Japanese and Chinese visual observations, A.D. 1054. Recorded by Japanese and Chinese astronomers, and a Middle Eastern medical doctor, the supernova also may have been recorded by Native Americans. (After John C. Brandt and Ray A. Williamson, "The 1054 Supernova and Native American Rock Art." *Archaeoastronomy, Supplement to the Journal for the History of Astronomy* 10 [1979]: S1–S38.)

under cloud cover during most of the time from July 4 to August 4, 1054, but it seems unlikely that the skies over all of Europe *and* the Arab lands to the south were so obscured. Astronomers, however, have searched and searched in vain until recently for a single record, however obscure, of this impressive event.

Sometimes the pursuit of science follows circuitous paths. In 1978, a *Newsweek* article mentioning astronomer John Brandt's and my interest in the supernova and citing the curious absence of records from Europe brought the problem to the attention of Israeli medical historians Elizabeth and Alfred Lieber. They had studied the medical journal of Ibn Butlan, a Christian doctor who traveled throughout the Near East in the eleventh century. Butlan apparently saw the star, for he described the appearance of a bright star in the constellation Gemini in A.D. 1054. Since the plague was raging in Constantinople at that time, Butlan, like the Chinese astrologers, thought there might have been a causal connection between the appearance of the star and the plague. He wrote:

> One of the well-known epidemics of our time is that which occurred when the spectacular star appeared in Gemini in the year 446 H. [A.D. 12 April 1054–1 April 1055]. In the autumn of that year fourteen thousand people were buried in [the cemetery of] the Church of [St.] Luke, after all the [other] cemeteries in Constantinople had been filled.
>
> As this spectacular star appeared in the sign of Gemini which is the ascendant of Egypt, it caused the epidemic to break out in Fustat [old Cairo] when the Nile was low, at the time of its appearance in the year 445 H. [23 April 1053–11 April 1054]. Thus Ptolemy's prediction came true: "Woe to the people of Egypt when one of the comets appears threateningly in Gemini!" . . . And this confirmed the wisdom of Ptolemy in saying: "When Saturn and Mars are in conjunction in the sign of Cancer the world will be shaken."[6]

Although his grasp of medical principles may have been poor, Butlan can be thanked for recording an appearance that Western astronomers apparently ignored. Butlan, in following the accepted medical practice of his day by watching the skies for signs of impending health or illness, left us an unexpected astronomical legacy.

Potential Native American Observations of the Supernova

The Anasazi were acute observers of the sky. So also were other Native American groups. Could they also have seen and recorded the "guest star"? A chance discovery in 1955 by astronomical photographer Bill Miller makes such a possibility seem probable.[7] While visiting archaeological sites in northern Arizona, he witnessed two intriguing examples of Native American rock art, one a petroglyph and the other a pictograph. Both seemed to represent the moon and some other celestial object, perhaps a star. The pictograph, however, presented an impossible physical situation. Stars can never come between the moon and the earth. Perhaps the images were an attempt to depict the near conjunction of an extremely bright star and the moon. In such a case, the bright star might appear to "spill over" onto the moon.

The answer to the puzzle may lie in the conjunction of the crescent moon and the guest star. The Chinese did not mention the phase of the moon, but with modern, high-speed computers, it is fairly simple to discover the moon's phase on July 4, 1054. When Miller checked this possibility, he found that the waning crescent moon came within 2° of the guest star (a distance about four times the diameter of the moon).

In the fictional account, I have described the event as any southwestern observer might have seen it. Actually, this spectacular conjunction would have been visible throughout all of western North America, from the Rockies to the California coast, from British Columbia to Baja California. Miller's examples are from northern Arizona, but many other possible supernova records are now known to exist in Baja California, California, Utah, Nevada, New Mexico, and Texas. Pecked or incised, painted in charcoal or hematite (a reddish pigment made from iron oxide), these images represent some of the earliest known Native American depictions of sky objects. Although they cannot yet be dated accurately, most examples we have discovered are found near habitation sites dating from the same era as the 1054 supernova.

Perhaps the best example of one of these possible supernova records is at the same site I described in chapter 5 as a possible sun watching site. The glyph panel exists on an isolated wall of Chaco Canyon in New Mexico. Situated a few hundred yards from the remarkable ellipsoidal Anasazi town of Penasco Blanco, the glyphs are painted on a sandstone outcrop in the canyon. Penasco Blanco is high above them on the mesa top.

The paintings are located about six yards above the canyon floor on the underside of an overhanging ledge and are painted with a reddish-brown pigment that appears to be hematite, which is commonly found in small deposits in the canyon. The image of a hand just above the crescent, which, according to Pueblo practice, marks the spot as sacred, is nearly life-sized. Just below the glyphs on the vertical wall is the sun symbol I described in chapter 5 — a painting of three concentric circles with a dot in the center. Taken as a whole, these glyphs probably mark a sacred sun watching site, a possibility made especially plausible by the existence of appropriate horizon features for sun watching on the eastern horizon. It also seems to be an especially striking record of the A.D. 1054 event.

These glyphs nearly exactly reproduce the astronomical circumstances of July 4, 1054. The star image appears south of the crescent, and the horns of the moon point westward. Furthermore, when the crescent and star were first seen, the sun was still below the horizon. This, too, is represented by the Chaco Canyon glyphs. The sun glyph appears below the star and crescent on the vertical wall, an apparent attempt to place the sun symbol below the horizon.

Although the Pueblo ruins of Chaco Canyon National Historical Park have been known to archaeologists for about a century, this remarkable glyph was recorded only in the early 1970s when a survey team of archaeologists scoured the entire monument for any evidence of prior occupation.

The workings of science are often surprising and full of false starts. The process is seldom the textbook case of discovery, hypothesis, and testing that we learn in the classroom. In the case of the Chaco glyph, the workings of chance also played a strong part in the scientific process. A park ranger who was also an amateur astronomer, Clarion Cochran, heard about the find from the survey team, photographed it, and measured it. He noted its similarity to Miller's crescent-star example and thought that it, too, might symbolize the remarkable appearance of the Crab supernova. His interest was the circumstance that brought the painting to the attention of archaeoastronomers.[8]

Shortly afterward, I happened to visit the canyon to investigate Casa Rinconada, Pueblo Bonito, and other ancient ruins in order to determine their alignments. I was, to say the least, surprised and excited to discover from Cochran that there might be a record of the

Distribution of suspected Native American records of the 1054 supernova.
In western North America, the supernova would have been seen near the
rising crescent moon just before sunrise. By the time the supernova was
visible in China, the moon had moved several degrees away from the
supernova.

1054 supernova in the canyon. When he showed it to me, this painting, perhaps deeply sacred to its makers, imparted a sense of awe
and wonder to me. Was this sheltered glyph indeed an ancient painting of the supernova put there to memorialize its appearance? Was it
instead just a marker for a sacred sun watching place? Perhaps it
served both purposes. These and similar questions crowded my
mind as I investigated this site with Cochran in 1972. Since then,

many other potential supernova records have been discovered in the West and Southwest, but none that so beautifully portray the circumstances of that July morning in 1054.

The Hypothesis Considered

The hypothesis that this and similar glyphs represent the supernova has its roots in several disparate facts. First, Native Americans followed the daily and yearly movements of the sun, moon, and stars with deep interest, and were therefore extremely likely to have observed the supernova or any other unusual sky event. Second, the appearance of the crescent and the star together was a spectacular occurrence; it surely drew the attention of more than just the sky watcher whose duty it was to survey the sky regularly. Third, the occurrence of crescents in rock art is relatively rare, a circumstance that makes it unlikely that the crescents we do find simply represent the moon alone or with another ordinary star such as the morning star.

Not everyone accepts this hypothesis for the origin of the crescent-star glyphs.[9] One strong objection is that none of the glyphs has yet been firmly dated. Even though most of them appear near ruins that were occupied at the time of the supernova, the glyphs themselves could have been placed there any time before or after the 1054 event. Another counterargument holds that the American Indians, unlike their Chinese contemporaries, were not inclined to record *unusual* events, no matter how spectacular. They were much more likely to record the common cyclical rhythms of the sky. By this hypothesis, the crescent-star association could represent the fairly common association of the crescent phase of the moon with the morning star. This position is based on the use of ethnographic analogy, a potentially powerful tool for analyzing an archaeological site. By looking at the historic practices of a group, we can learn about what to expect in analyzing their ancestors' material remains. I have used ethnographic analogy extensively in attempting to understand the many astronomical alignments my colleagues and I have found. Like all tools, however, it must be used judiciously.

For example, by using recent historic practices as a guide to what to look for in Anasazi buildings, one might completely overlook the very important cardinal alignments of Casa Rinconada in Chaco Canyon, because it is the intercardinals that have been most important in historic practice. Ironically, it was our ethnocentric view that the cardinal directions were important that led our archaeoastronomy team to look for and recognize such alignments there.

Another problem in using ethnographic analogy is that even among historic groups there are significant differences that make broad generalizations far too inexact. Though they have a keen interest in the day-to-day, and tend to de-emphasize the unusual occurrences of nature and society, the Pueblo of the recent past also paid a certain amount of attention to such infrequent unusual celestial events as eclipses. The Tewa of the Rio Grande, for instance, dreaded the eclipse of the sun, an event that takes place in a given area only a few times in a lifetime. According to their explanation of the event, when the burning shield of the Sun Father gives only a little light, he has moved away from the earth in displeasure with the people of this world who are fighting. When this happens, the Tewa fear that he will retire to his house in the underworld (just as he does at night) and never reappear. They even devised a ceremony to propitiate the sun and implore him to remain in his daily cycle. Their prayer to the sun during this ritual emphasizes what the loss of the sun would mean to them.

Let the earth be covered with all things beautiful. All trees, plants, flowers. Let the deer, antelope, mountain sheep and turkey roam over the earth that we may have food in plenty for our children. Let the eagle soar over the earth that we may have plumes to offer to our gods. Refresh our mother earth with rains that she may be happy.[10]

The Sky in Native American Art

It seems clear that with their well-developed observational interests, the North American native sky watchers must have witnessed more than just eclipses. They must have noted comets, novae, and other spectacular sky events as well. The Tewa, for instance, call comets "tailed stars" and view them as interlopers in the sky. "The comet seen in November, 1910 [Halley's comet], excited this interest of the Tewa."[11] The question is, what did they make of unusual appearances, and more important, just what celestial objects did Native Americans record and in what form? We are beginning to discover that celestial motifs play an important role in Native American art of all forms.

Among prehistoric and historic groups in the West and Southwest especially, the use of astronomical symbols is common. The Navajo use celestial motifs in their ceremonial objects, as well as on dry paintings. In addition, they also depicted the sun, moon, and stars in their rock art. Astronomical symbols abound in the kiva wall paintings and kiva altars of the Pueblo Indians as they were observed at the turn of the century by travelers and anthropologists. Unfortunately, largely because of the treatment these men and women accorded the native people they studied, many sacred objects or places are no longer available for scrutiny. The whites were often quite capable of intruding uninvited into sacred places. Lieutenant J. G. Bourke of the U.S. Army recorded various mythical or sacred beings as decorating the walls of a kiva at one of the Hopi pueblos. Among these were paintings of the sun, the moon, and the morning and evening stars. Though we may be grateful for some of his data today, his methods leave much to be desired. While at Santo Domingo Pueblo along the Rio Grande in New Mexico, Bourke attempted to gain entrance to secret kiva ceremonies by force and sheer bravado. As he frankly tells us, his rude behavior was reciprocated by like actions of his hosts.

As it might be a good thing to obtain a correct description of the little that was transpiring within the Estufas (kivas), Moran and I laid our heads together, and concluded that an attempt should be made to penetrate the larger edifice.

Our note-books were gripped tightly in one hand, and our sharpened pencils in the other, the theory of our advance being that, with boldness and celerity, we might gain an entrance and jot down a few memoranda of value before the preoccupied savages could discover and expel us.

My pulse beat high as we reached the roof and passed the sacred standard floating from the top of the ladder. Everything looked propitious, and I had gotten down four rungs of the ladder, within two of the bottom, when a yell was raised, repeated from point to point in warning tones, and from every conceivable spot — from out of the earth as it seemed to me — Indians fairly boiled.

The Estufa (kiva) itself buzzed like a hive of bees. Before I could count ten I was seized from above by the neck and shoulders, and from below by the legs and feet, and lifted or thrown out of the Estufa, the Indians yelling at the tops of their voices, "Que no entres, amigo, manana bueno" — "You mustn't enter, friend — to-morrow, to-morrow; you can come in to-morrow; it isn't good now."

There was no disguising the fact; I was "fired out," as the slang phrase is, and had to make the best of a bad bargain. My tailor had left too much "slack" in my pantaloons, and thus gave the Indians so much the better purchase when they seized me.[12]

As other early observers of Pueblo life also recorded, drawings and paintings of the sun, moon, and stars commonly appeared on kiva walls and on painted altar panels. In addition, the morning and evening star were also depicted in various forms, most often as an inflated four-pointed star. One particularly famous example is the sun watching shrine at the ancient village of Matsaki at Zuni Pueblo. On one level the symbols of sun, moon, and morning star that Frank Cushing, the anthropologist who lived in the pueblo for several years, saw there identified a place for sun watching, but they also served to remind the viewer that the sun, moon, and morning star themselves are sacred beings.

Astronomical symbols are also included by the historic Pueblo people on their ritual masks and headdresses. The Hopi kachinas Tawa, A'hul, A'Hote, and Sohu, which often bear paintings of the sun, moon, or star symbols, are also found today in surprising abundance in the modern paintings on display in the Hopi Cultural Center on Second Mesa. In attempting to revive the old traditions, the modern Hopi artists have resurrected the tradition of using flat earth colors and have incorporated ritual symbolism, much of which is astronomical, in their powerful paintings.

The Zuni kachina Hemucikwe sometimes has the morning star and a crescent painted on its mask. Further, headdresses worn by Zuni maidens at an August ceremony for rain depict the morning and evening stars, a crescent moon, and the sun. Finally, some modern potters, particularly those of San Ildefonso Pueblo in New Mexico, commonly make use of sun symbols on their finely decorated pottery.

Although celestial art is quite common among the southwestern tribes, they are by no means the only historic North American groups to demonstrate their interest in the sky through the medium of their art. Many Plains Indians (Sioux, Pawnee, Crow, Blackfoot, Kiowa, and Cheyenne) often decorated their lodges and tipis with stars, the sun, and the moon. Disks of white, black, or blue, as well as the more recognizable four-pointed crosses or small dots arranged in constellation patterns, may represent stars. The sun is usually shown as a yellow disk, while the moon may be represented either as a crescent or a colored disk.

Celestial motifs are common on Plains Indian war shields as well. One particularly fine Kiowa shield, a model of which is retained in the Smithsonian Institution collection, depicts the rays of the sun on one half of the shield, the stars at night on the other half of the shield, and a crescent moon and the Pleiades along the center line between them.

Prehistoric Art

Astronomical motifs from prehistoric times are somewhat less common but are nonetheless identifiable. The prehistoric Hopi of Siky-atki village decorated some of their pottery with stars, the sun, and occasionally the moon. The Mimbres of southern Arizona, who produced great quantities of finely wrought, delicately painted pottery also made use of astronomical motifs.

The sun is the celestial object most commonly represented in the prehistoric rock art of Arizona and New Mexico. Concentric circles, rayed circles, and quartered circles are all said to represent the sun. Some of the sun glyphs, of course, appear to mark sun watching sites. Some, though, may be more artistic in nature, carved or painted on the rock surfaces to satisfy an urge to represent the power of the sun. Stars seem to be particularly numerous among the abundant rock art panels along the Rio Grande in central and southern New Mexico. There, even a few crescents are seen. Crescents, stars, and the sun may be depicted independently or incorporated into other figures such as shields or animals. The prehistoric painted kivas of Kuaua and Pottery Mound near Albuquerque or of Awatobi on the Hopi reservation also contain celestial motifs shown explicitly or in the guise of anthropomorphic figures. The Utes and earlier Fremont cultures of eastern Utah also depicted the sun and stars in rock art.

In California, and along the Northwest Coast, the sun and stars are pictured along with deer, bighorn sheep, and human figures. One unusual panel at a site called Fern Cave in central California seems to show the 1054 supernova in two stages: when the star had just risen after the rising of the crescent moon and later after the crescent had moved away from the star.

It may seem surprising that pictographs of the sky might appear within the dark confines of a cave, under the surface of the ground. This cave was formed many thousands of years ago when a lava flow poured over the region. Trapped gases within the lava turned the interior of the flow into a lava "tube." Later, erosion and natural seepage of water opened an entrance into the tube and eventually the natives of the area discovered it and occupied it. One particularly good reason for drawing on the walls of this cave was that it was the artists' home, or perhaps a place of spiritual retreat. Another, however, was that it was the only place around to protect their drawings. The area just outside the cave made an especially good place to view the whole sky. The region is scrub desert — totally devoid of obscuring trees or nearby mountains. It is easy to imagine the native astronomer being greeted by the spectacular predawn phenomenon and returning to his home to paint the event in charcoal, his only medium, on the rough inner wall of the cave.

Other rock art in California, some of it very abstract in design, may represent specific constellations.[13] According to this theory, these glyphs, found with numerous realistic portrayals of animals, birds, and men on or near game trails, may have been an important component of their makers' hunting magic. Some examples of these "constellation figures" that have been investigated are more convincing than others. Indeed, the whole hypothesis is open to the criticism that in searching for design correspondences to stellar patterns one may find many accidental similarities of form in any two sets of random patterns.

Although they have not been particularly well studied to date for their astronomical content, enough examples of celestial motifs in Indian art occur across the continent, including the Midwest and East, to demonstrate that the sun, moon, stars, and even comets were the subject of considerable artistic interest. In deciding whether prehistoric Native Americans might have recorded the 1054 supernova, it would be useful to know whether they used their art to record celestial *events*. Picturing the sun, moon, or stars isolated from a particular event requires a wholly different attitude toward the world than making a record of it. The latter assumes the need or desire to remember or commemorate events, as happened, for example, in making the Bayeaux tapestry. The artists included a rendition of Halley's comet[14] that had appeared in the same year as the Norman invasion of England and must have seemed a portent or symbol of disaster for the British and of victory for William the Conqueror. Recording such events might have been a reference for dating or perhaps an expression of a wish to leave a record of certain events for the future.

The scanty evidence available suggests that Native Americans did record particular *events*. This is relatively rare, but we know of at least two historic examples: the unmistakable paintings of the Leonid meteor shower of 1833 made on buffalo skin by the Dakota Sioux and a depiction of the solar eclipse of August 7, 1869. The Dakota Sioux and other Plains Indian groups were interested in both these ephemeral events and used records of them as part of their so-called winter count to remind them of other events that took place during the same year.

Comets also are unusual occurrences and spectacular in their own way. They, too, seem to have been recorded. Among the wonderful cave paintings of the California Chumash are several figures that seem to represent comets. Other examples exist in California and Nevada in the form of petroglyphs. Yet another has been photographed in New Mexico near Los Alamos. The Navajo, who depict many celestial objects in their dry paintings, rarely use comets, as they are considered abnormal, and "acting contrary to established laws";[15] they are therefore inappropriate to a healing ceremony. They are only used when the Navajo Singer is using the image to help rid the patient of bad dreams or evil influences.

The Dating Problem

If it were possible to date a suspected supernova record accurately, the question of whether it represented the guest star's appearance could be solved. At the very least the range of options could be limited. However, the best that anyone has been able to do in dating rock art is to look at the style, the mode of execution, and the other nearby rock art. With these indications, a rough date can be suggested. Dating nearby habitations provides another clue. The difficulty with this last approach is that it is often only a guess whether the ruins and the glyph are contemporaneous. Paintings with an organic base could in theory be dated by carbon 14 dating methods, but so much of the pigment would be needed to determine the date accurately that the very process would destroy the painting.

For petroglyphs, the situation is more promising. Nuclear technology may eventually come to the aid of rock art research with a process called neutron activation analysis.[16] Boulders that have been exposed to the weather for a long period of time develop a brownish coating called desert varnish, caused by minerals leaching out of the rock over time. The thickness of this coating is in direct proportion to the length of time the surface has been exposed to the weather. After this coating is cut away in the process of making a petroglyph, the now "clean" surface begins to develop a new coating of desert varnish. By measuring the relative thickness of the two coatings — that on the petroglyph and that on the rock surface nearby — it would be possible to date the petroglyph. Only laboratory specimens have been dated so far, but as techniques improve, it may be possible to carry a nondestructive device into the field to measure the relative age of the petroglyphs.

Other, much cruder, methods of estimating the dates of rock art exist, such as comparing the relative amounts of lichen growing over a petroglyph surface, or the superimposition of one painting style over another. Neither these nor the more accurate methods, however, can be used to determine specific dates directly, such as the dates of possible supernova records. Improved methods, however, increase the prospect of using a variety of evidence to date certain glyphs.

In addition to proving the hypothesis that Native Americans recorded the supernova, one of the reasons it is of interest to date a few putative supernova records is that it would be useful to turn the problem around and use those records to date nearby glyphs and habitation. For example, many of the rock paintings of Baja California are not even roughly datable because so few material remains are available to study, and because the rugged country of the peninsula is particularly difficult to work in. Photographer and adventurer Harry Crosby has made an extensive study of the rock art of Baja California. One out-of-the-way painting in particular drew his interest because it may hold the key to dating other glyphs in the area. No buildings exist nearby, nor are there even many identifiable campsites. What material remains do exist are not well studied. The glyph that caught Crosby's attention is of a crescent and a round object with radiating rays next to it. The crescent seems to have been intended as a representation of the moon, since the remaining part of the circle is filled in by a faint red pigment, much as the dark part of the moon's surface is illuminated by earth light when the moon is in waning or waxing crescent phase. The rayed circle, which Crosby interprets to be a star, is to the right of the crescent.

If, as Crosby argues, the glyph depicts an event, then there is every likelihood that it is a record of the 1054 explosion. He reached this conclusion because the art of this area of Baja California is characterized by the "rarity of abstract symbols of any sort" and a "propensity for depicting real objects such as men, animals, arrows and spears."[17] Because conjunction of the moon and bright planets is a fairly common occurrence, we would expect to find more pictures of this kind if the prehistoric painters of these pictographs habitually depicted astronomical events. The very meager evidence now available for the dates of habitation of the area points to the years between A.D. 500 and 1500, a time period that includes the 1054 event.

Another intriguing petroglyph panel owned by a private collector presents us with another way to use the 1054 event to solve an anthropological problem. Unfortunately, in this case the panel was long ago removed from its surrounding glyphs. In the process, either by accident or intention, the records of its origin were lost. Fortunately, however, the rock itself contains all that is needed to place it as originating from a rather confined geographical area. The drawings are pecked on an unusual sort of rock, Moenkopi shale, which is found in only two large deposits, both northeast of Flagstaff, Arizona. This places it in an area inhabited by the Hopi in prehistoric times.[18]

The lizard, bear paw, snake, crane, and turtle are all Hopi clan symbols. Their presence here indicates that the glyphs were made by a Hopi hand. The star and crescent appear above three mountains. Traditionally, the San Francisco Peaks are represented in Hopi art by three similar humps. These mountains are important to the Hopi primarily because they are the traditional home of the rain spirits, the kachinas represented in Hopi festivals by the masked dancers. Art historian Seymour Koenig theorizes that the prehistoric Hopi artist who probably created the glyph would have been looking east, since in all likelihood the glyph was removed from a shale deposit west of the San Francisco Mountains. The presence of the clan symbols could mean that these particular clans were in their western migration in 1054 when the supernova appeared.

What interested Koenig about this glyph, perhaps more than the possibility that it is a record of the supernova explosion, is the male figure on the left-hand side of the panel. It appears to be wearing a mask similar to the Hopi kachinas of today. If so, and if the star and crescent represent the supernova, the panel would also be evidence of a very early introduction of the kachina cult into the Southwest. Hitherto, Polly and Curt Schaafsma have argued in their study of rock art along the Rio Grande in New Mexico and Texas that the kachina cult came up from Mexico by way of the Rio Grande and spread westward to the Hopi villages, where it became more highly developed and elaborate than in the eastern Pueblo villages along the Rio Grande.[19] Koenig's example would be contrary evidence to their claim. Whoever turns out to be correct in the light of further study, it is clear that the supernova event can provide an important dating mechanism if any of the various records we have assembled can be shown to be depictions of it.

Perhaps the greatest value in these studies, interestingly enough, lies not in whether they aid in proving this hypothesis but in the peripheral questions that have been raised or answered as the research has proceeded — questions of the age of certain petroglyphs and pictographs as well as the role of astronomical motifs in Native American rock art and culture. Perhaps eventually we will be able to date other presently undated pictographs and petroglyphs because a nearby glyph is an unmistakable record of the supernova.

Some astronomers have complained that too much emphasis has been placed on studies of the Crab Nebula to the detriment of other interesting supernova remnants. The Crab Nebula has certainly had its share of attention, perhaps even more than its share. But in studying the records and possible records of its appearance in 1054, we are led to understand a great deal more than the simple data about the physical details of the explosion. Because such a spectacular appearance is unique, it gives us a chance to explore the intellectual interests of eleventh-century peoples all over the world. Who recorded these events and why, and what impact they might have had on the lives of men and women, are questions surely worth investigating for their own sake.

The Disappearance of This Prehistoric Art

Students of Native American rock art, amateur and professional alike, face an increasingly difficult time in appreciating or attempting to understand the content of rock art. At the same time as knowledge grows, the body of art upon which the analysis rests is being chipped, eroded, carved, or even shot away. One of my early trips to investigate a possible supernova record proved a sad initiation to the problem of the losses we have already sustained in some areas. In attempting to show me a particularly fine rendition of a bird, my guide was shocked to discover it had disappeared, the apparent victim of a "collector" who had pried off the whole petroglyph. Not only did the vandal remove the bird from its location, but he or she badly damaged several other nearby petroglyphs in the process. Colonel Jim Bain of Albuquerque, who was my guide on this unhappy expedition, reported that such treatment was all too common in his experience. In his retirement years, Bain has catalogued thousands of New Mexican petroglyphs and pictographs, with the help of the many students he brings to similar rock art sites each year. Unfortunately, increasing population in the Southwest has resulted in greater destruction. At some sites, even portions of the rock are removed, as in this case. At others, panels are painted over, scratched, or used for target practice.

Recording the sites photographically, however, is an important resource for scholars in both the present and the future. They can use photographs or drawings to study the frequency of designs and styles, but these are a poor substitute for the original. Many subtleties of execution are often lost, as are important details of the design. Detailed studies of the modes of production require having access to the original art. So also does a full appreciation of the artistic content of a rock art panel. Beyond the possible losses to our opportunities for scholarly study, however, is the loss of a valuable heritage of artistic expression. Perhaps our increased awareness and understanding will bring with it an increased sensitivity to the need to preserve this important part of our Native American heritage for future generations to view, study, and enjoy.

If Seymour Koenig's example of Hopi rock art had been left in place so we could study it in the context of any other nearby images we might be much closer than we now are to answering the question of whether Native Americans witnessed and recorded the supernova explosion of 1054. As the evidence now stands, neither this nor any other example can *prove* the hypothesis.

9   Medicine Wheels and the Plains Indians

The Crow, Cheyenne and Sioux, Comanche, Kiowa, Blackfoot and Pawnee, and many other lesser-known Indian tribes who inhabited the Great Plains from the slopes of the Rockies east to Kansas and Missouri are generally thought of as the great Native American equestrians. To many around the world, it is the Plains Indian whose image comes to mind when they think of the American Indian — brilliant riders leading a charge of horses at dawn against a sleepy and off-guard U.S. Cavalry, or stealthy braves sneaking up to raid and plunder a fragile homestead. With war paint and feathered head-dresses, they are remembered as a people whose chief accomplishments were their ability to hunt buffalo, build tipis, and ride horses. This image is strongly supported by the movie scenarios but, of course, hardly touches the complexity of this real-life people who possessed a distinctive and diverse culture.

Though they contrived no written language and their artistic accomplishments were confined to a few highly portable and useful objects, like many other Native American groups, they had well-developed myths and folktales. They also possessed distinctive cosmologies and their own astronomy, which was well adapted to their needs for ritual and sustenance.

The phase of Plains Indian life we know the most about, of course, is that which developed after the Spaniards brought the horse to North America. This one addition alone changed their life immeasurably and in ways that made the Plains Indians of the eighteenth and nineteenth centuries a vastly different people from their forebears.

Although the arrival of the horse made them more mobile, even before Coronado the Plains people were constantly on the move, stopping at most only a few seasons before picking up and moving on again. In those days, they carried all they owned on their own backs or on a dog travois and walked from campground to campground. Though they hunted buffalo and deer, their ability to stalk and kill was severely limited by hunting on foot.

Because many of these tribes built no lasting habitations like their Anasazi neighbors in the Southwest, we know very little of their history. In particular, we are not even sure where the historic tribes originated. Their myths contain some geographical references, and their languages can often be traced linguistically to other tribes. In these ways their origins can be delineated or guessed at. On the whole, though, their nomadic ways and few cultural remains leave little for an archaeologist to study. There is one distinctive material feature, however, that is characteristic of the prehistoric Plains Indian. Throughout the Plains are thousands, perhaps millions, of stone circles 6 to 18 feet in diameter that these people built and left behind. We now call these stone circles tipi rings, on the assumption that they were used to hold down the edges of tipi covers and simply left behind as their users moved to another camp. The stones used were gathered from the local area, and most are about the size of a large loaf of bread. The existence today of the tipi rings, clustered in groups, indicates to archaeologists the size of the traveling groups, the size of their tipis, and their arrangement. This information, together with the bones of animals, broken pots, and other cultural remains from the campsites, gives us most of our information about the lives of the Plains Indians.

In addition to these numerous small stone circles, they also laid out mysterious large stone patterns: some of them simply long, low stone walls and alignments; others large stone effigies; and still others extended wheel-like structures that today have come to be called medicine wheels because of their association with sacred forces.

Medicine wheels are known in a variety of sizes and patterns, but most often they are made up of lines of loaf-sized stones laid out in a pattern that converges toward a central cairn (pile of rocks), much like the spokes of a wheel. They often have several other cairns along with them and sometimes circles of rock as well. Much larger than tipi rings, medicine wheels may approach 60 yards in diameter. Their central cairns can be as high as 3 or 4 yards and extend as much as 10 yards across — constructions that required several tons of rock to be lifted and carried to the site.

The effigies, the stone alignments, and the medicine wheels have long puzzled archaeologists, there being little additional cultural material nearby and no local lore to shed light on their function or meaning. A few years ago, however, astronomer John Eddy took an interest in the medicine wheels, and because of his careful investigations, we can now say with considerable assurance that at least some of the medicine wheels were built for calendric purposes.

The Bighorn Medicine Wheel

The Bighorn Medicine Wheel was the first of these structures that Eddy investigated.[1] At an altitude of nearly 10,000 feet, almost at the summit of Medicine Mountain in the Bighorn Mountains of Wyoming, it lies in an excellent location for sky watching — above the timberline with a horizon clear of human or natural obstructions. The wheel was apparently made by laboriously gathering numerous stones that lie about on the grassy terrain and piling them up in the wheel-like pattern. At its center lies a doughnut-shaped cairn nearly 10 feet in diameter, which is connected to the outer circle by twenty-eight spokelike straight lines. Six peripheral cairns, five outside the rim and one just inside, complete the pattern. These are much less massive than the central cairn, being only one to two courses high and 4 to 6 feet in diameter.

Eddy began his on-site investigation of the medicine wheel a few days before the summer solstice in 1972. The rigors of the local climate soon made themselves felt in the form of a summer snowstorm — more than a foot of snow fell on June 19. The wisdom of the wheel's builders was very soon evident. They had chosen a spot near the summit that not only boasted a clear view of the horizon but that is so swept by the wind that within a few hours the wheel was clear of snow. Two days later, Eddy was there again before dawn to observe and photograph the solstice sunrise.

What did Dr. Eddy expect to find on this frigid, windy morning? From an examination of an earlier map, and some initial calculations, he was convinced that it had been laid out along astronomical

Bighorn Medicine Wheel, summer solstice sunrise.

lines — in directions related to the summer solstice. At winter solstice, the other possibility suggested by the map, the summit area of Medicine Mountain is generally quite deep in snow, well above the height of the central cairn, so it could not have been used for sky observing.

His cold, uncomfortable wait for sunrise that morning was well rewarded, for as he stood just outside cairn E along a line between its center and the center of the central cairn, he watched the first gleam of the rising sun appear just above the center of the wheel. Hardly noticing the cold in his excitement, he photographed the phenomenon as the sun first appeared and then followed its path above the horizon and southward. By the time it reached the horizon, it was well south of the central cairn.

His sunset observations on the same day yielded similar confirmation of his measurements and calculations. In this case, while standing on cairn C he was elated to watch the sun set just to the south (left) of the central cairn's center. It was clear from his measurement and from his direct observation that the wheel might be designed to be used for observing the summer solstice. What about those other cairns? Solstice sunrise and sunset account for the sighting functions of only two of the auxiliary cairns.

Puzzled by that, Eddy investigated other possible pairings. Did any others demonstrate significant astronomical alignments? The available maps of the wheel, he had found, were woefully inadequate to the task of predicting astronomical significance. In some, the scale of the wheel was incorrect. In others, the angular relationships between the cairns were inaccurate. So, using a steel tape and a transit, and assisted by his family, he painstakingly remeasured the features of the wheel. In addition, he took care also to determine the altitude of the horizon around the wheel, for it is only by measuring both azimuth *and* altitude that it is possible to calculate which celestial objects might have risen along a given sight line.

The complexity of the potential alignments forced Eddy to eliminate as many of the cairn pairings as possible. Each two cairns result in two sighting directions — forward and reverse. The general equation governing these pairings is

$$\text{Number of pairs} = n(n-1),$$

where n is the integer number of cairns in the wheel. Thus, seven cairns yield forty-two such pairings. As has often been said, as the number of possible alignments grows, so does the potential for chance celestial alignments. Thus Eddy was faced with not only reducing the number of pairings to a manageable level but also selecting the ones that best fit the particular circumstances of the wheel's geographical location. He took four factors into account.

First, the alignments must be ones that could be used in the summer. Because of the deep snow that covers the mountain in late August or early September and often lasts until late May, the wheel would be unusable except in the summer months. Also, additional alignments should form a consistent set with the solstice alignments or be otherwise related to Plains Indian ritual or subsistence needs. Third, groups of alignments that use a single cairn for a foresight or

Table 3   Bighorn Medicine Wheel Survey of Cairn Directions

| Cairns | | 1972 survey | | |
Back-sight	Fore-sight	Separa-tion (m)	Horizontal dip angle (deg)	Azimuth (deg)
E	O	13.4	+0.18	55.0
C	O	12.5	−0.25	308.6
A	O	12.4	−0.5	196.5
B	O	12.3	−1.0	263.6
D	O	12.9	−0.2	348.5
F	O	12.1	+1.9	114.5
F	A		−0.6	65
F	B		0	99
E	B		−0.4	69

backsight should be considered as more likely than isolated single pairs. Fourth, only alignments to very bright stars should be considered.

With these considerations in mind, Eddy developed a list of directions that resulted in potentially intentional astronomical alignments for the present epoch. The first thing to note about his list is that no lunar or planetary possibilities exist. Apparently the wheel's builders had no interest in using it for sighting the moon or planets. This does not mean, of course, that they were not interested in those celestial bodies. On the contrary, as we will see in the next chapter, they had a deep significance for certain Plains Indians. What is striking about Eddy's list is that it contains three of the nine brightest stars in the northern celestial sphere. When this fact is combined

Celestial declination of rise (R) or set (S) (deg)	Indicated alignment (epoch 1972)		Declination difference (deg)	Azimuth difference (deg)
	Declination (deg)	Object		
+23.6 (R)	+23.4	Solstice sunrise	0.2	0.3
+25.5 (S)	+23.4	Solstice sunset	2.1	3.4
−43.8 (S)		?		
− 5.7 (S)		?		
+43.4 (S)		?		
−15.7 (R)	−16.7	Sirius rise	1.0	1.6
+16.6 (R)	+16.5	Aldebaran rise	0.1	0.1
− 6.7 (R)	− 8.2	Rigel rise	1.5	2.1
+14.1 (R)	+16.5	Aldebaran rise	2.4	3.8

From John A. Eddy, "Astronomical Alignment of the Big Horn Medicine Wheel," Science 184 (1974): 1035–43.

with the additional observation that the risings of all three stars can be observed using cairn F for a backsight (that is, Aldebaran–FA, Rigel–FB, Sirius–FO), it seems highly likely that the cairns were intentionally placed to observe these stars.

But what about stellar precession? Is it likely that alignments to stars at this epoch represent intentional alignments when the wheel was constructed? Archaeologists are not sure just how old the Bighorn Medicine Wheel might be, but it is certainly more than 100 years old. The primary archaeological evidence for its age comes from a tree-ring analysis of a piece of tree limb found lodged in cairn F. If this piece of wood had been placed there during construction, the cairn is no older than 220 years, corresponding to a construction date of 1760 or so.

What is the evidence from the stars? Although precession generally makes it impossible directly to witness potential stellar alignments constructed in an earlier era, it is also the case that the fact of precession can serve as a powerful tool for dating a structure. To do this one must generally be sure that substantial supporting evidence exists for the suspected stellar alignments. We lack such evidence for the Bighorn Medicine Wheel. But observe what happens when the positions of Aldebaran, Rigel, and Sirius are investigated as a function of time. At the present era, Aldebaran rises unseen in the predawn glare of the sun about one hour ahead of the sun on the solstice. It now makes its first dawn appearance some days after the summer solstice. However, because of precession, in previous centuries it was briefly visible just before the solstice sunrise. Such an appearance, also called a heliacal rise (that is, with the sun) would have served notice to the solstice watchers that it was about to occur, thus providing them with an additional, redundant observation for their calendar reckoning.

At the present time, the star Aldebaran is only 22° along the ecliptic from the summer solstice sun. That angle, however, was greater several centuries ago. In fact, the rate of angular decrease between the summer solstice sun and Aldebaran (1.4° per century) is such that in A.D. 1200 at the latitude of Bighorn Medicine Wheel, it would have risen heliacally. Because the exact moment of heliacal rising is a subjective matter depending on the experience and eye sensitivity of the observer, the rise of Aldebaran *could* have been used as late as A.D. 1700, implying that the wood sample was placed in cairn F at a later date than that at which the wheel was initially constructed. If Eddy's hypothesis is correct, three solstice alignments were operative: sunrise, sunset, and the heliacal rise of Aldebaran. At first glance these certainly seem overly redundant. However, as Eddy found, cloudy weather around the time of solstice is a strong possibility. Thus, having a sunset as well as a sunrise alignment would increase the possibility of actually observing the sun on the solstice. The Aldebaran alignment, on the one hand, would also enhance the effort to determine the solstice, but in a strikingly different way. Determining the precise day of solstice is difficult because the sun moves along the horizon very slowly at this time of year. On the other hand, an experienced observer is able to pick out the first yearly appearance of a star within no more than two or three days.

Celestial alignments, Bighorn Medicine Wheel.

Seeing the star Aldebaran appear briefly and then disappear in the predawn light several centuries ago, the users of the Bighorn Medicine Wheel could have increased their ability to choose the exact day of the summer solstice.

The significance of the alignment to Aldebaran is strengthened by the two remaining stellar alignments — Rigel and Sirius. In the same century that Aldebaran made its best heliacal solstice appearance, Rigel made its first yearly appearance about twenty-eight days after the solstice. Another twenty-eight days later, Sirius, the brightest star in the sky, rose heliacally. Cairn F is the point upon which one stands to observe star risings over cairns A, B, and O respectively.

For several years, the significance of cairn D remained uncertain. It was the only one that did not seem adequately to fit an astronomical hypothesis. The line DO suggested a possible north-south alignment, but it extends along an azimuth of 348.5°, which is 11.5° too far west to have served as an accurate indicator of the local meridian. More recently, however, astronomer Jack Robinson[2] found a possible astronomical use for cairn D. Postulating that it, like A, B, and C, might use cairn F as a backsight, he discovered that between A.D. 1050 and 1450 the bright star Fomalhaut rose heliacally along line FD about a month before summer solstice. This period is compatible with other evidence about the wheel, and further strengthens Eddy's findings.

It remains to understand the spokes and the rim. The number 28 seems highly suggestive of a lunar month. Though the time from new moon back to new moon (the synodic lunar month) is actually 29.5 days, the month is traditionally understood by many Native American groups as 28 days; the single day of invisibility of the moon is generally uncounted. According to the archaeological studies done on the wheel, the rim and spokes were added after the cairns. Perhaps the central cairn O and cairns E and C were the initial cairns built to mark the summer solstice. As the wheel's users gained more experience they may have added cairns F, A, and B to make the summer solstice determination more accurate and to mark the subsequent rise of Rigel and Sirius. The twenty-eight spokes of the wheel could then have served as day counters, each one subsequently marking the passage of one day between heliacal risings. Once noticed, the significance of the number 28 connected to the predawn appearances of bright stars would hardly have been lost on groups that were so attuned to the yearly cycle of the heavens. The rim itself seems not only to provide a fitting endpoint for the twenty-eight spokes but may have had considerable ritual significance for a people who lived in a state of continual alertness for calendar sky events along the rim of the world. For the Plains dwellers who presumably built the wheel, the uninterrupted sight of the rim of the world was a constant part of their visual experience. It is likely that this experience was, in part, the cause of their historic descendants' interest in and veneration for the wheel shape.

Given the windswept, inhospitable, isolated nature of the Bighorn Medicine Wheel's location, it seems hardly appropriate for the encampment of a large band. It seems much more plausible that it served the few whose priestly role gave them knowledge and the power to use its secrets for the guidance of the many. After making the pilgrimage to this lonely spot to ascertain the arrival of the summer solstice, they then could have brought their knowledge back to encampments lower down on the slope.

As we have seen in the Southwest, ethnographic data gathered from historic groups have provided important clues to the meaning and use of prehistoric structures. For the Bighorn Medicine Wheel, it is much more difficult to make use of the little ethnographic data available. Local Indians questioned at the turn of the century professed no knowledge of its builders. Though they recognized it as an ancient holy place, they were ignorant of (or reluctant to disclose) its function. In response to questions asked by the anthropologist S. C. Simms, local Crow tribal elders asserted nearly a hundred years ago that "it was made by people who had no iron."[3] That is, it is very old indeed. Two visiting Sioux Indians, when asked about the wheel, declared that it "belonged" to both the Arapaho and the Cheyenne.

After inspecting the diagram of it, which I had hastily drawn in order to make clearer the questions asked them through an able interpreter, each of the two Sioux drew a diametrical line through the wheel and, pointing to one half, said "Arapaho," and then pointing to the other half said, "Cheyenne."[4]

In other words, it reminded the Sioux of structures that were common to both tribes. A nearby trail furnishes evidence that the area had been visited often up to a hundred years ago, sometimes apparently for religious purposes. Beads and pieces of wampum, perhaps left in offering or prayer, have been found under stones of the wheel. In addition, Simms found a buffalo skull there on his first visit.

Upon the projecting slabs of the eastern side of the central structure [that is, cairn O] rested a perfectly bleached buffalo skull which had been so placed that it had the appearance of looking toward the rising sun.[5]

The similarity between the plan of the wheel and the ground plan of a medicine lodge has piqued the imagination of anthropologist and Indian alike. In the 1920s, the anthropologist George Grinnell questioned Cheyenne Indians and found the medicine wheel to be well known to them. They even told him of other wheels and of rock art depictions of such structures. When shown a drawing of the

Bighorn wheel, the Cheyenne Indian Elk River, a venerable man of more than a hundred winters at the time Grinnell spoke to him, professed immediately that it was

> the plan of an old time Cheyenne medicine lodge. The outer circle
> of stones he said represented the wall of the Medicine Lodge; the
> lines leading toward the center, the rafters — or, as he called them,
> the lodge poles — of the Medicine Lodge; and the small circle in
> the center of the large one, from which the so-called spokes radiate,
> represented the center pole of the Medicine Lodge. He added that
> the building to the northwest of the entrance, and within the circle
> and touching it, was the place from which the thunder came; and
> by this I understood him to mean what I call the altar — the place
> in the Cheyenne Medicine Lodge *which is especially sacred, and in
> which is the buffalo skull.* [Emphasis mine.][6]

Black Elk, a holy man of the Oglala Sioux, described the construction of a particular medicine lodge, the Sun Dance Lodge, in the following way, highly suggestive of the connection between the Sioux ceremony and the calendar.

> A little dance was held around the base of the tree, and the sur-
> rounding lodge was made by putting upright, in a large circle,
> twenty-eight forked sticks, and from the fork of each stick a pole
> was placed which reached to the holy tree at the center.
>   I should explain to you here that in setting up the sun dance
> lodge, we are really making the universe in a likeness; for, you see,
> each of the posts around the lodge represents some particular object
> of creation, so that the whole circle is the entire creation, and the
> one tree at the center, upon which the twenty-eight poles rest, is
> Wakan-Tanka, who is the center of everything. Everything comes
> from Him, and sooner or later everything returns to Him. And I
> should also tell you why it is that we use twenty-eight poles. I have
> already explained why the number four and seven are sacred; then
> if you add four sevens you get twenty-eight. Also the moon lives
> twenty-eight days, and this is our month; each of these days of the
> month represents something sacred to us: two of the days represent
> the Great Spirit; two are for Mother Earth; four are for the four
> winds; one is for the Spotted Eagle; one for the sun; and one for the
> moon; one is for the Morning Star; and four are the four ages; seven
> are for our seven great rites; one is for the buffalo; one for the fire;
> one for the water; one for the rock; and finally one is for the two-
> legged people. If you add all these days up you will see that they
> come to twenty-eight.[7]

Anthropologists have usually taken the connection between the

wheel and the Sun Dance Lodge to mean that the wheel was pat-
terned after the lodge. But the astronomically derived age of the
wheel might suggest the reverse — that the wheel served as the
pattern for the Sun Dance Lodge. However, such speculation ultimately seems moot, since the truth of the matter is lost in the
dimness of time. What seems both safe to say and worthy of note is
that the two seem to have sprung from similar traditions about the
sky and its use for ritual and calendrical functions. Further evidence, both historic and prehistoric, from other geographical areas
gives us some important clues about the wheel's possible meaning.

Other Medicine Wheels

After completing his research on the Bighorn Medicine Wheel, Eddy
began to study the other forty to fifty known medicine wheels on the
Great Plains for evidence of astronomical alignment. He found that
they came in a surprising array of shapes and sizes. Some lack
spokes, others have no rim, still others have been so disturbed that
their original shape and extent can only be guessed at.

The wheels are located in the northern Plains, mostly in Canada.
A few seem to have some astronomical significance, but for the most
part, they seem to have been built for purposes other than astronomical observation. Some, such as the Fort Smith Medicine Wheel on
the Crow reservation in Montana or a very primitive one on Trail
Ridge in northeastern Colorado, do display credible summer solstice
sunrise alignments, but the function of the remainder of the wheels
is very unclear.

A major exception to the lack of astronomical evidence for the
wheels is the Moose Mountain Medicine Wheel in southeastern Saskatchewan.[8] It, like all the wheels Eddy examined, lies on the top of
a hill with a clear view of the entire horizon circle, though the
feature from which it takes its name is not a mountain at all but a low
ridge extending across rolling farmland. The wheel is typical of the
Canadian wheels; it has a very large central cairn. Superficially, it
differs markedly from the Bighorn Medicine Wheel in other ways as
well. It is nearly twice as large and has fewer spokes and no rim,
though a small stone oval encloses the central cairn. Astronomically
speaking, however, there are some surprising similarities to its
southern cousin in Wyoming that become apparent when maps of

the two are placed side by side. Without the rim and the spokes of the Bighorn Medicine Wheel, the two would look remarkably alike. The similarities are even more apparent when their astronomical alignments are compared. Together with archaeologists Tom and Alice Kehoe, Eddy surveyed the Moose Mountain site and established that the wheel possesses a summer solstice sunrise alignment (EO), and alignments to the points of rise of the same three summer stars he discovered for the Bighorn wheel: Aldebaran (FA), Rigel (FB), and Sirius (FO). The three found no summer solstice sunset line in the wheel, a difference that is probably not significant since there already are two summer solstice determinants in the wheel (line EO and the line to the rise of Aldebaran).

They did discover an interesting feature that may have served as an important mnemonic device or indicator. Near cairn E, at the terminus of the line of stones between it and the central cairn, is a small stone mosaic resembling a sunburst. Was this cluster of stones and projecting "rays" put there to remind the sun watcher which cairn to stand at? Eddy has found a similar stone pattern at the Fort Smith Medicine Wheel; others were later discovered by the Kehoes in their investigation of Saskatchewan wheels — each one of which has solstice orientations. The device may, indeed, serve as a marker.

At the time Eddy conducted his study of the Moose Mountain Medicine Wheel, no one had examined it archaeologically. Thus, here again as in the Bighorn wheel, he attempted to date the structure by analyzing the astronomical alignments he found. This was the beginning phase of one of the most exciting stories in archaeoastronomical research to date.

As many scientists have noted over the years, dating archaeological structures by astronomical techniques is a procedure fraught with pitfalls, the greatest being that, because of precession, eventually some star has to align with a given horizon sight line. Some have suggested that the method should never be used. As Eddy has put it, however, a caution of this nature is "a good warning but a bad rule." At Moose Mountain there are several independent astronomical tests of the wheel's age. How well do they agree with one another?

Comparing the observed present alignments with rise positions for the three stars, Eddy found that the best fit for Aldebaran was from 150 B.C. to A.D. 150; for Sirius, A.D. 0 to A.D. 1000; and for Rigel, the

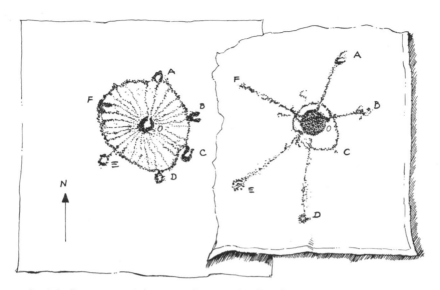

Celestial alignments, Bighorn Medicine Wheel and Moose Mountain Medicine Wheel compared. Although these wheels are separated by over a thousand miles, and perhaps a thousand years, the angular positions of the external cairns of the two wheels are remarkably similar. (After a drawing by John A. Eddy.)

modern era. Of the three, the position for Aldebaran provides the most sensitive test because its declination changes most rapidly. For A.D. 0, the rise position of Rigel is about 2° south of the measured alignments. Yet it is the closest bright summer star to the cairn alignment in the neighborhood. This, therefore, leaves the identification of the Rigel orientation in considerable doubt.

At a given latitude, the position of a star along the horizon depends entirely on its declination (its angular position perpendicular to the equator). However, its time of heliacal rise depends on the star's right ascension (its position parallel to the celestial equator). Suppose the first heliacal appearance of Aldebaran was observed at Moose Mountain in order to determine the date of summer solstice. Here the best fit lies between A.D. 180 and A.D. 580; the earlier date is sufficiently close to the latter limit of the horizon alignment that both methods could have been used effectively for a short time.

There is still another alignment that has an interesting consequence for the age of the wheel. Cairns D and O define a line that falls 6° east of north. Could this have been used as a crude north indicator? For a span of three centuries or so, centered on A.D. 50, the northern star Capella appeared to skim the horizon in its nightly circumpolar path. Because of precession, at its present declination (+46°) this bright star in the constellation Auriga now stays well above the Moose Mountain horizon. At this earlier time, however, it would have descended, disappeared briefly in the horizon haze, and then reappeared a few degrees east of geographic north. The line DO falls close enough to the point of reappearance of Capella at this epoch and near enough to north to have served as an effective north marker; moreover, it would have been highly visible in the northern sky. During those years, it reached its lower culmination between April and July, just at the period when the wheel could have been used most effectively as a summer solstice marker.

As Dr. Jack Robinson has pointed out, at the Moose Mountain wheel, as at the Bighorn Medicine Wheel, the line between F and D points to Fomalhaut.[9] Between A.D. 600 and A.D. 900 the star would have been seen rising heliacally about a week before the summer solstice; here, too, it could have been used to warn of the summer solstice. Assuming that it was so used, its presence in the wheel suggests a calendrical use for the wheel over hundreds of years.

With the exception of Rigel and Fomalhaut, all of the alignments fit a hypothesis that the Moose Mountain Medicine Wheel was built and used near the time of Christ for astronomical observations. When this conclusion was announced, the reaction of the archaeological community to this suggestion was, predictably, highly skeptical. Where was the archaeological evidence? Though archaeologists had little better notion themselves of the function of the medicine wheels, they were unsure of the work of this physical scientist, who, they feared, might overlook many of the very real problems inherent in making adequate sense of a prehistoric structure. Besides, they did not really understand some of his arguments, grounded as his interpretations were in the complexities of stellar and solar observation with the naked eye.

In keeping their eyes on the ground, so to speak, the archaeologists had neglected the sky and its demands and interests for a nomadic people who lived their lives predominantly out of doors. Whether they accepted it or not, Eddy had given them a hypothesis that could be checked. According to it, the Moose Mountain wheel was at least two thousand years old. Verifying the age of the wheel by archaeological methods would, in turn, check the hypothesis that gave rise to a construction date of A.D. 0, namely that the structure had been used as an astronomical observatory.

Tom and Alice Kehoe had become interested in Eddy's work because they had both worked on the problem of the medicine wheels for several years and had collaborated with him in analyzing the Canadian wheels. A year later, following Eddy's analysis and astronomical dating of the Moose Mountain wheel, the Kehoes decided to excavate it and study it by more traditional archaeological methods. Their results startled the archaeological community.[10]

Modern archaeologists have as one of their primary working assumptions the disturbance of as little as possible of the structures they investigate. They do this in order to leave as much as possible for future generations of archaeologists who could bring new techniques and different perspectives to the study. Thus the Kehoes actually excavated very little of the total structure of the wheel. More important to them was their desire to leave a relic of Plains Indian past intact for the tribes' descendants.

Although they excavated only a portion of the wheel, their investigation was carefully planned to develop a maximum of information about the putative astronomical orientations. Cairn E is the station from which to watch the summer solstice sunrise over the central cairn. By excavating at the edge of cairn E and along line EO, as well as on the circle and part of the central cairn, they hoped to discover whether the wheel had been constructed in sections over time, or whether it could have been built in one grand burst of activity. In other words, they wanted to establish the relative dating of parts of the structure. In addition, they hoped to find evidence of its absolute date, something to compare with Eddy's less traditional method of dating.

Both objectives were met to some extent, but excavating a structure made up of boulders laid together without benefit of mortar has its frustrations. Wind-blown or culturally deposited debris from later periods may find its way into the lower layer and complicate attempts to develop accurate stratigraphy.[11]

Nevertheless, they were able to say a few things with confidence. About a yard below the topmost boulders of the central cairn, they encountered the cairn's foundation, a layer of boulders that had been laid directly on the original surface layer of grass that covers the hill. The soil now present there contained small chunks of charcoal and pieces of red ochre, the former, as the Kehoes surmise, the result of burning off the surface grass prior to constructing the wheel.

The assemblage of collected charcoal bits was just large enough to make up a single radiocarbon sample that yielded an initial construction date of between 1080 and 440 B.C. From other evidence, the Kehoes regard the later date as the most likely.

Further, as they analyzed the available evidence for relative dating, they found no suggestion that the parts of the wheel had been constructed sequentially. The construction techniques and artifactual evidence point to its having been built over a single short time span. But here, as in much of archaeology in which samples of a structure are investigated, we must add a caveat. The Kehoes did not study the other cairns in the structure. Those cairns might tell a different story. However, given the spread of dates for the first sample, more accurate carbon dating than is currently available would be necessary to distinguish differences of a few hundred years with any assurance.

Assuming the Kehoes' date of 440 B.C. for construction of the central cairn, cairn E, and the line EO, it seems that the purpose of the wheel was to observe and establish summer solstice sunrise. As the builders used the cairns in this way, they may have discovered the utility of using the heliacal rise of Sirius to presage the end of the useful summer season and built cairns F and A to mark both directions. The use of Rigel seems less likely, since its point of rise lay so far from direction FB in A.D. 0, the most likely time for the heliacal rise data to have been discovered and used to build a calendar.

This information gives us a truly new picture of the Plains Indian. The Moose Mountain Medicine Wheel is a structure built and used two thousand years ago in ways we could not have guessed at as late as 1975. It is not an isolated example, either. Other "wheels" exist that were likely used to find the summer solstice, as we have seen. We can now see the American Indian as having far greater intellectual achievement than was thought even a few years ago. Here, as in so many cases, we are moved to ask what more would we know and appreciate about Native American culture had the Europeans who conquered North America cared to learn the extent of their achievements.

We have seen the relative paucity of ethnographic data about the Bighorn Medicine Wheel. The same is true of the Canadian wheels. The local Indians profess little knowledge of the meaning or use of the wheels the Kehoes investigated. One Cree reported that:

> Our elders tell us not to disturb them [the circles]; leave them alone, they belong to another creation; another time. There's one on our reserve, a big circle on the hill, facing southeast; our elders tell us to leave it alone.

About summer solstice, the same individual asserted that "we had ceremonies on that day. We prayed, we knew then another year was beginning on that day, we prayed at the start of another year." He went on to add that in those days, at the turn of the century, "we had calendar men. Back around 1929, the last calendar man died on my reserve. He had a lot of little sticks, handed down for generations, and two bags. Each day he'd put one stick from one bag into the other. He kept our dates for the [Sun Dance] camp. We relied on him for our calendar. Now we just look at the [printed] calendar." [12]

How exciting it might have been to explore this old man's knowledge of the calendar!

10 The Pawnee: Great Morning Star

It was just before dawn on April 22, 1838. After a long ritual preparation, Haxti, a captive Oglala Sioux girl about fifteen years old, walked proudly but hesitantly toward the approaching sunrise at the head of a stately procession of Pawnee.[1] Her entire right side, which faced the south, was painted red to symbolize the dawn. Her left, or north, side was painted black for the night that had just passed. She wore a long leather skirt, and around her shoulders she clutched a carefully tanned and painted elkskin robe. Her headdress was a hawk, the bird who carried messages from Morning Star.

Before her stood a wooden scaffold in the middle of a shallow rectangular pit lined with downy feathers. Each part of the scaffold reflected a close connection with one of the four world-quarters. The two upright posts were of elm (north) and cottonwood (south). The four rungs, reckoning upward from the bottom, represented the northeast (elm), southwest (box elder), northwest (cottonwood), and southeast (willow). Each rung had been tied with strips of animal skin associated with the appropriate direction — bear, mountain lion, wildcat, wolf. A second willow crossbar near the top of the two posts symbolized Heaven. It was attached with otterskin, which signified the renewal of life. The pit below the scaffold symbolized Evening Star's garden of germination in the west.

As the procession moved toward the sacred wooden structure, the priests and people sang four songs — about the girl, about Heaven, and about the powers of the four world-quarter beasts. Haxti paused only briefly before the scaffold.[2] Whether she yet fully realized her

Pawnee sacrifice of captured maiden to Morning Star. Every few years when the need to propitiate Morning Star was great and the celestial appearances were appropriate, the Pawnee captured a maiden from a neighboring tribe, and after months of ceremony, sacrificed her to Morning Star.

fate and wanted to escape would remain unknown, for she was quickly compelled to climb the scaffold. At each of the four rungs the assembly sang about the animal associated with the rung's direction. Two priests tied her between the two willow rungs with an elkskin thong, and then backed away to watch for Morning Star. Haxti, too, watched for Morning Star to appear, surrounded by the rosy light of dawn. The god of light, fire, and war, "the Morning Star [who] stands upon the dawn"[3] awaited his sacrifice.

Then, suddenly, the priest of the southeast, who had hidden himself until now, rushed out with a burning brand and touched her gently once near her right armpit and once near her groin. Another priest touched her in a similar way on the opposite parts. Then the man who had captured her from her village and dedicated her to Morning Star ran forth, and using a sacred bow and arrow, he shot Haxti through the heart. Her soul rose immediately to Tirawahat, the supreme god of the Pawnee. Tirawahat then gave her soul to Morning Star, who arrayed it in flint taken from his dawn fireplace. Haxti therefore became another of the stars in the heavens, to shine down in favor on the Pawnee.

Though Haxti's spirit had ascended to Heaven, she still possessed life that would aid the Pawnee. The chief priest now came forth and cut her above the heart with a flint knife. After smearing his face with streaks of Haxti's blood, he let some fall upon the dried heart and tongue of a buffalo that her captor held below her. Blood also fell upon the bed of downy feathers in the pit below as a symbol of growth and plenty. Each male who could wield a bow now came forth to send an arrow into her body. Others helped those too young to draw a bow themselves. The renewal of the earth was complete. Haxti had been overcome by Morning Star.

Although this account is a fictional composite of other similar human sacrifices carried out by the Pawnee, a teenage girl named Haxti was actually sacrificed in secret on the morning of April 22, 1838. Her sacrifice was probably the last ever held. The moral indignation of Western society[4] had been aroused, and the Pawnee, under extreme pressure from without and from some individuals within, stopped the practice, although they maintained other elements of the Morning Star ceremony in order to ensure the fertility of the land and the increase of the buffalo.

The practice of sacrifice to Morning Star was part of the rites of the Skidi band of the Pawnee, a group that had developed a unique relationship to the stars. Of all the Native American groups, no one had developed such an intricate and direct affinity to the stars. For them, the stars wore kindred souls; they took much of the direction of their life from the sky.

The Pawnee homeland was in the grasslands along the tributaries

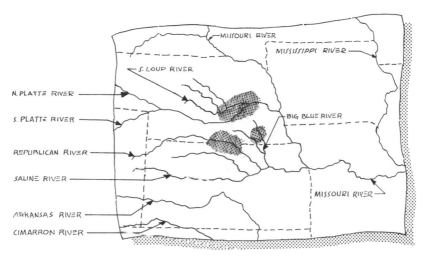

The Pawnee homeland (cross-hatched areas).

of the Missouri River in southeastern Nebraska. They built their earth lodges, miniature models of the cosmos, along the Loup, Republican, and Platte rivers. There they lived, and planted corn, beans, and squash, for the Pawnee were village Indians, distinguished from their Plains relatives to the west and northwest by their agricultural habits. Still, they also followed the buffalo. Each June, after planting was completed, the entire village would pack up and leave to take part in the annual buffalo hunt. From then until September, when they returned to harvest their well-laid crops, they would be on the move, following the buffalo and living in tipis similar to their Plains cousins. The time after harvest, before they set out on the winter buffalo hunt, was one of storytelling. It was then that the adults would remind themselves of the old stories and tell them for the first time to the youngsters who had grown up enough to listen to this wisdom of their elders.

Much of what we know about the Skidi Pawnee and their starlore derives from James R. Murie, whose mother was Skidi. Though he was raised and schooled basically as a white man, James Murie developed a deep interest in the traditions of his mother's people. Working primarily with anthropologists Alice Fletcher and George Dorsey, Murie gathered stories, purchased artifacts for the Field Museum in Chicago, and arranged for interviews with other Skidi Pawnee. He also attended as many ceremonies as he could.[5]

Stellar Guides

What drew the ire of the white citizens of the new America toward the Pawnee was the actual sacrifice of a maiden or a young boy. Most cared neither about the meaning of the ceremony nor about the intricate ritual that preceded the delivery of a soul to Morning Star. Yet this ceremony and the rituals that came before it lay at the very core of Skidi thought and response to the heavens. From Morning Star, or the Great Star, they derived their very being, and their rules for living. The sacrificial ritual they performed every few years when the heavenly signs were propitious was a re-enactment of the events that brought them to life.

> Over all is Tirawa (or Tirawahat), the One Above, changeless and supreme. From Tirawa comes all things: Tirawa made the heavens and the stars.
>
> In the west dwelt the White Star Woman, the Evening Star, who must be sought and overcome that creation might be achieved. From the east went forth the Great Star, the Morning Star, to find and overcome the Evening Star, that creation might be achieved. The Morning Star called to his younger brother: "Take the Sacred Bundle, bear it over thy shoulder and follow." And the Morning Star journeyed to the west. As ever as he journeyed, the Evening Star moved, came and drew him towards her. (For men may see how the Evening Star moves nightly. One night she is low in the heavens, another night she is high in the heavens. Even so she moved and drew the Morning Star.) Yet when the Evening Star beheld the Morning Star draw near, she placed in his path Hard Things to hinder his approach. Thus, even as the Morning Star first saw the Evening Star, she rose and looked on him and beckoned him. He started towards her, but the earth opened and waters swept down, and in the waters was a serpent with mouth wide opened to devour.[6]

Morning Star conquered the serpent by throwing a ball of fire into his opened mouth. In a similar manner he also conquered other hardships that he found in his way, ten in all, before he reached the lodge of Evening Star. Guarding her were the beasts of the four directions in the form of four stars. They were powerful, yet he also conquered them and gained entrance to the lodge.

And the Morning Star spoke [to the stars] and said, "I have conquered, and ye shall obey my command. Thou, Black Star, shalt
stand in the northeast, whence cometh night. Thou art Autumn.
Thou, Yellow Star, shalt stand in the northwest, where is the golden
setting of the sun. Thou art Spring. Thou, White Star, shalt stand in
the south, facing north, whence cometh the snow. Thou art Winter.
Thou, Red Star, shalt stand in the southeast. Thou art Summer.[7]

Then, before Evening Star would yield to Morning Star, Morning
Star had to perform more tasks. Because Morning Star was so powerful, he alone could conquer the Hard Things that Evening Star had
placed in his path, and endure the further trials that she posed for
him. One of these trials was to procure a specific cradleboard and its
appropriate trappings from a lodge in the heavens. After he had
stolen the cradleboard, he still had to procure otterskin tying strings,
a buffalo robe, and the skin of a wildcat, which were also part of the
ensemble. In symbolic recognition of the first cradleboard, Pawnee
examples were made up of these parts and, appropriately, were decorated with the symbol of the Morning Star, a large four-pointed star.

He also provided water in the form of rain, to keep Evening Star's
garden in the west ever green. After Morning Star lay with Evening
Star, he created the sun to provide light and heat for the earth. The
Pawnee say, "The Power of the Sun is from the Morning Star."[8]
Evening Star had opposed the creation of earth and of man. From the
union of Morning Star and Evening Star came a maiden who descended to earth and married a boy, the child of the moon and the
sun. Together, the two children grew and peopled the earth.

As astronomer Von Del Chamberlain suggests, the sacrifice of a captured maiden and the details of her capture and preparation are all
part of the symbolic re-enactment of the original conquering acts of
Morning Star, as seen in the heavens. The long sequence of earthly
events leading to the sacrifice began when one of the Pawnee warriors experienced a dream of Morning Star, who demanded sacrifice
for his original labors in bringing people to earth. In the dream,
Morning Star was a man adorned with red paint and with leggings
decorated with scalps. Upon waking, the warrior who had been chosen by the vision paused to see Morning Star himself in the rosy
streaks of dawn, and then loudly announced his dream to the village
as he ran quickly to the lodge of the Morning Star priest. He and the

Morning Star priest sat together and meditated four days, for the warrior was to represent Morning Star in capturing and sacrificing the maiden.

Each aspect of the succeeding ceremonies, from the preparation of the warrior to the capture and sacrifice, was steeped in significance related to the original myth of Morning Star and Evening Star. As the warrior made ready to depart, the Morning Star priest studied the sky for the appearance of the Great Star. On the warrior's forehead the priest painted a red bird's foot to represent the stars called by the same name, the Bird's Foot. Located in the Milky Way, this unidentified constellation was associated with Morning Star. The warrior also wore items from the sacred Great Star Bundle kept by the Morning Star priest. He then left the village as Morning Star appeared in the sky, accompanied by other warriors who personified the star gods of the four directions. They traveled under the protection of Morning Star, and each morning of their journey they watched carefully for him to rise and help them on their way.

During their last encampment, near the enemy village, the group ritually performed the journey of Morning Star in his quest for Evening Star. As the chosen leader acted out in mime Morning Star's journey, all members of the party took part in singing about the time of origins when Morning Star overcame Evening Star. While he circled the sacred fire they had kindled in honor of Morning Star, the leader also mimed the obstacles that Morning Star had to overcome. The others participated by singing the same songs that Morning Star sang as he searched for Evening Star. One last time, they watched carefully for Morning Star to rise. Then, while it was still well before dawn, they rode to the village. The warriors representing the four-quarter stars took their appropriate places outside the village; the one who personated Morning Star was on the east. As soon as they located and seized an appropriate young woman, her captor spoke the name of Morning Star, Opirikuts, thus dedicating her to the Great Star. She was then sacred to the Morning Star, and no harm or mistreatment must come to her.

The Identity of Morning Star

The care with which the Pawnee observed the sky and noted the celestial events suggests that the story of Morning Star and Evening

Star, in addition to serving as an explanation of the original events of the Pawnee universe, might also reflect actual celestial occurrences. Von Del Chamberlain has devoted considerable effort to deciphering the cast of stars referred to by Pawnee sources. He believes that the mythical journey of Morning Star can also be seen in the movements of the planets and other celestial bodies.

To understand the possible sequence of events that would represent the travels and trials of Morning Star, it is first essential to identify Morning Star. Many authors have attempted to associate him with one or another of the bright planets. However, in the opinion of Chamberlain, the only planet that will fit the known cases of sacrifice most appropriately is Mars. It is the *westward* migration of Mars that is likely to be "*the* key observational element in Skidi mythology and practice,"[9] he says.

This conclusion is supported by several observable facts, and strengthened by the story describing the journey of Morning Star. Let us examine the indications we have from the various commentators. Although they disagree over the identity of Morning Star, they generally agree that his color is red. Indeed, the Morning Star of the warrior's dream is clothed in red. Upon first being brought into the Pawnee village, the captive sacrificial maiden was also rubbed with red ointment symbolic of Morning Star. In addition, as we have seen, just before her sacrifice, her right side was painted red to represent the dawn, and also Morning Star. It is entirely conceivable, in fact, that the association of the color red with Morning Star derives from his physical association with the rosy dawn. Observationally, though, Mars is the only planet that has a reddish appearance. However, even if Mars is identified as Morning Star in this manner, it remains to be seen whether the Pawnee watched the sky for signs that Mars would be the morning star when the sacrifice took place. In other words, did the celestial signs have to be appropriate for the sacrifice to be carried out, or would other bright stars or planets serve in Mars's stead?

Chamberlain examined each of the known historic occurrences of the sacrifice and concluded that although different celestial objects were used as Morning Star besides Mars, Mars was the best fit to the available evidence. The distinction between finding the true Morning Star rising just before dawn and an acceptable candidate for the circumstances is an important one for Native American thought. The time for the sacrifice had to fit earthly as well as celestial events. Just as the sacrifice was not held every time Mars appeared ahead of the sun in the morning, it was also true that earthly circumstances sometimes required a sacrifice when the celestial phenomena failed to be exactly right. Faced with these circumstances, the vision might come to a warrior and the sacrifice be carried out before another morning star. It is apparent that the Pawnee priests understood the difference quite well but were prepared to deviate from the best celestial practice to satisfy earthly needs.

The 1838 sacrifice of the Sioux maiden Haxti is a most interesting example to illustrate the celestial positions. Although we have no account of the ceremony itself, Chamberlain has reconstructed the celestial events that accompanied the capture, and described the positions of the planets as the sun made ready to appear on the sacrificial morning. Tables of the positions of the planets, the sun, and moon are available to help us see where the brightest celestial objects were located. In thinking about this sequence of celestial events, it is helpful to recall that, like all planets, as Mars moves through the sky from night to night, it wanders among the stars, completing a full circuit through the sky every 780 days. Because Mars, like all planets, travels along the ecliptic, the sun's yearly apparent path, it appears in each of the four quarters of the sky at some time in its cycle. This is because the ecliptic lies at a 23.5° angle to the celestial equator. Indeed, Mars could be said to "overcome" certain bright stars that it encounters, including the stars of the four quarters, since, in its circuit, it appears in each of the semicardinal directions. In addition, because Mars's motion through the stellar field is irregular, and also appears to stop for a time near certain stars and even move backward among them,[10] the planet could even be considered to be doing battle with them. Unlike Venus or Mercury, which never appear to move very far from the sun, Mars can also appear well away from the sun, high up in the night sky.

Since other planets in addition to Mars, and even some stars, are involved in the celestial enactment of the myth of Morning Star and Evening Star, their parts must also be accounted for in searching for the appropriate signs for the capture and sacrifice. Although Haxti's sacrifice was recorded to have taken place on the morning of April 22, 1838, we have no record of when she might have been captured, nor therefore of what celestial occurrence might have prompted it.

However, Chamberlain has speculated that to the experienced observer, the close conjunction of Mars, Saturn, and Venus on October 2 and 3, 1837, just six months prior to the sacrifice, might have seemed an especially propitious time to seek a sacrificial victim. At that time, Venus was in the evening sky, and appeared to "come out to meet Mars, which was itself drawing close to Saturn."[11] The new crescent moon, which was growing in brightness at this time, passed close to this group of wanderers, creating an arresting apparition for anyone who viewed these bodies as gods having direct influence on human affairs. Well before this celestial spectacle (in June 1836), Mars had been a morning star, appearing in the northeast, at the same time that Venus was a bright evening star in the northwest. Mars then began its journey to the west, passing by Jupiter on its way. As Mars passed to the evening sky, it also traveled further south, until, after the conjunction with Venus and Saturn, it drew near the southernmost quarter of the sky and passed into the glare of the winter solstice sun. In early January, Venus remained a brilliant evening star, but then it, too, drew closer to the sun and disappeared. In late March, Venus reappeared as a morning star and reached its brightest state on April 9. Eleven days later, during the four-day presacrifice ritual, the waning crescent moon passed only four degrees away from Venus. Though it was not yet visible in the glare of the rising sun, Mars had become Morning Star once again. Thus, both Mars and Venus were together, we might say, in the House of the Morning Star. As Haxti was sacrificed two days later, Mars still remained invisible, but Venus shone brilliantly in the reddish dawn light. In his account of these planetary motions, Chamberlain reminds us that although the conjunction of Mars and Venus would have had considerable significance for Pawnee thought, so, too, would the appearance of the moon. As the Pawnee astronomer-priest followed the movements of all the celestial bodies across the sky, including the moon, he would have known that the waning crescent would slide eastward and pass near Venus before disappearing into the bright light of the rising sun. The moon played an important role in their creation myth, for it was the son of the moon and sun, as well as the daughter of the Morning Star and Evening Star, who peopled the world.

As Chamberlain points out in his analysis of these and other similar celestial events related to the creation myth, the periods of Mars and Venus are such that the Pawnee would have observed the journey of Mars from east to west every 2.14 years (the synodic period of Mars). This journey, when taken together with the movements of Venus from an evening star to a morning star and back again results every six and a half years in a propitious celestial pattern reminiscent of the myth.

The synodic period of Mars suggests an explanation of another pattern of Pawnee ritual life. Each of the four semicardinal directions had a sacred bundle associated with it, by tradition bequeathed to the Pawnee by the gods and cared for by the village of each semicardinal direction — the so-called leading villages, in recognition of the tradition that each village took a turn at leadership in the ceremonial cycle. Murie was sure that the cycle was astronomically based but was puzzled as to why it happened every two years, rather than every year. Chamberlain has suggested that the synodic period of Mars was the controlling factor, a hypothesis that seems to fit the conceptual patterns of the Skidi Pawnee very well.

Sun and Moon in Pawnee Thought

It is striking that the sun assumes a relatively minor role in the Pawnee conception of the cosmos and in its relationship to Pawnee ritual. This stance makes the Pawnee nearly unique among native North Americans. Even as these agriculturalists appreciated the warming power of the sun, they attributed his power either to Morning Star or to Evening Star.

Although the Pawnee were certainly fully aware of the extreme positions taken by the sun throughout its yearly cycle, their calendar apparently had as its basis the yearly appearance of certain stars, coupled with earthly signs of seasonal change such as the regular occurrence of thunder in the spring. Thus, in conformity with their predominant interest in the stars, they subordinated the yearly cycle of renewal and growth, and eventual cold retreat provided by the sun, to a stellar calendar. What mythological power the sun was imputed to have was also a subordinate kind. The sun gave power to the buffalo, and he also gave the bow and arrow to the people. The power he imparted directly to humans was thought to be directed primarily to the medicine men, who also gained assistance from animals. Their powers were therefore of lesser strength than those of the star priests, whose power derived directly from the stars.

The moon, a female, watched over earthly women, and also played a role in agriculture, for the Pawnee considered it important to plant their corn during the new moon. This takes place during the first new moon after the willow leaves appear. Like the sun, the moon also imparted special power to the medicine men.

Living by the Stars

According to their own stories, the Pawnee received much of their ritual direction from the stars. They claimed that at one time they organized their villages according to stellar patterns. Each village, they said, possessed a sacred bundle given to it by one of the stars. When the different villages assembled for a great ceremony, their spatial arrangement on earth reflected the celestial positions of the stars whose bundles they possessed. Then there were eighteen separate Skidi Pawnee villages, each associated with a different star.

As mentioned earlier, four of the villages belonged to the four semicardinal stars that Morning Star overcame in his quest for Evening Star. These villages were termed the leading villages because each took its turn in leading the annual ceremonial cycle, beginning when the various sacred bundles were opened in the spring after the Evening Star ritual.

According to Pawnee cosmology, the four world-quarter stars were related to one another. They served as the pillars of Heaven that held the sky away from the earth. In the traditional Pawnee earth lodge, the four posts that held up the roof represented the four stars that held up the sky. Each star was also associated with one of the beasts of the four quarters, and with a season. The northwest star, for example, was associated with spring, the mountain lion, yellow corn, and a female star, Yellow Star. Yellow Star was married to Red Star, who ruled over the southeast and the summer. Red Star was associated with red corn and the wolf. Big Black Star, which stood in the northeast, was the autumn star. He was associated with black corn and with the bear. He was married to the southwest, or white, star. She, in turn, ruled over winter and was associated with white corn and the wildcat.

The exact identity of the four world-quarter stars is not known from the ethnographic records. Part of the problem in naming them is that knowledge of the stars was, in part, sacred knowledge and therefore not readily accessible to uninitiated Pawnee. However, by using some of the clues at hand in the ethnographic notes and published papers, as well as a thorough knowledge of the sky, Chamberlain has postulated four likely candidates for these stars.[12] Working from the colors associated with the four stars, and assuming that they were bright enough to be seen near the horizon, he has suggested the following sequence: as Capella, a yellowish star, is setting in the northwest, Antares, a red star, rises in the southeast. Prior to that, Sirius, a bright white star, has set in the southwest as Vega rises in the northeast. Of course, neither Vega nor any other star could be considered black in color. However, if the other stars are identified correctly, then the diagonal pairing evident in this scheme leads directly to identifying Vega as the Big Black Star. One of the strongest arguments for Chamberlain's identifications is the fact that each of these stars "rules over" its respective season. In the spring, Capella is high in the sky just after sunset. Antares is visible all summer in the south, and Vega is a dominant star in the fall evenings. Last, Sirius is highly visible all winter long.

It is not clear how the name Big Black Star originated. Several ethnographers have puzzled over its origin but have reached no satisfactory conclusion. In some accounts, he is called Big Black Meteoritic Star, a reference perhaps to a fireball or large meteorite that may have once appeared in the northeast. A newly fallen meteorite is often black in color. Perhaps this is also why it was said that Big Black Star's sacred bundle once contained a meteorite. The Pawnee were well aware of meteors and fireballs, and claimed to have meteorites in their possession, which they thought to be Tirawahat's children and were therefore extremely powerful and highly revered. When going to war to help ensure success in battle, they carried bundles containing stones they considered to be meteorites.

We see the Pawnee attitude toward meteorites in a story about a warrior called Osage Sky-Seeing. While on a journey, Osage Sky-Seeing witnessed a falling star. It seemed to fall close to him, so the warrior searched and found a stone he believed to be the remnant of the falling star. Then, wrapping up the stone, he carried it with him as he continued on his journey. One night as he dreamed, a young man came to him and said,

My brother, I am the stone you have. I came from a star that stands in the heavens a little to the east, but south. Take me with you wherever you go. I shall make you successful when you go to capture ponies. When you are about to go on a long journey, put me in front of you, take your pipe filled, smoke straight up to the heavens, and then the different stars, the last to me. When I shine brightly, then you may know that I will be present with you.[13]

According to the story, Osage Sky-Seeing became a successful warrior and a deeply spiritual man. When he died, the ceremony that Osage Sky-Seeing learned from the stone passed on to others.

A Pawnee Star Chart

Interestingly, Big Black Star was also associated with learning. He was said to have distributed sacred healing bundles to the medicine men and given them their knowledge of healing. Big Black Star also gave humans other knowledge, including knowledge of the stars. Indeed, attached to his bundle was a detailed chart of the stars. It was painted on buckskin and was kept in a bag made from the scalp of a buffalo. Apparently, the chart was once also used to wrap a stone that was considered to be a meteorite.

The chart has been a puzzle for many years, as it seemed to some to be a bit too Westernized to be genuine. Waldo Wedel, the noted Plains archaeologist, once told me that he was highly suspicious of the chart because the leather seemed too supple and new to have been a genuine artifact of earlier Pawnee culture. Recent detailed analysis by Von Del Chamberlain has shown, however, that it was probably tanned using Pawnee methods, and was painted with mineral pigments that would have been available to the Pawnee. Although definite proof of its origin or of its age is not attainable, it appears to be genuinely Native American and rather old. The chart is extremely interesting to the study of ethnoastronomy because it appears to contain most of the constellations recognized by the Pawnee. It is not, however, as some have claimed, an accurate representation of the night sky in its entirety.[14] Indeed, it would have been contrary to Pawnee thought to concentrate on accurately depicting the sky. As a sacred object that therefore carried a lot of power, it was likely to be more important to the Pawnee to paint the crucial constellations as they understood them from their corpus of myths. In use, I suspect that the chart served to remind the owner of the bundle and his intimates of the stellar patterns and their stories. It was also likely to have been thought of as containing great power. When it was opened for a ceremony, this power would have been available to the Pawnee people.

The Pawnee recognized many different constellations in the night sky, but not all are identifiable with known Western constellation patterns. As with so many other important aspects of Native American life, much of the difficulty of identifying these stellar patterns with assurance is that the ethnographers began to ask their questions only after those who possessed the knowledge had died. Other difficulties arise because some of the knowledge was sacred and the priests were not willing to share it with outsiders. The identifications that have been made illustrate how important the stars were to Pawnee life. Nearly all of these constellations are visible on the buckskin star chart.[15]

The north star, whose name in Pawnee is literally "the Star That Does Not Walk Around," they compared to the god Tirawahat. North Star was chief over all the other stars and saw to it that they did not lose their way. As depicted on the star chart, the north star is among the largest stars, and certainly much larger than those near it. This is directly contrary to the actual celestial appearance of the north star, which is fainter than, for example, several stars near it in Ursa Major.

Rotating around the north star and nearest to it were the groups of stars that represented stretchers. According to the myth, in the first council, when decisions were being made about where the various gods would stand in the sky, two people became ill. The stars placed them on stretchers in order to carry them along. They still journey in the sky, traveling continually about the Star That Does Not Walk Around, and serving as a pattern for humans. The stretchers are the bowls of the Big and Little Dippers; the stars that follow (that is, the respective handles) are the Medicine Man, his wife, and Errand Man. These patterns are obvious on the chart. As Alice Fletcher has recorded, "the people took their way of living from the stars, so they must carry their sick and dead as shown, the mourners following."[16]

The chart is divided roughly in half by a series of small painted dots and tiny crosses that represent the Milky Way. Its placement on the star chart reflects the Pawnee understanding of the Milky Way, which was thought of as parting the heavens. It is referred to as the

Pathway of the Departed Spirits, because the Pawnee, as many other Native Americans, considered it the road to the world of the dead. Those who die of natural causes take the long branch of the Pathway, while those who die in battle or in other sudden ways take the short path. The common people often refer to it as the dust of the buffalo, in apparent reference to the cloud of dust that the buffalo kick up in running across the prairie.

Near the center of the chart and below the Milky Way is a large circle of eleven stars called the Council of the Chiefs, who were in the sky to watch over the people. They, in turn, were watched over by the north star. The Council of the Chiefs is known in Western lore as Corona Borealis, or Northern Crown. It served to remind the Pawnee of the original council of stars set up by Tirawahat. When the last Pawnee earth lodge was built in the early part of this century, Murie noted, "Women laced willow branches together and they were placed upon the slanting poles, and so formed a covering for the lodge, leaving only a round hole at the top. This circle represents the circle of stars in the heavens."[17]

Opposite the Council of the Chiefs on the other side of the Milky Way is the Pleiades, a compact group of six stars. The priests used the appearance of the Pleiades, as seen through the lodge smoke hole just after sunset in early spring, to establish the time for planting ceremonies. The Pleiades were thought of as six or seven brothers who had saved a girl from a rolling skull.

The arrival of spring, perhaps the most important time of the year, was watched for in the skies by the heliacal appearance of the two stars called the Swimming Ducks. These were identified by the astronomer Forest Ray Moulton as the stars Lambda and Upsilon Scorpio, which form the stinger of the Western constellation Scorpius. The arrival of spring was known not only by the stars but also by signs such as the frequent occurrence of thunder. Indeed, the ceremony of the Evening Star, which began the ritual year, was called the Thunder Ritual. Murie described the two observations:

> The time for the ceremonies of the Evening Star bundle was primarily determined by the recurrence of the thunder in the spring; but it should be understood that it was not at the very first sound of the thunder that the ceremony was held, for it might have thundered at any time. The approximate time was fixed by the appearance of two small twinkling stars (the Swimming Ducks) in the northeastern

[*sic:* this should read *southeastern*] horizon near the Milky Way. When low, deep, rumbling thunder was heard, starting in the west and rolling around the entire circuit of the heavens, then it was time for the Thunder Ritual to be recited.[18]

The Swimming Ducks appear on the star chart very near the Milky Way, on the same side as the Council of the Chiefs. To their right is the grouping that the Pawnee call the Snake. The latter pattern is made up of the stars that form the body of the Western constellation Scorpius. Antares, which also appears to be the red star of the southeast, forms the head of the snake. Interestingly, although the Swimming Ducks are seen in the sky as much fainter than Antares, in the star chart they are represented as slightly larger than that star. I suspect this is because of their ritual importance as harbingers of spring and the Evening Star ceremony.

The Thunder Ritual was a fundamental part of Pawnee ceremonial life, not only because it began the ceremonial year but because the ritual invoked the friendly response of the sky gods. The occurrence of thunder in the spring was thought to be the voice of Paruxti, the messenger of Tirawahat, through whose agency life was renewed. Paruxti was wind, cloud, lightning, and thunder combined in one powerful being.

Shortly after hearing Paruxti's voice in the spring, the priests of the four directions met, and opening the Evening Star bundle that governed this ceremony, they sang:

> They sang this song above, they have spoken.
> They have put new life into the earth.
> Paruxti speaks through the clouds,
> And the power has entered Mother Earth.
> The earth has received the powers from above.[19]

After repeating this song many times, the priests mimicked the sound of thunder from the four directions, and smoked. Many other songs were sung, telling of the clouds and Paruxti's power that shakes the earth. Then the priests sacrificed a dried buffalo heart and tongue to the gods. After cutting it up into ten pieces, they burned it in offering first to Tirawahat, and then to Morning Star and Evening Star. Four sacrifices they made to the Big Black Meteoritic Star who stands in the northeast, one to each of the gifts he gives to the Pawnee — healing, knowledge, buffalo, and skill in capturing enemy ponies. Next, they sacrificed to the sun, who rules over the day, and moon, who helps provide the fruits of the earth. Finally, they made their offering to the buffalo, saying, "The spirit of the buffalo skull shall whisper to the buffalo in the west so that they will start eastward toward our village, and we shall have plenty of buffalo."[20]

After singing more of Paruxti and his power, and purifying themselves in the smoke of smouldering sweet grass, they sat down to eat corn and other food. The corn, which was last year's crop, reminded each of the participants of the bounty of the gods who brought them Mother Corn. Finally, after all had eaten, to complete the ceremony the chief priest rose, and facing east to the entrance to the earth lodge, he said: "We are going to walk toward the entrance belonging to Mother-Corn, Mother-of-the-Dawn, Mother-Sunset-Yellow. Now, priests, we rise! We walk toward the entrance, belonging to Mother-Corn. Rise! Priests!"[21] The new cycle had begun — to bring, it was hoped, health and plenty to the Pawnee.

The buckskin star chart contains many other stars than those mentioned, including some of the stars of the four quarters of the world. Among the constellations of particular interest are the Bow, which is pictured between the Pleiades and the Milky Way, and the Deer, on the other side of the Pleiades. The Bow, which Murie suggests is the group of stars otherwise known as Delphinus, was said to represent the bow bestowed on the first man by Morning Star. This bow made it possible for the first man to kill buffalo and other animals.

The stars called the Deer present an interesting puzzle. They are said to be three stars in a line, following one another, which rise late in autumn in the southeast. Although this description fits the belt of Orion quite well, they were identified on the star chart by an informant as a group of seven stars. The seven stars resemble Taurus more than they do Orion. With the data available today, it is impossible to be sure which fits the original Pawnee conception more closely.

Most of the remaining numerous stars are unidentified, primarily because there is no Pawnee left capable of commenting on its meaning and explicating the messages it must have once conveyed to its owner. That it was of deep spiritual meaning to a people who took their rules for living from the stars, I have no doubt. The chart surely served as a sacred reflection and reminder of the star gods above.

11 Eastern Sun Worship

The Historic Southeast

The early French and Spanish explorers of the Southeast noted with more than passing interest that the various Indian groups they encountered worshiped and venerated the sun; for many the sun was the supreme deity. The particular customs and specific religious practices they witnessed varied throughout the region, but most commentators agreed on the power and importance of the sun in the daily lives of the natives they encountered.

For the Choctaw of Mississippi, the sun was an important force in their war expeditions. "It was through the influence of Hushtahli, or the sun, that they were enabled to find the bright path, which led them to victory, and returned them in safety to their homes."[1] They also associated fire directly with the power of the sun and imputed to fire the ability to inform the sun of mortals' activities.

Further east and south, in Florida, the Timucua worshiped the sun in a remarkable way. As the sixteenth-century French artist and explorer Jacques Le Moyne attested, they

> were accustomed every year, a little before their spring — that is, in the end of February — to take the skin of the largest stag they could get, keeping the horns on it; to stuff it full of all the choicest sorts of roots that grow among them, and to hang long wreaths or garlands of the best fruits on the horns, neck, and other parts of the body. Thus decorated, they carried it, with music and songs, to a very large and splendid level space, where they set it up on a very high tree, with the head and breast toward the sunrise. They then offered prayers to the sun, that he would cause to grow on their land good things such as those offered him. The chief, with his sorcerer, stands nearest the tree and offers the prayer; the common people,

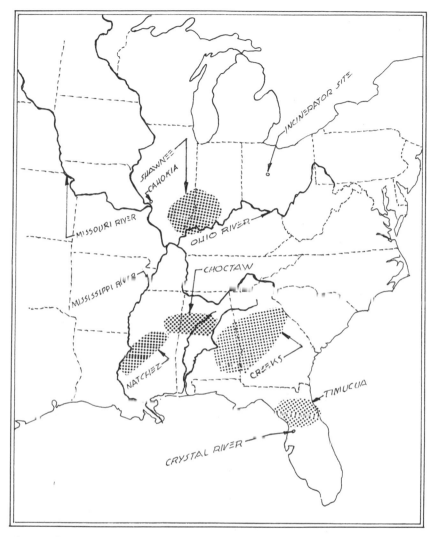

The southeastern tribes and archaeological sites mentioned in this chapter.

placed at a distance, make responses. Then the chief and all the rest, saluting the sun, depart, leaving the deer's hide there until the next year. This ceremony they repeat annually.[2]

Sun worship was not the only striking cultural feature the early explorers noted. When Hernando de Soto traveled along the Mississippi River in the early 1500s, he found natives who were organized into chiefdoms, the primary villages of which contained platform mounds. Surrounding villages paid tribute to the chief, who lived in large and sumptuous quarters atop one of the mounds. The chief villages contained storage bins "in which they bring together the tribute their people give them of maize, skins of deer and blankets of the country." The chiefs then redistributed them among the people as they saw fit.[3]

Nearly one hundred fifty years later, when the French explored along the Mississippi in the late 1600s, they encountered a tribe they called the Natchez Indians. This group erected great temple mounds and had a highly structured society for whom the sun was the principal deity. After visiting the Natchez, one French priest wrote:

> The sun is the principal object of veneration to these people, and as they cannot conceive of anything which can be above this heavenly body, nothing else appears to them more worthy of their homage. It is for the same reason that the great chief of this nation, who knows nothing on earth more dignified than himself, takes the title of brother of the sun, and the credulity of the people maintains him in the despotic authority which he claims.[4]

The Natchez considered their chief to be the earthly sun, and therefore called him Great Sun. This deity on earth lived in a wooden dwelling atop a large earthen mound that extended about three yards above the village plaza. His door opened to the east.

> Every morning as soon as the Sun appears, the great chief comes to the door of his cabin, turns himself to the east, and howls three times, bowing down to the earth. Then they bring him a calumet, which serves only for this purpose. He smokes, and blows the smoke of his tobacco toward the Sun; then he does the same thing toward the other three parts of the world. He acknowledges no superior but the Sun, from which he pretends to derive his origin.[5]

The Natchez had what could be called a solar theocracy. Great Sun took his authority from a supreme sky god whose son in the distant past had come to earth and bequeathed to the Natchez their customs, their arts, and their stories of the beginning. The latter then entered into a stone, revered and preserved by the Natchez in a temple atop a mound adjacent to that of Great Sun. Its door also opened east.

> In this temple they have a fire which is preserved continually; it is the sun which they say this fire represents and which they adore. That is why every morning, at sunrise, they make a fire before the door of the temple, and in the evening at sunset . . . There are four

temple guards who sleep there each during a quarter and who keep the perpetual fire.[6]

This fire was never used for any earthly purpose, as it was directly connected with the fire of the sun. John Swanton, an ethnologist with the Bureau of American Ethnology, took a deep interest in the sun worship of the eastern tribes. His view of the Natchez relationship to the sun probably extended to other groups living in the Southeast.

> Could we but bring back the Natchez nation as it once existed in its integrity, we should probably find their entire national life, its arts, industries, and the doings of daily life, as well as its religious rites and social organization, woven through and through with solar ideas.[7]

Earlier, the French developed an interest in the Natchez and recounted the details of Natchez life, which in some respects they regarded as highly civilized. Great Sun counted at least nine villages under his chiefdom. His subjects relied on farming, mainly corn, for much of their sustenance, but they also gathered local wild grains and nuts, and hunted deer, turkey, bison, and bear. The Natchez traded with others along the Mississippi, and kept the nearby tribes in a tributary status. According to the Natchez themselves, the tribe had previously occupied a much wider area prior to the era they were discovered by the French.

What de Soto and the other Spanish and French explorers encountered in the Southeast were native groups descended from or related to earlier peoples who painstakingly constructed the great mounds and earthworks of North America. Nestled along the rivers of the southeast and central regions, these earlier cultures, the Adena, the Hopewell, and the later Mississippian groups, demonstrated a high degree of organization and well-developed ceremonial activities. Poverty Point, Monks Mound, Etowah, Spiro Mounds — from Louisiana and Illinois to Georgia and Oklahoma, mounds and oddly shaped earthworks have also yielded evidence of an interest in celestial motions. Most of the historic cultures related to the builders of these mounds and earthworks disappeared soon after the arrival of European culture and new diseases to these shores. Thus, there is much less ethnographic material to draw upon than for elsewhere in the country. The archaeological remains of these and other eastern cultures demonstrate concern with a calendar and with celestial observations, suggesting the same general interest in the sky evidenced by other North American groups. However, nowhere among the mounds of the East is the evidence for celestial orientation stronger than at the Cahokia mounds in southwestern Illinois.

The Cahokia Mounds

It is easy to miss the Cahokia mounds as you speed by them on Interstate 55–70 in East St. Louis, Illinois; from the highway they look simply like overgrown piles of earth left behind by a creative bulldozer operator. Yet that area is the site of the largest prehistoric earth mound north of Mexico. Monks Mound, so named because a group of Trappists lived there briefly in the early 1800s, among North American mounds is exceeded in total volume only by the Pyramid of the Sun at Teotihuacán and the pyramid at Cholula. Monks Mound measures 1037 by 790 feet and is 100 feet high. As impressive as this individual structure is, however, the complex of smaller mounds of which it is a part is much more remarkable because of the size and complexity of the civilization that it implies. The entire site, which covers 3700 acres, is certainly the largest single prehistoric settlement north of Mexico.

The complex of 120 mounds and other Native American remains called Cahokia derives its name from an Indian group that lived in the area when the French settled there in the eighteenth century. However, the Cahokians looked upon these mounds as ancient artifacts and claimed no connection with their builders. Originally begun about A.D. 900 by the so-called Mississippian culture, which built other mounds throughout the area, the population center at Cahokia grew in size and importance over the years; it reached its peak of development between A.D. 1150 and 1250, with a population estimated at thirty to fifty thousand individuals.

Both the original builders and the later groups that added to the first mounds were undoubtedly drawn to the area by the rich flood plain. There, just a couple of miles east of the Mississippi River, they grew several varieties of corn, beans, and squash, and hunted small animals and deer. The city was probably the central focus of a large trading network, aided surely by the proximity of the Mississippi, the Illinois, and the Missouri rivers. In one grave alone, archaeologists have uncovered several trade goods that came from far distant regions: a roll of sheet copper a yard long and two-thirds of a yard wide that probably originated from the copper outcroppings around Lake Superior; black chert arrowheads that undoubtedly came from Arkansas or Oklahoma; and enough sheet mica, likely from North Carolina, to fill several bushel baskets. In many respects the most interesting items the grave yielded were fifteen carved and polished stone disks that may have come from the Southeast. Similar disks, about 4 inches in diameter and resembling concave hockey pucks, were used throughout the Southeast in historic times in a popular game the natives called chunky.[8] The game varied from tribe to tribe in its details, but the general object seems to have been to roll the disk along a smooth, leveled playing ground while opponents on either side threw long sticks at the disk, attempting to stop its course. The stick that ended up closest to the disk won its owner a point.

Although Cahokia clearly flourished until about A.D. 1250, and was probably a major trading center known throughout the region, it slid into a gradual decline. By A.D. 1500, the center of Mississippian culture had moved south and east. Although smaller groups continued to live in the area until the arrival of the Europeans, their numbers and level of organization were vastly reduced.

Although much of the area that made up the prehistoric center has been destroyed by twentieth-century urban sprawl, enough remains intact to confirm initial impressions of an extremely important prehistoric population center. Indeed, one of the early visitors, the Reverend Timothy Flint, was moved to commit his impressions of the site to verse:

> I lingered by some soft enchantment bound,
> And gazed enraptured on the lovely scene,
> From the dark summit of an Indian mound
> I saw the plain outspread of living green,
> Its fringe of cliffs was in the distance seen,
> And the dark line of Forest sweeping round.
>
> I saw the lesser mounds which round me rose;
> Each was a giant heap of mouldering clay;
> There slept the warriors, women, friends and foes,
> There side by side the rival chieftains lay;
> And mighty tribes, swept from the face of day,
> Forgot their wars and found a long repose.[9]

The Reverend Mr. Flint's romantic conceptions notwithstanding, Cahokia is indeed impressive. Even the casual tourist cannot fail to recognize the energy and grand conception that went into its construction. Cahokia represents a high level of Native American organization and achievement.

Four types of mounds were built at the Cahokia site over the centuries. Even Monks Mound, the largest one, was constructed laboriously, basketful by basketful, the builders taking earth dug from so-called borrow pits many yards distant and carrying it to the mound by hand — for here, as in other parts of North America, there were no large beasts of burden to help, nor were there wheeled carts to lighten the human load. Monks Mound, a unique stepped pyramid comprising four levels, contains an estimated 22 million cubic feet of earth. In addition, Cahokia boasts six smaller ridgetop mounds and seven conical mounds. The most common type, however, is the platform mound. This style appears in several shapes — round, oval, or square — and may have one or more platforms. Some platform mounds originally had wooden structures atop them. The ridgetop mounds and the conical mounds presumably served primarily as burial mounds, although archaeologists will have to do extensive additional excavation to verify this hypothesis.

Ridgetop mound 72, in the southern part of the site, provided archaeologist Melvin Fowler and his associates with intriguing evidence of astronomical orientation for the mounds complex.[10] In pondering the meaning of the ridgetop mounds, they noticed that of the total of six found at Cahokia, three are located at the extreme east, south, and west boundaries of the city. The southeast extremity of mound 72, however, is located on a line between the western edge of Monks Mound and the western edge of the southernmost ridgetop mound. This line falls along the local meridian; that is, it forms a north-south line. Further, mound 72 is oriented at an unusual angle for Cahokian mounds, 30° south of east. It is also located at the western edge of the largest borrow pit at Cahokia, about 800 yards south of Monks Mound. Fowler and his colleagues speculated that mound 72 helped to define a "carefully calculated north-south center line at Cahokia." They tested this hypothesis by sinking a trench where they expected this line to fall across the edge of mound 72.

While excavating, they came upon evidence (indicated by a soil stain left behind) of a timber whose base was about 2 feet across.

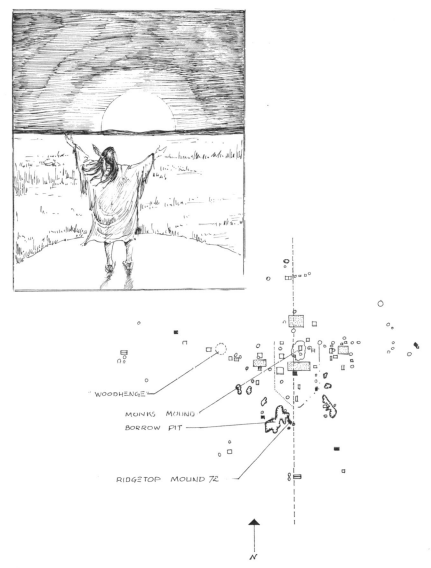

Mounds at Cahokia, Illinois, in East St. Louis. The Cahokia mounds were the site of a major civilization in the heartland of this country. The city that was Cahokia had more than 100 mounds and probably housed as many as 40,000 people at the height of its development. These mounds appear to have been laid out according to an astronomical plan designed around the cardinal directions. Monks Mound is the largest earth mound north of Mexico. Burial mound 72, a ridgetop mound, may have been deliberately aligned along the winter solstice sunrise and summer solstice sunset positions. (After Melvin L. Fowler, "A Pre-Columbian Urban Center on the Mississippi. *Scientific American* [August 1975]: 92–101.)

This confirmed their hypothesis that the north-south line was likely to have been intentionally constructed, for such a large-diameter post was also likely to project high above the surface, and therefore be highly visible throughout Cahokia. Such orientation represents a sophisticated level of planning that is emphasized by the careful positioning of other mounds in the group. Fowler and his colleagues also discovered that for several generations, the mound served as the burial ground for an elite. This and other evidence from other parts of Cahokia suggests that the social structure during the period that the marker post was erected (between A.D. 925 and 1035) was distinctly stratified.

What I find particularly interesting about mound 72 is its axial orientation approximately 30° south of east (or 30° north of west). At sunrise, the shadow of the post would fall right along the axis of the mound. As the sun rose and moved south, the shadow would move north of the ridge. Conversely, on the summer solstice, the setting sun would cause the post to cast its shadow along the axis of the ridge in the opposite direction. Although the present ridgetop shape of mound 72 was not reached until about a hundred years after its construction began, the orientation of the mound seems to merit further examination by archaeologists. The number of high-status burials that were found there, from several phases of construction, suggests that the mound was known as a sacred, special place for many years. Its orientation along the solstice directions may indicate a conceptual link between burial and the winter solstice direction. I do not believe that it would have been used for observing winter solstice sunrise or summer solstice sunset for the purposes of setting a calendar. A much higher degree of accuracy would be needed for such observations than is afforded in an earth mound. On the other hand, the mound is nearly 70 yards long. A post at the northwest end in precisely the right place with respect to the southeast post would create a reasonably accurate and impressive winter solstice sunrise or summer solstice sunset marking device. To date, the northwest end has not been excavated.

The American Woodhenge

Excavations centering on the era of occupation during which mound 72 was built, termed by archaeologists the Fairmount phase, have provided a partial glimpse into the grand schemes that may have

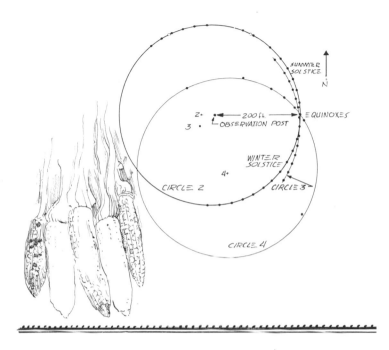

Woodhenge circles at Cahokia, Illinois. Constructed of cedar posts, these circles contain solar alignments that could have been used to define a solar calendar. The three posts of circle 2 that mark the solstices and the equinoxes have been reconstructed by archaeologist Warren Wittry in an attempt to see how they might have functioned for the Cahokians. (After Richard Norrish, "Woodhenge — Work of a Genius." *Cahokian* [February 1978]: 21–24.)

been held by Cahokia planners. They have also yielded evidence of a fascinating wooden structure from the same period, dubbed an American Woodhenge by its principal excavator, archaeologist Warren Wittry. Wittry first discovered evidence of a full circle of cedar posts, and several arcs of circles, while conducting salvage archaeology in the early 1960s in preparation for the construction of Interstate 55–70. What he and his crew found in their hurried excavations were several large oval pits revealed only by soil stains. Their seemingly unique shape, shallow on one end and deeper on the other, puzzled these investigators until a similar pit was found at an entirely different site with a log still in place in the deeper end. The oval pits were the remnants of post holes; the odd shape was the result of digging ramps to facilitate erecting especially large posts. An inclined ramp from the bottom of each hole to the surface makes it possible to slide a post nearly two feet in diameter and many feet long into the hole and then raise it up in stages.[11]

After learning the probable meaning of the odd-shaped holes, Wittry then realized that these remnants of post holes were arranged in arcs of circles. He now believes there are at least four, and possibly more, circles that were built at different times. Each circle has a similar radius but different post spacing and center. At least two of the circles (circles 2 and 3) seem to have astronomical significance.

While pondering the meaning of the data from his first excavations at the site, Wittry reached a striking conclusion.[12] An observer standing near the center of the original circle could watch the sun rise behind three of the poles on the summer and winter solstices and the equinoxes. Observing from the exact geometrical center of the circle, however, the placement of the solstice allows the summer solstice sun to rise a little north of the "solstice post," and the winter solstice sun a little south of its respective post. Yet further excavations at the site revealed a post hole 5 feet east of true center. Looking from this spot instead, the angles are precisely correct to observe the solstice sunrises behind the posts. Strangely, no signs of a post or other structure have been found at the center. Observing from the observation post, the angular diameter of the circle's posts are just slightly greater than the diameter of the sun, thus allowing an extremely accurate determination of the solstice. Since the sun appears to pause along the horizon for about four days at the solstices, when the sun disappeared completely behind the post in its yearly travels, the observer would have known that the solstice would occur in one or two days.

From viewing a small-scale diagram of circle 2, it is tempting to assume that the circle possessed posts located precisely at all four cardinal directions. Yet the area in which we would expect to find the western post has been destroyed. Although Wittry found the eastern post, nearly precisely on the east line, he discovered that the north and south posts are situated slightly west of geographic north and south as seen from the center. The posts themselves lie along a meridian, but their meridian passes about 1.5 feet west of the center. Thus, it would seem that the Cahokians intended the circle to contain posts at the cardinal directions but were less concerned with north-south *as seen from the center* than with the eastern equinox post. Actually, the discrepancy is small and may simply reflect the difficulties of locating holes for the posts any more accurately without benefit of advanced surveying tools. As they now stand, the divergence from true north and south as seen from the center is only about the angular diameter of the sun.

Circle 2 is about 410 feet across and was originally made up of forty-eight posts, set approximately 27 feet apart along the circumference of the circle. Cedar chips found in the post holes suggest that the posts were made of red cedar, a species that was common near Cahokia and seems to have ritual significance. Thirty-five post holes have been excavated in several seasons of fieldwork. The exact number of original posts is in doubt because the road builders, thinking they were safely beyond any important archaeological materials, dug a modern borrow pit across the west edge of the circle that obliterated thirteen probable post holes.

Two other circles are known at the site, circle 1 and circle 4. The latter circle yields a single carbon date of A.D. 815, which Wittry considers far too early, based on the level of civilization elsewhere in Cahokia at that epoch. However, this carbon-derived date can be used in a relative sense to place circle 4 in the sequence of other circles. His circle 1 does not intersect with the other circles, nor has it generated wood fragments that can be dated. There is some question in Wittry's mind whether it can be considered a Cahokian Woodhenge-type circle. However, it seems to have been intended to contain twenty-four posts. He suggests the following sequence.[13]

Circle	Epoch	Radius	Posts	Notes
1	?	117 ft.	24 (?)	Doesn't intersect
4	> A.D. 1000	205 ft.	36	7 posts known
2	c. A.D. 1000	205 ft.	48	35 posts known
3	c. A.D. 1150	224 ft.	72	Sunrise arc only

Circle 3 consists only of the sunrise arc, plus one extra post along the arc north of the summer solstice sunrise post. The center post of circle 3 is known as well. Only seven posts for circle 4 have been located to date, nor has anyone found the center post. Neither of these circles has been studied as extensively as circle 2.

Because one of the pits of circle 3 is superimposed on a pit belonging to circle 2, Wittry was able to show that circle 2 was built prior to circle 3. The pits of both circles yielded organic material that could be dated by carbon 14 techniques. For circle 2, six samples yield a range of dates extending from A.D. 810 to 1120 and leading to an average date of about A.D. 970.[14] Carbon dating of circle 3 indicated an average date of construction of about A.D. 1170. From artifactual and other evidence, Wittry believes that the average dates are a bit early for circle 2 and a bit late for circle 3. Wittry labeled the circles the American Woodhenge because it is reminiscent of the Wood-henge in Wiltshire, England, which is also made up of a large circular set of wooden posts and is also oriented to the summer solstice. There, however, the connection ends, for the British Woodhenge was built in the second millennium B.C., and is apparently the remnant of a large circular building. The American Woodhenge circles, by contrast, seem to be structurally unrelated to each other.

Whatever further fieldwork and theoretical calculations unearth at this site, it seems clear that circle 2 was designed to witness the solstices and the equinoxes. One find at the site is especially intriguing in this regard. In a fire pit that was found on top of the rampway dug to facilitate raising the winter solstice post of circle 2, excavators found a potsherd whose design may represent the winter solstice. The design is highly reminiscent of the quartered-circle symbols of the Pueblo region and consists of crossed lines in the center of a double circle, outside of which are short radiating lines. Wittry suggests that the crossed lines represent the world, and the lines outside the second circle signify the power of the sun. Finally, and most important to his entire thesis, an open pathway on the lower right may represent the winter solstice.

Although Wittry, like others, has speculated on possible lunar alignments in the circle of posts, he finds no evidence of an interest in observing lunar standstills at the site. If observations were made, they were solar observations of solstice and equinox. Wittry has arbitrarily taken the point where the sun last touches the horizon as the observation that most interested the Cahokians. In the moisture-laden atmosphere around the American Bottoms, it would often be reasonably comfortable, if not entirely safe, to observe the sun until it rose above the horizon. The ethnographic evidence of sun watching in this geographic region is tenuous. A Menomini myth collected many miles north of Cahokia mentions observing the sun when it "stands on the treetops," an account consistent with Wittry's assumption.

Excavating for the posts is exacting work, requiring a practiced eye and careful examination of every detail. Evidence for post holes exists several inches below the plow-zone layer, where in the past plows have dug up and disturbed the soil. After stripping this layer off, the area of the suspected posts is carefully scraped and examined. If nothing appears, excavators sprinkle water over the surface to enhance the contrast between soil stains around the missing post. Then, "they just pop out," as Wittry explains. If not, they scrape some more and water again. The striking thing is, once the archaeologists determine what the pattern is, in most cases they are able to find post holes near where they calculate them to be. Although it is often possible to determine the center of the post hole near the top of its depth, Wittry carries each excavation to the bottom of the post pit. There, it is generally possible to find the impression made by the weight of the original post. He then determines the center of the post hole by measuring the center of the impression.

Seven posts in the southwest sector of circle 2 showed evidence that the original post had been removed and another put in its place. In some cases, the prints at the bottom of the hole indicated that the second post had been shifted slightly from the first. In one case, however, the second post was completely separated from the first impression. Just why the builders of the circles might have removed a post and replaced it is not clear. The original one may have deteriorated over time and been replaced by a new post, or it may even have been struck by lightning. If the modern experience at Cahokia is any guide to the past, lightning damage appears to have been a particular problem. In an attempt to demonstrate to the public the possible use of circle 2 for calendrical purposes, Wittry reconstructed three of the eastern posts and the observer's post. In 1980, the observer's post was struck by lightning and shattered. The winter solstice post shows some signs of lightning damage as well. Another possible cause for removal is that the builders were unsatisfied by the angular placement of certain posts and replaced them to correspond more closely to their plan.

Originally, finding the circle patterns required painstaking mapping of every feature on the site and pulling away all those features that could be identified as house foundations, storage pits, or other known artificial features. Considering the fact that a total of 170 house foundations were found in and around the site, this was a major undertaking in itself. Once the pattern of circles was suspected, it then became a matter of fitting circumferences and centers in a trial-and-error procedure to locate individual circles.[15]

The City's Plan

Treating Cahokia as a whole, there is every reason to believe that its builders put to use a well-developed blend of rudimentary astronomy and geometry in planning their city.[16] Instead of being scattered randomly, the placements of the individual mounds give every appearance of having been planned deliberately. Most mounds cluster about the major east-west axis at the site and are roughly oriented along the cardinal directions. The mounds also seem to be grouped to form smaller units of platform mounds, plazas, and burial mounds within the overall city limits.

Their apparent attention to overall city planning as well as the mound form and orientation have suggested to many that perhaps the Mexicans influenced Cahokian thought. For example, Monks Mound and many other mounds are oriented along axes about 5° east of north. Many Mexican pyramids display similar orientations, though at angles between 7° and 15° east of north. Although it is tempting to make the connection with Mexico on the basis of this evidence, much more evidence will have to be gathered to prove the hypothesis. The grave goods suggest trade over great distances, but none can be traced directly to Mexico. By contrast, there is ample material evidence of trade links between the Anasazi and the Hohokam of the Southwest and the Mexicans. In addition, many of the other traits in evidence at Cahokia, such as the form of burials, are not traceable to Mexico. Cahokian astronomy could have been conceptually linked to Mexico, but no astronomical alignments we have seen at Cahokia particularly stand out as Mexican traits. In particular, the attention to the solstices and the equinoxes is a North American, as well as Mexican, trait.

Incinerator Site, Ohio

The Mississippian mounds culture is not the only prehistoric group in the center of the country for which astronomical alignments seem to have been a significant part of the cultural practice. Near the Great Miami River in Dayton, Ohio, is a prehistoric village that exhibits some surprising astronomical alignments. The present humble surroundings of the site, located near Dayton's incinerator and sewage-treatment plants, belie the importance it has for understanding the ancient culture of the area. This village had a close scrape with oblivion, for it had been scheduled to serve as the site of sludge-treatment ponds for the city of Dayton; however, after an extensive salvage excavation led by the Dayton Museum of Natural History, which discovered the wealth of interesting material at the site, in 1974 the village was placed on the National Register of Historic Places and preserved for further study.[17]

The Incinerator Site was inhabited by a group of Native Americans from the so-called Anderson Focus of the Fort Ancient culture, who lived in the area during the twelfth century. Archaeologists will likely be working the site for many years, but to date they have discovered that the original village consisted of more than fifteen houses arranged about a central open plaza. The houses were constructed from lath and daub over a wooden post framework and probably had thatched roofs. The site was originally surrounded by a nearly circular stockade 400 feet in diameter; its overlapping walls and gatehouses suggest that the inhabitants experienced problems with their neighbors.

The largest structure in the village (House I/71) is 22 by 30 feet. About 10 yards north of this house is a building that archaeologist James Heilman believes may have served an important ceremonial purpose (House I/78). With a slightly smaller ground plan than its companion to the south, this structure had walls that were nevertheless supported by larger-diameter posts sunk deeper in the soil. Larger posts may mean that this lodge was considerably taller than its nearby counterparts, giving it a more imposing appearance. It may have served a ceremonial function. Indeed, the presence of several burials nearby, whose contents indicate high-ranking individuals, suggests that it was more important than others in the village. This theory derives additional support from the fact that the archaeologists discovered remains of burnt corn affiliated with pipes and other exotic material buried between these lodges. These finds suggest that the corn was ritually burnt as a ceremonial offering. These two houses are pulled forward toward the plaza and have greater spacing around them than other houses in this village, which gives them a more conspicuous presence.

Analysis of the storage and trash pits shows that the villagers made pottery, flint, stone, and bone tools, and lived primarily off corn, beans, and squash and the meat of deer, elk, turkey, and raccoon. Flotation techniques have recovered substantial evidence of locally gathered nuts, fruits, and grain. In short, the people who lived at this site knew well how to use the bounty of nature for their sustenance and how to schedule their economic routines. They also looked up to view the heavens as well as down to till the soil, for the structure of the village indicates that they developed a calendar tied to ritual needs as well as agricultural.

Nearly 27 yards east of this ceremonial area, near the center of the village plaza, excavators discovered the remains of a large eastern red cedar center post. From the fact that two distinct ramps had been dug, they surmise that the post had been erected at the same place at least twice. The size of the post's base (over 2 feet in diameter) suggested to Heilman that it may have served some special function. Then, when he discovered four additional smaller posts precisely arranged in a parallelogram around the larger one, he sought the aid of astronomer Roger Hoefer to help interpret what he and his colleagues were finding.

This sort of collaboration is becoming increasingly common in archaeology as archaeologists discover material that more traditional archaeological techniques cannot explain. What they found by collaborating is far more intriguing than either could have discovered working independently. The parallelogram that surrounds the large post is about 6 yards long and 2 yards wide (between post centers), and the large post is seated precisely on the long axis of the parallelogram. This center line, which lies along an azimuth of 73.5° (16.5° north of east), if extended west-southwest, stretches right through House I/71, the largest house in the village. What especially drew the interest of Heilman and Hoefer was the fact that the extended axis of the parallelogram falls directly across the socket of a post located inside House I/71. This post was somewhat thicker than the average post and set off by itself. Just south of this line is the hearth; it is the only example in the village of a hearth not located in the center of the house, which, along with the exotic nature of the garbage near the house and the special spatial consideration given to this house, leads Heilman to believe it may have served a special purpose.

Hoefer surmised that this alignment might even have some calendrical significance. If it did, it signified dates between the vernal and the autumnal equinoxes. At this latitude, summer solstice occurs at an azimuth of 58.75°, so the line falls too far south to indicate a solstice alignment. Still, archaeological evidence from the site indicates the villagers burned corn ceremonially, perhaps in a version of the green corn ceremony that was witnessed by early explorers in the southeastern part of the country. The pair's measured orientation suggests an alignment based both on planting corn and on the green corn ceremony. A sunrise azimuth of 73.5° occurs on April 24 and August 20, therefore spanning a period of 118 days. By April 24, Dayton is, on the average, free of killing frost. According to the collaborators' theory, when the sun falls along this line at sunrise 34

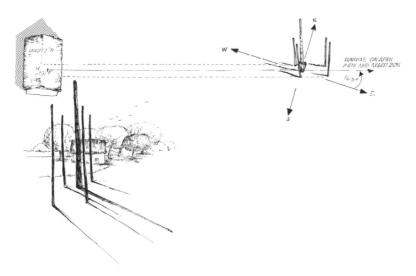

Solar alignment at Incinerator Site, Ohio. Several solar alignments are found at this important Fort Ancient site in Dayton, Ohio. This one illustrates the important alignment formed by a parallelogram of four posts surrounding a larger post with House I/71. At sunrise on April 24, the start of the corn planting season in the Ohio Valley, and August 20, about the time of the historic green corn ceremony of some eastern Indian groups, the large post casts a shadow in the direction of a small post (F) set up to the north of the hearth (H). The large post was made of cedar, a wood sacred to historic groups in the region.

days after the vernal equinox, the villagers would have begun planting corn, safe in the knowledge that the corn would not germinate
before killing frosts had passed.

Using the parallelogram as a guide, with the central large post and
the post in House I/71, it would be possible to time the ceremonial
planting or harvesting quite precisely. In the spring, the day just
before the sun reached the critical planting stage, it would first appear above the horizon along a line between the southern posts of the
parallelogram and the central post. The next day, because the angular diameter of a two-foot post as seen from House I/71 is greater than
the sun's disk, the sun would not appear on the horizon but would
appear to rise from behind the large central post. The sun priest
would then know that the day to begin planting had arrived. From
that day on, the sun would rise north of this line, turn around at the
summer solstice, and return to fall along the same line in late August, 32 days before the autumnal equinox. At that point, though the
corn would have filled out the husk, it would still be too immature to
harvest. It would, however, be ready for ritual sacrifice in thanks for
the bounty of nature. The sun, in its journey south, would again
appear between the posts of the parallelogram in such a way that the
officials who observed the sun could announce the ceremony just
prior to the proper time. If the fire pit in House I/71 was being used in
this green corn ritual, a shaft of sunlight would strike this hearth on
the day of the green corn ritual. One of the universals that anthropologist John Witthoft notes for the green corn ritual is the ritual
lighting of the new fire,[18] which Heilman believes was taking place
in this hearth in House I/71. The drama would certainly have been
increased with this shaft of sunlight striking the hearth as the "new
fire" was ignited.

The inhabitants of the Incinerator Site may have also observed the
equinox. Along a line 114 feet due west of the large central post, the
villagers placed three large trash pits containing what seem to be
ceremonial deposits. In excavating the pits, the archaeologists were
able to determine that they had been dug and filled in sequence
starting with the westernmost pit, indicating that the placement of
the pits was not a chance occurrence. In addition, beyond them
north and south of the equinox line are two lines of small post holes
that seem to form a lane 3 feet wide and 45 feet long. This lane ends
abruptly in a line of posts that cut across nearly perpendicular to the

equinox line. Thus, an observer standing or crouching before these posts could see the equinox sun appear from behind the plaza's center post and shine down the narrow avenue of smaller posts. Other observers would see the shadow cast by the large central post fall briefly right across the ceremonial trash pits and along the avenue before it swept north as the sun moved south through the sky.

I suspect that the slow sweep of the central post's shadow across the village as the sun rose would have made an exciting visual display for the entire village. A 20-foot-high post still casts a long shadow when the sun has been up for several hours. Thus, as the sun rose, say at the equinox, the post would first cast a shadow along the avenue of small posts. As the sun moves up from the horizon and southward, the shadow would swing north to sweep across the houses on the northwest side of the plaza. By about 7:00 A.M., however, its shadow would fall only on the plaza; there it would be extremely obvious even to the casual observer, and could serve as an effective sundial. During the period around the summer solstice, because the sun climbs higher in the sky the post's shadow would be relatively short most of the day. In fact, the noon shadow would be less than 6 feet in length. Around the winter solstice, it would extend to nearly 39 feet, about twice the length of the pole. Given the obvious visibility of the post's shadow in the plaza, it would be of considerable interest to investigate the area north of the central post for indications that the villagers might have used the post in this way to determine the meridian.

Deciding whether the solstices were of particular interest to these Native Americans will require further work at the site. The strongest indication at this stage is that the line passing between the summer solstice sunset and winter solstice sunrise runs right through a sweat lodge and then along the southern wall of House I/77, a structure that has a highly unusual trapezoidal ground plan. The parallelogram around the central post could also have been used to help define the summer solstice sunrise and winter solstice sunset. In addition, there are four post holes just beyond the sweat lodge to the northwest of the central post. They, too, could have been used to help define the two solstice events.

As they continue to explore this interesting site, Heilman and his colleagues will examine other possible alignments. It will also be particularly important to extend this work to other Fort Ancient sites, since it is of considerable interest to know whether the astronomical orientations uncovered in this village are common to the culture or whether this was a unique place.

When I visited the Incinerator Site, I was particularly struck with how much care the inhabitants had taken to lay out and organize their modest village. Though pouring rain and deep mud prevented a thorough examination of the structures, it was obvious that the intimacy of the enclosed village would have made the orientations Heilman and Hoefer have hypothesized visible to any inhabitant, not solely to a trained few. Once again, as in so many prehistoric sites throughout this vast country, astronomy formed an intimate part of people's lives.

The Green Corn Ceremony

Corn from Mexico became an essential part of the native diet throughout North America in the middle part of the first millennium A.D. Wherever it was cultivated, there seem also to have arisen special ceremonies to commemorate its importance to the Native American diet. Among other groups in the East, the Creek, Iroquois, and Cherokee celebrated especially when the corn was ripe enough to fill the husk but was still green. In all of these tribes, it was taboo to taste the green corn until eating it ritually at the ceremony. Even if its corn reached the proper stage of ripeness well before the ceremony, a family would live on roots and other foods or even fast rather than break the taboo.

The Iroquois still hold a four-day festival that begins in late August or early September, depending on when the corn is at the proper stage of ripeness.[19] On the first day, the new children are named, and a general thanksgiving is made to the spirits. The day ends with feather dances and, finally, a feast. Each subsequent day is marked by thanksgiving, feasting, and dancing. On the fourth day, the tribe plays the "great bowl game," the last of the four sacred ceremonies. The men divide into two groups, or moieties, and play against each other for possession of bean counters. One moiety takes the part of the creator and the other the part of his evil twin who, in the beginning, struggled with the creator for possession of the earth. When one side has won all 102 beans, the game ends, and the final ceremonies conclude the four days of ritual. This game is of particular importance because of the cosmic struggle it represents. The number *four*, representative of the four directions, is central to this ceremony.

The Creek Nation also held a four-day or an eight-day green corn ceremony called a busk (from the Creek word *posketa*, meaning "a fast"), which corresponded to their new year.[20] The details of the ceremony varied from town to town. Prior to the event, the chiefs held meetings to prepare for the ceremony, and to set its date (usually in late July or early August). They then prepared a sanctified square. On each side of the square were three-sided log shelters open to the square. The square was proscribed to women for the period.

In preparing the town for the ceremony, the men purged it of debts and quarrels by the first day of the busk. They also fasted until the ritual, and purged their bodies in order to be worthy of the new fire that was kindled on the first day. After all fires in the village were extinguished, the priest then prepared the new fire. From each corner of the square, men entered, each one carrying an oak log for the new fire. They placed the butt of each of the four logs toward the direction from which it came, to form a cross extending to the four directions. Then, using a wooden fire drill, the priest kindled the new fire. After the new fire took hold, the youths of the village lighted torches and carried them away from the fire toward the cardinal directions to light the village's hearth fires anew. Women waiting at the four corners of the square with their own torches then took the new fire to their homes.

After kindling the new fire, the chiefs prepared themselves spiritually for drinking the famous (or infamous) "black drink," an infusion of cassine (*Ilex vomitoria*) roots and leaves in water. The men of the tribe sat in the four buildings facing the square; the chiefs sat in two diagonal lines with their backs to opposite corners. After singing the appropriate song three times, the chiefs took the black drink from a conch shell and expelled it lustily, as the purgative qualities of the cassine act quickly and thoroughly.

The purification ritual may last just for the first day, or it may be repeated again the next day. In any event, the men are forbidden to eat until the busk is destroyed by cooking the new corn. When it was time to cook the green corn, four men entered the square again, one from each of the four corners, carrying corn to be cooked in the new fire. The ceremonies that followed included hunting, feasting, dancing, ball games, and perhaps a mock battle on the sacred square.

These historical accounts of roasting and ritually burning ears of corn demonstrate the deep relationship between the calendar, the four directions, and the production of foodstuffs for the village. It is highly likely that these rituals, or some form of them, accompanied the introduction of corn to the eastern part of the country. As archaeologist Heilman believes, the presence of burnt corn along with other material apparently of ritual origin at the Incinerator Site in Dayton lends particular weight to his interpretation of the site's astronomical orientations. Of especial interest to him is the fact that the Creek also used a large center pole in their busk ceremonies. As he notes, a shaft of sunlight would hit the fire pit in House I/71 on August 20, or about the same time the later groups held their green corn ceremonies.

Crystal River, Florida

Along the Crystal River, some 75 miles north of Tampa Bay on the west coast of Florida, a group of shell mounds exhibits several potential astronomical alignments. Built over centuries between about 30 B.C. and A.D. 1200, the site consists of six mounds of various shapes, and two standing steles, or sculptured stone pillars — the only ones known in the eastern United States. Archaeologist Clark Hardman, who has studied this site in detail, believes that it may have solstitial and equinoctial alignments, as well as possible north-south alignments. As he suggests, "this important ceremonial site can be interpreted as a giant calendar of sand, shell and stone."[21]

The shell mounds of Crystal River have been studied since the early years of the twentieth century, but it was only during a clearing operation in 1964 that stele 1 was uncovered.[22] As Hardman much later realized, it is this feature more than any other at the site that suggests the potential for astronomical sight lines. Stele 1 is an irregular limestone boulder 5 feet high. What qualifies it to be labeled a stele is a pecked and incised anthropomorphic petroglyph on the northeast side of the stone. Though the surface of the stone is rough and pitted, which therefore prevented the prehistoric artist from giving the figure finely articulated features, it is possible to make out a head and shoulders. From the top of the head extends hair or a feathered plume. Additional detailed features include eyes, a mouth, and a right ear with an attached earspool such as was worn by Florida tribes in historic times. The orientation of the boulder causes the figure to face toward summer solstice sunrise.

Modern excavations around stele 1 yielded some particularly interesting data suggesting it may have served as a shrine; because of its orientation, it also appears to be dedicated to the sun. The surface of the earth in the direction of solstice sunrise was excavated nearly a foot and a half deep by the shell mound people, who apparently erected the stele and wedged it in place with a small limestone rock. The excavations uncovered several limestone chips, suggesting that the stele was also shaped during placement. The builders then laid a cobblestone path in front of the petroglyph about 2 feet wide and nearly twice as long. They set a flat-topped limestone rock some 16 inches across and as many deep at the end of the cobblestones. Covering the cobblestones at the time of excavation were bits of charcoal, sand, and long-decayed remains of food, perhaps placed there as offerings. Over all, the builders of this shrine scattered another layer of mottled brown sand and yellow-gray sand. The soil that covers it all may have been deposited over the centuries since the stele was erected. The charcoal yielded a radiocarbon date of A.D. 440, showing that the stele itself was probably set up and used for votive or propitiatory offerings around the time that the South Temple Mound was built. If it was also used as a calendar device in that same epoch, it would be part of one of the older known calendar sites in North America.

Hardman suggests that the Native Americans who lived at this site deliberately planned the placement and orientation of the mounds and the stele to track the sun as it rose and set throughout the year. The fact that the figure on stele 1 faces the sunrise at summer solstice suggests its part in ritually observing that important solar date. However, it is also possible to develop an accurate calendar using parts of the mounds and the stele.

Still, not all of the orientations Hardman suggests are convincing. Part of the difficulty in determining probable orientations is that the vegetation in the area is particularly thick. The fact that many tall trees grow around and even through the site today implies that unless special sighting paths were cleared, it would have been impossible to view the sun along the horizon. Conversely, the builders of the mounds might have been satisfied with a high local horizon. Another obstacle in estimating how the features of the site might have been used is that the mounds are typically gently rounded, which makes determining the highest points or edges especially difficult. That, in turn, makes discovering precisely what constituted an appropriate sight line extremely hard. Nonetheless, it is worth investigating the possible alignments at the site for what they reveal about the potential for deliberately orienting earth, shells, and stones.

Stele 2 presents the best backsight for orientations. It is about 4.5 feet high, nearly the same width at the base, and from 5 to 12 inches thick. It has no markings, but excavations show that it, too, was probably deliberately erected at the site. Limestone chips around the foundation suggest that it was also specially shaped for some reason. Using stele 2 as a backsight, it is possible to witness winter solstice sunrise just above stele 1. Then, turning around, winter solstice sunset can be determined by observing from stele 2 across the top of North Shell Mound. The equinox can be estimated within a day or two by observing from stele 2 across the center of the burial mound to its east. Finally, from stele 2 the summer solstice sun can be observed rising above the north edge of the burial mound.

Although they are less convincing as deliberate orientations, it is also possible to construct two intriguing north-south lines through the mounds. From the east and west ends of the North Temple Mound, meridian lines fall, respectively, across stele 1 and through the center of the burial mound. As Hardman demonstrates, several other alignments are possible to construct at the site, but they all suffer from severe lack of precision or from the absence of a well-defined horizon. In short, they are unconvincing in the extreme.

That the later Florida tribes watched the sun seems clear from the few extant accounts left by the early European explorers. The Crystal River site suggests that the ancestors of these groups had also developed their skills along the same lines. The presence of the steles suggests that the site's builders may have been influenced by visitors from Mexico, especially from the Maya area. Ripley Bullen, the archaeologist who uncovered stele 1, notes that it, like the stele of the Maya, faces away from South Temple Mound to its southwest, and suggests that travelers "from southeastern Mexico (Veracruz or Yucatán), did get to the Crystal River Site around A.D. 500."

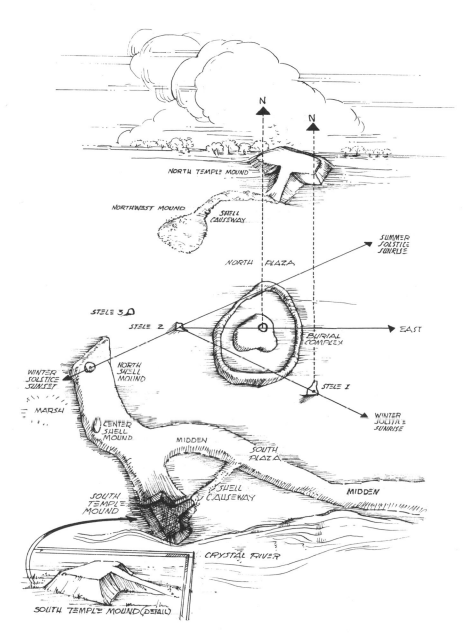

Potential astronomical alignments at the Crystal River, Florida, shell mounds.
These shell mounds may have been constructed in the early centuries of
the first millennium A.D. by native North Americans who were influenced
by visitors from southeastern Mexico.

Others have suggested that the Crystal River mounds and associated artifacts demonstrate cultural affinities with the Hopewell culture of the Ohio River Valley.[23] However, though these similarities are many, it is not clear whether they are the result simply of trade or of a transfer of customs between tribes. The case is as yet unproved.

Because the archaeoastronomical studies of this site were done in the late 1960s, before the general upsurge of interest in archaeoastronomy in North America and the greater knowledge about ethnoastronomy that is now available, I hope that someone will re-examine the shell mounds of Crystal River for their astronomical content. In light of the extensive studies that have been done elsewhere in North America, it would also be in order to study the historical records and other archaeological findings from the area that may relate to astronomical practice.

Chambers and Standing Stones

The Northeast presents the archaeoastronomer with a panoply of unusual problems, centered around the dispute over what constitutes the appropriate material to study. If you mention New England stone chambers to a northeastern archaeologist, at best you are likely to receive a knowing sigh in response. What follows might even be a lengthy discourse deriding the "nuts" of New England archaeology, those poor benighted men and women who chase around the landscape looking for evidence that the builders of the many stone chambers or various megaliths and standing stones found throughout New England, New York, and Pennsylvania are the remnants of an earlier European culture.

In the fall of 1977, I participated in a conference held to discuss these puzzling stones.[24] Are they historic constructions, or were they left by the ancestors of Native American tribes? Or, and I suspect this was the primary reason for holding the conference in the first place, were they put there primarily by Europeans who then either returned home again or intermarried with the various native groups of the eastern forests?

The question of the origins and meaning of these stones and stone structures is not a trivial one, nor is it apparently amenable to a few months' research in the historic archives. Surprisingly, there is very little known about them. I had been invited to participate in the conference because of my interest and expertise in archaeoastronomy. Dr. Warren Cook, the organizer of the conference, wanted someone who could comment on the putative astronomical alignments that had been found. Although several colleagues warned me that attending the conference might be a serious waste of time, I was curious about the antiquities of New England and especially about the potential for astronomical orientation. Besides, I thought it might be diverting to watch the various sides argue out the issues. I was not disappointed on either count. The conference turned out to be an uneasy mix of serious amateurs who have spent many years poking around the New England countryside in an effort to understand the remains of earlier peoples, some genuine nuts, and several professional archaeologists and anthropologists who attended primarily to discredit everyone else. Of primary importance to me was the chance to visit some of the stone chambers (or root cellars, as they are also called) and to hike through the Vermont countryside at the height of its autumn colors.

I was also able to see firsthand why the issues about the putative ancient structures are so difficult. The fact is that until fairly recently, the upright stones, stone chambers, large cairns, and other evidence of human handiwork not claimed by recent history had been poorly studied. Even today they have not been thoroughly catalogued. Studying these lithic remains is particularly difficult because potentially extremely old structures are intermixed with recent ones; sometimes they are even integrated into buildings, stone fences, and other artifacts that clearly are of the recent historic period. Prior to attending the conference, I thought that studying the astronomical orientations of some of the structures would be a way to help sort out some of the questions. However, I did not realize how strong the feelings were among the several sides, and how difficult it was for serious amateurs to discuss some issues with professional archaeologists. Nor did I realize how little archaeological study had been devoted to the stone chambers. At the time of the Vermont conference, there had been no systematic study of the stone chambers of New England, much less the many standing stones, rock cairns, and other lithic remnants of pre-nineteenth-century human activity. Today, although significant attempts have been made toward a better understanding of these remains, controversy reigns.

Nevertheless, the archaeoastronomical research at some of the

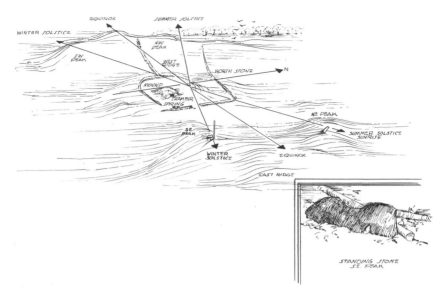

Calendar I site, Vermont. This site contains several solar alignments that may have been placed there intentionally by prehistoric Native Americans. The origins of these and other putative astronomically aligned structures in the Northeast are highly controversial. (After Byron E. Dix and James W. Mavor, Jr., "Two Possible Calendar Sites in Vermont," in *Archaeoastronomy in the Americas*, edited by Ray A. Williamson [Los Altos, Calif.: Ballena Press, 1981]: 115.)

sites suggests that some of the chambers and/or standing stones may have been intentionally aligned. In spite of superficial similarities between some of these remains and similar ones in Great Britain and Europe, it is highly unlikely that the two sets are related to each other.

The most thoroughly studied New England site is a complex of stone chambers, worked standing stones, and historic lithic features in central Vermont. Named Calendar I by the principal investigators of this area, amateur archaeologists Byron Dix and James Mavor, the cluster of structures and standing stones presents an intriguing picture of alignments to natural features as well as to worked megaliths.[25] The site itself is a natural bowl surrounded by ridges to the east, west, and north. In the center of the bowl, 50 yards from a year-round spring, is a stone chamber. Along the east ridge are two standing stones that may have astronomical significance. The west ridge is crowned by a stone wall constructed, as are most New England stone walls, from the many granite boulders found lying in the surrounding fields. Dix and Mavor postulate that past inhabitants of the area, with a thorough observational knowledge of astronomy, set up the two standing stones and used them, together with the natural topography of the east and west ridges, to define a calendar. They view the Calendar I site as a spot potentially sacred to its inhabitants and recognized as such through the ages.

Of most obvious astronomical interest at the site was the stone chamber west of the spring. Made up of irregular-shaped granite and mica schist boulders laid up without benefit of mortar, the chamber proper is about 3 yards long, 2 yards wide, and 5 feet deep. Although its entrance passage is aligned to an azimuth of 104.6°, because of the relatively high eastern horizon (15°), an extension of a line along its axis meets the horizon just where the equinox sun rises. This same axis extended toward the back of the chamber falls across a hole, 4 inches across and 10 inches deep, carved in the floor near the center of the chamber. Thus, for an observer located at the back of the chamber, the sun would appear to rise directly over this hole at the equinox.

Surface material and archaeological excavations demonstrated that the chamber was used in the historic period. In view of the orientation, however, it is of considerable importance to determine when it might have been built. The chamber currently has no roof, and there is no historic record of the sort of roof it might have had. However, the rubble on the floor contained several pieces of log, suggesting that it might once have had a wooden roof, dating probably from the historic period. Excavations of the chamber also revealed that it was built around a rectangular pit cut into the bedrock; in some places, the quarrying extended up to 1 yard deep. The fill inside and outside the chamber yielded historic artifacts down to about 8 inches above the bedrock. However, below that level, Dix and Mavor found several stones, which they suggest may be archaic tools, but no historic artifacts. In addition, they discovered polished stones in the northwest, southwest, and southeast corners of the chamber, which they surmise might be prehistoric stone offerings, or "magic stones." Lastly, they found remnants of a possible door frame and two historic door lintels in the passage outside the chamber. With the other historic artifacts (nails, pieces of leather, broken dishes), these latter certainly indicate historic occupation or use of the site.

What is not yet clear, even after excavation, is when the chamber might have been constructed. Even if it had been built during the historic period, it may have been deliberately placed over the earlier pit carved in the bedrock. If the chamber itself was already there when the first settlers arrived in Vermont, some of them may have added the door and made other improvements. Not even the construction methods reveal information about the chamber's builders, for they used fieldstones from the local area and laid them up dry, and used no special techniques that would set this chamber apart from similar ones elsewhere in the world, where similar materials are available.

Although the eastern orientation of the chamber near the spring is what originally drew Dix to the Calendar I site, he soon discovered that the topography offered the possibility for readily defining a complete yearly calendar. He has noted that by standing at a certain point north of the chamber, it is possible to witness sunrise and sunset at both solstices and at the equinoxes. Along the western ridge, entirely natural features define these important solar dates. Along the eastern ridge, two stones, apparently purposely erected, define the solstices. The equinoxes are marked by a shallow natural minimum in the horizon contour. No marker exists to define the point from which to observe these events.

Excavations of the area around the standing stone that defines the winter solstice horizon point show that it was apparently deliberately placed on a foundation slab 1 yard below the surface. The stone itself is about 5 feet long and as much high. A deep notch in the top of the horizontal surface serves as a sighting device for winter solstice sunrise as seen from the appropriate observation point within the bowl.

The problem with Dix's hypothesis is the fact that the proper place to stand within the bowl to witness these orientations is completely unmarked. It is possible, of course, that a later farmer removed the marker (if it existed in the first place) to clear the area. Assuming for the sake of argument that Dix's hypothesis is correct, it is also entirely possible that the people who first noticed the happy accident of the local horizon topography and erected the two standing stones may have denoted the place to stand with a wooden marker that has long since decayed. However, it seems extremely unlikely that a people who would use permanent stone horizon markers would use so evanescent a material as wood for as important a marker as this. If there had been a wooden post there, excavation might find its remnants.

Dix and Mavor have suggested a total of eighteen possible solar and lunar alignments and several stellar alignments at the site, based on the various unusual stone features they have discovered. Of these, the most persuasive are the solar ones just described. The major concern I have about Dix's hypothesis for Calendar I is reflective of my skepticism about his and Mavor's conclusions concerning other sites. Their ability to find astronomical alignments may be more a function of their own cultural bias than the reality of an earlier culture at the site. The lack of useful ethnographic data is a genuine handicap in interpreting and understanding their finds. In the Southwest and many other areas in North America, we have much more data from the early historic record about the native inhabitants than exists from Vermont and New Hampshire. The valleys and forests of central Vermont were inhabited in early historic times by a group called the Western Abenaki. However, as one writer put it, "the Western Abenaki have always been something of an unknown quantity to historians and ethnographers."[26] Because they lived well away from the coast, they were encountered by the English relatively late, when war, disease, and the general pressures of European expansion had already reduced their numbers considerably. Their settlements were small palisaded villages and their houses were bark-covered rectangular buildings that had room enough for several families. There is no record of these people having built or used stone chambers, or of their working with stone in any way. Nor is there much understanding of their ritual life. However, this is not to say that their ancestors, whoever they might have been, did not work with stone, or that the Western Abenaki might not have used stone chambers or erected special stones for ritual purposes. The fact is, however, without supporting evidence from the ethnographic record, Dix and Mavor are at a distinct disadvantage in arguing their hypotheses.

The astronomical alignments that Dix and Mavor and others have demonstrated in New England leave us still with a deep question about the intentionality of the people, whoever they were, who built the chambers and erected the various standing stones of the New England landscape. The archaeology, while highly suggestive that ancient peoples built some of these structures, is inconclusive at present. Much more research needs to be done to establish the probable construction dates of the chambers.[27] Because even prehistoric chambers may have seen historic use and modification, this work will need to be done by archaeologists open to a variety of possibilities and who will take the archaeoastronomical results seriously.

It has now been shown in other parts of the country that Native Americans paid much attention to the skies. It would be an anomaly if the native peoples who inhabited New England in the past did not also regard the celestial sphere with deep interest, and commemorate their interest using materials from the local landscape.

12 California Indians: Maintaining the Cosmic Balance

La Rumorosa

It is early dawn on the winter solstice near the little Mexican town of La Rumorosa in Baja California. A group of sleepy hikers, grumbling good-naturedly about the early hour, pile out of their van and fumble with their boot ties or reach for their gear. After slinging camera-filled packs on their backs, they strike out through the piñon and juniper for a rock shelter decorated with pictographs some 1000 yards away. They are in an anticipatory mood as they walk through the narrow valley, for the brightening sky promises a clear morning for viewing sunrise. There is no path through the scrub trees and undergrowth, but accurate dead reckoning by their guide brings them to the pictograph site with a minimum of lost motion.

Calculating that they have about half an hour until the sun appears on the distant southeast horizon, they spend their time unloading photographic gear and setting it up to take sequential photographs of the play of light and shadow across pictographs on the inside of the shallow cave. Their guide, anthropologist Ken Hedges, had observed part of the phenomenon the year before, but a fast-moving bank of clouds prevented him from viewing the full display he expected to witness there on the winter solstice. This solstice, however, the skies promise to remain clear.

There is just time for the novices in the group to examine the pictographs on the back wall of the shelter before the sun appears

A few of the many Native American groups in California.

above the distant southeast hills. The left-hand painting is a pair of white semicircles connected by a short white line; the center is a red anthropomorph with wavy hornlike appendages on its head; the right-hand image is a red bisected circle.

One of their number stands watch atop a large boulder in front of the shallow cave to time the exact moment of local sunrise. After the sun appears above the horizon, their expectations and excitement build, but it is about twenty minutes into its daily trip across the heavens before the play of light and shadow begins within the shelter. As sunlight reaches into the shelter, the group watches the two semicircles and the cave wall below them slowly brighten. Cameras click, whir, and snap as a triangular band of light grows and spreads to the right toward the little red figure. Someone gasps. Surprisingly, the light slips over the figure and lights up the wall to its right without touching the face of the figure. In the dim light of early dawn, the group had previously failed to notice that the red figure was painted across a very slight depression in the wall. Sunlight could not reach its face until the sun moved higher and a bit further south. "Look!" exclaims one excited participant. Slowly, a small patch of light to the figure's right creeps left across its eyes. The two small dots, carefully executed in black pigment, seem to sink back in its head as the sun's rays hit them. As the group continues to watch, sunlight creeps down to bathe the entire figure with light — except for the horns, which continue to remain in shadow. The group's excitement and awe is so great that it is only after the light beam fades that anyone in the group is able to articulate a complete sentence.

The entire play of light and shadow takes only about twenty min-

Winter solstice sunlight striking painting in rock shelter near La Rumorosa, Baja California. At sunrise on and around the winter solstice, in a moving display of light and shadow, sunlight enters a small, shallow cave and falls across the eyes of this painted figure. (After Ken Hedges, "Preliminary Report on a Winter Solstice Rock Painting at La Rumorosa, Baja California." Paper presented at the Fourth Annual Rock Art Symposium, May 1977, Tempe, Arizona.)

utes, but its effect on the solstice watchers lingers long after. As they talk about their observations, they begin to realize that no one individual saw the complete display. The streaks of light on the back wall are only part of the show. One beam of light, entering the upper part of the shelter, fell across a shallow depression in the horizontal rock surface in the back of the cave, thought to be a milling slick for grinding pigments or seeds. The resulting effect emphasizes the presence of the grinding area. Is this intentional? Other patterns were also noticed by various members of the group. Their observations led to many questions. What does the display of light mean? Who painted these symbols? Why did they do it? Unfortunately, little is known about the site, as it has not been excavated, nor has the general area been studied in any detail.[1]

Judging from the meager archaeological evidence nearby, it seems that the depictions were probably executed by a band of Kumeyaay Indians, a group who lived in southern California and northern Baja California. Information supplied by the few remaining survivors shows that they, like most California Indian groups, observed the solstices in order to participate in the ordering of the universe. Thus, at the critical time of the solstices, when Sun was at his extreme position, and the earth and the rest of the cosmos were in mortal danger of impending imbalance, it was necessary to intervene with Sun, to encourage him back to his proper path by supernatural means. This is much the same conception that we recognize among the Pueblo Indians. However, in the hierarchical society of southern California, the duty to encourage, or pull back, the sun devolved on highly placed shaman-priests who had a deeply developed awareness of natural cycles and of how to read and influence them. These priests led solstitial ceremonies and also worked with Sun directly by private prayer and ritual acts. Among the Chumash, for example, a group who lived near what is now Santa Barbara, the ritual leaders even assumed titles related to this role, such as "Image of the Sun," and "Splendor of the Sun." As a Franciscan priest who observed the Costanoan Indians near Mission San Jose wrote, "They adored the sun when it receded towards the south pole. They thought it was angry and they held dances in its honor and offered it seeds, etc., until they knew it was about to return to them."[2]

The site near La Rumorosa may well have served to determine the solstice, or, like many sites that are known in the Southwest, it may rather have been used to celebrate the passage of the solstice and been used by a Kumeyaay priest as a place to perform ritual acts designed to turn the sun around again. The latter hypothesis seems the most likely one. The horizon southeast of the cave is suitably rough to serve for direct observation of the winter solstice and a highly accurate determination of its occurrence. When standing outside the shelter atop the large boulder just in front of it, it is possible to witness the winter solstice sunrise at the bottom of a distinctive notch in the horizon. Ken Hedges surmises that the Indian or Indians who used it may have chosen the spot originally because it afforded the proper place to stand to witness the winter solstice sunrise. He further hypothesizes that the shaman then realized that the shelter made an excellent place to serve as a ritual site, and painted the back wall with the figures that currently appear there.

Both sorts of solstice sites appear elsewhere in California. The California Indians observed the solstices, kept accurate calendars, and generally observed the other celestial bodies with great interest.

The Data

The astronomical practices of the California Indians are only of relatively recent interest among scientists who study American ethnoastronomy and archaeoastronomy. They have tended to focus their attention on groups who built monumental structures in Mesoamerica, or the American Southwest. Part of this is because the tribes and tribelets of California constructed no monumental buildings. The archaeology of the region seemed to yield no evidence of astronomical interest among the California Indians, and the many references to astronomical practices gathered by the ethnologists were buried in the various journal articles or lost in their extensive unpublished notes. Another important reason the California groups were relatively neglected is that anthropologists have tended to ignore the important role that the study of the heavens has had in cultures that are not predominantly agricultural. Among agricultural peoples the need for an accurate calendar to support their other observations is obvious. The success of the farming enterprise, especially in certain climatic areas, depends on an accurate knowledge of the seasons, especially their turning points, as well as farming technology. However, the Native Americans who lived in California relied heavily on hunting and gathering for their sustenance, and until recently the importance of a calendar to hunters and gatherers has been ignored. We have the work of astronomers and anthropologists among the California groups to thank for an appreciation and understanding of how such groups might respond to the changing of the seasons and how they determine their yearly seasonal guide. They have now accumulated a vast amount of evidence to show that these groups observed the sun and other celestial objects closely. It is now clear that beyond serving the narrow functional use of organizing the planting and harvesting activities of sedentary groups, a calendar also serves to coalesce a group. It provides a standard of reference that everyone in the society can understand and to which everyone can relate.

Although a few early anthropologists asked questions of the California Indians about the sky, their data are spotty and poor. Part of the problem was that astronomical knowledge was restricted to the elite. Most of what we know about California Indian astronomy we owe to J. P. Harrington, an eccentric ethnographer who worked for the Bureau of American Ethnology. Harrington was a tireless accumulator of miscellaneous information about the western and southwestern Indians. It is to him, for instance, that we owe thanks for recording the fact that the Zuni and the Tewa Pueblos of New Mexico had a well-developed sense of the constellations and of the movements of the stars. He gathered his Zuni data while visiting the archaeological excavations in Chaco Canyon in June and July of 1929. On that occasion, Harrington interviewed Nachiapani, a Zuni member of the work crew on the archaeological dig, and apparently sat out with him under the stars on at least one night. Although Harrington's knowledge of the Zuni language was limited, having apparently been formed during a three-week stay in the canyon, he was able to elicit considerable information on the names and the nature of Zuni constellations.[3] While in Chaco Canyon, he also assembled the beginnings of a Zuni dictionary. However, true to the difficulty he had in making or finding time to publish much of his work, these and many other boxes of notes lay dormant for years before modern researchers, digging through archives, became fully aware of the extent of his notes.

In Pueblo country, Harrington was far afield from his usual haunts among the California groups. Harrington was troubled by the very real concern that the natives of California were disappearing or be-coming assimilated at a dramatic rate. He was acutely aware that although there had been an estimated three hundred to three hundred fifty thousand Native Americans living within the area when the Spanish first arrived to conquer and settle in the late 1700s, by 1900 only a few thousand were left. Unless he and his compatriot ethnographers worked day and night to gather valuable information, from as many elders as remembered it, on the language, myths, legends, and customs of the many California tribelets, these cultural data would be lost along with the people with whom they originated.

So consuming was his desire to gather data that he repeatedly ignored the pointed commands of his superiors at the bureau to publish his findings. His work of gathering ethnographic data obsessed him. He would go into hiding and refuse to answer letters for weeks at a time. His marriage, to an intelligent and resourceful woman whom he trained to help him in his work, ended in divorce.[4] Probably because he was more devoted to his work than to his wife, we owe J. P. Harrington a debt of thanks for many of our most important observations on the astronomy of California groups. Harrington apparently had a good command of celestial knowledge himself, and made it a point to include questions about the sky when interrogating his informants. Thus, celestial information in myths and legends and in various rituals is available for study today. However, in his quest for a broad variety of data, he glossed over many of the details of celestial names and practices that we now find important. His data are necessarily incomplete and often require considerable guess-work or other complementary information to understand them fully.

The California People

In addition to being well populated prior to the Spanish Entrada, the land that now constitutes the state of California was also highly diverse linguistically. More than seventy-five languages and three hundred different dialects are known to have existed in the lands between the majestic redwood forests of the northwest and the barren deserts of the southeast.

The California Indians were organized in very small groups the anthropologists call tribelets, groups smaller than a tribe but large enough to have a distinct identity — a separate language or dialect, social structure, and cultural background. The individual patterns each tribelet developed in response to its natural and cultural environment varied, but most developed a culture that is identifiably Californian. Each tribelet was autonomous and might consist of one or more villages governed by a single village in which resided the chief who presided over all. Although it is dangerous to summarize in a few words the salient characteristics of so diverse a group of peoples as the California Indians, some generalizations may be made. The California tribelets, as distinguished from, for example, the Pueblo villages, were structured along hierarchical lines. The astronomer-shamans were part of the elite that ruled and maintained the tribelets, and to them belonged a large measure of the protection and viability of the tribelets.

Because wild foods were abundant, the economy of most tribelets was based on hunting, fishing, and gathering.[5] In the south and inland there was limited agriculture as well. Along the coast, fishing and gathering of shellfish were important parts of the tribal subsistence. Toward the interior, hunting and gathering of plant foods were more common. The groups displayed regional differences, too. Those tribelets in the northwest area bore strong resemblances to their neighbors further north on the Pacific Northwest Coast. Those in the eastern deserts showed the influence of trading with their Pueblo neighbors in the Southwest. Like them, they had maize agriculture and pottery. Generally, the archaeological finds and ethnographic and historical sources substantiate that within each tribelet, the native Californians reached a high level of cultural achievement. They also demonstrated a striking level of political and social integration. The elite apparently exercised influence through trade, ritual activities, and political alliances all over California. Interestingly, these alliances often cut across environmental zones, a practice that gave them high economic viability.

In short, the picture of the California natives that was common only a few years ago of simple societies, highly fragmented and unconnected to one another, has given way in recent years to a more integrated view, one that places the Californians' cultural achievements on a much higher level. Thanks to the earlier work of the ethnologists, we have available a wealth of data on the practices of the native Californians near the turn of the century. Added to this work in recent years are the detailed studies of the many archaeologists who work in California. The latter are able, quite literally, to give substance to the words of the ethnologists and linguists by the material culture they unearth.

Chumash Astronomy

Of all the three hundred or so California groups, the Chumash and their astronomy and ritual astronomical practices are the most intensely studied.[6] A people who lived on the western coast and nearby islands beyond the Santa Barbara Channel near the present city of Santa Barbara, as well as inland, the Chumash are known for their highly decorated fine baskets, their wooden plates and bowls, their carefully constructed plank canoes, and an especially well-developed tradition of rock painting. Chumash rock paintings, executed on the interior walls of caves and rock shelters, are some of the most spectacular and elaborate of any in North America.[7] The Chumash also made many small tools, articles of adornment, and excellent cordage for ropes, twine, and nets.

Prior to European entry into the area, the Chumash numbered about fifteen thousand and spoke several related languages. Some individual villages reached populations of one thousand or more. Their natural resources were many and varied. They lived by hunting small animals, gathering plants and seeds, fishing, and collecting mollusks. Since they neither farmed nor herded animals, their calendar, an intricate one based on the sun and moon and perhaps Venus, was not developed in response to a cycle of planting and harvesting. Rather, it functioned to support the Chumash desire to understand, predict, manipulate, and control the forces that determined their "supernatural" environment.

Unfortunately, the calendar and other astronomical practices that the Chumash developed are only imperfectly understood today. The Franciscan priests and other early explorers and conquerors who interacted with the Chumash two centuries ago had a unique opportunity to probe the Indians' beliefs and cultural achievements. They chose not to study Native American beliefs, but rather to suppress these "pagan" beliefs and rituals. What the priests knew about native worship of the sun, they generally ignored. Once, when sent an *interrogatorio*, which included questions about native religion, the priests among the Chumash specifically replied that the Indians around them did not worship or adore the sun and the moon.

Harsh punishment and ridicule awaited those native Californians who were found to continue in their superstitious ways. Consequently, the Spanish writings yield virtually nothing about Chumash knowledge of astronomy or about their cosmology. Far from destroying native practices, however, the church and secular authorities caused them to go underground, much as the early Christian church in Europe was forced to do two millennia earlier. Part of the reason that it was possible for them to maintain many of their sacred practices was that for them, as for other Native Americans, the secular and the sacred were closely intertwined. Sacred sources of power were everywhere to be tapped — in animals, in plants, in other human beings, and especially in those celestial bodies that daily circled their local cosmos. Many of these practices lay hidden from view until uncovered during the early part of the century, but it was only recently with the work of anthropologist Travis Hudson and his colleagues that their astronomy became widely known.[8]

Data on astronomical practices were difficult to obtain because these data were tightly held by astronomer-priests who also wielded considerable political power among the Chumash. They were members of a religious cult called *'antap*, whose adherents conducted the community ceremonies and advised the chief of the province politically. Some of the *'antap* were also shamans, men or women whose duty and privilege it was to use supernatural powers for the good of the Chumash in their area.

One of the reasons we can speak of a Chumash astronomy is that the *'antap* cult extended throughout Chumash territory. Each village had its *'antap* members, among whom were included the village political leaders. These men and women knew the *'antap* rituals and esoteric practices, but their political leadership gave them special status in the society and enabled them, along with their counterparts from other villages, to exercise political and ritual power over the whole region. That the members of the *'antap* organization were looked up to and sometimes feared can be divined from the many stories of their power. To them belonged the responsibility of maintaining the balance of power in the universe — the course of the sun and moon, the dynamic balance of the seasons, and the outcome of critical human events. They controlled the weather, cured the sick, sought visions by means of the drug datura, and generally endeavored to maintain the cosmic balance. In addition, they used the calendar that they devised and maintained to regulate the political, economic, legal, and ritual activities of the community. Nearly our entire body of data regarding *'antap* astronomical knowledge and how they put it to work has survived because a few native observers were able to tell J. P. Harrington what they knew about the *'antap* cult. Although Harrington's efforts came too late to allow direct questioning of any members of the *'antap* cult, some of their relatives and friends knew enough about *'antap* practices to allow anthropologists to infer their astronomical and cosmological lore, especially when these data are combined with other information from tribes geographically and culturally related to the Chumash.

For the Chumash the entire universe and the supernatural powers within it were constantly in flux. Without supernatural intervention from humans, the powers of the world could readily produce events with cataclysmic results. The astronomers of the *'antap* cult, who were referred to by the name *'alchuklash*, had within their province the duty to seek out the necessary knowledge from the celestial beings, to foresee the future, and to take the proper steps to alter the upcoming course of events for the well-being of their fellow Chumash.

According to Chumash stories, each night, celestial teams led by Sun and by Sky Coyote played a gambling game called *peon*. On the night before winter solstice, the winners of each game for the year were tallied to see which team had won most often. Moon keeps score. Moon's count is the number of days before or after new moon to the winter solstice. The consequences of Sky Coyote's victory would be a rainy year and an abundance of food for humans. If Sun and his team won the yearly tally, food would be scarce and human lives would be lost. It was the duty of the astronomer-shaman to read the results of the *peon* game and to take corrective steps to avoid disaster if the count came out in favor of the sun.

The *'alchuklash* also were thought to possess the power to make it rain, or to avert or divert a powerful storm. Among these duties, it was their place to name children according to the solar and lunar periods of the calendar, and the bright stars and planets visible at birth. They were thus astrologers as well as astronomers and divined the fates of their fellow tribal members.

In short, the political, astrological, and weather-controlling duties of the *'alchuklash* made them persons of great power in the community. They were present at births and presided during puberty rituals. In addition, they gave advice and controlled the powers of the cosmos for their fellow humans during life, cured their sickness, and were present also at death. They touched all the life cycles of their tribesmen, and of the cosmos.

For the Chumash, the separation between humans and nature that is the basis of modern philosophical thought and science would have been totally foreign. The *'alchuklash* conducted their lives and made their observations of the skies under the basic assumption that the world of humans and everything else in the world were inextricably bound together. The appropriate human actions could influence the workings of the rest of the cosmos, and vice versa. The animate realm was, for them, a cycle of continual re-creation. Life comes from life. Animate matter is not destroyed, only reconstituted in another form.

The Chumash understood the universe to be made up of three (five in some accounts) circular, flat worlds. Humans lived in the Middle World between the above and below. With the proper skills, a shaman could travel to any of these worlds, either to learn the secrets of the supernaturals who inhabited them or to intercede for the good (or ill) of their fellows.

Powerful and dangerous supernaturals inhabited the Lower World. The Upper World, supported by a giant eagle, was the home of the celestial beings. By moving his wings, he caused the phases of the moon. The center of the Middle World was a sacred spot called *'antap*, a dangerous place where spirits lurked and danced at night. Harrington recorded this account of the place from one of his informants:

> The place the *'antaps* are is a tiny pond in a canyon near Mount Pinos and beyond Cuddy Valley. The water flows not to, but away from here. You hear bullroarers and flutes and whistles and shouting. Also dogs barking. There were many people in there. It is like a fiesta. And in a cave, underground, the sacred deer bone whistles used by the *'antap* are kept — four of them [for each of the four directions?]. The ancients never went near that vicinity. The wind blows strong there and the earth quakes. If you get in there you never get back out again. Once the soldiers from the fort went up there to make shakes — lots of fine pines up there. In the night they saw fires lit in the mountains, and the soldiers quickly departed. All was quiet again the next day.[9]

The Chumash regarded the area around Cuddy Valley (about 40 miles northwest of Santa Barbara) as the most sacred place in the Chumash world, and went there deliberately to experience supernatural happenings. It was a center from which radiated the four directional lines (apparently cardinal) that divided the Chumash world into four quarters. As with most other Native American groups, the four directions were very important to the Chumash; they prayed to them regularly in order to restore balance to the world. For them, the ritual centers were places where balance could be struck, where, in the words of one anthropologist, "cosmic or sacred time and space and spiritual beings met with secular time and space and human beings."[10] The entire Middle World, where human beings live, was for the Chumash a center, a place to which humans could draw the supernatural powers from above and below.

The Sun

Though considered a dangerous force by the Chumash, the sun, a male deity, was also the greatest supernatural being. The Ventureno Chumash gave him a name which meant "the radiance of the child born on the winter solstice."

The sun lived in the Upper World with his two daughters in a house made of quartz crystal. His wives were the morning and evening stars. In his daily travels across the sky, he not only carried the sun torch to light the world but also preyed on humans below. His only clothing was a feather band around his head, into which he would stuff an occasional Chumash child as he traveled. Much as the Greek god Helios followed a chariot path across the heavens, the Chumash Sun carefully followed a cord that stretched across the world, taking care not to break it lest he fall down to the Middle World. He held his torch carefully — neither too low nor too high lest those below freeze or burn up. When he stopped to rest, which he did three times a day, he rested in a sand dollar's hole, leaving his rays outside. After reaching his house again at sunset, Sun would dine on the humans he chanced to gather up during the day.

The sand dollar was a highly appropriate symbol of the sun for this seafaring people. The shape and construction of the sand dollar resemble the circular form of Sun and the rays that emanate from his heart. One name for the sand dollar meant "the shadow of the child of the winter solstice."[11]

Sand dollars. The sand dollar was considered by the Chumash Indians of southern California to represent the sun. At noon, Sun was said to rest for a time in a sand dollar's hole before continuing his journey.

Sun was a powerful being who brought life in the form of heat and light but could also bring death — presumably to those who deserved it, for he served as a moral symbol as well. "Never do anything that is prejudicial or unlawful and think that no one will see you," said one Chumash. "For while the sun is shining, an eye is here . . ."[12] Just as humanity needs the sun, Sun also needs humans to intervene in his travels, especially at the critical times of the solstices.

Sun was, however, a fearsome creature. As he travels, he picks up whichever humans he might choose and carries them home.

> He arrives home in time for supper, and at first when he enters the house there is a dense fog. He throws the adults down in the doorway and then takes the babies from his *ciwin* (headband) and throws them down too. And when the fog clears away, there stands Sun with his firebrand. He and his two daughters just pass the people through the fire two or three times and then eat them halfcooked. And they don't drink water like we do, but blood.[13]

The winter solstice was seen as a particularly dangerous time by the Chumash, as it was for most Native American groups. It was a time when all the force of their supernatural powers was needed to restore order and balance to the world by encouraging Sun to move northward again. On the actual winter solstice, the Chumash remained indoors lest they be taken up and eaten by the sun at the end of his daily journey. After the sun's turn north, they celebrated his choice with considerable rejoicing.

The effort to turn the sun northward meant both public and private rituals presided over by the 'antap. These included ceremonies honoring the dead and offerings to the sun. Preparations for the winter solstice celebrations started in the fall, when the 'alchuklash would predict the appropriate date and give orders for the manufacture of necessary ritual regalia. By continually observing the sun's progress along the features of the horizon, and comparing it to their daily count, they could calculate an accurate solstice date.

During the first day of the winter solstice ceremony itself, the people settled all their debts, perhaps as a way of beginning the approaching new year with a "clean slate." The second day was devoted to a ceremony to "pull" the sun northward again. On the previous day, they had prepared for the ceremony by digging a hole in the plaza about 12 to 18 inches across. Then, on the afternoon of the solstice, the chief priest, called Image of the Sun, and his twelve assistants, the Rays of the Sun, erected a sunstick in the hole they had previously prepared. The role of the sunstick was to urge the sun northward once again.

The sunstick itself was a 15- to 18-inch-long stick atop which was affixed a stone disk. They called the sunstick by a word that meant "to divide or separate in the middle" because the sun at noon is in the middle. It was thought to be at the center of the earth (that is, at the intersection of the four cardinal points on a circular horizontal plane) and, at the same time, a projection from the navel of the earth, in a deliberate analogy to the human body. In the afternoon, at about 3:00, the Image of the Sun entered the plaza, carrying the sunstick. Assisted by two old men, the priest erected the sunstick in the hole he and his twelve helpers had prepared earlier. Then, after the sunstick was standing by itself in the hole, the Image of the Sun would stand. In the meantime, the twelve Rays of the Sun would have arranged themselves in a circle about the sunstick, each holding a goose or eagle down feather in his hands. At the right moment they tossed their feathers into the air and let them fall in simulation of rain as the sun priest chanted, "It is raining! You must go in the house!" Twice he hit the stone disk to release its supernatural powers. Then he gave a ritual speech in which he reminded the people that the sunstick signified the axis of the earth and the power of the sun.

> A miracle! Here is the force of the Sun — see how it drives this into the earth. Believe! Courage! Pay attention! Bring all your children to see, so they can see the staff of Hutash. Look! It is going to stand! Observe it in its place and always remember it so! Yes, always remember![14]

His speech ended with predictions about the state of the food supply and weather to come in the ensuing year. Dances by the Rays of the Sun closed this stage of the winter solstice ceremony.

That night, the priests and people returned to dance around longer, decorated poles called sunpoles. Painted, and adorned with feathers and beads, later these poles would be erected outside the village. Until midnight the people danced in a clockwise, or sunwise, direction. After midnight, they reversed direction and danced in anti-sunwise circles. During this night, the normal strict prohibition against sexual promiscuity and adultery was relaxed in honor of the sun. During the dancing, a man could choose any woman, married or not, by singing to her. When his song was over, it was her duty to accompany him into the bushes and give herself to him sexually. Only at sunrise did the dancing stop. The ethnographic record is not absolutely clear precisely what ceremony was held as the sun rose, but it is plausible from the context of Harrington's notes that at sunrise, the people assembled around the sunstick to implore Sun to return and to "enter the Staff of Hutash" (that is, the axis of the earth). As the sun rose, three old men sang

> Come out, Sun!
> Come out so that you may
> see your grandfather![15]

Shortly after, six women took up the singing while motioning with arms extended to Sun to come back and to enter the sunstick.

After dark, the people gathered once again to perform the Dance of the Widows for any women or girls who had become widows or orphans during the year. After midnight passed, the assembly would weep in memory of the passing year, at the decease of husbands and fathers, in anticipation of the arrival of the sun, and at the renewal that the new year represented. The sun was returning to the center. For the next six months, the sun would be traveling north.

The final morning of the ceremony, the sunstick was taken down and carefully placed in a box inlaid with shell. Both were then put away for another year. The Chumash's prayers had been answered. The sun again was returning. They then carried the five feather poles to their customary locations outside the village and "planted" them in the earth. The first pole they erected to the west of the village. On their way to the next location, they stopped twelve times to dig a hole in the earth and deposit an offering consisting of a small bundle of sage. When they reached the next location at the top of a nearby hill, they planted three feather poles. One last pole remained, and it was erected on a higher hill by two men especially chosen for the task. This completed the ceremony.

The place at which the three poles were planted was a shrine dedicated to the dead. It was called 'Iwayɨk't, or "mystery," and objects belonging to the dead were deposited at the base of the poles in memory of the dead. Dolls, beads, mortars, even old boots, might be scattered about at this "Depository of the Things of the Dead."

Although with the available information it is impossible to understand the full meaning of the events of the last day of the solstice ritual, the attempt nevertheless may provide some insights for later research on the place of astronomy in Chumash ritual.

They planted five feathered sunpoles. Although it is nowhere explicitly stated why the Chumash chose to plant five poles, it is reasonable to assume that they represent the four cardinal directions plus the above (connected with the sun). With the emphasis that the Chumash placed on bringing back the sun, the additional sunpole could more explicitly represent the upward movement of the renewed sun. This hypothesis is given further credence by the fact that during the Chumash Mourning Ceremony, which was held during the harvest festival of Hutash, a pole called the "pillar of the sun" was erected over the place where offerings to the dead had been burned.

In addition, when the fifth and final pole was emplaced, the '*alchuklash* said, "This is the pole symbolizing the center of the earth, this is our kingdom." Thus the pole represented both the center and the connection between the center and the above.

The three poles, planted in a row from north to south, may represent an asterism that the Chumash called the Three Kings. Anthropologist Travis Hudson, who has done the major work on Chumash astronomy, has suggested that this asterism, mentioned in several places in Harrington's notes, is formed by the stars alpha (Altair), beta, and gamma Aquila.[16] Shortly after sunset near the winter solstice, these three stars are visible on the western horizon, aligned from north to south. Hudson is guided by the fact that the asterism would have been directly over the Chumash Land of the Dead at the same time that the winter solstice ceremonies honoring the dead were performed.

The Chumash sunsticks appear to be unique among Native American astronomical artifacts. From ethnographic accounts we know that they were constructed from small disks of stone painted green or blue, through which was inserted a shaft of wood. The sunstick's maker also painted on the stone a black or red crescent representing the moon. One end of the stone disk represented the sun, and the sunstick as a whole represented the axis of the world.

No actual specimens identified by informants as sunsticks have survived, but several objects that fit their description were found about a century ago in Bowers Cave in Los Angeles County. Housed for years in museums, the objects had been misidentified as stone clubs, but more recently Travis Hudson realized they were probably astronomical instruments.[17]

His identification of the "club" as a ritual artifact and astronomical instrument is an excellent example of the use of ethnology to aid in understanding archaeological artifacts. It also illustrates how cultural bias can cloud our understanding. Not being aware of the intense astronomical interests of the Chumash, the archaeologists who originally examined the sunsticks relegated them to a relatively mundane role in the daily life of the Chumash. Only four have survived the ravages of time and museum care; three are in the Peabody Museum at Harvard, and one is now in a collection in Australia.

The three specimens from the Peabody Museum are quite similar. Although Hudson emphasizes that we cannot be certain that the sticks of Bowers Cave are Chumash sunsticks, they fit the ethnographic description remarkably well. All are made of fine-grained, worked sandstone through which a wooden shaft has been inserted and fixed by asphaltum and cord. All have markings that may be related to the yearly horizon positions of the sun. In two of the examples, the attached stick makes a slight angle to the perpendicular — 10° and 18° respectively.

Chumash sunstick. On the winter solstice, a Chumash priest placed in the ground a sunstick similar to this one that was found a few years ago in the collection of Harvard University's Peabody Museum. The stick represented the axis of the world; the stone represented the sun.

Hudson has suggested that the angular cant is meant to reflect the angle of the sun from the vertical on the summer solstice (11.5°) and during the month of August (19°) in the area near Bowers Cave. According to his theory, which is supported by the ethnographic accounts of the summer solstice ceremony I have just related, the sunstick was "planted" with the stone atop the stick. If it was placed in such a way that the plane of the disk was parallel to the plane of the earth, then the shadow of the stone disk would fall along the sunstick, since the stick was set at an angle from the vertical equal to that of the sun.

Possible Chumash sun symbols. The two top images are from Chumash rock paintings. The bottom one reproduces the painting on one of the Chumash sunsticks found in Harvard University's Peabody Museum by anthropologist Travis Hudson and archaeologist Evan Hadingham. (After Travis Hudson and Ernest Underhay, *Crystals in the Sky: An Intellectual Odyssey Involving Chumash Astronomy, Cosmology and Rock Art* [Los Altos, Calif.: Ballena Press, 1978]: fig. 8.)

Hutash

Hutash was a unifying metaphor for the Chumash, for it referred not only to the axis of the earth but also to the earth itself, as well as the month of harvest and the festival at which the bounty of the earth was celebrated. As one Chumash explained:

> Here where we live is Hutash. You know that each body has its place where the sense of feeling is. All mankind lives in the sphere of Hutash. The sphere of Hutash is everything that contains the human race, and for the Indians the sphere of Hutash is the land. All are born of the earth, and the sun revivifies all creatures. That is where the word "love" triumphs. Love is the basic motivation. From the abundance of the heart the mouth speaks.[18]

Hutash was also the name of the evening star, so chosen, apparently, because its presence in the night sky signaled the arrival of the month of Hutash. In addition, Hutash was the name of the coffeeberry plant. The shrub seems to have received its name from the fact that it was very common and produced most heavily at this time of year.

This multiple use of a single name, which seems rather surprising to Western ears, was nevertheless a useful device to remind the Chumash of the importance of the land and all it contributed to Chumash life. Repetition, either through metaphorical use of a visual symbol or through a verbal symbol such as Hutash, was a common part of the Native American experience.

As the harvest month Hutash was a critical time in the Chumash calendar. Among other things, it was the occasion for planning for the winter solstice ceremony. As the Chumash said, "Hutash is the mirror of the Sun, and the Sun is the mirror of Hutash."[19]

The sun ceremony in the month of Hutash was used to prepare the people for the coming winter solstice ceremony and also to set its date. In one account, the crucial meeting was held in the house of one of the 'antap. The group assembled in midmorning. To start the ceremony, the old men ('antap) brought out several mysterious articles, among which was a whale vertebra painted with an image of the sun. Each ray of the sun painting represented one of the twelve months of the year. After the persons attending placed offerings in several baskets that had been put there for the purpose, one of the old men, who had been sitting on the west side of the room facing east, began to sing three songs of gratitude to the sun as they all waited for the sun to rise symbolically. A young boy then took the

Possible Chumash sun painting. This is believed to be similar to a sun symbol painted on the vertebra of a whale and displayed during a Chumash ceremony preparing for the winter solstice. (After Fernando Librado, *The Eye of the Flute* [notes of John P. Harrington, edited by Travis Hudson et al.]. Santa Barbara: Santa Barbara Museum of Natural History, 1977: 51.)

painted sun, which had been lying horizontally on the floor, raised it up with a stick, and held it vertically for all to see. The sun had risen. Each woman with a babe still suckling brought him in and held him up to the sun painting. Then the leader warned them all to respect Sun and lectured them to follow the proper path and to avoid the dangers to life and property that exist at this time of year. "None of us in this assembly control our destiny, for we live in the shadow of the Sun."[20]

The data are not entirely complete about the connection of this ceremony with the winter solstice ritual, but either just after this ceremony or on another day close to it, the *'antap* gathered to formulate their plans for the coming winter solstice ceremony. At this time, the *paha*, or leader, took on his role as sun priest and his twelve helpers explicitly became the Rays of the Sun. They used the occasion to set the date of the winter solstice ritual and to specify the preparation of the necessary feathered sunpoles. This important time, therefore, not only served the purpose of organizing future events, but also began to build people's expectations and to strengthen the importance of the winter solstice ceremony to come.

The Solstice and Other California Groups

The Chumash celebrated the winter solstice with elaborate ritual, and prepared for it long in advance of the day the sun turned and the year began again. So also did many other California groups. Though the accounts of the actual rituals are few, they make it clear that the solstices were as important for most California tribelets as for many other North American groups. Even where data on a given tribelet are unavailable, it is more likely that the omission is because of the failure of the observers to ask the right questions than because the practice of watching for the solstices did not exist. Although they more often attempted to ignore or suppress the native rituals, the mission fathers reveal in their accounts that some were aware of the importance the natives placed on the sun and determinations of the sun's position.

> They celebrated with more pomp and attention the sun's arrival at the Tropic of Capricorn [winter] than for the Tropic of Cancer [summer], for they were pleased with the sun's approach towards them. Its return meant much to them for it ripened their fruits and

seeds, gave warmth to the atmosphere, and enlivened again the fields with beauty and productivity.[21]

This response of the Juaneño-Luiseño (near Mission San Juan Capistrano) to the winter solstice is typical of most North American groups and most of the California tribelets as well. But what methods did they use to discover the crucial day? How and from what sites did they observe the sun? From what we can learn by reading the ethnographic accounts, they used both direct observation (sunrise and/or sunset along the horizon) or indirect observations (images of light and shadow against a backdrop). The pictograph shelter near La Rumorosa is a site at which indirect observations were probably made. There, apparently, the sun priest observed the play of light and shadow across painted features. Other similar sites involving rock art are also known throughout California, some in Chumash territory. In other cases involving indirect observation, the tribes observed the sunbeam strike marks on the floor, wall, or center post of a ceremonial structure. At least ten different California tribes used this method to note the solstices.

The practice of making direct observations of the sun seems to have been more widespread. The ethnographic accounts record examples of solstice watching using direct methods in sixteen tribes. We can use these accounts to test the validity of suggestions that certain archaeological sites were used as sun watching locations. The accounts agree that the solstice watchers determined the solstice by noting when the sun appeared to stop and turn around in its northward or southward journey. In one account, a Chumash sun watcher observed the sun with reference to three distant mountain peaks:

> The sun would pass the middle peak on the way south, pass the valley, remain two days, and on the third day would come up again over the middle peak on its way north. He would notify the other Indians of the New Year.[22]

Kumeyaay Sun Watching

Although no specific record of direct sun watching is known for the Kumeyaay Indians of southern California, near San Diego, it can be inferred from joining ethnographic and archaeological data about an archaeological site on Viejas Mountain in San Diego County. From records taken near the turn of the last century, we know that the Kumeyaay held a yearly ceremony (probably winter solstice) on the mountain to honor the sun. The single surviving account of this ceremony is worth quoting here for its poetic rendering as well as for the information about Kumeyaay practices it conveys:

> The Indians made a pilgrimage once a year to its [Viejas Mountain] very top to watch In'ya (Sun) come out of En-yak' (East), and praise and honor him with song and dance. For In'ya (Sun) was the great Ruler of All Things. He governed the universe; he commanded the earth; nothing grew unless he caused it; he even dominated the bodies of men, some of whom he made energetic and strong, others weak and lazy. When he disappeared at night he cast a drowsiness o'er the world, so that everything slept until it was time for him to come again in the morning. Such a great ruler as he, received due reverence and worship.
>
> When all had reached the summit, the ritualistic ceremonies began. With song and dance in the blushing dawn, they watched for In'ya (Sun), Ruler of All. Opalescent streamers of golden radiance and flaming banners of crimson flaunting across the pearly tints of the receding night, heralded his arrival; while the people chanted songs of praise in honor of his wonderful light, and made obeisance in the dance in homage of his great power over all things.[23]

While investigating the area for signs of the dance circle that once existed on Viejas Mountain, anthropologist Ken Hedges found instead a group of rocks laid out in a crude cross. Although he found it impossible to date the pattern of stones, their weathered upper surfaces led him to believe that the alignment was quite old. The long axis of this cross was oriented to the southeast and pointed to a mountain named Buckman Peak more than 16 miles away. At the winter solstice, as seen from this cross, the sun rises directly over Buckman Peak; immediately after first gleam, the summit of the peak can be seen to bisect the sun. Unfortunately, as Hedges found on a later trip to the area, the cross has now been destroyed by campers who moved the stones for a campfire.[24]

Another possible alignment in the Kumeyaay area occurs on Cowles Mountain in the Cowles–Fortuna Mountain Regional Park in San Diego, where an archaeological survey revealed a circle formed from small and medium stones bisected by a straight line of stones. Here, as with the cross, the growth around the stones and the condition of the stones themselves indicated that the feature was not of recent construction. As determined by actual observations on the winter solstice, the circle's bisector lies along the direction of winter solstice sunrise and points to a prominent rocky outcrop some 14 miles to the southeast. Just after the first gleam of the winter solstice sun occurs, the peak bisects the sun. The site and distant peak work together to constitute a very accurate indicator of the solstice, for with an effective horizon at a distance of 14 miles, small movements of the sun along the horizon would be easily detected by an observer on Cowles Mountain. Thus, the solstice could be determined within a few days. The exact placement of the circle or the precise angle of the circle's bisector turn out to be not very important at such distances. The marker simply acts to point out the proper direction in which to look.

If the two sites were once used by the Kumeyaay for determining the winter solstice, as Hedges has suggested, they give a clue for hypothesizing what constituted the moment of sunrise for calendrical purposes for this group of California Indians. Soon after first gleam, the sun is much too bright to gaze at directly, and any horizon features are lost in the sun's overpowering glare. Thus, in order to have observed the horizon against the rising sun, it appears that the Kumeyaay noted sunrise either at first gleam or just slightly afterward. For them, it appears that this was the crucial moment to observe the sun to set the calendar.

Other Possible Solstice Sites

Both of the preceding examples rely on manmade surface features to indicate the proper place to observe the solstice sunrise, but several investigators have suggested that elsewhere rock art exists that depicts solstice sunrise and thereby also suggests where to stand to observe.

Two such sites exist in the tribal territory of the Tubatulabal Indians near the Kern River in south-central California. One, known by the unromantic name Ker-17, is located right above the Kern River and consists of three panels of pictographs painted on granite boulders. The central panel includes a painting that, as suggested by investigators Victor Slaboszewicz and Robert Cooper, may very well represent the sun standing above the horizon.[25] In fact, a perpendicular to the central panel extends to the east-southeast in the general direction of winter solstice sunrise. In other words, an observer standing with his or her back to the panel faces the direction of winter solstice sunrise. As confirmed by observations on the solstice, the sun rises along the left side of a broad (about 2°) notch along the horizon. As it rises, the sun illuminates all of the rock art panels evenly since the site is quite open. If the horizon features of interest consisted solely of the notch and the peak to the north of it, this site would doubtless be of little interest for archaeoastronomical studies, for the width of the notch is too broad to define the winter solstice with any accuracy. However, the slope of the mountain to the north is nearly equal to the angle of the sun's path as it rises above the horizon. Thus, on one day about three weeks before the winter solstice sunrise, the sun just skirts the horizon for about half an hour before rising above the peak. The very next day brings an abrupt jump in the horizon position of the rising sun. It does not appear at all above the horizon until it emerges from behind the peak, but the sky above it remains very bright. An experienced observer would then know that the winter solstice would occur eight days later. The method is capable of high accuracy (one to two days) and is reminiscent of similar techniques known to be used by the Hopi for accurately determining the solstices.

Just across the river from the site are the remains of a Tubatulabal village, so they would have had ready access to it. The site itself in modern times was described by a related tribe as a fishing spot, and it may have been so used in prehistoric times. Whether the Tubatulabal actually used the site as suggested is highly plausible, but not proven. However, it does suggest an area for fruitful investigation in the future. As it now stands, it is the only California site known for which the winter solstice sunrise could be determined in such a manner.

About thirty miles away, in an area also occupied in prehistoric times by the Tubatulabal, is a second suspected solstice site that Robert Schiffman selected by examining the records of rock art of California for design elements that appear to depict the sun near the horizon. All of the pictographs at the site, Ker-317, are abstract. None appears to represent humans, plants, or animals. Though abstract, one design in particular stands out as a possible depiction of solar phenomena. Schiffman interprets this pictograph to predict the location of sunrise on both the summer and the winter solstices, by presenting a mirror image of the horizon features opposite the site.

Standing in front of the pictograph, the observer faces east and is able to see both summer and winter solstice sunrise positions on the mountain range opposite. As interpreted, the two spirals and the amorphous symbol to the right represent distinct mountain peaks on the horizon. The set of short horizontal lines indicates where to look for summer and winter solstice sunrise. The spoked circle to the left is thought to represent the relatively fainter light and heat of the winter solstice sun.[26]

Although the interpretation proffered for this site is interesting and imaginative, it has several drawbacks, the most serious being that the abstract symbols are not consistently applied to the patterns on the horizon. The two spirals Schiffman interprets to apply to two prominent peaks, but he identifies the amorphous symbol on the left

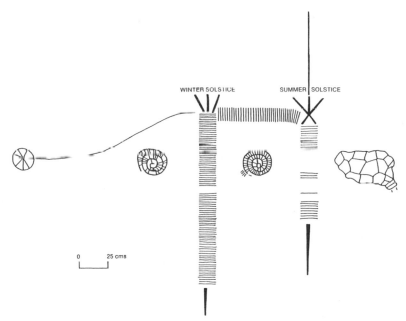

The Ker-317 pictograph in California. Painted on the east side of a granite boulder in pinkish-red pigment, this panel of abstract symbols has been interpreted to represent the directions in which to look to identify the summer and winter solstice sunrise. Anthropologist Robert Schiffman suggests that the painter intended the viewer to stand in front of the pictograph panel to view the eastern horizon. (Drawing by Robert Schiffman.)

with a prominent peak. In addition, the meaning of the sets of horizontal lines is unknown, as is the single set of short vertical lines that link the two "solstice positions." Finally, the meaning of the spoked circle on the right is unclear. If, as suggested, it represents constrained light of the winter solstice sun, why, then, does it not appear at the winter solstice location? In the end, upon further investigation, this site may prove to have an entirely different meaning. Still, it stands as an interesting example of the attempt to link certain glyphs with sun watching locations.

The Other Cosmic Players

The California astronomer-priests were primarily interested in satisfying two major needs — maintaining the food supply and sustaining the cosmic balance. To aid in these two complementary aims, they carried their interest in the celestial sphere well beyond sun watching. They also watched the stars, the moon, and even the planets with great care. As in the studies of traditional cultures from so many other geographical areas, until the 1970s and 1980s, the data on California Indian knowledge about the stars was spread throughout the anthropological literature or left hidden away in anthropologists' notes. However, thanks to the extensive work of anthropologists Travis Hudson and Thomas Blackburn, as well as others, many of these data have been discovered, assembled, and interpreted in the context of California native culture.

What they show is that California Indian knowledge of the stars was extensive. The constellations they recognized included Orion, the Pleiades, Ursa Major, and Ursa Minor, as well as many other star associations whose particular groupings would be unfamiliar to Western eyes. Certain individual bright stars, such as Aldebaran, Altair, Antares, Capella, Spica, and Vega, also held particular meaning for some groups. Since specifics about the sky were closely held by an elite group of astronomer-shamans, however, the common tribal citizen was not privy to knowledge of the stars. We can only infer from what we do know that many specifics of their understanding of the stars and other celestial beings were lost with the deaths of the shamans. On the one hand, much specific knowledge is lost forever. On the other, because they clothed much of their understanding in the trappings of stories, it may eventually be possible to infer even more about the extent of their knowledge of the stars and other celestial bodies. In their myths, the First Beings wandered between the earthly and the celestial realm with ease, and some of their experiences relate directly to the location and movements of specific celestial bodies. Indeed, as one Luiseño storyteller put it, "All those [the First Beings] that are now the stars went up in the sky . . . hoping in that way to escape death." This was from the time "when animals were people." Thus, many of the creation stories about certain animals apparently relate to their place and purpose in the celestial realm. Although there is a wealth of skylore, little of it has yet been mined for the information that it might yield.

The California astronomers were well attuned to the practical uses of the stars. As one Cahuilla Indian put it:

> The old men used to study the stars very carefully and in this way could tell when each season began. They would meet in the ceremonial house and argue about the time certain stars would appear, and would often gamble about it. This was a very important matter, for upon the appearance of certain stars depended the season of the crops. After several nights of careful watching, when a certain star finally appeared, the old men would rush out, cry and shout, and often dance. In the spring, this gayety was especially pronounced, for it meant that they could now find certain plants in the mountains. They never went to the mountains until they saw a certain star, for they knew they would not find food there previously.[27]

For the native Californian, the celestial realm was a place of power and danger. By carefully timing their intercessions with the beings who peopled the Upper World, the shamans who understood the movements of the sky could wrest some of the celestial power to their own uses. Because that power could also be highly dangerous, the shamans had to be especially careful to watch for just the right moment, lest they bring ill to the people for whom they strove to understand and use the power of the cosmos.

13 Living the Sky

> Look as they rise, up rise
> Over the line where sky meets the earth;
> Pleiades!
> Lo! They are ascending, come to guide us,
> Leading us safely, keeping us one;
> Pleiades,
> Teach us to be, like you, united.[1]

Thus sang the Pawnee in one of their ceremonies, making explicit their link to the sky and its patterns. They and most other Native Americans directly associated their lives, indeed their very being, to the sky, and to the earth. Everyday Native American customs reflect celestial patterns of space and time.

Knowledgeable visitors entering a Sioux tipi will walk around to the left in a sunwise direction. They therefore move from east to south and thence to the west to reach their destination across the tipi. In a traditional Mescalero Apache dwelling in northwestern New Mexico, persons entering also follow a sunrise direction. By contrast, the Hopi priest of Arizona generally makes his prayers to the four directions in the anti-sunwise direction: northwest, southwest, southeast, northeast. In their ritual dances, the California Chumash danced to each of the four directions in turn. When building a hogan, the Navajo orients the doorway to the rising sun. In the green corn ceremony of the southeastern Indians, the sacred fire is fed by four logs that are laid along north, south, east, and west. The roofs of Pawnee earth lodges were supported by four roof posts representing stars of the four intercardinals. These and numerous other spatial patterns of Native American life are an important part of their cultural response to the rhythms of the cosmos.

Another set of responses related to the cosmic rhythms illustrates Native American interest in and use of numbers related to time. When telling stories, the Zuni repeat important phrases four times, once for each direction. Crucial periods in the story last four days, four weeks, or four years. The Mescalero Apache say that man passes through four stages of life. The Oglala Sioux use twenty-eight poles to erect their Sun Dance Lodge, a number they relate to the length of a lunar month. Hopis who are about to travel away from the village for a period of time spread four lines of cornmeal across their entranceway to seal the door. No one will enter while they are absent. Cherokee practitioners of the green corn ceremony held a seven-day festival whose center was a seven-sided ceremonial house. During this ceremony they sacrificed seven ears of corn. Throughout their lives, formulas such as these, related to the celestial sphere, guided the traditional behavior of Native Americans.

Although it is highly simplistic to speak of Native Americans as if they constitute a uniform, related whole, there are nonetheless many similarities among the tribes and groups of North America, especially with respect to their view of the cosmos. The particular ways in which different groups respond to the motions of the celestial bodies or to the demands of their local environment vary dramatically across the continent. Native Americans from different tribes, however, often share similar views about universals. What is especially interesting about their responses to astronomical phenomena is that they contrast sharply with the Western, scientific view of the world.

For human beings in general, the stories we tell, the choices we make, the directions or numbers we prefer, and the ways in which we live, all reflect our view of the world and the assumptions we make about it. Seldom are these assumptions very explicit or systematic. We usually leave the task of articulating our metaphysical and cosmological assumptions to the philosopher or to an outside observer. However, within our culture, we nevertheless share certain basic assumptions about our own human nature and, more generally, about the nature of reality, our presumptions about the present, our hopes for the future, and our view of the world. These views, taken as a whole, determine the characteristics of our culture.

In Western society, thousands of years of cultural development have led to the presumption that humans and nature have separate states of being. Further, in order to better our own lives, we must learn to conquer nature and to subdue it to our own ends. These notions were first most ably articulated by the Frenchman René Descartes and the Englishman Sir Francis Bacon in the seventeenth century. As Descartes wrote:

> We may find a practical philosophy by means of which, knowing the force and the action of fire, water, air, the stars, heavens, and all other bodies that environ us, as distinctly as we know the different crafts of our artisans, we can in the same way employ them in all those uses to which they are adapted, and thus render ourselves the masters and possessors of nature.[2]

Bacon echoed these sentiments in different words:

> If a man endeavor to establish and extend the power and dominion of the human race itself over the universe, his ambition (if ambition it can be called) is without doubt both a . . . wholesome and a . . . noble thing.[3]

Today, we hardly find these views of mastering and possessing nature remarkable, for the twentieth century has seen them come to maturity in deed as well as thought. We have now developed enormous power to change our environment and, recently, even our genes. In some respects, we have gone far beyond the imagination of Descartes and Bacon, for we now have the power to control and to change life on earth unalterably. However, running counter to the trend of mastering and controlling nature is the realization that we might attempt to live in accordance *with* nature rather than in spite of it.

"HEAT YOUR HOME WITH SOLAR POWER," announces a headline. "Take a sunshower," proclaims a recent advertisement for solar water heaters. In the years ahead, the 1970s and 1980s will be known as the decades when we rediscovered the sun as a source of energy and life-giving power. As much as 20 percent of our total energy requirements in the United States could be supplied by direct and indirect solar energy by the end of this century if we had the will to pursue such a goal.

Exacerbated by the realities of a limited supply of oil and gas, this new view of the sun has helped to give us a new perspective on the world and our use of its resources. Two other relatively recent developments have profoundly altered our view of the world and our relationship to it. Foremost, perhaps, is the realization among some that we are better off living with nature than in opposition to it. Slowly, we are learning to note the yearly progression of the sun and to orient our buildings to accept the sun fully in winter and to shield its rays in summer. In short, we are relearning in practical ways that we are truly part of nature — it affects us as we affect it. This is a view of the world that we do not accept easily. Underlying the current public debate over the energy issue, I suspect, is the worrisome perception of some that we aren't, after all, fully in control of our lives.

The other recent development is the view we now have of the earth from space. Buckminster Fuller coined the phrase *Spaceship Earth* in the mid 1950s to connote a connected, interrelated planet Earth. A few years later we could all see just what he was talking about in pictures from space. His metaphor conveys a message of wholeness and oneness. Indeed, it is extremely hard to view the photographs of Earth taken from space without becoming aware of the intimate connections between the different parts of Earth. The object that faces us in these photographs has an integrated, interdependent being that is hard to conceive solely from an earthbound perspective. We are just beginning to understand the Earth from this new vantage point.

How different is the world of the traditional Native Americans! Theirs is an animate world in which everything is related to everything else — rocks, trees, animals, insects, humans, are intimately connected. For them, nature has a vastly different meaning. The difference is apparent even in the common modes of speech. For example, when I, as a scientist, speak or write of the sun or the stars, I tend to treat them as objects, inanimate and separated from my being, except in the essential way that we are all composed of matter. By contrast, the traditional Native American personifies the sun, and calls him Sun Father. The sky is Sky Old Man; the earth is Earth Old Woman. This view of the world has many important consequences, not the least of which is that humans can affect the animate powers active in the world and can turn them to our own benefit. Thus, when the Native American studies the world in action, the motions of the sun and the stars, the clouds and wind, he or she does so for

the immediately practical. Understanding is for the sake of influenc-
ing the powers that lurk behind the motions of the world.

It is unlikely that Westerners will ever fully trade their view of
nature for a more traditional one. The view of nature as an object of
exploitation has been too successful in supplying the creature com-
forts that we enjoy, and in establishing the hegemony of Western
culture over much of the globe. This view of nature also carries with
it a profound optimism about humankind's role in the evolution of
the universe — we can, if we desire, quite literally create our own
world. Indeed, the advocates of building space colonies — self-
contained, self-sustaining units of human habitation — propose to
do just that. Theirs is a profoundly Cartesian view of the universe,
optimistic and exploitative. However, it is rather striking that along
with the newfound interest in the practicalities of solar energy,
which many future colonizers of space share because of its obvious
utility in powering a space colony, our civilization has also begun to
look back in time to recover, as it were, earlier perceptions of the sun
and its relationship to man. Hence, I believe it is hardly accidental
that a deep interest in archaeoastronomy and ethnoastronomy has
emerged at the same time we have also rediscovered the power of the
sun. Dr. Ed Krupp, an astronomer with a deep interest in archaeoastronomy, put it this way:

> It [archaeoastronomy] is useful. It has a humanizing influence. It
> changes the way we look at people, at our ancestors. Through that it
> changes the way we look at ourselves. And attitude is the real
> bonanza. Whenever you have something that prompts people to see
> themselves and the world more clearly, more sympathetically, more
> humanistically, you are talking about enhancing social cohesion and
> the richness of life. That sounds like a tool for survival to me.[4]

Whatever world view we hold, it has arisen in response to our
basic need to understand the world. In our attempt to make sense out
of the panoply of confusing sensory data that the world presents us,
we hypothesize about the basic structure of the world. That structure
serves as the foundation of our knowledge of the way things are.
From this process arises our own collection of myths, our various
stories about the way things are. These stories serve as a way of
talking about an often unfriendly world.

A central component in our collection of myths is the way in
which we understand the sky — and conversely how that under-

standing affects the way in which we live. What we are experiencing in our rediscovery of the sun is a partial reordering of our Western philosophical foundations, a change in our own received mythology, as it were. For the modern homeowner who wishes to take full advantage of the sun for winter heating, direction assumes a profound importance. Structures that use a lot of glass in the south are simply much more efficient at garnering the rays of the sun than those that do not. This may seem all too obvious, especially today, but for years, architects and builders in most U.S. cities gave very little thought to how their buildings were oriented with respect to the sun and its yearly cycle. Local topography and street alignments have assumed a much greater importance than cosmic direction.

It is ironic that modern homeowners who seek to make their homes most efficient must rediscover principles that the Native Americans of the eleventh and twelfth centuries knew almost intuitively. Direction is essential to life. It establishes our place on this earth. However, direction without the sky for guidance is purely arbitrary and depends solely on local geography. By contrast, the cardinal directions that establish our worldly context are defined by the motions of the sky. The prehistoric Native Americans understood this and used this invaluable information to survive in an often unfriendly world. Their descendants who have kept the traditional ways also remain aware of these facts and use them in their daily lives.

Before the Europeans arrived, Native Americans lived very close to the land. Whether they were hunters and gatherers or agriculturalists, all groups depended heavily on the grace of nature and their own wits to survive. They had to learn the weather patterns, the cycles of plant growth, and the movements of game in order to live. Beyond that, they shared with each other, and indeed with all humans, the need to understand and explicate their world. They told stories that made sense of the happenings around them and lived in accordance with their views.

Thus, at the turn of the century, when scholars began to turn their attention to the thoughts and knowledge of the North American Indian, they found a well-developed cosmology, explained metaphorically in story form, and ritual practices that indicated these groups paid close attention to the sky. Many of these metaphors survive today in the practices of native groups.

In her sympathetic examination of the present-day Mescalero
Apache who live in the White Mountains of New Mexico, anthropologist Claire Farrer has illustrated just how deeply cosmic
notions may be incorporated into all parts of native life. Indeed, as
Farrer has suggested, "The Mescalero can truly be said to be 'living
the sky.' "

Ask an Apache well-versed in traditional Apache lore to describe
the universe and he or she will draw a simple circle, bisected along
the cardinal directions. This metaphor is consciously and deliberately repeated in the construction of the Holy Lodge of the girls'
puberty ritual, held every year during the first week of July. Although the lodge is a twelve-pole structure, the first four poles constitute the base structure representative of the entire universe. They
are "The Four Grandfathers who hold up the universe for us." They
restate the visual metaphor of the quartered circle. The four poles
also reflect the story of the beginning:

> At that time [the beginning] there was nothing in the universe ex-
> cept — for the Great Spirit, God. And He — He made the world in
> four days. First came Father Sun and Mother Earth; then the sky
> elements and Old Man Thunder and Little Boy Lightning. Next
> came animals and on the fourth day came man, the Apaches.

Of the Ceremonial Lodge they say:

> The main ceremonial lodge is made of twelve evergreen fir trees.
> These poles . . . represent eternal life for us. And the twelve repre-
> sent the twelve moons of the year . . . The four main structure poles
> [the Four Grandfathers] . . . correspond to the four directions of the
> universe, the four seasons, the four stages of life — for in the natu-
> ral world everything is based on four.[5]

As in the visual metaphor of the four poles, the story of the beginning is in fours and is also balanced; according to this account, first
our worldly surroundings are created, and then animals and man.

The girls' puberty ritual continues the metaphor, for it lasts four
days and four nights. Further, the ceremony contains other visual
and verbal metaphors that the Mescalero explicitly intend to be the
"same thing" as the bisected circle. Each night of the ceremony, the
Mountain Gods dance, and their impersonators wear a costume,
upon which is painted transformations of the universal metaphor. A
crescent or a four-pointed star is common. It is not obvious to the

uninitiated observer that these could be related to the bisected circle, or that the other motifs that may appear on the costume, eight-pointed stars or lightning, are the "same thing" as the four-pointed star. Yet, to the Mescalero, the latter images are indeed the same thing as the four-pointed star. Even the groups of four triangles on the headdress represent the same thing. They evolve from a simple construction, and then a series of geometrical transformations performed on the original, first figure.

The Mescalero Apache's thought process follows a highly logical and metaphorical process. As Farrer and her collaborator Bernard Second have explained, the Mescalero Apache begin with the first four poles of the Grandfathers along the cardinal axes, then add the remaining eight poles of the Holy Lodge. These twelve poles represent the twelve months of the year. Connected by an imaginary circle, the poles form the primary image of the universe. The four-pointed star may now be formed by adding a second set of four intercardinal points on a smaller radius inside the first and connecting the points. Two of the intercardinal points lie on an arc whose extremities intersect the diameter of the circle. The circle and the arc together form a crescent. Thus are the primary metaphorical images understood to be related to one another. By cutting the star at one point and laying it out, a mountain symbol is formed. Then lightning is constructed by joining two such zigzag lines. Other geometrical shapes may be formed from the same basic four-pointed star; they are still considered by the Mescalero Apache as the same symbolic metaphor.

These symbolic reflections of the cosmos permeate other parts of the ceremony as well. For example, when blessing the girls, pollen is sprinkled to the cardinal points in a circle around the head, then from the top of the head to the forehead and then perpendicular to this, from shoulder to shoulder. The crescent, symbolic of the moon and of womanhood, is formed by dusting pollen across the bridge of the nose. These simple motions call forth the powers of the universe and remind both the girls and the audience of the creation.

Although these symbols are most apparent and most consciously presented in a ceremony such as the girls' puberty ritual, their force extends throughout Mescalero Apache life. The ideal way to live is presented by the lessons of the creation and the movements of the heavens — in balance, and always in the proper direction. Because

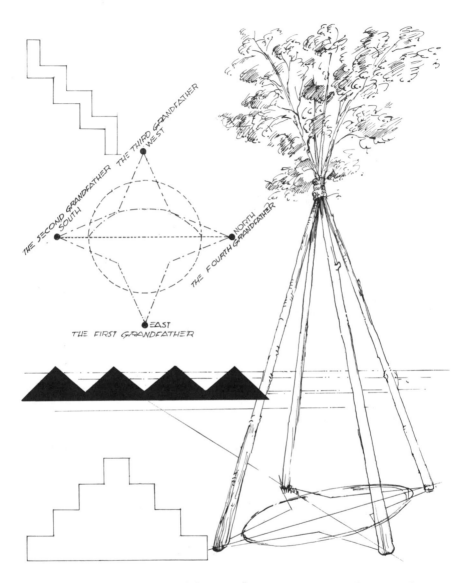

Mescalero Apache symbols of the four directions. The Mescalero Apache
repeat these symbols in many different ways. From top left: lightning;
star, crescent moon, and the sunwise movement; mountains; and clouds.
The four poles on the right are the primary structure of the Holy Lodge
four-pole tipi. (After Claire Farrer and Bernard Second, "Living the Sky:
Aspects of Mescalero Apache Ethnoastronomy." In *Archaeoastronomy in
the Americas*, edited by Ray A. Williamson. Los Altos, Calif.: Ballena
Press, 1981.)

the sun moves clockwise, it is therefore proper upon entering an Apache building to move clockwise, around to the left. Dance movements, too, are circular and proceed in a clockwise, or sunwise, direction. The number *four*, connected with the four primary directions and the four days of creation, is of central importance. Humans live through four stages — infancy, childhood, adulthood, and old age. In the first and last stages they are understood to be dependent on others; in the two middle stages they are independent.

Conscious directional images are not unknown in Western society, though they are much attenuated in use. How many visitors to the nation's capital, for example (how many even of its residents), are aware of the precise orientation of the entire city? Washington, D.C., was deliberately laid out along the cardinal lines. The original designer of the capital, the Frenchman Pierre L'Enfant, skillfully used the existing topography, cardinal orientations, and a system of diagonals to effect a highly pleasing and meaningful design, appropriate to the capital of a great nation. European cathedrals of the Middle Ages and later were often oriented to the cardinal directions for similar reasons. Earlier in history, Vitruvius, the influential Roman architect of the first century B.C., prescribed the proper orientation of the Greek and Roman temple:

> The quarter toward which temples of the immortal gods ought to face is . . . the western quarter of the sky. This will enable those who approach the altar with offerings or sacrifices to face the direction of the sunrise in facing the statue in the temple, and thus those who are undertaking vows look toward the quarter from which the sun comes forth and likewise the statues themselves appear to be coming forth out of the east.[6]

There is in these examples, and in the orientation of the U.S. capital, a sense of participation with the natural world. For the Native American, however, there is no clear-cut distinction between the "natural world of the cosmos" and the world of humans. Beings pass back and forth between these realms at will. However, it is possible to draw certain distinctions between the two worlds. Though Sun follows a prescribed path through the sky from which he never deviates, he always has a choice not to. It is an important component of Native American thought that Sun have a choice. By the same token, it is also important that humans remind Sun of his duty. What distinguishes Sun from the world of humans and the myriad choices that we face every day is that Sun *always* chooses to follow the proper path. Thus, when Sun returns northward after pausing at the winter solstice, he is doing his duty and responding to the right choices that the celebrants of the winter solstice ceremony demonstrate for him.

The lesson of right action for Sun and for humans is illustrated by the story of Coyote and Sun. The listener knows that where Coyote is involved, there will be trouble, for this comic character can never seem to make the right choices. It requires Coyote to show us the choice, and by his contrary decision, like the actions of the Native American sacred clown, to illustrate the wisdom of doing his duty.

For the Chumash, this lesson is in the form of a myth similar to the Greek myth of Helios and Phaëthon or the Hopi myth of Coyote and Sun. The difference between the Greek story and the Native American stories is that the former is tragic, while the latter are deliberately comic. Typically of Native American thought, comic indirection indicates the way of right action.

Coyote had come to Sun's house to visit with his daughters. When Sun arrived home from his daily travels, he was highly displeased to find this scruffy visitor from the lower world, but consented to let him stay. The next morning, the unwelcome visitor had the temerity to ask Sun whether Coyote could travel with him that day. Sun resisted strenuously, but after Coyote pleaded, Sun finally allowed him to come along on condition that he behave himself. The two started off with Sun in front and Coyote right behind, studying carefully all Sun did, as they followed Sun's trail along a cord stretched around the world. "Wouldn't it be better to cut that string?" Coyote asked, just to annoy Sun. Sun responded quickly. "No, to cut the cord would mean falling to Earth. Under no circumstances could we cut the cord!"

All this time Coyote watched Sun carefully to see how he held the torch that lights up the world. At midday, they both rested in a sand dollar's hole. While they restored their strength, Sun left his torch standing outside so Earth might still be well lit. Then, when Sun made ready to continue on his way, Coyote implored Sun to let him carry the torch for part of the journey. "I have watched you carefully. I can carry it the proper way."

Sun at first refused, warning, "If you make a mistake and let the torch come too close to Earth, you could burn up the whole world down below." But after Coyote begged and implored, Sun relented and gave him the torch with a stern warning. "Stick close to the path of the cord and don't let it drop."

Coyote started off paying close attention to his duty, but after just a little way, he began to think about other things, and the torch slipped from his hands and almost burned up the world before Sun could dash downward to retrieve it. Coyote was much chastened (for the moment) by his experience. Thereafter, he stayed behind Sun and followed him, dejected, until they reached the western side of the world. Then the two of them returned to Sun's crystal house by way of the south. Sun's path and Sun's torch no longer held much fascination for Coyote.[7]

Order and Chaos

Coyote's exploit with the sun torch is perhaps the grandest theme of our struggle to understand the world — the opposition between order and chaos. Without ordering principles, the panoply of sense impressions we continually take in remains meaningless. Indeed, much of our folklore and mythology, the many stories we tell about our lives and the world around us, are attempts to order the world of sense impressions. It seems that not only must humans order their world to be able to survive, it is their special duty as well, for from chaos comes great evil. Elements of the tension between chaos and order run throughout the corpus of myth throughout the world. Consumed by jealousy of his wife, Desdemona, Othello, the Moor of Venice, speaks eloquently of the anguish we feel when we lose our ordering principles:

> Excellent wretch! Perdition catch my soul
> But I do love thee! and when I love thee not,
> Chaos is come again.[8]

The human struggle with chaos is seen in a different way in the Greek tale of Pandora's box. It succinctly captures the human dilemma we face in maintaining order in spite of human desires.

Married to the god Epimetheus, the brother of Prometheus, Pandora was the most beautiful, most gifted woman in the world. She had but one fault — unquenchable curiosity to view the contents of a beautiful golden box that the messenger-god Hermes had given her as a wedding gift. In giving Pandora the box, Hermes cautioned that she must never open it, for if she did, great harm would come to her and to all the world. Though she struggled mightily to leave the box alone, and even buried it away out of sight, her desire to know its contents overcame her. Finally, convincing herself that Hermes' warning was another one of his tricks, open it she did, and unhappily loosed upon the world all manner of loathsome, noisome creatures. Composed of embodied chaos, these beings infected the entire world with human plagues and troubles — old age, sickness, insanity, vice, and passion. That is why today, chaos is with us always, continually threatening the order within which we attempt to live.

In Native American thought, it is often the trickster, Coyote, or some other animal who brings a chaotic element into the otherwise orderly world. Ruled entirely by his passions, both cunning and credulous, and forever getting into trouble, Coyote often acts entirely counter to social and sacred order. In that role, he makes it possible to experience in speech actions that are not permitted to humans. The trickster, however, though he looses disorder upon the world, is not evil or a devil. He is truly a necessary figure for understanding the sacred. As the Chumash, and indeed the Hopi, stories about Coyote and Sun illustrate, not only does the trickster by his contrary actions illuminate the proper way by indirection, he also reflects an awareness of the nature of the chaotic element.

A Model Universe

Opposed to the chaos represented by Coyote are the ordered motions of the sky. In fact, one important reason that traditional societies developed a deep interest in the sky was that it was the source of quite obvious and predictable regularities. They were principles the traditional society, with its limited technology, could depend upon. In the midst of varied and chaotic sense impressions, the regularity of the heavens must have seemed a comfort. The heavens also provided an ordering principle for humans. The nearness of the moon's synodic period to a woman's menstrual cycle may have suggested direct connections between the celestial realm and the earthly human sphere. The cycle of the seasons, following predictably (or nearly so) upon the motions of the sun, moon, and stars, provided another close and obvious tie. What better way to bring order and structure into our own life on earth than to model the regularities of the heavens in daily life? Virtually every Native American tribe or social group developed models of the celestial realm that were part of their everyday patterns of life.

In his famous treatise on the author of the *Odyssey*, Samuel Butler opined that "art is only interesting as it reveals an artist."[9] The Pawnee's artful response to the heavens reveals the structure of their world view and the complexity of their notions about space and time. In many respects their example serves as a paradigm of Native American cosmology in general. The earth lodge is of particular interest since it was a conscious and deliberate reflection of the cosmos, structured to incorporate the essential features of the sacred celestial realm. As such, it served as a continual reminder of the essential underlying order of the world. Pawnee concepts of time and space meet in the earth lodge. This cosmic structure gave the Pawnee the foundation on which to model the rest of their world. For example, not only did the lodge and its central fire reflect the celestial realm, it also served as an image of a turtle.

> You see our fireplace. It is the Morning Star. That is where our sun
> comes from. It is also the picture of a turtle where really it is the
> Morning Star. You see the head of the turtle is towards the east.
> That is where the gods do their thinking in the east. While in the
> west all things are created and you see the hind end of the turtle in
> the west. The four legs are the four world quarter gods [that] uphold
> the heavens.[10]

The structure of the Pawnee earth lodge was dictated by the god Paruxti, the Wonderful Being, who was the spokesman of the creator Tirawahat. The circular floor of the Pawnee earth lodge was a symbol of the earth that meets the sky in a circle. The roof, supported by four posts, represented the sky. Each major roof post represented one of the four world-quarter stars, which, according to the origin myths of the Pawnee, were to be painted the colors associated with the stars. The stars themselves told the people, "You must see how I am painted, and you must paint the posts in the lodge as you see me. The posts must be yellow, white, red, and black," in accordance with the colors of the pillars of the sky.[11]

As astronomer Von Del Chamberlain has explicated in detail, everything in the Pawnee earth lodge represented a portion of the natural world outside. The two posts on either side of the entranceway represented the stars of day and night. The south post represented Morning Star and the day. It was the protector of humans. By the same token, the north post, which represented Big Black Meteoritic Star and night, was the protector of animals. Thus, to walk into a Pawnee earth lodge was to come under the protection of these two stars and the ordering principles of night and day.

As a model of the abode of the gods, the entire earth lodge was sacred. However, the west end of the lodge was especially sacred, for it held the sacred bundle. When not in use, the bundle hung from a roof pole. However, when opened and spread out, the bundle became an altar representing the garden of the Evening Star. On the altar rested a buffalo skull whose spirit still lived and conferred benefits upon the occupants of the lodge. As the anthropologist George Dorsey explained, "Upon this rectangular space, or garden, the sun descends and gives light and understanding to all men, for it is in this garden that the sun goes to renew its magic potency."[12]

Imagine what it must have been like to grow up and live in such a model of the universe, in which every part had a symbolic sacred meaning. Virtually every act, whether deliberately sacred or merely mundane, would take on special meaning in such a structure. Just after a Pawnee child was born, he or she was dedicated to Morning Star, and placed in a cradleboard decorated with an image of Morning Star. The baby was physically secure while bound up in the cradleboard, and its spiritual state was watched over by the star whose representation was found on the head of the board. The baby's earliest impressions inside the lodge were of a highly structured, spatially oriented environment in which every element was charged with supernatural meaning. Safe in its immediate surroundings, when the child looked up, it saw the rounded dome of the lodge, which mimics the dome of the sky. When it looked around, it saw the supporting poles painted as the stars they represented. When it looked through the smoke hole at night, it could see the brighter stars of the celestial sphere shining down through the smoky haze. Because the doorway pointed east, the entire structure was oriented to the cosmic plan. This also meant that the family that resided within was oriented to the east and to the influence of Morning Star as well as to the rest of the celestial influences. Finally, the circular shape of the lodge's floor reflected the horizon circle outside.

As important as were the spatial, structural elements of the lodge to the Pawnee, and to the education of the child, they constituted only a small part of its total exposure to the Pawnee view of the world. Because the lodge had only one room, even before the child could fully comprehend the significance of what transpired around it, the child witnessed the yearly ritual cycle and heard the stories of the beginning. Thus he or she grew up in a context of looking to the mythic past for guidance, for the proper patterns of behavior. For the attentive child, this was easy to do, because the spatial elements of the lodge, which represented the celestial sphere, also reflected sacred time in which the beginning recurred again and again as the ritual year played itself out. And in another image that was implicitly, if never explicitly, stated, the Pawnee astronomers, who were also medicine men and priests, sat within a model of the cosmos in order to witness through the smoke hole above the play of time displayed in the stars.

This notion of cyclical time was crucial to the Pawnee and to other Native Americans as well. For them, sacred events recur again and again in a pattern that repeats the cycles of the celestial sphere. Thus, time does not progress along a linear path but moves in a cyclical manner so as to provide an enclosure or total setting in which events occur. Past, present, and future all exist together because the cycles turn continually upon themselves. We can see this especially in the acts surrounding the Morning Star ritual. In performing the dances and singing the songs of the beginning, the Pawnee participate in the acts of the origins. While they do so, Morning Star and the ancestors are there also, re-enacting their own beginnings. Thus the ancestors and the gods were constantly around them, sharing in daily events, and teaching them the proper way to live.

It is impossible to overstress the pervasive influence of the gods and the ancestors in the Native American way. It is also impossible to overstate how completely these ways of thinking have faded from history for many groups. For the Pawnee, their order began to break down and disintegrate with the coming of the Europeans to this continent. Some Pawnee began to question the validity of their ways and converted to white men's ways. Others simply died, the victims of new diseases, war, or old age. Similar stories of the total loss of traditional ways could be told by other tribes, if they still existed. However, some tribes, in spite of deep deprivation and dispersal, have been able to maintain traditional ways in the face of great pressure to convert to Western customs. The traditional Navajo, for example, have learned and incorporated Western modes of being in their lives, while maintaining their old ways. For them, the Navajo gods reign supreme, even though pressures from European-derived civilization constantly threaten. The Navajo maintain a deep interest in string games. However, they are not just games, as they are for children of Western influence. In a revealing discussion with Navajo friends about their string games, folklorist Barre Toelken captured the essence of Spider Woman's influence on the education of children.

> "Where did you learn those designs?" we ask. The children confer with their father for a while, then answer, "I don't know. I guess it's all from Spider Woman. They say if you fall into Spider Woman's den she won't let you out unless you can do all these. And then if you do these in the summer you won't get out at all anyway."
> "Why is that?"
> "Well, we're only supposed to do it in the winter when the spiders are hibernating, because it's really their kind of custom to do things with string."
> "The Spider Woman taught us all these designs as a way of helping us think. You learn to think when you make these. And she taught us about weaving, too," a teen-age daughter puts in.
> "If you can think well," the first boy adds, "you won't get into trouble or get lost. Anyway, that's what our father says."
> Then Toelken asked: "But Spider Woman didn't teach *you* these things, right? Where did *you* learn them?"
> "Well, we probably picked them up from each other and from our father, but they were already around, you know. All the people know about them. Spider Woman taught us."

After making figures of stars, including the constellation Dilyehe, with the string, and then some comic figures, the children's father then explained the relationship between the string, the patterns of the gods, and Navajo life. What he said about the Navajo approach to the world could also be said about most Native American groups.

> These are all matters we need to know. It's too easy to become sick, because there are always things happening to confuse our minds. We need to have ways of thinking, of keeping things stable, healthy, beautiful. We try for a long life, but lots of things can happen to us.

So we keep our thinking in order by these figures and we keep our lives in order with the stories. We have to relate our lives to the stars and the sun, the animals, and to all of nature or else we will go crazy, or get sick."[13]

The Calendar

One way to relate to the sky is to pattern ritual behavior according to the sun and stars. Another way is to develop a calendar that relates directly to its rhythms. To the Native Americans, both were important. Native American rituals reflected their calendars, and their calendars in turn established the patterns for their rituals. Another way of expressing this is that for most Native Americans, reckoning time was for the sake of integrating their lives with nature and with the supernatural influences that pervaded their universe.

The Agriculturalists

Ritual recognition of the cosmological directions gave order to Native American lives, but the calendar provided power — power to participate fully with their environment and power over its vagaries. Beyond this basic understanding, however, the function of an organized celestial calendar has often been a source of dispute and some misunderstanding among anthropologists. Some have simply assumed that the importance certain Native American groups seem to place on either accuracy or precision was a direct outgrowth of their agricultural needs. Others have rightly stated to the contrary that neither extreme accuracy nor precision is needed for making planting or harvesting decisions. This question holds particular importance for interpreting prehistoric remains, since one is never sure just how much accuracy might have been intended by the builders of the structure or calendrical device. For example, when planting or harvesting, a celestial calendar, while helpful, is not always necessary for crop safety. The signs of the natural world are many and varied and often provide sufficient evidence of the appropriate times for these activities. It is therefore normally enough to use rather crude celestial signs, such as the position of certain constellations, in addition to other available indications. However, in some cases, and in some regions, the need for greater accuracy would be essential. In planting my own garden in the early spring, I have discovered to my sorrow that ignoring the calendar can be disastrous. Although the local signs of spring are everywhere, if I plant too early a killing frost may still wipe out all my hard work. The lesson is that an accurate calendar and careful observation of weather patterns can help to prevent disaster.

Such considerations have important implications for archaeoastronomy. Where the climatic patterns in the past have made planting too early or harvesting too late particularly precarious, we may expect to find more careful attention to an accurate calendar. For example, in the area around Hovenweep National Monument, tree-ring analysis yields considerable evidence that drought conditions prevailed in the thirteenth century. With their society under climatic stress, the local Anasazi inhabitants undoubtedly needed every available means to assure survival in harsh conditions, and apparently turned to the celestial motions to help them out. If my hypothesis is correct, it is thus not at all surprising that the Anasazi built several examples of accurate calendar devices at Hovenweep. Indeed, their careful attention to the calendar for reasons of survival may have then resulted in greater interest in setting the dates for rituals related to assuring the growth and survival of the crops such as we find even today among the traditionalists of the Hopi.

However, when studying a particular structure, it is very difficult to know in advance how accurate we might expect a calendrical device to be. The lessons of ethnoastronomy tell us that attention to accuracy varies considerably among agricultural tribes. The Hopi, for example, seem to place a very high premium on setting the dates of ceremonies with great accuracy. They also achieve a precision from year to year of a day or two. Others, like the Havasupi further west in Arizona, bestow less importance on an accurate celestial calendar. However, where great accuracy of time is required, it often seems to be related to ritual needs rather than to strictly subsistence ones. In other words, it is important to have the ceremony at precisely the right time. However, a calendrical structure that is also used for ritual may be very inaccurate. For example, at Casa Rinconada in Chaco Canyon, the sun enters the northeast porthole and shines on the opposite wall niche for at least a week on either side of the solstice. There, apparently, the priests relied on other means to determine the proper date for the ceremony. The beam of the rising sun was then available when needed for ceremonial purposes.

The Hunter-Gatherers

The most exciting recent development in understanding the Native American use of calendars is the realization, primarily from anthropologist Travis Hudson's studies in California, that hunters and gatherers also made extensive use of celestial calendars. This finding has led to a much more sophisticated understanding of the role of calendars in traditional societies as a whole.

Anthropologists previously have tended to ignore the importance of a calendar to hunter-gatherer societies, apparently on the assumption that local seasonal signs would be entirely sufficient to their purpose. However, a member of the Cahuilla tribe in California, whose immediate ancestors relied primarily on hunting and gathering for their sustenance, articulated just how important the celestial signs had been for his tribe:

> When the sun swung to the north and the moon showed quartered by day overhead, or west, they knew by the signs of the sun and the moon when the seeds of certain plants were ripe, and they got ready to go away and gather the harvest. Every plant that grew, the nesting time of all the birds, the time for the young of all the animals, the time of the young eagles, everything they learned by the signs of the sun and the moon.
>
> They studied the north star, how it turns about, and the seven stars [the Great Dipper] and the morning star — all this helped to know when to go and gather their food. The month that the road runner flies means certain things, and the habits of many animals all meant something to these older people who studied the signs of the sun and the moon and the stars and the animals.[14]

Like the native groups who based their food economy mainly on agriculture, the Cahuilla and other California hunter-gatherers used a celestial calendar extensively to support their survival. They recognized the utility of the calendar for such purposes and pursued their celestial observations to make it possible to use it for such directly practical purposes. On the other hand, the fascination of human beings for order gives a much greater importance to the celestial calendar than it might otherwise have for purely functional needs. There, too, hunters and gatherers developed attitudes similar to the agriculturalists toward the development of calendars to serve their ritual interests. To restate an earlier assertion, their calendars served ritual interests at the same time that ritual gave additional status to the development of the calendar.

In most societies, people believed that the calendar was ordained by the gods. The gods told the people how to watch the sky. They also set the length of the month and year. According to a Chemehuevi story from the time When the Animals Were People, the first beings began to order the earth by establishing four seasons. But when it came time to determine the number of months in the year, Coyote and Burrowing Owl began to argue.

Coyote, who preferred to have everything in groups of four, loudly exclaimed, "*Haik^{y}a, haik^{y}a!* The seasons shall be four months long —*aik^{y}a!*"

Burrowing Owl just kept quiet. In response to the boisterous exclamations of Coyote, he merely held up his three-toed foot.

Coyote insisted, and repeated his previous choice in the same unpleasant manner. Burrowing Owl continued to hold up his three toes, but remained totally silent. A third time Coyote repeated his desire. A third time Burrowing Owl silently displayed his three-toed foot.

Then, still maintaining silence, Burrowing Owl left the assembly, and hiding out in the thicket nearby, he cried out three times, "*Parangkwingkwi'i, parangkwingkwi'i, parangkwingkwi'i.*"

Coyote was so angry that he lept into the brush to find Burrowing Owl, but the latter animal, fully expecting Coyote to follow him, turned himself into Rattlesnake and bit Coyote, severely.

Coyote's fourth outburst settled the matter. "*Haik^{y}a, haik^y, haik^y!*" Coyote yelped, "I give up — *aik^{y}a!* I give up — *aik^{y}a!* The seasons shall consist of three months each — *aik^{y}a!*"[15]

The Passage of Time

As I have emphasized throughout this book, the many ways of keeping a celestial calendar depend on direct observation, on patterns of light and shadow, and on human artifice. Rarely does counting seem to enter into the picture except to establish the time of a particular sacred ritual within the ceremonial year. Unlike their cousins to the south, with rare exceptions, the native North Americans seem also not to have recorded intervals of time. In fact, it is fair to say that the Native American was thoroughly uninterested in intervals of time that were unconnected to the celestial patterns.

Beyond a year, the passage of time became vague and generally uninteresting. Even the Winter Counts of the Plains Indians were kept primarily as mnemonics of past events of particular importance to the individual who painted them, not to record the passage of time. The fact that one could count the years was incidental to their essential meaning. As time progressed, men and women were born, grew up, and grew old, but that was a reflection of the observable cycles of nature where the seasons caused the plants and simple animals to follow a similar course over a year. In a society that pays deep attention to those cycles, this is understandable. The progression of time along a developmental path was a concept foreign to Native Americans until the Europeans forced them into history.

Even the so-called histories of some of the tribes are an intricate and, to readers trained in the Western European traditions of history, puzzling mixture of objective fact and origin myth. This is mainly because, in their conceptual framework, in which cycles turn on cycles, the Native American ancestors are always present and considered an integral part of their current life. Indeed, according to their own accounts, their knowledge of the calendar was imparted to them by their ancestors. In many tribes, this knowledge is repeated in ritual prayers at the solstices or other important ceremonial times.

The sky turns, and in turning, measures out our lives. To live in harmony with the world and its cycles is the goal of traditional Native Americans. Their patterns for living derive from a deeply held attention to the rhythms of the sky and earth. The lessons of archaeoastronomy and ethnoastronomy instruct us that whether as architects, weavers, hunters, potters, or storytellers, traditional Native American men and women weave their perceptions of the celestial patterns into their lives in order to participate directly in the ways of the universe.

Notes
Bibliography
Index

Notes

1. Myth, Buildings, and Myth Building

1. John A. Eddy, "Astronomical Alignment of the Big Horn Medicine Wheel," *Science* 184 (1974): 1035–43; "Medicine Wheels and Plains Indian Astronomy," in *Native American Astronomy*, ed. Anthony F. Aveni (Austin: University of Texas Press, 1977), 147–69. See citations in both articles for ethnographic references to the medicine wheels.

2. The term *prehistoric* in the American context generally refers to the time prior to the arrival of Columbus to these shores, though histories of some tribes were not recorded until late in the last century.

3. Anthony F. Aveni, Sharon L. Gibbs, and Horst Hartung, "The Caracol Tower at Chichén Itzá: An Ancient Astronomical Observatory?" *Science* 188 (1975): 977–85.

4. Anthony F. Aveni, "Concepts of Positional Astronomy Employed in Ancient Mesoamerican Architecture," in *Native American Astronomy*, ed. Anthony F. Aveni (Austin: University of Texas Press, 1977), 3–19.

5. Anthony F. Aveni, *Sky Watchers of Ancient Mexico* (Austin: University of Texas Press, 1980), 3–19.

6. Anthony F. Aveni, "Horizon Astronomy in Incaic Cuzco," in *Archaeoastronomy in the Americas*, ed. Ray A. Williamson (Los Altos, Calif.: Ballena Press, 1981), 305–18; R. Tom Zuidema, "Inca Observations of the Solar and Lunar Passages Through Zenith and Anti-Zenith at Cuzco," in *Archaeoastronomy in the Americas*, 319–42.

7. Aeschylus, *Agamemnon*, in David Grene and Richmond Lattimore, eds., *The Complete Greek Tragedies* (Chicago: University of Chicago Press, 1958), lines 824–28.

8. Frances Densmore, *Smithsonian Institution Bureau of American Ethnology Bulletin* 151 (1953): 219.

9. The effect on archaeoastronomy of astronomer Gerald Hawkins's study of Stonehenge has been extremely important. For individuals like myself, *Stonehenge Decoded* was important in drawing attention to the astronomical possibilities of ancient monuments. I was fascinated by his book. The academic controversy it aroused and the ensuing rebuttals from British prehistorians and archaeologists served to draw the interest of the press and the general public. Less well known is the work of Alexander Thom, a Scottish engineer with a passion for precise survey work. Thom has surveyed the stone circles of the British Isles for many years, and reached the conclusion that the circles have geometric and astronomical properties that speak of a high level of intellectual development on the part of their builders. Both men have fought hard the skepticism of other professionals toward their views of the British stone circles.

10. The first published mention of the terms *archaeoastronomy* and *ethnoastronomy* that I know of is in Elizabeth Chesley Baity, "Archaeoastronomy and Ethnoastronomy So Far," *Current Anthropology* 14 (1973): 389–449.

11. Their papers were collected in *Archaeoastronomy in Pre-Columbian America*, ed. Anthony F. Aveni (Austin: University of Texas Press, 1975). This book, together with a later volume, *Native American Astronomy*, ed. Anthony F. Aveni (Austin: University of Texas Press, 1977), which derived from the conference at Colgate University, became the visible evidence of considerable interest in the astronomy of traditional Native American groups, both historic and prehistoric.

12. R. Tom Zuidema, "The Inca Calendar," in *Native American Astronomy*, ed. Anthony F. Aveni (Austin: University of Texas Press, 1977), 219–59.

13. Many of the papers presented at that conference were published in a single volume. See *Archaeoastronomy in the Americas*, ed. Ray A. Williamson (Los Altos, Calif.: Ballena Press, 1981). In addition to scholarly papers on different tribes or geographical areas, this volume includes a group of papers on the state of the discipline of archaeoastronomy.

2. The Native American

1. See the references and excellent reconstruction of events surrounding this chance encounter in J. Wesley Huff, "A Coronado Episode," *New Mexico Historical Review* 26 (1951): 119–27.

2. Huff notes some confusion on the interval between pilgrimages. By some accounts they occur every four years. However, Huff notes, "Observations in recent times indicate the Zunis count the ceremonial seasons — winter and summer — each as a 'year' so that actually the pilgrimages have been taking place with regularity every second calendar year."

3. *The Columbus Letter of March 14, 1493.* (Chicago: The Newberry Library, 1953), 6–10, quoted in Virgil J. Vogel, *This Country Was Ours* (New York: Harper & Row, 1972), 34.

4. Benjamin Keen, trans., *The Life of the Admiral Christopher Columbus by His Son Ferdinand* (New Brunswick, N.J.: Rutgers University Press, 1959), 59.

5. [Pedro de Castañeda de Najera], "Relacion Postrera de Cibola," in *Narratives of the Coronado Expedition*, George P. Hammond and Agapito Rey, eds. (Albuquerque: University of New Mexico Press, 1940), 310.

6. [Pedro de Castañeda de Najera], "Relacion del Suceso," in Hammond and Rey, *Narratives of the Coronado Expedition*, 293.

7. Clark Wissler and D. C. Duvall, *Mythology of the Blackfoot Indians*, Anthropological Papers of the American Museum of Natural History II, 68, No. 6, New York (1909).

8. Leslie Marmon Silko, *Ceremony* (New York: New American Library, 1977), 53.

9. Joseph Epes Brown, ed., *The Sacred Pipe: Black Elk's Account of the Seven Rites of the Oglala Sioux* (Norman: University of Oklahoma Press, 1953), 5–6.
10. The text of Sayatasha's Night Chant appears in Ruth Bunzel, "Zuni Ritual Poetry," *Smithsonian Institution Bureau of American Ethnology Annual Report* 47 (1932): 611–835. In retranslating Bunzel's text, M. Jane Young of the University of Texas discovered the remarkable amount of calendrical data the poem contains. See M. Jane Young, "Translation and Analysis of Zuni Ritual Poetry," Master's Thesis, University of Pennsylvania, 1978.
11. Barbara Tedlock, "The Clown's Way," in *Teachings from the American Earth*, ed. Dennis Tedlock and Barbara Tedlock (New York: Liveright, 1975).
12. Matthew W. Stirling, "Origin Myth of Acoma and Other Records," *Smithsonian Institution Bureau of American Ethnology Bulletin* 135 (1942): 33.
13. Stirling, "Origin Myth of Acoma," 37.
14. John G. Neihardt, *Black Elk Speaks* (Lincoln: University of Nebraska Press, 1961), 192.
15. Barre Toelken, "Seeing with a Native Eye: How Many Sheep Will It Hold?" in *Seeing with a Native Eye*, ed. Walter Holden Capps (New York: Harper & Row, 1976), 18, 19.

3. Celestial Motions and the Roots of the Calendar

1. Because the atmosphere, the land mass, and the oceans store heat, the seasons lag behind the position of the sun.
2. Franz Boas, "Keresan Texts," *Publications of the American Ethnological Society* VII, Pts. 1&2 (1928): 31–32. The Twins mentioned here are the same ones born to an earthly mother after being impregnated by Sun. They are also considered to be Morning Star and Evening Star among some Pueblos (see chapters 4, 5, and 6).
3. Franc J. Newcomb, *Navaho Folk Tales* (Santa Fe: Navajo Museum of Ceremonial Art, 1967), 80.
4. The early Romans had a very complicated and inaccurate lunar calendar; it was so notorious that centuries later Voltaire was moved to remark, "Les generaux romains triomphaient toujours, mais ils ne savaient pas quel jour ils triomphaient." It was so far out of adjustment that when Julius Caesar reformed the calendar in 46 B.C., three additional months were required to bring it into proper relationship with the celestial position of the sun. The Julian calendar was very similar to our modern Gregorian calendar. It was based on the sun and had 365 days with a leap year every four years.

The Gregorian calendar, which is still in use today, was introduced in A.D. 1582 by Pope Gregory XIII. By 1582, the calendar had slipped once again until the vernal equinox fell ten days earlier than it should. Pope Gregory's reform made a small, but necessary, correction. This correction is necessary because the solar year is 365.24220 days, 0.0098 days too short per year. Every four years, on leap year, we correct the calendar by adding a day to the month of February. However, over a hundred years, this gives us a day too much. Therefore, on the century year, which would otherwise be a leap year, we neglect to add the day. Thus, the years 1700, 1800, and 1900 were not leap years. However, the year 2000 *will* be a leap year because every four hundred years, the calendar will fall one day behind the sun's cycle.

5. See R. Tom Zuidema, "The Inca Calendar," in *Native American Astronomy*, ed. Anthony F. Aveni (Austin: University of Texas Press, 1977), 219–59.

6. The Greek astronomers became very interested in these wandering stars and attempted to account for their motions by means of mathematical models. The most well known of these models were those of the second-century astronomer Ptolemy. His system of circles turning within circles in which Earth was at the center of the universe survived until, and somewhat beyond, the sixteenth century, when the astronomer Nicolaus Copernicus developed a different model using circles, but with the sun as the center of motion.

7. See Aileen O'Bryan, "The Dine: Origin Myths of the Navaho," *Smithsonian Institution Bureau of American Ethnology Bulletin* 163 (1956): 16–17. I am indebted to Von Del Chamberlain for pointing this out to me.

8. For quick survey work, a compass and a portable sighting level are also very useful in certain situations, although the accuracy they allow is generally not great enough for anything more than survey.

4. Southwestern Children of the Sun

1. This is a retranslation by M. Jane Young of the University of Texas of a text collected by Ruth L. Bunzel, "Zuni Ritual Poetry," *Smithsonian Institution Bureau of American Ethnology Annual Report* 47 (1932): 635.

2. Alexander M. Stephen, "Hopi Tales," *Journal of American Folklore* 42 (1929): 3.

3. Stephen, "Hopi Tales," 4.

4. Stephen, "Hopi Tales," 5–6.

5. Frank H. Cushing, "Outlines of Zuni Creation Myths," *Smithsonian Institution Bureau of American Ethnology Annual Report* 13 (1896): 428–29. The rather flowery rendition of the Zuni into English is Cushing's attempt to impart to his readers a sense of Zuni ritual speech. It is as unlike mundane speech as the King James version of the Bible is modern English.

6. I am indebted to M. Jane Young of the University of Texas for pointing out this fact. "The word for 'earth' or 'earth mother' (that is, the ground in which seeds are planted), *a'"witelin*, derives from the word for 'four,' *a'witen*." See M. Jane Young, "Translation and Analysis of Zuni Ritual Poetry," Master's Thesis, University of Pennsylvania (1978): 14.

7. This estimate is based on the presence of eighteen pit houses excavated at the village. See Frank H. H. Roberts, "Shabik'eshchee Village," *Smithsonian Institution Bureau of American Ethnology Bulletin* 92 (1929). In this report, Roberts notes that in Navajo, the name Shabik'eshchee means Sun Picture Place, a reference to a large petroglyph depicting the sun within a shield that the Navajo once cut into the eastern face of a large boulder on the trail from Chaco Wash up to the Basket Maker village at the top of the mesa.

8. Bryant Bannister, "Tree-Ring Dating of the Archaeological Sites in the Chaco Canyon Region, New Mexico," Southwestern Monuments Association *Technical Series* 6, Pt. 2 (1965). Although this report refers to a specific geographical area, it gives an excellent introduction to the use and interpretation of tree-ring dates.

9. Matthew W. Stirling, "Origin Myth of Acoma and Other Records," *Smithsonian Institution Bureau of American Ethnology Bulletin* 135 (1942): 18–19.

10. Matilda Coxe Stevenson, "The Sia," *Smithsonian Institution Bureau of American Ethnology Annual Report* 11 (1894): 29–30. Note the colors associated with these materials. The Sia, or Zia, associate white with the east, turquoise with the west, red with the south, and yellow with the north.

11. The Niman kachina dances have been described in many places, but one of the earliest accounts from several Hopi villages appears in Jesse Walter Fewkes, "A Few Summer Ceremonials at the Tuysayan Pueblos," *Journal of American Ethnology and Archaeology* 2 (1892): 1–160.

5. Pueblo Sun Watching

1. Frank H. Cushing, *My Adventures in Zuni* (Palmer Lake, Colo.: Filter Press, 1967), 40–41. This is a facsimile reprint of Cushing's original articles published in *Century Magazine*. The book is a delightful description of life in Zuni in the 1890s when Cushing lived there, and of his experiences with the Zuni people.

2. For more about Hopi shrines and their uses, see Jesse Walter Fewkes, "Hopi Shrines Near the East Mesa," *American Anthropologist* 11 (1906): 346–75.

3. Alexander M. Stephen, *Hopi Journal*, ed. Elsie Clews Parsons, *Columbia University Contributions to Anthropology* 23, 2 vols. (1936), 23–24. For a different but related account, see Jesse Walter Fewkes, "Sun Worship of the Hopi Indians," *Annual Report of the Smithsonian Institution* (1918): 496–526. Stephen worked for Fewkes for a time and much of the latter's published material derived in various ways from Stephen's notes and letters to Fewkes.

4. Stephen, *Hopi Journal*, 24.

5. Matilda Coxe Stevenson, "The Zuni Indians," *Smithsonian Institution Bureau of American Ethnology Annual Report* 23 (1904): 119–20.

6. Stevenson, "The Zuni Indians," 140.

7. Although the particular form of the rituals the Anasazi may have had will remain unknown, we can obtain some clues regarding the sacred matters they emphasized by investigating in more detail the rock art and certain material objects they left behind and their relationships with historic Pueblo ritual practice. Archaeoastronomy and ethnoastronomy also provide many clues as well. See in particular, Polly Schaafsma, *Indian Rock Art of the Southwest* (Albuquerque: University of New Mexico Press, 1980); and R. Gwinn Vivian, Dulce N. Dodgen, and Gayle H. Hartmann, "Wooden Ritual Artifacts from Chaco Canyon, New Mexico," *Anthropological Papers of the University of Arizona* 32 (1978).

8. Florence H. Ellis and Laaurens Hammack, "The Inner Sanctum of Feather Cave, a Mogollon Sun and Earth Shrine Linking Mexico and the Southwest," *American Antiquity* 33 (1968): 25–44.

9. This and the next example are discussed in Ray A. Williamson, Howard J. Fisher, and Donnel O'Flynn, "Anasazi Solar Observatories," in *Native*

American Astronomy, ed. Anthony F. Aveni (Austin: University of Texas Press, 1977), 203–17.

10. Ray A. Williamson, "Sky Symbolism in a Navajo Rock Art Site, Chaco Canyon National Historic Site, N.M.," *Archaeoastronomy* 6 (1983).

11. Michael Zeilik and Richard Elston, "Wijiji at Chaco Canyon: A Winter Solstice Sunrise and Sunset Station," *Archaeoastronomy* 6 (1983).

12. Ruth F. Benedict, *Zuni Mythology* (New York: AMS Press, 1969), vol. II, 66, 67.

13. Luis E. Arochi, *La Piramide De Kukulcan* (Mexico City: Editions Orion, 1981).

14. Neil H. Judd, "Material Culture of Pueblo Bonito," *Smithsonian Institution Miscellaneous Publications* 24 (1964).

15. Polly Schaafsma, *Indian Rock Art of the Southwest* (Albuquerque: University of New Mexico Press, 1980), chap. 7.

16. Fewkes, "Sun Worship of the Hopi Indians," 505.

17. Alexander M. Stephen, "Hopi Tales," *Journal of American Folklore* 42 (1929), 13.

18. Ray A. Williamson and M. Jane Young, "An Equinox Sun Petroglyph Panel at Hovenweep National Monument," *American Indian Rock Art* 5 (1978): 70–80.

19. Joe Winter et al., *Hovenweep 1974, Hovenweep 1975* (San Jose: San Jose State University, 1976).

20. Jonathan Reyman, in "An Anasazi Solar Marker?" *Science* 209 (1980): 858–59, appropriately questions the assumption that the Fajada Butte site is Anasazi. My own view, based on careful examination of the petroglyph and the site's surroundings, is that it is probably Anasazi, though it is impossible to tell from what era in Anasazi occupation it might date.

21. Anna Sofaer, Volker Zinser, and Rolf Sinclair, "A Unique Solar Marking Construct," *Science* 206 (1979): 283–91.

22. Elsie Clews Parsons, "Isleta," *Smithsonian Institution Bureau of American Ethnology Annual Report* 47 (1930): 292.

23. Parsons, "Isleta," 393.

24. Parsons, "Isleta," 368.

25. Michael Zeilik, "Anticipation in Ceremony: The Readiness Is All," presented at the conference "Astronomy and Ceremony in the Prehistoric Southwest," Maxwell Museum, University of New Mexico, Albuquerque, October 12–14, 1983.

26. Evelyn B. Newman, Robert K. Mark, and R. Gwinn Vivian, "Anasazi Solar Marker: The Use of a Natural Rockfall," *Science* 217 (1982): 1036–38.

27. Jesse Walter Fewkes, "A Few Summer Ceremonials at the Tusayan Pueblos," *Journal of American Ethnology and Archaeology* 2 (1892): 32–33.

28. Stephen C. McCluskey, "The Astronomy of the Hopi Indians," *Journal of the History of Astronomy* 8 (1977): 174–95.

29. Elsie Clews Parsons, "A Pueblo Indian Journal," *American Anthropological Association Memoirs* (1925): 1–123.

6. Ancient Pueblo Sun Buildings

1. Most of my early research at Hovenweep National Monument was done with the support of a National Geographic Society research grant. I began my work there in 1976, and have returned nearly every summer since to continue my investigations of this amazing set of Anasazi buildings.

2. Frank H. Cushing, *My Adventures at Zuni* (Palmer Lake, Colo.: Filter Press, 1967), 41. This is a continuation of the passage quoted at the beginning of chapter 5. Although Zuni Pueblo is about 150 miles south of Hovenweep National Monument, the practice of using ports for marking the solstices is common throughout the pueblos. See also Kendrick Frazier, "Solstice Watchers of Chaco," *Science News* 114 (1978): 148–51, who discusses a Hopi example, and Charles H. Lange, *Cochiti: A New Mexico Pueblo, Past and Present* (Carbondale and Edwardsville: Southern Illinois University Press, 1959), 56, 249.

3. Ruth F. Benedict, *Zuni Mythology* (New York: AMS Press, 1969), vol. II, 46.

4. See Jackson's descriptions and sketches in William H. Jackson, "Ancient Ruins in Southwest Colorado," *Eighth Annual Report of the Hayden Geological Survey for 1874*, 369–420. These pages have been reprinted in a small volume entitled *Mesa Verde and the Four Corners* (Ouray, Colo.: Bear Creek Publishing Co., 1981).

5. See the extensive bibliography in Albert Schulman, "Pre-Columbian Towers in the Southwest," *American Antiquity* 4 (1950): 288–97. Of special interest is J. Walter Fewkes, "Prehistoric Villages, Castles, and Towers of Southwestern Colorado," *Smithsonian Institution Bureau of American Ethnology Bulletin* 70 (1919).

6. I investigated this possibility more extensively with a research tour out of the Crow Canyon campus of the Center for American Archaeology in 1983. It appears as if the northern corner of the tower would have to be extended 8 feet further north of where we thought it should end in order for this suggested alignment to work. However, direct observations of summer solstice sunrise are still needed to settle the issue. Other effects may also be occurring there.

7. The unit-type house was named by Dr. T. M. Prudden, a medical doctor who became deeply interested in the ancient Pueblo ruins, particularly of the San Juan watershed. He was the first to investigate in detail the small mesa-top ruins that now bear the name Prudden Units. They are so called because they typically contain five to ten rooms and a small kiva south of the dwelling generally connected to it by a narrow tunnel. Presumably they housed one to several families. At Unit-Type House at Hovenweep National Monument, the kiva is built right into the structure, presumably because there is no more room to the south. As it is, the kiva extends right to the edge of the mesa.

8. We were also drawn to walk along Square Tower Canyon at that time of day because as soon as the sun has been up for a few hours and has had a chance to heat the north side of the canyon, it becomes an extremely pleasant place to hike. Commonly, in the low humidity conditions of Hovenweep, the temperatures, especially along the east-west canyons, reach up above 50°F or so even on days when the low for the morning is 0°F.

9. See the excellent treatment of great kivas in Gordon Vivian and Paul Reiter, "The Great Kivas of Chaco Canyon and Their Relationships," *School of American Research and the Museum of New Mexico, Monograph* 22 (1960). This book, while extremely helpful in our research, also confused us for a time because the north arrows on the drawings of Casa Rinconada point to magnetic north rather than geographic north. The difference (about 12°) is significant, and nowhere do the authors indicate which is being used. The confusion is exacerbated by the fact that the drawings for the Pueblo Bonito great kivas use geographic north as the reference. Archaeologists often do not distinguish between the two reference points in their research, which creates a special problem for anyone wishing to use archaeologists' maps. If the structure is still open and available for study, it is generally important to remap it with reference to geographic north. This is also important because the height of the horizon is generally critical to determining the possible astronomical orientation of the structure (see chapter 3).

10. Ray A. Williamson, "Casa Rinconada, a Twelfth-Century Anasazi Kiva," in *Archaeoastronomy in the New World*, ed. Anthony F. Aveni (Cambridge, England: Cambridge University Press, 1982), 205–19. See also Howard J. Fisher, "Astronomy and Geometry at Casa Rinconada," *Archaeoastronomy* 1, no. 3 (1978): 5–6.

11. The probable error of 19′ arc is a remarkably low 3 percent. In calculating the average distance between niches we ignored the angular distance between niches 27 and 28, a value of 22°16′.

12. Because it is unknown whether the opening to the northeast functioned as a window or a doorway to the exterior room, this observation needs to be tempered with the caveat that it may never have been used to observe the sun or to celebrate its arrival at the summer solstice. However, even if the opening functioned as a doorway, it would have been feasible for there to have been an opening in the exterior room that would have allowed the light of the summer solstice sun to enter and illuminate the low niche.

13. Matthew W. Stirling, "Origin Myth of Acoma," *Smithsonian Bureau of American Ethnology Bulletin* 135 (1942): 19.

14. Vitruvius suggests a similar method for determining north. See Morris Hicky Morgan, trans., *Vitruvius: The Ten Books of Architecture* (New York: Dover Publications, 1960), 26–27.

15. Pueblo Bonito was the first town in Chaco Canyon to be explored with any thoroughness. Richard Wetherill, the discoverer of the extensive ruins at Mesa Verde as well as the Basket Makers of Grand Gulch, in the late nineteenth century set up a trading post on the west side of Pueblo Bonito and dug for pots and other items in the ruin. See Frank McNitt, *Richard Wetherill: Anasazi* (Albuquerque: University of New Mexico Press, 1957). Shortly thereafter, with Wetherill's help, George H. Pepper carried out more systematic excavations of the building. See George H. Pepper, "Pueblo Bonito," *Anthropological Papers of the American Museum of Natural History* 27 (1920). Neil M. Judd, however, did the most exhaustive work at the pueblo. Supported by the National Geographic Society, Judd spent seven years in the 1920s excavating and reconstructing the pueblo. See Neil M. Judd, "The Material Culture of Pueblo Bonito," *Smithsonian Institution Miscellaneous Collections* 124 (1954), and "The Architecture of Pueblo Bonito," *Smithsonian Institution Miscellaneous Collections* 147 (1964).

16. Ray A. Williamson, Howard J. Fisher, Abigail F. Williamson, and Clarion Cochran, "The Astronomical Record in Chaco Canyon, New Mexico," in *Archaeoastronomy in Pre-Columbian America*, ed. Anthony F. Aveni (Austin: University of Texas Press, 1975), 33–43; Ray A. Williamson, Howard J.

Fisher, and Donnel O'Flynn, "Anasazi Solar Observatories," in *Native American Astronomy*, ed. Anthony F. Aveni (Austin: University of Texas Press, 1977). These articles also describe more details about archaeoastronomy at Chaco Canyon, including mention of passageways at Pueblo Bonito that are aligned, perhaps intentionally, to the winter and summer solstices. For more about Pueblo Bonito and possible winter solstice alignments, see Jonathan Reyman, "Astronomy, Architecture, and Adaptation at Pueblo Bonito," *Science* 193 (1976): 957–62.

17. Ray A. Williamson, "Pueblo Bonito and the Sun," *Archaeoastronomy* 1, no. 2 (1978): 5. See also Ralph Knowles, *Energy and Form* (Cambridge, Mass.: MIT Press, 1974), 34–45.

18. The amount of heat generated in the summertime would, of course, be unwanted. Though the reconstructed models of Pueblo Bonito don't include reference to cooling shades, or ramadas, in the desert climate of Chaco Canyon, they were undoubtedly used by the inventive Anasazi. Such simple structures would have been an excellent antidote to the direct heat of the sun.

7. The Navajo: In Beauty May They Live

1. Aileen O'Bryan, "The Diné: Origin Myths of the Navaho Indians," *Smithsonian Institution Bureau of American Ethnology Bulletin* 163 (1956): 13.

2. Frank Mitchell, *Navajo Blessingway Singer*, ed. Charlotte J. Frisbie and David P. McAllester (Tucson: University of Arizona Press, 1978), 175.

3. This rendering of the Navajo origin myth and the building of the first hogan is a composite of several versions: O'Bryan, "Origin Myths of the Navaho Indians," 13; Mitchell, *Navajo Blessingway Singer*, 171–75, 244, 245; Franc J. Newcomb, *Navaho Folktales* (Santa Fe: Museum of Navaho Ceremonial Art, 1967), 192–203; and Cosmos Mindeleff, "Navaho Houses," *Smithsonian Institution Bureau of American Ethnology Annual Report* 17 (1898): 469–517. I have chosen to build a composite story and thus, in a manner, a composite "first hogan," on the grounds that each story brings a slightly different slant to the whole. No single published story is detailed enough to show the richness of the conception of the sacred, cosmic quality of the hogan. Together, the pieces convey an impression of the first hogan as one of great literal beauty, one that is fit for the task of planning the creation of the Navajo world.

4. There are many different versions of the hogan songs. This was taken from Leland C. Wyman, *Blessingway* (Tucson: University of Arizona Press, 1970), 115. See also Charlotte J. Frisbie, "Ritual Drama in the Navajo House Blessing Ceremony," in *Southwestern Indian Ritual Drama*, ed. Charlotte J. Frisbie (Albuquerque: University of New Mexico Press, 1980).

5. Mindeleff, "Navaho Houses," 505.

6. There are several excellent general introductions to the Navajo. Though somewhat dated, one of the best is Clyde Kluckhohn and Dorothea Leighton, *The Navaho* (New York: Doubleday, 1962).

7. Anglo employers who hire bright, energetic, and hard-working Navajo but fail to recognize this important fact often become disappointed with their Navajo employees, whose notions of ownership and family are sometimes radically different from conventional Anglo-American approaches.

Navajos tend to view property as belonging to a very broad group of relatives. Because of this, the relative who works in town at a salaried job may, in effect, be supporting many more than his or her immediate family. That employee's first and foremost loyalties are to the extended family and its material and ritual needs. This often causes situations where family and religious duties override agreed-upon work schedules and responsibilities.

8. This account derives primarily from Mindeleff, "Navaho Houses," 487–93.

9. All accounts agree that the proper direction for the doorway is east. However, in the literature there is some confusion as to whether this means due east, roughly east, or the direction of the rising sun on the day the hogan is built. Also, most references to the orientation of the entranceway allude to its easterly, or sunwise, direction, but few specify whether or not it is related to an observation. However, several authors assert that the sunrise orientation of the hogan at time of construction is to receive the blessing of the rising sun.

The hogan is a winter home. In the warm months, the Navajo who still keep the traditional ways live out of doors in temporary shelters of various kinds. Since winter homes are more likely to be constructed during the summer or early fall before the weather becomes too cold for outdoor living, one would expect the most common orientation to be northeastward or eastward, with few entries facing southeast. However, too little archaeological or ethnographic work has been done to determine whether or not there is a preferred building season.

In eighteenth-century hogans, northeasterly and eastern orientations are most common, although southeast and even northerly ones are known as well. Northern orientation represents a deviation from a pattern of orienting the entries to sunrise, since the sun never reaches due north in its yearly horizon journey. See S. C. Jett and V. E. Spencer, *Navaho Architecture* (Tucson: University of Arizona Press, 1981), 17.

10. Mindeleff, "Navaho Houses," 507.

11. Jett and Spencer, *Navaho Architecture*; David P. McAllester and Susan W. McAllester, *Hogans* (Middletown, Conn.: Wesleyan University Press, 1980).

12. Berard F. Haile, *Starlore Among the Navaho* (Santa Fe: Museum of Navajo Ceremonial Art, 1947). The creation story reproduced here is also taken from Father Haile, who learned it from the Nightway chant.

13. Haile, *Starlore*, 4.

14. Coyote Star is in some texts referred to as Canopus. At the mean latitude of the Navajo (about 36°), Canopus would appear only 2° to 3° above the horizon. This seems a less likely choice than Antares for the Coyote Star.

15. Franc Johnson Newcomb, Stanley Fishler, and Mary C. Wheelwright, "Navajo Symbolism," *Papers of the Peabody Museum of Archaeology and Ethnology* 23, no. 3, 1956.

16. Sallie P. Brewer, "Notes on Navaho Astronomy," in *For the Dean, Essays in Anthropology in Honor of Byron Cummings* (Tucson: University of Arizona Press, 1950), 133–36.

17. Since Revolving Male is mainly composed of stars in the familiar Western constellation Ursa Major, it is a particularly handy constellation for the reader to use to test these observations. Following sunset, and just when it is fully dark in late May (about 9:00 P.M.), the Big Dipper will be oriented with the dipper turned toward the earth and the handle parallel to the horizon. As the night progresses, the handle of the dipper will swing upward and counterclockwise around the pole star.

18. Haile, *Starlore*, 33.

19. W. W. Hill, "The Agriculture and Hunting Methods of the Navaho Indians," *Yale University Publications in Anthropology* 18 (1938): 26.

20. Donald Sander, *Navaho Symbols of Healing* (New York: Harcourt Brace Jovanovich, 1979), 204.

21. Newcomb et al., "Navajo Symbolism," 26.

22. Alfred M. Tozzer, "A Note on Star-Lore Among the Navajos," *Journal of American Folklore* 21 (1909): 28–32.

23. Clarion Cochran, who acted as my guide early in these researches, "owns" a ceremonial rattle given to him by a Navajo friend. It is about 6 inches long, has a wooden handle that extends through the gourd which holds the bits of turquoise and shell that constitute the rattling material. It is fastened to the gourd by means of a leather thong.

24. I am indebted to Thomas K. Simpson for pointing out these remarkable patterns and suggesting that they might represent constellations, though I hardly understood their relevance to Navajo starlore at the time. Clarion Cochran suggested that I might compare them with the patterns on ceremonial rattles.

25. Von Del Chamberlain originally recorded these glyphs and kindly shared his photographs with me.

26. Artist and rock art expert Polly Schaafsma first suggested to me that the white sun symbol might be Navajo. She has found many instances where archaeologists have mistakenly attributed Navajo glyphs to the Pueblo.

27. Brewer, "Notes on Navaho Astronomy," 136.

28. See C. Britt, "Early Navajo Astronomical Pictographs," in *Archaeoastronomy in Pre-Columbian America*, ed. Anthony F. Aveni (Austin: University of Texas Press, 1975), 89–108.

8. Omens of the Sky: Bright Star and Crescent

1. I have chosen to use the Zuni name "Seeds" for the constellation Pleiades, which rose heliacally at this time of year. The setting is the Anasazi town of Penasco Blanco, in Chaco Canyon.

2. An ancient Chinese observatory often had four observers, one for each quarter of the sky. See J. Needham, *Science and Civilization in China*, vol. 3 (Cambridge, England: Cambridge University Press, 1959). Because the moon's monthly movement is from west to east at a rate of one lunar diameter per hour, by the time the moon was visible from China, it preceded the rise of the guest star by about one hour.

3. See the extensive bibliography in John C. Brandt and Ray A. Williamson, "The 1054 Supernova and Rock Art," *Archaeoastronomy, Supplement to Journal for the History of Astronomy* 10 (1979): S1–S38.

4. For a general scholarly discussion of the historical and astronomical data about supernovae, see D. H. Clark and F. R. Stephenson, *The Historical Supernovae* (Oxford, England: Oxford University Press, 1977).

5. Ho Peng-Yoke, F. W. Paar, and P. W. Parsons, "The Chinese Guest Star of A.D. 1054 and the Crab Nebula," *Vistas in Astronomy* 13 (1972): 1–13.
6. Kenneth Brecher, Elizabeth Lieber, and Alfred E. Lieber, "A Near Eastern Sighting of the Supernova Explosion of 1054," *Nature* 268 (1978): 728–30.
7. William C. Miller, "Two Possible Astronomical Pictographs Found in Northern Arizona," *Plateau* 28 (1955): 6–12.
8. Clarion Cochran also made the first survey of the extensive rock art in the canyon. It was through his records that Donnel O'Flynn was able to locate the Navajo/Anasazi site east of Wijiji Pueblo. Colonel James Bain has in recent years taken his rock art school to Chaco Canyon to make a thorough catalogue of the canyon's petroglyphs and pictographs.
9. For example, see Florence H. Ellis, "A Thousand Years of the Pueblo Sun-Moon-Star Calendar," in Anthony F. Aveni, ed., *Archaeoastronomy in Pre-Columbian America* (Austin: University of Texas Press, 1975), 59–87.
10. Matilda Coxe Stevenson, notes, National Anthropological Archives, n.d.
11. John P. Harrington, "The Ethnogeography of the Tewa Indians," *Smithsonian Institution Bureau of American Ethnology Annual Report* 29 (1916): 49.
12. J. G. Bourke, *The Snake Dance of the Moquis* (New York: Charles Scribner's Sons, 1884).
13. See Dorothy Mayer, "Star Pattern in Great Basin Petroglyphs," in *Archaeoastronomy in Pre-Columbian America*, ed. Anthony F. Aveni (Austin: University of Texas Press, 1973), 88–130; "An Examination of Miller's Hypothesis," in *Native American Astronomy*, ed. Anthony F. Aveni (Austin: University of Texas Press, 1975), 59–87.
14. The English astronomer Edmund Halley, while studying the orbital paths of comets, found in 1704 that the bright comets of 1456, 1531, 1607, and 1682 had nearly the same orbital characteristics. Notice that its reappearance occurs about once every seventy-five years. He used this fact to predict its subsequent appearance in 1758. It was named Halley's comet after him. Working backward in time, this was the same comet that appeared in 1066. Its much earlier appearance in A.D. 66 was considered the herald of the destruction of Jerusalem in A.D. 70. It appeared in 1910 and will be seen again in 1985 when it will be the object of an intensive study by Soviet, European, and Japanese spacecraft.
15. Franc Johnson Newcomb, Stanley Fishler, and Mary C. Wheelwright, "Navajo Symbolism," *Papers of the Peabody Museum of Archaeology and Ethnology* 23, no. 3 (1956): 25.
16. J. C. Bard, F. Asaro, and R. F. Heiser, "Perspectives on Dating of Great Basin Petroglyphs by Neutron Activation Analysis of the Patinated Surfaces," *Archaeometry* 20 (1978): 85–88.
17. Harry Crosby, *The Cave Paintings of Baja California* (La Jolla: Copley Books, 1978), 30.
18. Seymour H. Koenig, "Stars, Crescents, and Supernovae in Southwestern Indian Art," *Archaeoastronomy, Supplement to the Journal for the History of Astronomy* 10 (1979): S39–S50.
19. Polly Schaafsma and Curtis F. Schaafsma, "Evidence for the Origins of the Pueblo Katchina Cult as Suggested by Southwestern Rock Art," *American Antiquity* 39 (1974): 535–45.

9. Medicine Wheels and the Plains Indians

1. John A. Eddy, "Astronomical Alignment of the Big Horn Medicine Wheel," *Science* 184 (1974): 1035–43.
2. Jack H. Robinson, "Fomalhaut and Cairn D at the Big Horn and Moose Mountain Medicine Wheels," *Archaeoastronomy* 3, no. 4 (1980): 15–19.
3. S. C. Simms, "A Wheel-Shaped Stone Monument in Wyoming," *American Anthropologist*, new series 5 (1903): 107.
4. Simms, "Wheel-Shaped Stone Monument," 107.
5. Simms, "Wheel-Shaped Stone Monument," 108.
6. George Grinnell, "The Medicine Wheel," *American Anthropologist*, new series 24 (1922): 307.
7. Joseph Epes Brown, *The Sacred Pipe: Black Elk's Account of the Seven Rites of the Oglala Sioux* (Norman: University of Oklahoma Press, 1953), 80.
8. John A. Eddy, "Medicine Wheels and Plains Indian Astronomy," in *Native American Astronomy*, ed. Anthony F. Aveni (Austin: University of Texas Press, 1977), 147–69.
9. Robinson, "Fomalhaut and Cairn D."
10. Alice B. Kehoe and Thomas F. Kehoe, "Solstice-Aligned Boulder Configurations in Saskatchewan," *Canadian Ethnology Service Paper No. 48*. Ottawa, Canada: National Museum of Man Mercury Series (1979).
11. Archaeologists depend heavily on the cultural material found in each layer of an excavation to give them a picture of the evolution of a structure or site over time. Stratigraphic data are extremely important to this endeavor.
12. Kehoe and Kehoe, "Solstice-Aligned Boulder Configurations," 32.

10. The Pawnee: Great Morning Star

1. This account is a composite drawn from accounts by Gene Weltfish, *The Lost Universe* (Lincoln: University of Nebraska Press, 1977); Ralph Linton, "The Sacrifice to the Morning Star by the Skidi Pawnee," *Field Museum of Natural History Anthropological Leaflets* 6 (1923): 1–18; George A. Dorsey, "The Skidi Rite of Human Sacrifice," *Proceedings of the Fifteenth International Congress of Americanists* (1906): 65–70; and from Von Del Chamberlain, *When Stars Came Down to Earth* (Los Altos, Calif.: Ballena Press, 1982). Each account is sufficiently different that no agreement on some details is possible. The reader is referred especially to the accounts of Chamberlain and Weltfish for details of the ceremonies preceding the sacrifice to Morning Star, and for a detailed rationale behind some of the ritual actions.
2. Certain similarities between the Pawnee sacrifice and the scaffold sacrifice of the Aztecs have been noted in the literature, especially by Clark Wissler and Herbert J. Spinden, "The Pawnee Human Sacrifice to the Morningstar," *American Museum Journal* 16 (1916): 49–55. Although it is tempting to impute these similarities to contact between the Aztecs and the Pawnee, the differences between their practices far outweigh the possible similarities. For one thing, as Chamberlain has pointed out (*When Stars Came Down*, 68), the Aztec religion was oriented to the sun. The Pawnee religion was oriented to the stars. In addition, the Aztec sacrifice was merely one of many sacrificial ceremonies.
3. George A. Dorsey (n.d.), quoted in Chamberlain, *When Stars Came Down*, 57.

4. The moral indignation of the whites toward this ceremony was exceeded only by their own systematic slaughter of the Pawnee and other Indian tribes from whom the Pawnee took their victims. Pressed on all sides — by the settlers who took their land and slaughtered the buffalo, and passed on crippling diseases, and by other tribes that sold them into slavery when they could — the Pawnee were virtually exterminated. By 1900, only six hundred Pawnee remained of the thousands that roamed the Plains before the coming of the European settlers.

5. Murie worked with Fletcher and then with Dorsey for several years. The materials he gathered are now, after many years, published in James R. Murie, *The Ceremonies of the Pawnee*, Douglas Parks, ed. (Washington D.C.: Smithsonian Institution Press, 1981). Other information can be found in George A. Dorsey's publications, and in *The Lost Universe* by Gene Weltfish. Few of Fletcher's notes on the Pawnee were published by her, though many found their way into Weltfish's book. The descriptions of Skidi starlore in this chapter are taken primarily from Von Del Chamberlain's excellent book.

6. For a more detailed rendition of this beautiful story, told by Murie, see Natalie Curtis, *The Indian's Book: Songs and Legends of the American Indians* (New York: Dover Publications, 1968), 91–144.

7. Curtis, *The Indian's Book*, 101.

8. Curtis, *The Indian's Book*, 103.

9. Chamberlain, *When Stars Came Down*, 80. His sympathetic and thoughtful treatment of the extensive materials available to the scholar are assembled in his book. He presents there (pp. 71–90) the detailed evidence related to Morning Star's identity.

10. This "retrograde motion" is typical behavior for the planets, and was a subject of great interest to the Greek astronomers. It comes about because we see the planets moving against a field of stars at the same time that Earth moves through space around the sun.

11. I have taken this account from Chamberlain's rendition (*When Stars Came Down*, 75), which was aided by his use of the Albert Einstein Spacearium at the National Air and Space Museum.

12. Chamberlain, *When Stars Came Down*, 95–106.

13. George A. Dorsey (n.d.). This story is quoted in Chamberlain, *When Stars Came Down*, 147.

14. In a *National Geographic* article (July 1944), Matthew W. Stirling stated, "So accurate is the workmanship that astronomers can calculate its approximate date by the positions of the major planets." This is surely imagination working overtime.

15. Ralph N. Buckstaff, "Stars and Constellations of a Pawnee Sky Map," *American Anthropologist* 29 (1927): 279–85, described the star chart and attempted to identify constellations that appear on it. Examination of the chart bears out only a few of his identifications — the most obvious ones. As Chamberlain complains, "Buckstaff's paper is confusing, unclear, and very inconsistent" (*When Stars Came Down*, 192).

16. Alice C. Fletcher, "Pawnee Star Lore," *Journal of American Folklore* 16 (1903): 14–15.

17. James R. Murie (n.d.). Quoted in Chamberlain, *When Stars Came Down*, 139.

18. See Murie, *Ceremonies of the Pawnee*, 53. The identification here of the

Swimming Ducks as northeastern stars led Chamberlain on a sort of "wild duck" chase, until he realized that elsewhere Murie and also Dorsey identified these two stars as situated near the constellation Serpent and rising in the southeast. The tail of Scorpius is certainly meant. Errors such as this transposition are not uncommon in Murie's writings.

19. Ralph A. Linton, "The Thunder Ceremony of the Pawnee," *Field Museum of Natural History Anthropological Leaflets* 5 (1922): 10.

20. Linton, "Thunder Ceremony," 15.

21. Linton, "Thunder Ceremony," 19.

11. Eastern Sun Worship

1. Allen Wright, *The Missionary Herald* 24 (1828): 179–80.

2. Jacques Le Moyne, *Narrative of Le Moyne, an artist who accompanied the French expedition to Florida under Lauonniere, 1564.* Translated from the Latin of De Bry. (Boston: 1875): 13.

3. See *Gentleman of Elvas, Narratives of the career of Hernando de Soto . . . As told by a Knight of Elvas,* Buckingham Smith, trans., reprint edition (Gainesville, Fla.: Palmetto Books, 1968), 23–33.

4. Father Le Petit, Letter to d'Avaugour, in Reuben Gold Thwaites, ed., *Jesuit Relations and Allied Documents. Travels and explorations of the Jesuit Missionaries in New France, 1610–1791,* vol. 68 (Cleveland: 1896–1901), 126–27.

5. See Pierre F. X. de Charlevoix, in *French's Historical Collection of Louisiana* (New York: 1851), 163. Quoted in John R. Swanton, "Indian Tribes of the Lower Mississippi Valley," *Bureau of American Ethnology Bulletin* 43 (1911): 174.

6. Pierre Margry, *Descouvertes et estabilissements des Francis dans l'Ouest e dans le Sud l'Amerique Septentrionale (1614–1754). Memoires et Documents Originaux Recueillis et Publies par Pierre Margry,* 6 vols. (Paris: 1875–1886). Quoted in Swanton, "Indian Tribes," 159.

7. Swanton, "Indian Tribes," 175.

8. See John R. Swanton, "The Indians of the Southeastern United States," *Smithsonian Institution Bureau of American Ethnology Bulletin* 147 (1946): 682–84. He mentions that the Creek and the Cherokee played chunky, as did the Choctaw, Natchez, and various tribes along the Mississippi River.

9. Melvin L. Fowler, "The Cahokia Site," in "Explorations into Cahokia Archaeology," Melvin L. Fowler, ed., *Illinois Archaeology Survey Bulletin* 7 (1973): 8.

10. Actually, Fowler's first attempt produced nothing indicating an alignment. Then, realizing that an error had been made in his original calculation, he sunk another test pit. This produced the described results. Melvin L. Fowler, "A Pre-Columbian Urban Center on the Mississippi," *Scientific American* (August 1975): 92–101.

11. Warren L. Wittry, "The American Woodhenge," in "Explorations into Cahokia Archaeology," 43–48.

12. See Richard Norrish, "Woodhenge — Work of a Genius," *Cahokian* (February 1978): 21–24; Warren L. Wittry, "Cahokia Woodhenge Update," *Archaeoastronomy* 3, no. 1 (1980), 12–13.

13. Dr. Wittry kindly supplied me with these figures.

14. Dr. Wittry cautions that one should not take these carbon dates too seriously. They indicate that the construction of two circles was separated in time, and give an estimate of how much that separation might be. However, taking a simple average overlooks the fact that some pieces of wood might have come from a replacement post, so they yield later dates. In addition, it is impossible to tell from what part of the tree they came. Samples from the center can differ in carbon 14 age from samples near the outside. Finally, the carbon 14 dating, even if it were 100 percent accurate, only determines the cutting date of the log, and there is no way of telling when the logs might have been cut relative to their use.

15. Wittry has been criticized for not being precise enough. However, this seems to be more a matter that Wittry himself has published relatively little about his investigations. In an apparent effort to be as definitive as possible, he has continued to study the site and understand as many of its ramifications as possible. He also speculates freely about the various possibilities. Other commentators, attempting to examine the validity of Wittry's hypotheses, have used either information from popular accounts or Wittry's own sketches of the site that have appeared in the literature. The latter are admittedly inaccurate, as they are drawn to illustrate the circles, not to be used for further calculations. The former are also inaccurate in other ways. First, the popular accounts invariably get some of the details wrong. Second, they report some of Wittry's speculations, which, given the nature of speculation, he may soon find are incorrect. For example, at one point Wittry thought two unusual posts in circle 2 might be aligned to the star Capella. This was reported in one detailed account. He has more recently realized that these posts belong to a different circle. Therefore, the putative Capella orientations have turned out to be unconfirmed. If he is to be faulted, it is for speculating openly about the meaning of his finds. In print, he is much more cautious, commendably so.

16. See the arguments in Nelson A. Reed, "Monks and Other Mississippian Mounds," in Fowler, ed., "Explorations": 31–42; and Fowler, "A Pre-Columbian Urban Center."

17. James M. Heilman and Roger Hoefer, "Possible Astronomical Alignments in a Fort Ancient Settlement at the Incinerator Site in Dayton, Ohio," in *Archaeoastronomy in the Americas*, Ray A. Williamson, ed. (Los Altos, Calif.: Ballena Press, 1981), 157–72.

18. See John Witthoft, "Green Corn Ceremonialism in the Eastern Woodland," *Occasional Contributions from the Museum of Anthropology of the University of Michigan* 13 (1949).

19. See Anthony F. C. Wallace, *The Death and Rebirth of the Seneca* (New York: Alfred A. Knopf, 1970), 57–58.

20. Witthoft, "Green Corn Ceremonialism."

21. Clark Hardman, Jr., "The Primitive Solar Observatory at Crystal River and Its Implications," *The Florida Anthropologist* 24 (1971): 135–68.

22. Ripley P. Bullen, "Stelae at the Crystal River Site, Florida," *American Antiquity* 31 (1966): 861–65.

23. David S. Brose, "An Interpretation of the Hopewellian Traits in Florida," in *Hopewell Archaeology*, ed. D. S. Brose and N. Greber (Kent, Ohio: Kent State University Press, 1979).

24. See Warren E. Cook, ed., *Ancient Vermont* (Castleton, Vt.: Castleton State College Press, 1978).
25. Byron E. Dix and James W. Mavor, Jr., "Two Possible Calendar Sites in Vermont," in Williamson, ed., *Archaeoastronomy in the Americas*, 111–32; Byron E. Dix and James W. Mavor, "Heliolithic, Ritual Sites in New England," *New England Antiquities Research Association Journal* 16 (1982): 63–83.
26. Gordon M. Day, "Western Abenaki," in *Handbook of the North American Indians, Northeast* (Washington, D.C.: Smithsonian Institution, 1978), 149.
27. Giovana Neudorfer, *Vermont's Stone Chambers* (Montpelier: Vermont Historical Society, 1980), discusses the possible origins of the Vermont stone chambers and concludes that they were probably constructed in historic times. However, Dix and Mavor criticize her book on the grounds that it contains numerous small factual errors and that Neudorfer was biased in her approach. My own view is that the problem needs more work before one or the other claim can be substantiated.

12. California Indians: Maintaining the Cosmic Balance

1. Ken Hedges, "Preliminary Report on a Winter Solstice Rock Painting at La Rumorosa, Baja California," Paper presented at the Fourth Annual Rock Art Symposium, May 1977, Tempe, Arizona.
2. Maynard Geiger and Clement Meighan, *As the Padres Saw Them* (Santa Barbara: Santa Barbara Mission Archive Library, 1976).
3. See M. Jane Young and Ray A. Williamson, "Ethnoastronomy: The Zuni Case," in *Archaeoastronomy in the Americas*, ed. Ray A. Williamson (Los Altos, Calif.: Ballena Press, 1981), 183–92.
4. For an insightful and highly readable, if biased, account of J. P. Harrington, see Carobeth Laird, *Encounter with an Angry God* (Banning, Calif.: Malki Museum Press, 1975). Carobeth Laird was Harrington's wife.
5. Although it is not generally appreciated, as California anthropologist Travis Hudson has pointed out to me, the highest population densities in prehistoric North America were not among agriculturalists but among the hunter-gatherers in California and the Pacific Northwest Coast. To take on the burden of agriculture in this abundant land would have been to work harder for less food.
6. See the bibliography in Travis Hudson and Ernest Underhay, *Crystals in the Sky: An Intellectual Odyssey Involving Chumash Astronomy, Cosmology and Rock Art* (Los Altos, Calif.: Ballena Press, 1978).
7. See Campbell Grant, *The Rock Paintings of the Chumash* (Berkeley and Los Angeles: University of California Press, 1965).
8. See especially Hudson and Underhay, *Crystals in the Sky*, and Travis Hudson, "California's First Astronomers," in *Archaeoastronomy and the Roots of Science*, Edwin Krupp, ed. (Washington, D.C.: Westview Press, 1984).
9. Quoted and annotated by Hudson in *Crystals in the Sky* (p. 41), from J. P. Harrington's notes.
10. Lowell Bean, "Power and Its Applications in Native California," in *Na-*

tive Californians: A Theoretical Retrospective, Lowell Bean and Thomas Blackburn, eds. (Ramona, Calif.: Ballena Press, 1976), 415.

11. J. P. Harrington's notes, *Crystals in the Sky*, 51.

12. See Travis Hudson et al., eds., *The Eye of the Flute: Chumash Traditional History and Ritual as Told by Fernando Librado to John P. Harrington*, second edition (Santa Barbara: Santa Barbara Museum of Natural History, 1981), 34.

13. Thomas C. Blackburn, ed., *December's Child: Stories Collected by J. P. Harrington* (Berkeley: University of California Press, 1975), 93.

14. Hudson et al., *Eye of the Flute*, chap. 13.

15. Hudson et al., *Eye of the Flute*, 60.

16. Hudson et al., *Eye of the Flute*, 106, n. 71.

17. Hudson and Underhay, *Crystals in the Sky*, 63–68.

18. Hudson et al., *Eye of the Flute*, chap. 12.

19. Hudson et al., *Eye of the Flute*, 53.

20. Hudson et al., *Eye of the Flute*, 52.

21. Fray Geronimo Boscana, *Chinigchinich*, Alfred Robinson, trans., P. T. Hanna, ed. (Santa Ana, Calif.: Fine Arts Press, 1933), 65–66.

22. Thomas Blackburn, "A Manuscript Account of the Ventureno Chumash," *University of California Archaeological Survey Annual Report 1962–1963* (1963): 141.

23. Mary Elizabeth Johnson, *Indian Legends of the Cuyamaca Mountains* (San Diego: privately printed, 1914), 24–25.

24. Ken Hedges, "Winter Solstice Observatory Sites in Kumeyaay Territory, San Diego County, California," in Ray A. Williamson, ed., *Archaeoastronomy in the Americas* (Los Altos, Calif.: Ballena Press, 1981), 151–56.

25. Victor J. Slaboszewicz and Robert M. Cooper, "Ker-17: A Possible Tubatulabal Winter Solstice Observatory," in *Visions of the Sky: Archaeological and Ethnographic Studies of California Indian Astronomy*, ed. Travis B. Hudson, John B. Carlson, and Robert A. Schiffman. (Ramona, Calif.: Acoma Books, in press).

26. Robert A. Schiffman, "A Native American Solstice Observatory," in *Visions of the Sky*.

27. Lucile Hooper, "The Cahuilla Indians," *University of California Publications in American Archaeology and Ethnology* 16 (1920): 315–80.

13. Living the Sky

1. Alice Fletcher, "The Hako: A Pawnee Ceremony," *Smithsonian Institution Bureau of American Ethnology Annual Report* 22, Pt. 2 (1904): 151–52.

2. René Descartes, "Discourse on the Method of Rightly Conducting the Reason," in *The Philosophical Works of Descartes*, trans. Elizabeth S. Haldane and G.R.T. Ross (Cambridge, England: Cambridge University Press, 1911), 119.

3. Francis Bacon, *The New Organon and Related Writings*, ed. Fulton H. Anderson (Indianapolis: Bobbs-Merrill, 1960), 119.

4. E. C. Krupp, "A Glance into the Smoking Mirror," in Ray A. Williamson, ed., *Archaeoastronomy in the Americas* (Los Altos, Calif.: Ballena Press, 1981), 59.

5. Claire R. Farrer and Bernard Second, "Living the Sky: Aspects of Mescalero Apache Ethnoastronomy," in Williamson, ed., *Archaeoastronomy in the Americas*, 137–50.

6. Vitruvius, *The Ten Books on Architecture*, Morris Hicky Morgan, trans. (New York: Dover Publications, 1960), 116.

7. See Thomas C. Blackburn, *December's Child: Stories Collected by J. P. Harrington* (Berkeley: University of California Press, 1975), 200–201.

8. William Shakespeare, *Othello*, act III, scene 3.

9. Samuel Butler, *The Authoress of the Odyssey* (Chicago: University of Chicago Press, 1967), 6.

10. George Dorsey, unpublished notes, quoted in Von Del Chamberlain, *When Stars Came Down to Earth* (Los Altos, Calif.: Ballena Press, 1982), 160–61.

11. Alice Fletcher, unpublished notes, quoted in Chamberlain, *When Stars Came Down*, 100.

12. George Dorsey, unpublished notes, quoted in Chamberlain, *When Stars Came Down*, 157.

13. Barre Toelken, *The Dynamics of Folklore* (Boston: Houghton Mifflin, 1979), 95–96.

14. Francisco Patencio, *Stories and Legends of the Palm Springs Indians* (Los Angeles: Times-Mirror Press, 1943), 113.

15. Carobeth Laird, *The Chemehuevis* (Banning, Calif.: Malki Museum Press, 1976), 157–58.

Bibliography

General Archaeoastronomy and Ethnoastronomy

Archaeoastronomy: Bulletin of the Center for Archaeoastronomy. Center for Archaeoastronomy, Space Sciences Bldg., University of Maryland, College Park, Md. 20742.

Archaeoastronomy: Supplement to the Journal for the History of Astronomy. Science History Publications Ltd., Halfpenny Furze, Mill Lane, Chalfont St. Giles, Bucks., England HP8 4NP.

Aveni, Anthony F. "Archaeoastronomy." In *Advances in Archaeological Method and Theory* 4:1–77. Princeton: Academic Press, 1981.

Baity, Elizabeth Chesley. "Archaeoastronomy and Ethnoastronomy So Far." *Current Anthropology* 14 (1973): 389–449.

Brecher, Kenneth, and Michael Feirtag, eds. *Astronomy of the Ancients.* Cambridge, Mass.: MIT Press, 1979.

Cornell, James. *The First Stargazers.* New York: Charles Scribner's Sons, 1981.

Hadingham, Evan. *Early Man and the Cosmos.* New York: Walker, 1984.

Hawkins, Gerald S. *Beyond Stonehenge.* New York: Harper & Row, 1973.

Hodson, F. R. "The Place of Astronomy in the Ancient World." *Philosophical Transactions of the Royal Society of London* 276, no. 1257 (1974): 1–276.

Krupp, E. C. *Echoes of the Ancient Skies: The Astronomy of Lost Civilizations.* New York: Harper & Row, 1983.

———, ed. *In Search of Ancient Astronomies.* New York: Doubleday, 1978.

———, ed. *Archaeoastronomy and the Roots of Science.* Washington, D.C.: Westview Press, 1984.

Santillana, Giorgio de, and Hertha von Dechend. *Hamlet's Mill.* Boston: Gambit, 1969.

Native American Sources

Autrey, Nev E., and Wanda R. Autrey. "Zodiac Ridge." In *Archaeoastronomy in the Americas,* edited by Ray A. Williamson. Los Altos, Calif.: Ballena Press, 1981.

Aveni, Anthony F. *Skywatchers of Ancient Mexico.* Austin: University of Texas Press, 1980.

———. "Archaeoastronomy Today." In *Archaeoastronomy in the Americas*, edited by Ray A. Williamson. Los Altos, Calif.: Ballena Press, 1981.

———, ed. *Archaeoastronomy in Pre-Columbian America*. Austin: University of Texas Press, 1975.

———, ed. *Native American Astronomy*. Austin: University of Texas Press, 1977.

———, ed. *Archaeoastronomy in the New World*. Cambridge, England: Cambridge University Press, 1982.

———, and Gary Urton, eds. *Ethnoastronomy and Archaeoastronomy in the American Tropics*. Annals of the New York Academy of Sciences, vol. 385, 1982.

Benedict, Ruth. *Zuni Mythology*. 2 vols. New York: Columbia University Press, 1935.

Blackburn, Thomas C. *December's Child: A Book of Chumash Oral Narratives*. Berkeley and Los Angeles: University of California Press, 1975.

Brandt, John C., et al. "Possible Rock Art Records of the Crab Nebula Supernova in the Western United States." In *Archaeoastronomy in Pre-Columbian America*, edited by Anthony F. Aveni. Austin: University of Texas Press, 1975.

Brandt, John C., and Ray A. Williamson. "The 1054 Supernova and Native American Rock Art." *Archaeoastronomy*, supp. to *Journal for the History of Astronomy*, no. 1 (1979).

Brinton, D. G. *Myths of the New World: A Treatise on the Symbolism and Mythology of the Red Race of America*. 1896. Reprint. New York: Haskell House, 1968.

Brown, Joseph Epes. *The Sacred Pipe: Black Elk's Account of the Seven Rites of the Oglala Sioux*. Norman: University of Oklahoma Press, 1953.

Bunzel, Ruth L. "Introduction to Zuni Ceremonialism; Zuni Katchinas; Zuni Origin Myths; Zuni Ritual Poetry." *Smithsonian Institution Bureau of American Ethnology Annual Report* 47 (1932).

Carlson, John B. "Archaeoastronomy and Education." In *Archaeoastronomy in the Americas*, edited by Ray A. Williamson. Los Altos, Calif.: Ballena Press, 1981.

Castetter, E. F., and W. H. Bell. *Pima and Papago Indian Agriculture*. Albuquerque: University of New Mexico Press, 1942.

Chamberlain, Von Del. *When Stars Came Down to Earth: Cosmology of the Skidi Pawnee Indians of North America*. Los Altos, Calif.: Ballena Press, 1982.

Cook, Warren L., ed. *Ancient Vermont*. Castleton, Vt.: Castleton State College Press, 1978.

Crow Wing. *A Pueblo Indian Journal, 1920–1921*. Edited by E. C. Parsons. *Memoirs of the American Anthropological Association* 32 (1925).

Curtis, Frank H. *The North American Indian, Vol. 12: The Hopi*. 1922. Reprint. New York: The Plimpton Press, 1970.

Cushing, Frank H. "Outlines of Zuni Creation Myths." *Smithsonian Institution Bureau of American Ethnology Annual Report* 13 (1896).

———. *Zuni Folk Tales*. New York: G. P. Putnam's Sons, 1901.

———. *My Adventures in Zuni*. Santa Fe: Peripatetic Press, 1941.

Daniel-Hartung, Ann L. "Archaeoastronomy at a Selection of Mississippian Sites in the Southeastern United States." In *Archaeoastronomy in the*

Americas, edited by Ray A. Williamson. Los Altos, Calif.: Ballena Press, 1981.

Dix, Byron E., and James W. Mavor, Jr. "Two Possible Calendar Sites in Vermont." In Archaeoastronomy in the Americas, edited by Ray A. Williamson. Los Altos, Calif.: Ballena Press, 1981.

Douglass, William B. "A World-Quarter Shrine of the Tewa Indians." Records of the Past 2 (1912).

Dozier, E. P. Hano, A Tewa Indian Community in Arizona. New York: Holt, Rinehart & Winston, 1966.

Dutton, Bertha P. Sunfather's Way. Albuquerque: University of New Mexico Press, 1963.

Eddy, John A. "Astronomical Alignment of the Big Horn Medicine Wheel." Science 184 (1974).

———. "Medicine Wheels and Plains Indian Astronomy." In Native American Astronomy, edited by Anthony F. Aveni. Austin: University of Texas Press, 1977.

———. "Medicine Wheels and Plains Indian Astronomy." In Astronomy of the Ancients, edited by Kenneth Brecher and Michael Feirtag. Cambridge: MIT Press, 1979.

———. "Some Thoughts on Archaeoastronomy Today." In Archaeoastronomy in the Americas, edited by Ray A. Williamson. Los Altos, Calif.: Ballena Press, 1981.

Eggan, Fred. Social Organization of the Western Pueblos. Chicago: University of Chicago Press, 1950.

Eidenbach, Peter L. "Wizard's Roost and Wally's Dome, Continuing Investigations of Prehistoric Observatory Sites in the Sacramento Mountains, New Mexico." Jornada Mogollon Archaeology, edited by Beckett and Wiseman. New Mexico State University, 1979.

Ellis, Florence H. "A Thousand Years of the Pueblo Sun-Moon-Star Calendar." In Archaeoastronomy in Pre-Columbian America, edited by Anthony F. Aveni. Austin: University of Texas Press, 1975.

———. "Datable Ritual Components Proclaiming Mexican Influence in the Upper Rio Grande of New Mexico." In Collected Papers in Honor of Marjorie Ferguson Lambert. Albuquerque: Archaeological Society of New Mexico, 1976.

Evans, John H., and Harry Hillman. "Documentation of Some Lunar and Solar Events at Casa Grande, Arizona." In Archaeoastronomy in the Americas, edited by Ray A. Williamson. Los Altos, Calif.: Ballena Press, 1981.

Farrer, Claire R., and Bernard Second. "Living the Sky: Aspects of Mescalero Apache Ethnoastronomy." In Archaeoastronomy in the Americas, edited by Ray A. Williamson. Los Altos, Calif.: Ballena Press, 1981.

Fewkes, Jesse Walter. "A Few Summer Ceremonials at the Tusayan Pueblos." American Ethnology and Archaeology 2 (1892).

Fowler, Melvin L. "A Pre-Columbian Urban Center on the Mississippi." Scientific American 233 (1975).

———. "The Cahokia Site." Explorations into Cahokia Archaeology. Illinois Archaeological Survey, Bulletin 7, 1977.

Hardman, Clark. "The Primitive Solar Observatory at Crystal River and Its Implications." Florida Anthropologist 24 (1971).

Harrington, John P. "The Ethnogeography of the Tewa Indians." *Smithsonian Institution Bureau of American Ethnology Annual Report* 29 (1916).

Hartung, Horst. "The Role of Architecture and Planning in Archaeoastronomy." In *Archaeoastronomy in the Americas*, edited by Ray A. Williamson. Los Altos, Calif.: Ballena Press, 1981.

Hedges, Ken. "Winter Solstice Observatory Sites in Kumeyaay Territory, San Diego County, California." In *Archaeoastronomy in the Americas*, edited by Ray A. Williamson. Los Altos, Calif.: Ballena Press, 1981.

Heilman, James M., and Roger R. Hoefer. "Possible Astronomical Alignments in a Fort Ancient Settlement at the Incinerator Site in Dayton, Ohio." In *Archaeoastronomy in the Americas*, edited by Ray A. Williamson. Los Altos, Calif.: Ballena Press, 1981.

Hicks, Ronald. "Archaeoastronomy and Related Problems: Old World Approaches vs. New." In *Archaeoastronomy in the Americas*, edited by Ray A. Williamson. Los Altos, Calif.: Ballena Press, 1981.

Hudson, Travis, and Thomas Blackburn. "The Integration of Myth and Ritual in South-Central California: The 'Northern Complex.'" *Journal of California Anthropology* 5 (1978).

Hudson, Travis, Georgia Lee, and Ken Hedges. "Solstice Observers and Observatories in Native California." *Journal of California and Great Basin Anthropology* 1 (1979).

Hudson, Travis, and Ernest Underhay. *Crystals in the Sky: An Intellectual Odyssey Involving Chumash Astronomy, Cosmology and Rock Art.* Socorro, N.M.: Ballena Press, 1978.

Kehoe, Thomas F., and Alice B. Kehoe. "Solstice-Aligned Boulder Configurations in Saskatchewan." *National Museum of Man Mercury Series*, Canadian Ethnology Service Paper No. 48 (1979).

Koenig, Seymour H. "Stars, Crescents, and Supernovae in Southwestern Indian Art," *Archaeoastronomy*, supp. to *Journal for the History of Astronomy*, no. 1 (1979).

Krupp, E. C. "A Glance Into the Smoking Mirror." In *Archaeoastronomy in the Americas*, edited by Ray A. Williamson. Los Altos, Calif.: Ballena Press, 1981.

Librado, Fernando. *The Eye of the Flute* (notes of John P. Harrington, edited by Travis Hudson et al.). Santa Barbara: Santa Barbara Museum of Natural History, 1977.

———. *Breath of the Sun* (notes of John P. Harrington, edited by Travis Hudson). Banning, Calif.: Malki Museum Press, 1979.

McCluskey, Stephen C. "The Astronomy of the Hopi Indians." *Journal for the History of Astronomy* 8, part 2 (1977).

———. "Transformation of the Hopi Calendar." In *Archaeoastronomy in the Americas*, edited by Ray A. Williamson. Los Altos, Calif.: Ballena Press, 1981.

Marshall, James A. "American Indian Geometry." *Ohio Archaeologist* 28, no. 1 (1978).

———. "Geometry of the Hopewell Earthworks." *Early Man* (Spring 1979).

Miller, William C. "Two Possible Astronomical Pictographs Found in Northern Arizona." *Plateau* 27 (1955).

Neihardt, John G. *Black Elk Speaks.* Lincoln: University of Nebraska Press, 1961.

Norrish, Richard. "Woodhenge — Work of a Genius." Cahokian (February 1978). Collinsville, Ill.: Cahokia Mounds Museum Society.

Ortiz, A. The Tewa World. Chicago: University of Chicago Press, 1969.

———. "Ritual Drama and the Pueblo World View." In New Perspectives on the Pueblos, edited by Alfonso Ortiz. Albuquerque: University of New Mexico Press, 1972.

Packard, Gar, and Maggy Packard. Suns and Serpents. Santa Fe: Packard Publications, 1974.

Parsons, Elsie C. "The Origin Myth of Zuni." Journal of American Folklore 33 (1923).

———. "Isleta, New Mexico." Smithsonian Institution Bureau of American Ethnology Annual Report 47 (1930).

———. "Zuni Tales." Journal of American Folklore 43 (1930).

———. Pueblo Indian Religion. 2 vols. Chicago: University of Chicago Press, 1939.

Reed, Nelson. "Monks and Other Mississippian Mounds." Explorations into Cahokia Archaeology. Illinois Archaeological Survey Bulletin 7 (1977).

Remington, Judith Ann. "Mesoamerican Archaeoastronomy: Parallax, Perspective, and Focus." In Archaeoastronomy in the Americas, edited by Ray A. Williamson. Los Altos, Calif.: Ballena Press, 1981.

Reyman, Jonathan. Mexican Influence on Southwestern Ceremonialism. Ph.D. diss., Southern Illinois University, 1971.

———. "The Nature and Nurture of Archaeoastronomical Studies." In Archaeoastronomy in Pre-Columbian America, edited by Anthony F. Aveni. Austin: University of Texas Press, 1975.

———. "Sun Temple, Mesa Verde National Park: A Re-evaluation." Paper presented at a symposium held at Colgate University, September 23–26, 1975.

———. "Astronomy, Architecture, and Adaptation at Pueblo Bonito." Science 193 (1976).

———. "Archaeoastronomy at Pueblo Bonito." Science 79 (1977).

———. "Wupatki: Rejecting False Profits." American Antiquity 43 (1978).

———. "Some Observations on Archaeology and Archaeoastronomy." Archaeoastronomy 2, no. 2 (1979).

———, and J. Eddy. "Big Horn Medicine Wheel: Why Was It Built?" Science 188 (1975).

Risser, Anna. "Seven Zuni Folk Tales." El Palacio 58 (Santa Fe, 1941).

Schaafsma, Polly. Indian Rock Art of the Southwest. Albuquerque: University of New Mexico Press, 1980.

Silverberg, Robert. The Mound Builders. New York: Ballantine Books, 1970.

Sims, S. C. "A Wheel-Shaped Stone Monument in Wyoming." American Anthropologist new series, vol. 5 (1903).

Sofaer, Anna, Volker Zinser, and Rolf Sinclair. "A Unique Solar Marking Construct." Science 206 (1979).

Stephen, Alexander M. Hopi Journal of Alexander M. Stephen. Edited by E. C. Parsons. Columbia University Contributions to Anthropology vol. 23 (2 vols). New York, 1936.

Stevenson, Matilda Coxe. "The Zuni Indians." Smithsonian Institution Bureau of American Ethnology Annual Report 23 (1904).

Stirling, M. W. "The Origin Myth of Acoma and Other Records." *Smithsonian Institution Bureau of American Ethnology Bulletin* 135 (1942).

Swanton, John R. "Sun Worship in the Southeast." *American Anthropologist* 30 (1928).

———. "The Indians of the Southeastern United States." *Smithsonian Institution Bureau of American Ethnology Bulletin* 137 (1946).

Taleyesva, D. *Sun Chief.* Edited by Leo W. Simmons. New Haven: Yale University Press, 1942.

Tedlock, Dennis. "The Girl and the Protector: A Zuni Story." Transcription of a performance by Walter Sanchez. *Alcheringa* (n.s.) Vol. 1, no. 1 (1975).

Titiev, Mischa. "Old Oraibi: A Study of the Hopi Indians of Third Mesa." *Papers of the Peabody Museum of American Archaeology and Ethnology* 22, no. 1. Cambridge, Mass.: Harvard University Press, 1949.

Tyler, Hamilton. *Pueblo Animals and Myths.* Norman: University of Oklahoma Press, 1964.

———. *Pueblo Gods and Myths.* Norman: University of Oklahoma Press, 1964.

———. *Pueblo Birds and Myths.* Norman: University of Oklahoma Press, 1979.

Urton, Gary. "The Use of Native Cosmologies in Archaeoastronomical Studies: The View from South America." In *Archaeoastronomy in the Americas*, edited by Ray A. Williamson. Los Altos, Calif.: Ballena Press, 1981.

———. *At the Crossroads of the Earth and the Sky.* Austin: University of Texas Press, 1981.

Vivian, G., and P. Reiter. "The Great Kivas of Chaco Canyon and Their Relationships." *School of American Research and the Museum of New Mexico, Monograph* 22. Sante Fe, 1960.

Wedel, Waldo R. *Prehistoric Man on the Great Plains.* Norman: University of Oklahoma Press, 1961.

———. "Native Astronomy and the Plains Caddoans." *Native American Astronomy*, edited by Anthony F. Aveni. Austin: University of Texas Press, 1977.

Weltfish, Gene. *The Lost Universe.* New York: Basic Books, 1965.

Williamson, Ray A. "Archaeoastronomy at Pueblo Bonito." *Science* 79 (1977).

———. "Pueblo Bonito and the Sun." *Archaeoastronomy Bulletin* (Maryland), 1978.

———. "Hovenweep National Monument — Field Report," *Archaeoastronomy, the Bulletin of the Center for Archaeoastronomy* 2, no. 3 (1979).

———. "North America: A Multiplicity of Astronomies." In *Archaeoastronomy in the Americas*, edited by Ray A. Williamson. Los Altos, Calif.: Ballena Press, 1981.

———, H. J. Fisher, and D. O'Flynn. "Anasazi Solar Observatories." In *Native American Astronomy*, edited by Anthony F. Aveni. Austin: University of Texas Press, 1977.

———, H. J. Fisher, A. F. Williamson, and C. Cochran. "The Astronomical Record in Chaco Canyon, New Mexico." In *Archaeoastronomy in Pre-Columbian America*, edited by Anthony F. Aveni. Austin: University of Texas Press, 1975.

————, and M. J. Young. "An Equinox Sun Petroglyph Panel at Hovenweep National Monument." *American Indian Rock Art* 5 (1979). El Toro, Calif.: American Rock Art Research Association.

Wilson, Michael, Kathie L. Road, and Kenneth J. Hardy. *Megaliths to Medicine Wheels: Boulder Structures in Archaeology.* Calgary, Alberta: University of Calgary Archaeological Association, 1981.

Witthoft, John. "Green Corn Ceremonialism in the Eastern Woodlands." *Occasional Contributions from the Museum of Anthropology of the University of Michigan* 13. Ann Arbor: University of Michigan Press, 1949.

Wittry, Warren. "An American Woodhenge." *Explorations into Cahokia Archaeology,* Bulletin 7. Illinois Archaeological Survey, 1973.

Young, M. Jane, and Ray A. Williamson. "Ethnoastronomy: The Zuni Case." In *Archaeoastronomy in the Americas,* edited by Ray A. Williamson. Los Altos, Calif.: Ballena Press, 1981.

Zuidema, R. T. "Anthropology and Archaeoastronomy." In *Archaeoastronomy in the Americas,* edited by Ray A. Williamson. Los Altos, Calif.: Ballena Press, 1981.

European Archaeoastronomy

Brown, Peter Lancaster. *Megaliths, Myths and Men.* Poole, Dorset: Blanford Press, 1976.

————. *Megaliths and Masterminds.* London: Robert Hale, 1979.

Burl, Aubrey. *Stone Circles of the British Isles.* New Haven: Yale University Press, 1976.

————. *Prehistoric Avebury.* New Haven: Yale University Press, 1979.

————. *Prehistoric Stone Circles.* Aylesbury, Bucks.: Shire Publications, 1979.

————. *Rings of Stone.* London: Frances Lincoln, 1979.

————. *Rites of the Gods.* London: J. M. Dent & Sons, 1981.

Hadingham, Evan. *Circles and Standing Stones.* New York: Walker, 1975.

Hawkins, Gerald S., in collaboration with John B. White. *Stonehenge Decoded.* Garden City, N.Y.: Doubleday and Company, 1965.

Heggie, Douglas C. *Megalithic Science.* London: Thames and Hudson, 1981.

————. *Archaeoastronomy in the Old World.* Cambridge, England: Cambridge University Press, 1982.

Hoyle, Fred. *On Stonehenge.* San Francisco: W. H. Freeman, 1977.

Lockyer, Sir J. Norman. *Stonehenge and Other British Stone Monuments Astronomically Considered.* London: Macmillan and Company, 1906.

MacKie, Euan. *Science and Society in Prehistoric Britain.* London: Elek Books, 1977.

Thom, Alexander. *Megalith Lunar Observatories.* Oxford, England: Oxford University Press, 1971.

————. *Megalithic Sites in Britain.* Oxford, England: Oxford University Press, 1967.

Wood, John Edwin. *Sun, Moon and Standing Stones.* Oxford, England: Oxford University Press, 1978.

Index